RANDOM
HOUSE
LARGE
PRINT

The SOUL of
AMERICA

JON MEACHAM

The SOUL of AMERICA

The Battle for Our Better Angels

RANDOM HOUSE
LARGE PRINT

FRONT ENDPAPER: In George P. A. Healy's **The Peacemakers**,
President Abraham Lincoln meets with General William T.
Sherman, General Ulysses S. Grant, and Rear Admiral David
Dixon Porter on Tuesday, March 28, 1865, aboard the
steamer **River Queen**.

TITLE PAGE: Franklin and Eleanor Roosevelt, pictured here in
1941 at the president's third inauguration, presided over the
country from March 1933, in the depths of the Great
Depression, until FDR's death in April 1945, on the verge of
victory in World War II.

BACK ENDPAPER: The Reverend Martin Luther King, Jr.,
at the March on Washington for Jobs and Freedom,
Wednesday, August 28, 1963.

Cover design by Tom McKeveny

The Library of Congress has established a
Cataloging-in-Publication record for this title.

ISBN: 978-1-9848-3208-5

www.penguinrandomhouse.com/large-print-format-books

FIRST LARGE PRINT EDITION

Printed in the United States of America

10 9 8 7 6 5 4 3 2

This Large Print edition published in accord
with the standards of the N.A.V.H.

To Evan Thomas and Michael Beschloss

History, as nearly no one seems to know, is not merely something to be read. And it does not refer merely, or even principally, to the past. On the contrary, the great force of history comes from the fact that we carry it within us, are unconsciously controlled by it in many ways, and history is literally present in all that we do.

—JAMES BALDWIN

The Presidency is not merely an administrative office. That's the least of it. It is more than an engineering job, efficient or inefficient. It is pre-eminently a place of moral leadership.

—FRANKLIN D. ROOSEVELT

Nothing makes a man come to grips more directly with his conscience than the Presidency. . . . The burden of his responsibility literally opens up his soul. No longer can he accept matters as given; no longer can he write off hopes and needs as impossible.

—LYNDON B. JOHNSON

CONTENTS

||||||||||||||||||||||||||||||||||||||||||||||||||

The SOUL of AMERICA

"For only the President represents the national interest,"
JFK said. "Upon him alone converge all the needs
and aspirations of all parts of the country . . .
all nations of the world."

TO HOPE RATHER THAN TO FEAR

||||||||||||||||||||||||||||||||||||||||||||||||||

Back of the writhing, yelling, cruel-eyed demons who break, destroy, maim and lynch and burn at the stake, is a knot, large or small, of normal human beings, and these human beings at heart are desperately afraid of something. Of what? Of many things, but usually of losing their jobs, being declassed, degraded, or actually disgraced; of losing their hopes, their savings, their plans for their children; of the actual pangs of hunger, of dirt, of crime.

—W.E.B. Du Bois, **Black Reconstruction in America,** 1935

We are not enemies, but friends. We must not be enemies. Though passion may have strained it must not break our bonds of affection. The mystic chords of memory, stretching from every battlefield and patriot grave to every living heart and hearthstone all over this broad land, will yet swell the chorus of the Union, when again touched, as surely they will be, by the better angels of our nature.

—Abraham Lincoln, First Inaugural Address, 1861

||||||||||||||||||||||||||||||||||||||||||||||||||

THE FATE OF AMERICA—or at least of white America, which was the only America that seemed to count—was at stake. On the autumn evening of Thursday, October 7, 1948, South Carolina governor Strom Thurmond, the segregationist Dixiecrat candidate for president of the United States, addressed a crowd of one thousand inside the University of Virginia's Cabell Hall in Charlottesville. The subject at hand: President Harry S. Truman's civil rights program, one that included anti-lynching legislation and protections against racial discrimination in hiring.

Thurmond was having none of it. Such measures, he thundered, "would undermine the American way of life and outrage the Bill of Rights." Interrupted by applause and standing ovations, Thurmond, who had bolted the Democratic National Convention in July to form the States' Rights Democratic Party, was in his element in the Old Confederacy. "I want to tell you, ladies and gentlemen," Thurmond had said in accepting the breakaway party's nomination in Birmingham, Alabama, "that there's not enough troops in the army to force the Southern people to break down segregation and admit the nigra race into our theaters, into our swimming pools, into our homes, into our churches."

The message was clear. He and his fellow Dixiecrats, he told the University of Virginia crowd, offered "the only genuine obstacle to the rise of socialism or communism in America." Civil rights, Thurmond declared, were a Red plot against the Free World: "Only the States Rights Democrats—and we alone—have the moral courage to stand up to the Communists and tell them this foreign doctrine will not work in free America."

Nearly seventy years on, in the heat of a Virginia August in 2017, heirs to the Dixiecrats' platform of white supremacy—twenty-first century Klansmen and neo-Nazis among them—gathered in Charlottesville, not far from where Thurmond had taken his stand. The story is depressingly well known: A young counter-protestor, Heather Heyer, was killed. Two Virginia state troopers died in a helicopter crash as part of an operation to maintain order. And the president of the United States—himself an heir to the white populist tradition of Thurmond and of Alabama's George Wallace—said that there had been an "egregious display of hatred, bigotry and violence on many sides," as if there were more than one side to a conflict between neo-Nazis who idolized Adolf Hitler and Americans who stood against Ku Klux Klansmen and white nationalists. The remarks were of a piece with the incumbent president's divisive language on immigration (among many other subjects, from political foes to women) and his nationalist rhetoric.

Extremism, racism, nativism, and isolationism, driven by fear of the unknown, tend to spike in periods of economic and social stress—a period like our own. Americans today have little trust in government; household incomes lag behind our usual middle-class expectations. The fires of fear in America have long found oxygen when broad, seemingly threatening change is afoot. Now, in the second decade of the new century, in the presidency of Donald Trump, the alienated are being mobilized afresh by changing demography, by broadening conceptions of identity, and by an economy that prizes Information Age brains over manufacturing brawn. "We are determined to take our country back," David Duke, a former grand wizard of the Ku Klux Klan, said in Charlottesville. "We are going to fulfill the promises of Donald Trump. That's what we believed in, that's why we voted for Donald Trump. Because he said he's going to take our country back. And that's what we gotta do."

For many, the fact that we have arrived at a place in the life of the nation where a grand wizard of the KKK can claim, all too plausibly, that he is at one with the will of the president of the United States seems an unprecedented moment. History, however, shows us that we are frequently vulnerable to fear, bitterness, and strife. The good news is that we have come through such darkness before.

This book is a portrait of hours in which the politics of fear were prevalent—a reminder that periods of public dispiritedness are not new and a reassurance that they are survivable. In the best of moments, witness, protest, and resistance can intersect with the leadership of an American president to lift us to higher ground. In darker times, if a particular president fails to advance the national story—or, worse, moves us backward—then those who witness, protest, and resist must stand fast, in hope, working toward a better day. Progress in American life, as we will see, has been slow, painful, bloody, and tragic. Across too many generations, women, African Americans, immigrants, and others have been denied the full promise of Thomas Jefferson's Declaration of Independence. Yet the journey has gone on, and proceeds even now.

There's a natural tendency in American political life to think that things were always better in the past. The passions of previous years fade, to be inevitably replaced by the passions of the present. Nostalgia is a powerful force, and in the maelstrom of the moment many of us seek comfort in imagining that once there was a Camelot—without quite remembering that the Arthurian legend itself was about a court riven by ambition and infidelity. One point of this book is to remind us that imperfection is the rule, not the exception.

With countries as with individuals, a sense of proportion is essential. All has seemed lost before, only to give way, after decades of gloom, to

On Thursday, December 1, 1955, Rosa Parks, who worked as a seamstress at the Montgomery Fair department store, was arrested after refusing to give up her seat to a white passenger in Jim Crow–era Alabama. She is pictured here in 1956.

light. And that is in large measure because, in the battle between the impulses of good and of evil in the American soul, what Lincoln called "the better angels of our nature" have prevailed just often enough to keep the national enterprise alive. To speak of a soul at all—either of a person or of country—can seem speculative and gauzy. Yet belief in the existence of an immanent collection of convictions, dispositions, and sensitivities that shape character and inform conduct is ancient and perennial.

There is a rich history of discussion of what the Swedish economist Gunnar Myrdal, writing in 1944, called the American Creed: devotion to principles of liberty, of self-government, and of equal opportunity for all regardless of race, gender, religion, or nation of origin. Echoing Myrdal, the historian Arthur M. Schlesinger, Jr., wrote, "The genius of America lies in its capacity to forge a single nation from peoples of remarkably diverse racial, religious, and ethnic origins. . . . The American Creed envisages a nation composed of individuals making their own choices and accountable to themselves, not a nation based on inviolable ethnic communities. . . . It is what all Americans should learn, because it is what binds all Americans together."

I have chosen to consider the American soul more than the American Creed because there is a significant difference between professing adherence to a set of beliefs and acting upon them. The war between the ideal and the real, between what's right and what's convenient, between the larger good and personal interest is the contest that unfolds in the soul of every American. The creed of which Myrdal and Schlesinger and others have long spoken can find concrete expression only once individuals in the arena choose to side with the angels. That is a decision that must come from the soul—and sometimes the soul's darker forces win out over its nobler ones. The message of Martin Luther King, Jr.—that we should be judged on the content of our character, not on the color of our skin—dwells in the American soul; so does the menace of the

Ku Klux Klan. History hangs precariously in the balance between such extremes. Our fate is contingent upon which element—that of hope or that of fear—emerges triumphant.

Philosophically speaking, the soul is the vital center, the core, the heart, the essence of life. Heroes and martyrs have such a vital center; so do killers and haters. Socrates believed the soul was nothing less than the animating force of reality. "What is it that, present in a body, makes it living?" he asked in the **Phaedo.** The answer was brief, and epochal: "A soul." In the second chapter of the book of Genesis in the Hebrew Bible, the soul was life itself: "And the Lord God formed man of the dust of the ground, and breathed into his nostrils the breath of life; and man became a living soul." In the Greek New Testament, when Jesus says "Greater love hath no man than this, that a man lay down his life for his friends," the word for "life" could also be translated as "soul."

In terms of Western thought, then, the soul is generally accepted as a central and self-evident truth. It is what makes us **us,** whether we are speaking of a person or of a people, which Saint Augustine of Hippo, writing in **The City of God,** defined as "an assemblage of reasonable beings bound together by a common agreement as to the objects of their love."

Common agreement as to the objects of their love: It's a marvelous test of a nation. What have Americans loved in common down the centuries? The answer sheds light on that most essential of questions: What is the American soul? The dominant feature of that soul—the air we breathe, or, to shift the metaphor, the controlling vision— is a belief in the proposition, as Jefferson put in the Declaration, that all men are created equal. It is therefore incumbent on us, from generation to generation, to create a sphere in which we can live, live freely, and pursue happiness to the best of our abilities. We cannot guarantee equal outcomes, but we must do all we can to ensure equal opportunity.

Hence a love of fair play, of generosity of spirit, of reaping the rewards of hard work, and of faith in the future. For all our failings—and they are legion—there is an abiding idea of an America in which anyone coming from anywhere, of any color or creed, has free access to what Lincoln called the "just and generous and prosperous system, which opens the way for all." Too often, people view their own opportunity as dependent on domination over others, which helps explain why such people see the expansion of opportunity for all as a loss of opportunity for themselves. In such moments the forces of reaction thrive. In our finest hours, though, the soul of the country manifests itself in an inclination to open our arms rather than to clench our fists; to look out rather than to turn inward; to accept rather than to reject. In so doing, America has grown ever stronger, confident that the choice of light over dark is the means by which we pursue progress.

For reasons ranging from geography to market capitalism to Jeffersonian ideas of liberty, Americans have tended to believe, without irony, that Thomas Paine was right when he declared that "we have it in our power to begin the world over again." In the twilight of his life, Franklin D. Roosevelt recalled the words of his old Groton School rector, Endicott Peabody, who had told him, "Things in life will not always run smoothly. Sometimes we will be rising toward the heights—then all will seem to reverse itself and start downward. The great fact to remember is that the trend of civilization itself is forever upward; that a line drawn through the middle of the peaks and the valleys of the centuries always has an upward trend."

Roosevelt quoted that observation in his final inaugural address in the winter of 1945, and American power and prosperity soon reached epic heights. The Peabody-Roosevelt gospel seemed true enough: The world was not perfect, nor was it perfectible, but on we went, in the face of inequities and inequalities, seeking to expand freedom at home, to defend liberty abroad, to conquer disease and go to the stars. For notably among nations, the United States has long been shaped by the promise, if not always by the reality, of forward motion, of rising greatness, and of the expansion of knowledge, of wealth, and of happiness.

So it has been from the beginning—even before the beginning, really, if we think of 1776 as the birth of the nation. "I always consider the settlement of America with Reverence and Wonder," John Adams wrote in 1765, "as the Opening of a grand scene and Design in Providence, for the Illumination of the Ignorant and the Emancipation of the slavish Part of Mankind all over the Earth." Jefferson, too, spoke of the animating American conviction that tomorrow can be better than today. In his eighty-second year, Jefferson wrote of a "march of civilization" that had, in his long lifetime, passed "over us like a cloud of light, increasing our knowledge and improving our condition. . . . And where this progress will stop no one can say."

In the middle of the nineteenth century, the minister and abolitionist Theodore Parker defined "the American idea" as the love of freedom versus the law of slavery. Frederick Douglass, the former slave who became a leading voice for equality, believed deeply in America's capacity for justice. "I know of no soil better adapted to the growth of reform than American soil," Douglass said after the Supreme Court's **Dred Scott** decision in 1857. "I know of no country where the conditions for affecting great changes in the settled order of things, for the development of right ideas of liberty and humanity, are more favorable than here in these United States." Eleanor Roosevelt, niece of TR, wife of FDR, and global human rights pioneer, wrote, "It is essential that we remind ourselves frequently of our past history, that we recall the shining promise that it offered to all men everywhere who would be free, the promise that it is still our destiny to fulfill."

Self-congratulatory, even self-delusional? At times and in part, yes. It's an inescapable fact of experience, though, that from John Winthrop to Jefferson to Lincoln, America has been defined by a sense of its own exceptionalism—an understanding of destiny that has also been tempered by an appreciation of the tragic nature of life. "Man's capacity for justice makes democracy possible," the theologian and thinker Reinhold Niebuhr wrote in 1944, "but man's inclination to injustice makes democracy necessary." We try; we fail; but we must try again, and again, and again, for only in trial is progress possible.

Deep in our national soul we believe ourselves to be entitled by the free gifts of nature and of nature's God—and, in a theological frame, of our Creator—to pursue happiness. That ambient reality has been so strong that even the most clear-eyed among us have admitted the distinctive nature of the nation. "Intellectually I know America is no better than any other country; emotionally I know she is better than every other country," the novelist Sinclair Lewis remarked in 1930. He was not alone then, nor would he be alone now.

To know what has come before is to be armed against despair. If the men and women of the past, with all their flaws and limitations and ambitions and appetites, could press on through ignorance and superstition, racism and sexism, selfishness and greed, to create a freer, stronger nation, then perhaps we, too, can right wrongs and take another step toward that most enchanting and elusive of destinations: a more perfect Union.

To do so requires innumerable acts of citizenship and of private grace. It will require, as it has in the past, the witness and the bravery of reformers who hold no office and who have no traditional power but who yearn for a better, fairer way of life. And it will also require, I be-

"When in the course of human events . . ." John
Trumbull's depiction of the presentation of the
first draft of the Declaration of Independence to the
Second Continental Congress on Friday, June 28, 1776,
in the Assembly Room of the Pennsylvania State
House in Philadelphia.

lieve, a president of the United States with a
temperamental disposition to speak to the country's hopes rather than to its fears.

In the 1790s, with the Alien and Sedition Acts,
the Federalists sought not just to win elections
but to eliminate their opponents altogether. In
the Age of Jackson, South Carolina extremists
threatened the Union, only to be put down by a
president who, for his manifold flaws, believed in
the Union above all. Anti–Roman Catholic sentiment, driven by immigration, gave rise to a major

The experience of World War II, where Americans
fought with valor from Iwo Jima to Normandy, taught
us, President Truman said, that "recognition of our
dependence upon one another is essential to life, liberty,
and the pursuit of happiness of all mankind."

political movement, the Know-Nothings, in the
years before the Civil War. The Reconstruction
era featured several instances of progress and light
in the passage of crucial constitutional amendments concerning equality and in U. S. Grant's
1870–71 stand against the Ku Klux Klan, only to
give way to Jim Crow laws and nearly a hundred
years of legalized segregation.

In just the past century, during World War I
and after the Bolshevik Revolution of 1917, a
new Ku Klux Klan, boosted in part by the movie

The Birth of a Nation, took advantage of American anxiety to target blacks, immigrants, Roman Catholics, and Jews. The fear that the "huddled masses" of Emma Lazarus's poem "The New Colossus" would destroy the America that whites had come to know helped lead to the founding of the twentieth-century Klan, a nationwide organization that staged massive marches down Pennsylvania Avenue in Washington in 1925 and 1926. Isolationists and Nazi sympathizers took their stand in the 1930s; their influence evaporated only with the Japanese bombing of Pearl Harbor on Sunday, December 7, 1941, and Adolf Hitler's subsequent declaration of war on the United States. Then there was the anti-Communist hysteria of the early Cold War period and the white Southern defense of segregation in the civil rights era.

Our greatest leaders have pointed **toward** the future—not **at** this group or that sect. Looking back on the Dixiecrat challenge, Harry Truman—the man who won the four-way 1948 presidential campaign, triumphing over the segregationist Thurmond, the Progressive candidate Henry A. Wallace, and the Republican Thomas E. Dewey—once said: "You can't divide the country up into sections and have one rule for one section and one rule for another, and you can't encourage people's prejudices. You have to appeal to people's best instincts, not their worst ones. You may win an election or so by doing the other, but it does a lot of harm to the country." Truman understood something his legendary immediate predecessor had also grasped: that, as Franklin D. Roosevelt observed during the 1932 campaign, "The Presidency is not merely an administrative office. That's the least of it. It is more than an engineering job, efficient or inefficient. It is pre-eminently a place of moral leadership. All our great Presidents were leaders of thought at times when certain historic ideas in the life of the nation had to be clarified."

As Truman and Roosevelt—and Jackson and Lincoln and Grant and TR and Wilson and Eisenhower and Kennedy and Lyndon Johnson and Ronald Reagan, among others—understood, the president of the United States has not only administrative and legal but moral and cultural power. "For only the President represents the national interest," John F. Kennedy said. "And upon him alone converge all the needs and aspirations of all parts of the country, all departments of the Government, all nations of the world." There was nothing, Lyndon Johnson remarked, that "makes a man come to grips more directly with his conscience than the Presidency. Sitting in that chair involves making decisions that draw out a man's fundamental commitments. The burden of his responsibility literally opens up his soul. No longer can he accept matters as given; no longer can he write off hopes and needs as impossible." The office was a crucible of character. "In that house of decision, the White House, a man becomes his commitments," Johnson said. "He understands who he really is. He learns what he genuinely wants to be."

I am writing now not because past American presidents have always risen to the occasion but because the incumbent American president so rarely does. A president sets a tone for the nation and helps tailor habits of heart and of mind. Presidential action and presidential grace are often crucial in ameliorating moments of virulence and violence—and presidential indifference and presidential obtuseness can exacerbate such hours.

We are more likely to choose the right path when we are encouraged to do so from the very top. The country has come to look to the White House for a steadying hand, in word and deed, in uneasy times. As Woodrow Wilson observed more than a century ago, the president is "at the front of our government, where our own thoughts and the attention of men everywhere is centered upon him."

About that there has long been little debate.

"His person, countenance, character, and actions, are made the daily contemplation and conversation of the whole people," John Adams wrote in 1790. After his own presidency, Adams observed, "The people . . . ought to consider the President's office as the indispensable guardian of their rights," adding: "The people cannot be too careful in the choice of their Presidents." In 1839, his son John Quincy Adams wrote that "the powers of the executive department, explicitly and emphatically concentrated in one person, are vastly more extensive and complicated than those of the legislature." The British writer and statesman James Bryce, in his **American Commonwealth,** published in 1888, described the presidency as "this great office, the greatest in the world, unless we except the papacy, to which anyone can rise by his own merits." The political scientist Henry Jones Ford, writing in 1898, observed, "The truth is that in the presidential office, as it has been constituted since Jackson's time, American democracy has revived the oldest political institution of the race, the elective kingship."

The emphasis on the presidency in the following pages is not to suggest that occupants of the office are omnipotent. Much of the vibrancy of the American story lies in the courage of the powerless to make the powerful take notice.

"One thing I believe profoundly: **We make our own history**," Eleanor Roosevelt, who knew much about the possibilities and perils of politics, wrote shortly before her death in 1962. "The course of history is directed by the choices we make and our choices grow out of the ideas, the beliefs, the values, the dreams of the people. It is not so much the powerful leaders that determine our destiny as the much more powerful influence of the combined voice of the people themselves."

We are a better nation because of reformers, known and unknown, celebrated and obscure, who have risked and given their lives in the conviction that, as Martin Luther King, Jr., said, "The arc of the moral universe is long, but it bends toward justice." This is not sentimental. "Surely, in the light of history," Mrs. Roosevelt remarked, "it is more intelligent to hope rather than to fear, to try rather than not to try."

Of course, history's stories of presidential leadership in hours of fear can be as often disappointing as they are heroic. The Civil War was the hinge of our national saga, and our brief survey will begin in earnest in the shadow of Appomattox. Southern anxiety was a critical factor in the coming of the Civil War—the fear that the "peculiar institution" of slavery could not survive, much less thrive, within the Union. And fear fundamentally shaped American life and politics in the Reconstruction period well into the twentieth century—the white fear of ceding too much power to free blacks, an anxiety that knew no regional boundary. The most profound issues of freedom and power, of domination and subordination, were in play. From decade to decade, the white fear of people of color and of immigrants played significant, sometimes decisive, roles in the imaginations and the actions of the powerful. Writing in 1903, the scholar, historian, and activist W.E.B. Du Bois observed that "the problem of the Twentieth Century is the problem of the color-line," and, while Du Bois was surely right, it is correct, too, to say that color in some ways remains the problem of American history as a whole.

Such talk is uncomfortable in the twenty-first century. After King, after Rosa Parks, after John Lewis, after the watershed legislative work of Lyndon B. Johnson in passing the civil rights bills of the mid-1960s, many Americans are less than eager to acknowledge that our national greatness was built on explicit and implicit apartheid. Yet for all that the United States has accomplished—and we have been a country that people take pains to come to, not to leave—we remain an imperfect union.

Fear, as the political theorist Corey Robin has brilliantly argued, has been with us always.

Understood by Robin and many scholars both ancient and modern as an anticipation of danger to oneself or to a group to which one belongs—including economic, racial, ethnic, religious, or other identity groups—it is among the oldest of human forces. "Political fear . . . arises from conflicts within and between societies," Robin wrote in his 2004 book **Fear: The History of a Political Idea,** adding that political fear can be "sparked by friction in the civic world" and "may dictate public policy, bring new groups to power and keep others out, create laws and overturn them." In the most elemental of terms, masters of such politics are adept at the manufacturing or, if the fear already exists, the marshaling of it at the expense of those who one believes pose a threat to one's own security, happiness, prosperity, or sense of self.

As Aristotle wrote in his **Rhetoric,** fear "is caused by whatever we feel has great power of destroying us, or of harming us in ways that tend to cause us great pain." **Whatever we feel:** Fear can be rational—Thomas Hobbes believed fear of the state of nature, a milieu without government and order, was the primary motivation for men to enter into society, forming mutual bonds of protection—but it is often irrational. To be concerned is not necessarily the same thing as being fearful; fear is more emotional, more destabilizing, more **maddening.** Fear, Aristotle observed, does not strike those who are "in the midst of great prosperity." Those who are frightened of losing what they have are the most vulnerable, and it is difficult to be clear-headed when you believe that you are teetering on a precipice. "No passion," Edmund Burke wrote, "so effectually robs the mind of all its powers of acting and reasoning as **fear.**"

The opposite of fear is hope, defined as the expectation of good fortune not only for ourselves but for the group to which we belong. Fear feeds anxiety and produces anger; hope, particularly in a political sense, breeds optimism and feelings of well-being. Fear is about limits; hope is about growth. Fear casts its eyes warily, even shiftily, across the landscape; hope looks forward, toward the horizon. Fear points at others, assigning blame; hope points ahead, working for a common good. Fear pushes away; hope pulls others closer. Fear divides; hope unifies.

"The coward, then, is a despairing sort of person; for he fears everything," Aristotle wrote. "The brave man, on the other hand, has the opposite disposition; for confidence is the mark of a hopeful disposition." In Christian terms, fear, according to Saint Augustine, was caused by "the loss of what we love." Building on Augustine, Saint Thomas Aquinas wrote that "properly speaking, hope regards only the good; in this respect, hope differs from fear, which regards evil."

Augustine and Aquinas viewed the world in theological terms; in due historical course, the Puritans and successive generations of Americans would also see our national story in a religious context. To be sure, as Shakespeare wrote, "The devil can cite Scripture for his purpose," and the Bible has been used to justify human chattel, to cloak Native American removal with missionary language, and to repress the rights of women. At the same time, the great American reform movements have drawn strength from religious traditions and spiritual leaders. "I do not know if all Americans have faith in their religion—for who can read the secrets of the heart?—but I am sure that they think it necessary to the maintenance of republican institutions," Alexis de Tocqueville wrote in the Age of Jackson. "That is not the view of one class or party among the citizens, but of the whole nation; it is found in all ranks."

There was a genius about the American Founding and the emergence of American democratic politics. That genius lay in no small part in the recognition that the Republic was as susceptible to human passions as human beings themselves.

The Founders expected seasons of anger and frustration; they anticipated hours of unhappiness and unrest. Fear frequently defies constitutional and political mediation, for it is more emotional than rational. When the unreconstructed Southerner of the late nineteenth century or the anti-Semite of the twentieth believed—or the nativist of the globalized world of the twenty-first **believes**—others to be less than human, then the protocols of politics and the checks and balances of the Madisonian system of governance face formidable tests. Mediating conflicting claims between groups if one of the groups refuses to acknowledge the very humanity of the others is a monumental task. Our Constitution and our politics, however, have endured and prevailed, vindicating the Founders' vision of a country that would require amendment and adjustment. That the nation was constructed with an awareness of sin and the means to take account of societal changes has enabled us to rise above the furies of given moments and given ages.

And while those furies sometimes ebb, they also sometimes flow. In a November 1963 lecture that formed the basis of a **Harper's** cover story and of a book, the Columbia historian Richard Hofstadter defined what he called "the paranoid style in American politics," a recurring

popular tendency to adhere to extreme conspir-
atorial theories about threats to the country.
"The paranoid spokesman sees the fate of conspiracy in apocalyptic terms—he traffics in the
birth and death of whole worlds, whole political
orders, whole systems of human values," Hofstadter wrote. "He is always manning the barri-
cades of civilization. He constantly lives at a
turning point: it is now or never in organizing
resistance to conspiracy. Time is forever running
out."

The measure of our political and cultural
health cannot be whether we all agree on all
things at all times. We don't, and we won't. Dis-
agreement and debate—including ferocious dis-
agreement and exhausting debate—are hallmarks
of American politics. As Jefferson noted, divisions of opinion have defined free societies since
the days of Greece and Rome. The art of politics
lies in the manufacturing of a workable consensus for a given time—not unanimity. This is an
art, not a science. There is no algorithm that can
tell a president or a people what to do. Like life,
history is contingent and conditional.

In the American experience—so far—such
contingencies and conditions have produced
a better nation. Strom Thurmond's fate in the
1948 election is, in a way, itself an encouraging

example. The Dixiecrat carried just four states—Louisiana, Mississippi, Alabama, and Thurmond's native South Carolina. Given a choice, a sufficient number of American voters believed Truman the right man to bet on. In electing the Democratic nominee to a full term, the people were picking a president who, in 1947, had addressed the National Association for the Advancement of Colored People at the Lincoln Memorial—a first for an American president—and who had commissioned a report, **To Secure These Rights,** which offered a devastating critique of racial discrimination and detailed a civil rights program to bring African Americans into the mainstream.

Truman's motivations were both strategic and moral. The black vote was important in urban areas outside the Old Confederacy, and elections mattered. Principle and politics were intertwined: In Truman's view, candidates who carried the day at the polls would be able to do more in victory than they could in defeat. "It is my deep conviction," the president had told the NAACP, "that we have reached a turning point in the long history of our country's efforts to guarantee freedom and equality to all our citizens. . . . It is more important today than ever before to insure that all Americans enjoy these rights." He added: "When I say all Americans I mean all Americans." The president had written the "all Americans" sentence in his own hand on a draft of the address.

On the Fourth of July, 1947—he had spoken to the NAACP just the week before—President Truman delivered a speech at Monticello, Thomas Jefferson's mountaintop house. In the wake of World War II, Truman said, "We have learned that nations are interdependent, and that recognition of our dependence upon one another is essential to life, liberty, and the pursuit of happiness of all mankind." Everything was linked. "So long as the basic rights of men are denied in any substantial portion of the earth, men everywhere must live in fear of their own rights and their own security," Truman said. "No country has yet reached the absolute in protecting human rights. In all countries, certainly including our own, there is much to be accomplished."

History, Truman knew, is not a fairy tale. It is more often tragic than comic, full of broken hearts and broken promises, disappointed hopes and dreams delayed. But progress is possible. Hope is sustaining. Fear can be overcome. What follows is the story of how we have endured moments of madness and of injustice, giving the better angels of which Lincoln spoke on the eve of the Civil War a chance to prevail—and how we can again.

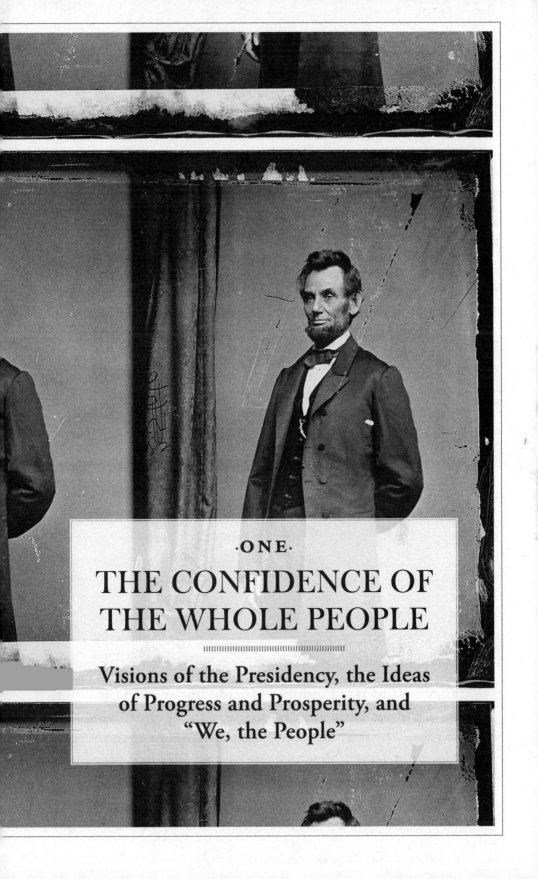

THE CONFIDENCE OF
THE WHOLE PEOPLE

Visions of the Presidency, the Ideas
of Progress and Prosperity, and
"We, the People"

DREAMS OF GOD AND OF GOLD (NOT necessarily in that order) made America possible. The First Charter of Virginia—the 1606 document that authorized the founding of Jamestown—is 3,805 words long. Ninety-eight of them are about carrying religion to "such People, as yet live in Darkness and miserable Ignorance of the true Knowledge and Worship of God"; the other 3,707 words in the charter concern the taking of "all the Lands, Woods, Soil, Grounds, Havens, Ports, Rivers, Mines, Minerals, Marshes, Waters, Fishings, Commodities," as well as orders to "dig, mine, and search for all Manner of Mines of Gold, Silver, and Copper."

Explorers in the sixteenth and seventeenth centuries sought riches; religious dissenters came seeking freedom of worship. In 1630, the Puritan John Winthrop, who crossed a stormy Atlantic aboard the **Arbella,** wrote a sermon, "A Model of Christian Charity," that explicitly linked the New World to a religious vision of a New Jerusalem. "For we must consider that we shall be as a City upon a hill," Winthrop said, drawing on Jesus's Sermon on the Mount. (Forever shrewd about visuals, Ronald Reagan added the adjective **shining** to the image several centuries later.)

We've always lived with—and perpetuated—fundamental contradictions. In 1619, a Dutch "man of warre" brought about twenty captive Africans—"negars"—to Virginia, the first chapter in the saga of American slavery. European settlers, meanwhile, set about removing Native American populations, setting in motion a tragic chain of events that culminated in the Trail of Tears. And so while whites built and dreamed, people of color were subjugated and exploited by a rising nation that prided itself on the expansion of liberty. Those twin tragedies shaped us then and ever after.

As did basic facts of geography. There was a breathtaking amount of room to run in the New World. The vastness of the continent, the wondrous frontier, the staggering natural resources: These, combined with a formidable American work ethic, made the pursuit of wealth and happiness more than a full-time proposition. It was a consuming, all-enveloping one.

For many, birth mattered less than it ever had before. Entitled aristocracies crumbled before natural ones. If you were a white man and willing to work, you stood a chance of transcending the circumstances of your father and his father's father and of joining the great company of "enterprising and self-made men," as Henry Clay put it in 1832.

The next year, President Andrew Jackson appointed one such man to be postmaster of Salem, Illinois. Though a Whig at the time—Jackson was a Democrat—Abraham Lincoln was happy to accept. Lincoln's rise from frontier origins became both fable and staple in the American narrative. He understood the power of his story, for he knew that he embodied broad American hopes. "I happen, temporarily, to occupy this big White House," Lincoln told the 166th Ohio Regiment in the summer of 1864. "I am a living witness that any one of your children may look to come here as my father's child has."

No understanding of American life and politics is possible without a sense of the mysterious dynamic between the presidency and the people at large. Sundry economic, geographic, and demographic forces, of course, shape the nation. Among these is an unspoken commerce involving the most ancient of institutions, a powerful chief, and the more modern of realities, a free, disputatious populace. In moments when public life feels unsatisfactory, then, it's instructive—even necessary—to remember first principles. What can the presidency be, at its best? And how should the people understand their own political role and responsibilities in what Jefferson called "the course of human events"?

In the beginning, at the Constitutional Convention in Philadelphia in 1787, the presidency was a work in progress. Ambivalent about executive authority, many of the framers were nevertheless anxious to rescue the tottering American nation. Governed by the weak Articles of Confederation—national power was diffuse to nonexistent—the country, George Washington wrote in November 1786, was "fast verging to anarchy & confusion!" The Constitutional Convention, which ran from May to September of 1787, was focused on bringing stability to the unruly world of competing state governments and an ineffectual national Congress.

In 1776's **Common Sense,** Thomas Paine had suggested the title of "President" for the leader of a future American government. Still, the colonial suspicion of monarchial power was evident in Paine's pamphlet. "But where, say some, is the king of America?" Paine wrote. "I'll tell you, friend, he reigns above, and doth not make havoc of mankind like the royal brute of Great Britain. . . . For as in absolute governments the king is law, so in free countries the law ought to be king, and there ought to be no other."

The tension between the widespread Paine view (that central authority was dangerous) and the practical experience of the Revolutionary War and the Confederation period (that a weak national government might be even more dangerous) shaped the thoughts and actions of the delegates who gathered in the Pennsylvania State House, now known as Independence Hall, in May 1787. Physically diminutive but intellectually powerful, James Madison, who laid out a plan for the new government with care, admitted the proper executive structure was a perplexing problem. "A national Executive will also be necessary," Madison wrote fellow Virginian Edmund Randolph before the convention. "I have scarcely ventured to form my own opinion yet, either of the manner in which it ought to be constituted, or the authorities with which it ought to be clothed."

Madison's uncertainty reflected the reality of the time. There were competing schools of thought. On the floor of the convention, Alexander Hamilton of New York proposed a president to be elected for life; others favored plans by which the legislative branch would select the executive, effectively creating a parliamentary system. Even when the drafting was done, the precise nature of the presidency—of its powers and relative role in guiding the nation—was an open mystery to the framers. Yet they were willing to live with ambiguity.

Why? Because of George Washington. It was generally assumed that General Washington, a man with Cincinnatus-like standing who had voluntarily surrendered military power at the close of the Revolutionary War, would be the first to hold the presidential post. (The delegates did provide that the president had to be a natural-born citizen, "or a citizen of the United States at the time of the adoption of this Constitution," suggesting that there has always been a wariness of foreign influence and of the foreign-born.) All in all, given the expectation of a President Washington, the creation of the office was an act of faith in the future and an educated wager on human character. From the start Americans recognized the elasticity of the presidency—and hoped for the best.

Such hopes have not always been realized. Near the end of Donald Trump's first year in power, for instance, **The New York Times** reported that, before taking office, he had "told top aides to think of each presidential day as an episode in a television show in which he vanquishes rivals."

This Hobbesian view of the presidency—that **every single day** is a war of all against all—is novel and out of sync with much of the presidential past. In his 1867 book **The English Constitution**, Walter Bagehot delineated the elements crucial to the government of a free people: "First, those which excite and preserve the reverence of the population—the **dignified** parts . . . and next, the **efficient** parts—those by which it, in fact, works and rules." Bagehot argued that the projection of aspirations above the usual run of political business was vital. "The dignified parts of government," Bagehot wrote, "are those which bring it force—which attract its motive power."

In the American context, this is especially true of the presidency, for the president, in the words of James Bryce, had become "the head of the nation." Speaking in Bagehot's vernacular, Bryce also observed: "The President has a position of immense dignity, an unrivalled platform from which to impress his ideas (if he has any) upon the people." His influence could therefore be nearly total. "As he has the ear of the country," Bryce wrote, "he can force upon its attention questions which Congress may be neglecting, and if he be a man of constructive ideas and definite aims, he may guide and inspire its political thought."

In a twenty-first-century hour when the presidency has more in common with reality television or professional wrestling, it's useful to recall how the most consequential of our past presidents have unified and inspired with conscious dignity and conscientious efficiency. "Every hope and every fear of his fellow citizens, almost every aspect of their wealth and activity, falls within the scope of his concern—indeed, within the scope of his duty," Harry Truman said. "Only a man who has held the office can really appreciate that." Reflecting on his historic push for civil rights after President Kennedy's assassination, Lyndon Johnson recalled: "I knew that, as President and as a man, I would use every ounce of strength I possessed to gain justice for the black American. My strength as President was then tenuous—I had no strong mandate from the people; I had not been elected to that office. But I recognized that the moral force of the Presidency is often stronger than the political force. I knew that a President can appeal to the best in our people or the worst; he can call for action or live with inaction."

To hear such voices is to be reminded of what

we have lost, but also what can one day be re-captured.

The possibilities of a powerful president in-formed several of Hamilton's contributions to **The Federalist,** his joint effort, with Madison and John Jay, to support the ratification of the Constitution. Hamilton defended article 2, the establishment of the executive, with characteris-tic eloquence. In his **Federalist** published on Tuesday, March 18, 1788, Hamilton wrote, "En-ergy in the Executive is a leading character in the definition of good government. It is essential to . . . the security of liberty against the enter-prises and assaults of ambition, of faction, and of anarchy."

Still, Hamilton's enthusiasm had its limits. Eight days later, in a subsequent **Federalist** essay, he observed, "The history of human conduct does not warrant that exalted opinion of human virtue which would make it wise in a nation to commit interests of so delicate and momentous a kind, as those which concern its intercourse with the rest of the world, to the sole disposal of . . . a President of the United States." The Founders saw, then, that the executive office would require check and balance.

With Hamilton and Madison's counsel, Presi-dent Washington gave the institution its founding form. "As the first of everything, in **our situation** [it] will serve to establish a Precedent," he wrote Madison, "it is devoutly wished on my part, that these precedents may be fixed on true principles." As Thomas Jefferson, the first secretary of state, recalled it, Hamilton once said that "the President was the center on which all administrative questions ultimately rested, and that all of us should rally around him, and support with joint efforts measures approved by him." In 1792, when farmers in western Pennsylvania were gathering forces to rebel against a federal excise tax on whiskey, Hamilton urged Washington to take a direct hand. "Moderation enough has been shown; it is time to assume a different tone," Hamilton argued. "The well-disposed part of the community will begin to think the Executive wanting in decision and vigor."

Washington agreed, writing, "Whereas it is the particular duty of the Executive 'to take care that the laws be faithfully executed' . . . the permanent interests and happiness of the people require that every legal and necessary step should be pursued" to avoid "violent and unwarrantable proceedings."

Within two decades, Thomas Jefferson, after serving in the highest office himself for eight years, had come to share something of Washington's understanding of the presidency. "In a government like ours it is the duty of the Chief-magistrate, in order to enable himself to do all the good which his station requires, to endeavor, by all honorable means, to unite in himself the confidence of the whole people," Jefferson wrote in 1810. "This alone, in any case where the energy of the nation is required, can produce an union of the powers of the whole, and point them in a single direction, as if all constituted but one body & one mind: and this alone can render a weaker nation unconquerable by a stronger one."

Many of even our most divisive figures have drawn on this Jeffersonian vision. Before Andrew Jackson, for example, power tended toward the few, whether political or financial. After Jackson, government, for better and for worse, was more attuned to the popular will. In the American experiment, Jackson proved that a leader who could inspire the masses could change the world.

He was the most contradictory of men—but then, America was, and is, among the most contradictory of nations. He had massacred Indians in combat, executed enemy soldiers, fought duels, and imposed martial law on New Orleans. A champion of even the poorest of whites, Jack-

son was an unrepentant slaveholder. A sentimental man who adopted an Indian orphan, he
was one of a line of leaders who drove Native
American tribes from their homelands. An
enemy of the Second Bank of the United States,
Jackson would have given his life to preserve the
central government.

Jackson spoke passionately of the needs of
"the humble members of society—the farmers,
mechanics, and laborers" and made the case for
popular politics and a more democratic understanding of power. He did so in part because he
had begun his life as one of that "humble" class.
A self-made man who had risen to the highest
levels of a slaveholding society, he wanted to
open the doors of opportunity for men like him.
Today we find many of his views morally short-
sighted, but in his time he was a figure of democratic aspiration.

In the presidency, compromise was a little-
remarked Jacksonian virtue. No other president
fulminated more passionately or threatened his
foes more forcefully, but Jackson believed in the
union with all his heart. To him, the nation was
a sacred thing, hallowed by his family's blood,
for he had lost his mother and brothers in the
Revolutionary War. We were then, and are now,
what Jackson called "one great family."

To Jackson, anger could be a means to an end.

He understood himself and how others saw him, and he turned his vices into virtues. In facing down disunionists in South Carolina in 1832–33, Jackson thundered on about leading troops into the state and hanging his opponents. Yet in the evenings, in the White House, he wrote carefully constructed letters to his allies on the ground about how to bring the crisis to a peaceful resolution.

In the first days of December 1832, Jackson was standing at his desk in his office on the second floor of the White House, a steel pen in hand, drafting what would become an essential document in the story of presidential power. South Carolina was threatening to nullify federal law—a tariff to which the state objected—and Jackson believed the maneuver an unacceptable blow against national authority. In a draft of his message to South Carolina, he wrote that he was speaking "with the feelings of a father" when he argued that nullification was "**incompatible with the existence of the Union, contradicted expressly by the letter of the Constitution, unauthorized by its spirit, inconsistent with every principle on which it was founded, and destructive of the great object for which it was formed.**" He wrote so quickly that the ink did not have time to dry before he was on to the next page.

The proclamation was intended to put down

rebellion and to put the presidency itself in the breach, defending both the ideal and the reality of the Union. Jackson believed his was the only voice in the country that could speak decisively in such a moment. "The President," Jackson wrote elsewhere, "is the direct representative of the American people"—an innocuous observation from the perspective of the twenty-first century, but in Jackson's time the assertion of the centrality of the president in the American system was controversial.

The claim provoked fury from John C. Calhoun, Jackson's great rival and the architect of nullification. "Infatuated man!" Calhoun said on the floor of the Senate. "Blinded by ambition—intoxicated by flattery and vanity! Who, that is the least acquainted with the human heart; who, that is conversant with the page of history, does not see, under all this, the workings of a dark, lawless, and insatiable ambition?"

The nullification crisis with South Carolina, the president believed, was an existential moment for the Union. "If I can judge from the signs of the times, nullification and secession, or, in the language of truth, **disunion**, is gaining strength," Jackson wrote his secretary of war, Lewis Cass. "We must be prepared to act with promptness and crush the monster in its cradle before it matures to manhood." In the proclamation, issued on Monday, December 10, 1832, Jackson called on South Carolinians to think of more than self-interest:

> Contemplate the condition of that country of which you still form an important part. Consider its government, uniting in one bond of common interest and general protection so many different States, giving to all their inhabitants the proud title of **American citizen,** protecting their commerce, securing their literature and their arts, facilitating their intercommunication, defending their frontiers, and making their name respected in the remotest parts of the earth! Consider the extent of its territory, its increasing and happy population, its advance in arts, which render life agreeable, and the sciences which elevate the mind! See education spreading the lights of religion, morality, and general information into every cottage in this wide extent of our Territories and States! Behold it as the asylum where the wretched and the oppressed find a refuge and support! Look on this picture of happiness and honor, and say, **We too are citizens of America.**

Taken together, the Nullification Proclamation of 1832 and Jackson's conviction that the presidency was the ultimate repository of the interests of the people gave his successors precedents for bold action in consequential times. And, critically, Jackson had spoken in the vernacular of hope and of unity to combat fear and disunion. To him it was a father's role—and a president's.

As did so much else, it fell to Abraham Lincoln to bring together the elements of the presidency that Jefferson and Jackson had articulated. The interval between Jackson and Lincoln had been largely marked by a Whig retreat from using executive power, a pattern rooted in the very foundation of the Whig—that is, the anti-Jacksonian—Party. In a series of executive actions during the Civil War era, ranging from summoning the militia to suspending the right of habeas corpus to, most notably, the emancipation of slaves in the seceded states, Lincoln broadly drew on Jefferson's and Jackson's examples. "Certain proceedings are constitutional when, in cases of rebellion or invasion, the public safety requires them, which would not be constitutional when, in absence of rebellion or invasion, the public safety does not require them," Lincoln remarked in 1863.

He increased his power in the broadest of causes: not only the rescue but also the redemption and rededication of the Union. At Gettysburg, Pennsylvania, on Thursday, November 19, 1863, the president invested the Civil War with overarching meaning. Gone was the temporizing of his first inaugural, with its reassurances that slavery could stand in the places where it had taken root. To the Lincoln of Gettysburg, the war was no ordinary contest. It was not about territory or spoils. It was not about the boundaries of a nation or the control of its commerce. It was, Lincoln was saying now, about democracy and equality. "Four score and seven years ago our fathers brought forth on this continent, a new nation, conceived in liberty, and dedicated to the proposition that all men are created equal," Lincoln said in words that would live ever after. "Now we are engaged in a great civil war, testing whether that nation, or any nation so conceived and so dedicated, can long endure." The task of the present generation, Lincoln said, was to ensure "that these dead shall not have died in vain—that this nation, under God, shall have a new birth of freedom—and that government of the people, by the people, for the people, shall not perish from the earth."

Fifteen months later, in his second inaugural, Lincoln continued his theme of calling on our better angels from four years earlier. "With malice toward none," he said, "with charity for all, with firmness in the right as God gives us to see the right, let us strive on to finish the work we are in, to bind up the nation's wounds, to care for him who shall have borne the battle and for his widow and his orphan, to do all which may achieve and cherish a just and lasting peace among ourselves and with all nations." Stirring words, but the work of peace was just that: **work,** an unfinished effort to reunite America, to confront the legacy of slavery, to rebuild the South, and to press on through shadow and twilight.

The president's commitment to making that perilous journey was clear to his contemporaries—even to those who sometimes found him, with his political sensitivities and calculations, too much the compromiser. After delivering the second inaugural, Lincoln received Frederick Douglass at the White House. What, Lincoln asked, had Douglass, himself one of the great orators of the day, made of the speech? No sycophant—he had fearlessly pressed Lincoln face-to-face on important questions in the past, including the unequal treatment of black soldiers in the Union army—Douglass rendered his verdict.

"Mr. Lincoln," Douglass said, "that was a sacred effort."

It was surely that. Yet Douglass's considered view of the Great Emancipator in the years to come sheds light on the enduring ambiguities

Frederick Douglass, who met with Lincoln
to argue that blacks should be treated fairly in
the Union's armed forces, once said: "I know
of no soil better adapted to the growth of
reform than American soil."

within the American soul. In April 1876, on the
eleventh anniversary of Lincoln's assassination,
Douglass spoke at the unveiling of a statue of
Lincoln on Capitol Hill. To be known as the
Freedmen's Monument, it was paid for by dona-
tions from former slaves.

"Truth is proper and beautiful at all times and
in all places," Douglass said, "and it is never more
proper and beautiful in any case than when
speaking of a great public man whose example is

likely to be commended for honor and imitation long after his departure to the solemn shades, the silent continents of eternity. It must be admitted, truth compels me to admit, even here in the presence of the monument we have erected to his memory, Abraham Lincoln was not, in the fullest sense of the word, either our man or our model. In his interests, in his associations, in his habits of thought, and in his prejudices, he was a white man." Douglass continued:

> He was preeminently the white man's President, entirely devoted to the welfare of white men. He was ready and willing at any time during the first years of his administration to deny, postpone, and sacrifice the rights of humanity in the colored people to promote the welfare of the white people of this country. . . . The race to which we belong were not the special objects of his consideration. Knowing this, I concede to you, my white fellow-citizens, a preeminence in this worship at once full and supreme. First, midst, and last, you and yours were the objects of his deepest affection and his most earnest solicitude. You are the children of Abraham Lincoln. We are at best only his step-children; children by adoption, children by forces of circumstances and necessity.

Despite all this, Lincoln had come through in the end, Douglass said, and liberated a people. Addressing white America, Douglass said "while Abraham Lincoln saved for you a country, he delivered us from a bondage." Though a white man with many of the prejudices of white men, Lincoln had proved worthy of the trust of an oppressed race:

> Our faith in him was often taxed and strained to the uttermost, but it never failed. . . . We saw him, measured him, and estimated him; not by stray utterances to injudicious and tedious delegations, who often tried his patience; not by isolated facts torn from their connection; not by any partial and imperfect glimpses, caught at inopportune moments; but by a broad survey, in the light of the stern logic of great events, and in view of that divinity which shapes our ends, rough hew them how we will, we came to the conclusion that the hour and the man of our redemption had somehow met in the person of Abraham Lincoln.

Douglass understood history and the men who made it. Perfection was impossible; greatness was reserved for those who managed to move forward in an imperfect world:

His great mission was to accomplish two things: first, to save his country from dismemberment and ruin; and, second, to free his country from the great crime of slavery. To do one or the other, or both, he must have the earnest sympathy and the powerful cooperation of his loyal fellow-countrymen. . . . Had he put the abolition of slavery before the salvation of the Union, he would have inevitably driven from him a powerful class of the American people and rendered resistance to rebellion impossible. Viewed from the genuine abolition ground, Mr. Lincoln seemed tardy, cold, dull, and indifferent; but measuring him by the sentiment of his country, a sentiment he was bound as a statesman to consult, he was swift, zealous, radical, and determined. . . .

The trust that Abraham Lincoln had in himself and in the people was surprising and grand, but it was also enlightened and well founded. He knew the American people better than they knew themselves, and his truth was based upon this knowledge.

Shot on Good Friday, 1865, the sixteenth president has loomed over the White House as grandly and as completely as he does over American history itself. He was a vibrant presence in the imagination of Theodore Roosevelt, the most compelling personality to hold the office since April 1865. In some ways a creature of his time—especially as an adherent of ultimately discredited theories of genetic white superiority—TR was also an unabashed champion of progressive causes and delighted in the possibilities of the presidency as a "bully pulpit." He had used the phrase one evening in his library while reading over a draft of a presidential message. As a friend recalled, TR "had just finished a paragraph of a distinctly ethical character, when he suddenly stopped, swung round in his swivel chair, and said: 'I suppose my critics will call that preaching, but I have got such a bully pulpit!' Then he turned back to his reading again."

TR recalled the typical American for whom he had governed. In his **Autobiography,** the former president reprinted a cartoon of an elderly, bewhiskered man, his feet by a fire, reading a copy of "The President's Message" in a newspaper. The caption: "His Favorite Author." TR loved it. "This was the old fellow whom I always used to keep in my mind," Roosevelt recalled. "He had probably been in the Civil War in his youth; he had worked hard ever since he left the army; he had been a good husband and father;

he brought up his boys and girls to work; he did not wish to do injustice to any one else, but he wanted justice done to himself and to others like him; and I was bound to secure justice for him if it lay in my power to do so."

TR firmly believed in the centrality of his office—and of himself. He was, he said, a president in the mold of Jackson and of Lincoln, not of James Buchanan. "I declined to adopt the view that what was imperatively necessary for the Nation could not be done by the President unless he could find some specific authorization to do it," Roosevelt recalled. "My belief was that it was not only his right but his duty to do anything that the needs of the Nation demanded unless such action was forbidden by the Constitution or by the laws."

As a political scientist before entering the arena, Woodrow Wilson wrote insightfully about the national experiment. In principle, he observed in **Constitutional Government in the United States,** the series of lectures he published in 1908, the American system was Newtonian—balanced, ordered, immutable. "Every sun, every planet, every free body in the spaces of the heavens, the world itself," Wilson wrote, "is kept in its place and reined to its course by the attraction of bodies that swing with equal order and precision about it, themselves governed by the nice poise and balance of forces which give the whole system of the universe its symmetry and perfect adjustment."

In practice, though, things were very different. "The trouble with the theory is that government is not a machine, but a living thing," Wilson said. "It falls, not under the theory of the universe, but under the theory of organic life. It is accountable to Darwin, not to Newton. It is modified by its environment, necessitated by its tasks, shaped to its functions by the sheer pressure of life. . . . Government is not a body of blind forces; it is a body of men . . . with a common task and purpose." Wilson continued:

> Fortunately, the definitions and prescriptions of our constitutional law, though conceived in the Newtonian spirit and upon the Newtonian principle, are sufficiently broad and elastic to allow for the play of life and circumstance. Though they were Whig theorists, the men who framed the federal Constitution were also practical statesmen with an experienced eye for affairs and a quick practical sagacity in respect of the actual structure of government, and they have given us a thoroughly workable model. If it had in fact been a machine governed by mechanically automatic

balances, it would have had no history; but it was not, and its history has been rich with the influences and personalities of the men who have conducted it and made it a living reality. The government of the United States has had a vital and normal organisc growth and has proved itself eminently adapted to express the changing temper and purposes of the American people from age to age.

Wilson also discussed the ideal role the president could play. "His position takes the imagination of the country," he said. "He is the representative of no constituency, but of the whole people. When he speaks in his true character, he speaks for no special interest. If he rightly interpret the national thought and boldly insist upon it, he is irresistible; and the country never feels the zest of action so much as when its President is of such insight and caliber."

Which makes the character of the president critical, and character manifests itself in temperament. On Wednesday, March 8, 1933, the newly inaugurated thirty-second president of the United States, Franklin D. Roosevelt, called on retired Supreme Court justice Oliver Wendell Holmes, Jr. The two men chatted a bit—Roosevelt asked about Plato, whom Holmes was reading—and FDR sought counsel on the crisis of the Depression. "Form your ranks and fight," Holmes advised. After the president left, Holmes was in a nostalgic mood. "You know, his [Cousin] Ted appointed me to the Supreme Court," Holmes remarked to a former clerk. The justice then added: "a second-class intellect, but a first-class temperament!"

Temperament is one of those terms that brings the late Supreme Court justice Potter Stewart's definition of hardcore pornography to mind: We know it when we see it. Or, in this case, **sense** it. The word itself derives from the Latin meaning "due mixture." Discerning human temperament is more a question of intuition and impression than of clinical or tactile perception, and it is a chancy undertaking.

As Justice Holmes noted on that early March day in 1933, though, it is a vital one. And FDR's was indeed first-rate. Like most politicians, it is true, Roosevelt loved attention and approval in equal measure. Once, after watching himself in a newsreel, he remarked: "That was the Garbo in me." On meeting Orson Welles, the president called out: "You know, Orson, you and I are the two best actors in America!" Reflecting on Roosevelt's determination to seek a third and then a fourth term as president, Harry Truman observed: "I guess that was his principal defect, that growing ego of his, which probably wasn't too minuscule to start with, though perhaps it was his only flaw."

FDR had the gifts of self-knowledge and a compassion for the plight of others—saving graces that enabled him to become one of a handful of truly great and transformative presidents. As important as he believed popular leadership to be—the Fireside Chats, the careful cultivation of public opinion, the weekly press briefings—he understood, too, that less was sometimes more.

"I know . . . that the public psychology and, for that matter, individual psychology cannot, because of human weakness, be attuned for long periods of time to a constant repetition of the highest note in the scale," Roosevelt wrote in a 1935 letter. His first two years in office had been tumultuous as he launched assault after assault on the Great Depression. Now he believed the public needed something of a breather. "There is another thought which is involved in continuous leadership—whereas in this country there is a free and sensational Press, people tire of seeing the same name day after day in the important headlines of the papers, and the same voice night after night over the radio." A leader's balancing act, then, was the education and the shaping of public opinion without becoming overly familiar or exhausting.

Dignified theatricality is an essential element of power. Whether on stage or on a throne, whether in the Oval Office or in the House of Commons, great leaders are often great performers, able to articulate national purposes and hopes, projecting strength and resolve in moments that threaten to give way to weakness and despair. On the night before Agincourt, Shakespeare's Henry V was racked by doubt and anxiety and fear, only to emerge in the sunlight to transform his men into a fabled "band of brothers."

FDR's point in his 1935 observation about the need to ration his exposure was that Agincourts are the exception, not the rule. Dwight Eisenhower, who served in the years of the rise of television, used to make the same argument. "I keep telling you fellows I don't like to do this sort of thing," Ike told advisers who urged him to go on the air more often. "I can think of nothing more boring, for the American public, than to have to sit in their living rooms for a whole half hour looking at my face on their television screens."

Presidents, as John Kennedy once observed, are subject to "clamorous counsel"—everyone, it can seem, has thoughts on how they could do the job better. When he was being told what to do and how to do it, Eisenhower—who, beneath his serene surface, had more than a bit of a temper—

would reply: "Now, look, I happen to **know** a little about leadership. I've had to work with a lot of nations, for that matter, at odds with each other. And I tell you this: you do not **lead** by hitting people over the head. Any damn fool can do that, but it's usually called 'assault'—not 'leadership.' . . . I'll tell you what leadership is. It's **persuasion**—and **conciliation**—and **education**—and **patience**. It's long, slow, tough work. That's the only kind of leadership I know—or believe in—or will practice."

TR would have agreed. In a letter written from the White House in December 1902, the first President Roosevelt described the nature of the office.

> Well, I have been President for a year and a quarter, and whatever the future may hold I think I may say that during that year and a quarter I have been as successful as I had any right to hope or expect. Of course political life in a position such as this is one long strain on the temper, one long acceptance of the second best, one long experiment of checking one's impulses with an iron hand and learning to subordinate one's own desires to what some hundreds of associates can be forced or cajoled or led into desiring. Every day, almost every hour, I have to decide very

big as well as very little questions, and in al-most each of them I must determine just how far it is safe to go in forcing others to accept my views and standards and just how far I must subordinate what I deem expedient, and indeed occasionally what I deem morally desirable, to what it is possible under the given conditions to achieve. . . . Often when dealing with some puzzling affair I find my-self thinking what Lincoln would have done. It has been very wearing, but I have thor-oughly enjoyed it, for it is fine to feel one's hand guiding great machinery, with at least the purpose, and I hope the effect, of guiding it for the best interests of the nation as a whole.

Sound and sensible, and not a bad standard for any president: The way to stand the "long strain on the temper" is to embrace compromise, seek balance, and strive to serve the national in-terest, which will be, in the fullness of time, in the personal historical interest of the individual president himself. Seemingly banal points, true, but recent history shows us that what we've long accepted as obvious isn't always as self-evident to a controlling portion of the electorate as one might think, or hope.

The essential question for voters, then, is discerning the nature of the man or woman who will be standing alone at what Kennedy described as the "vital center of action." For, as the Greeks knew, character is destiny.

What counts is not just the character of the individual at the top, but the character of the country—its inclinations and its aspirations, its customs and its thought, its attachments to the familiar and its openness to the new. "The form of government which prevails," Ralph Waldo Emerson wrote, "is the expression of what cultivation exists in the population which permits it." Americans are driven by many forces, and chief among those forces—and thus a formative element in the country's soul—is the "pursuit of happiness" of which Jefferson wrote in the Declaration of Independence.

When he composed those words in his rented second-floor quarters at Seventh and Market in Philadelphia in late June, 1776, Jefferson was not thinking about happiness in only the sense of good cheer. He and his colleagues were contemplating something more comprehensive— more revolutionary. Garry Wills's classic 1978 book on the Declaration, **Inventing America**, put it well: "When Jefferson spoke of pursuing happiness," Wills wrote, "he had nothing vague or private in mind. He meant public happiness which is measurable; which is, indeed, the test and justification of any government."

Until Philadelphia, the pursuit of happiness had never been granted such pride of place in a new scheme of human government—a pride of place that put the governed, not the governors, at the center of the project. Reflecting on the sources of the thinking on which he drew to draft the Declaration, Jefferson credited "the elementary books of public right . . . Aristotle, Cicero, Locke, Sidney, & c."

To understand the Declaration, then, we have to start with Aristotle. Happiness, he wrote, is the end and the purpose of action—the whole point of life. It was an ultimate good, worth seeking for its own sake. Given the Aristotelian insight that man is a social creature whose life finds meaning in his relation to other human beings, Jeffersonian **eudaimonia**—the Greek word for happiness, which can also mean "flourishing"—evokes virtue, good conduct, and generous citizenship. Happiness in the ancient and American traditions is as much about the public weal as it is about an individual's endorphins.

As Arthur M. Schlesinger, Sr., once wrote, a broad understanding of happiness informed the thinking of patriots such as James Wilson ("the happiness of the society is the **first** law of government") and John Adams ("the happiness of society is the end of government"). Beginning with the Declaration of Independence, the pursuit of happiness—the pursuit of the good of the whole, because the good of the whole was crucial to the genuine well-being of the individual, and vice versa—became part of the fabric (at first brittle, to be sure, but steadily stronger) of the young nation. For Jefferson and his contemporaries—and, thankfully, for most of their successors in positions of ultimate authority—one of the main points of public life was to enable human creativity and ingenuity and possibility, not to constrict it. In **The Rights of Man,** his 1791–92 celebration of the centrality of the individual and of the possibilities of human endeavor, Thomas Paine wrote: "From the rapid progress which America makes in every species of improvement, it is rational to conclude that if the governments of Asia, Africa, and Europe had begun on a principle similar to that of America, or had not been early corrupted therefrom, that those countries must, by this time, have been in a far superior condition to what they are."

The progress of which Paine wrote and its enabling agents—reform and revolution— have deep philosophical and political roots. As traced by the Columbia sociologist Robert A. Nisbet, the idea that human nature could advance is found as early as the Greek poets Hesiod and Xenophanes ("The gods did not reveal to men all things in the beginning," the latter wrote, "but men through their own search find in the course of time that which is better") and in the myth of Prometheus, who gave men fire. Beyond the pagan world, Saint Augustine spoke of life as a pilgrimage from darkness to light: "The education of the human race, represented by the people of God, has advanced, like that of an individual, through certain epochs, or, as it were, ages, so that it might gradually rise from earthly to heavenly things, and from the visible to the invisible."

For the American Founders, Enlightenment thinkers such as John Locke, Anne-Robert-Jacques Turgot, the Marquis de Condorcet, and Adam Smith permeated the age with the hope that progress would be possible through inquiry, argument, agitation, and finally reform. At the Sorbonne in December 1750, Turgot articulated the doctrine of progress. "The whole human race, through alternate periods of rest and unrest, of weal and woe, goes on advancing, although at a slow pace, towards greater perfection," he said in the lecture later published as **A Philosophical Review of the Successive Advances of the Human Mind.** "Like the ebb and flow of the tide, power passes from one nation to another, and, within the same nation, from the princes to the multitude and from the multitude to the princes. As the balance shifts, everything gradually gets nearer and nearer to an equilibrium, and in the course of time takes on a more settled and peaceful aspect." Of the American Revolution, Turgot wrote: "America is the hope of the human race."

Reason, religion, and capitalism were the tributaries that met to form the powerful American river that so impressed Turgot and his contemporaries. By replacing revelation and hereditary authority with rationality and republicanism, the American nation gave political form to the idea that the divine rights of monarchs and prelates had to surrender to the primacy of individual conscience and equality. No longer would certain men, by an accident of birth (kings) or an incident of election (popes), be granted absolute power over the humblest of others. This view of the intrinsic equality of every person—or at least of nearly every propertied white man— drew on secular philosophical insights, the ethos of the Protestant Reformation, and the prevailing culture of the Scientific Revolution.

The rise of market economics was critical, too, for the ability to prosper by dint of one's own initiative created citizens with a stake in preserving and advancing the very society that had given them their chance. "Every man, as long as he does not violate the laws of justice, is left perfectly free to pursue his own interest his own way," Adam Smith wrote in **The Wealth of Nations,** "and to bring both his industry and capital into competition with those of any other man, or order of men." To those who worried that the prosperous would close the doors of opportunity behind them, Smith argued that by "pursuing his own interest he frequently promotes that of the society more effectually than when he really intends to promote it." Moreover, in **The Theory of Moral Sentiments,** published in 1759, Smith wrote that "how selfish soever man may be supposed, there are evidently some principles in his nature, which interest him in the fortune of others and render their happiness necessary to him, though he derives nothing from it except the pleasure of seeing it." In Smith's view, the human capacity for sympathy and fellow feeling could be as much a part of the nature of things as the desire for wealth, and this capacity was essential to the life of a republic.

Liberty itself, meanwhile, was dependent on the moral disposition of the populace. "Machiavelli, discoursing on these matters," Algernon Sidney, the seventeenth-century English theorist and politician, wrote, "finds virtue to be so essentially necessary to the establishment and preservation of Liberty, that he thinks it impossible for a corrupted People to set up a good Government, or for a Tyranny to be introduced if they be virtuous." Put another way, a republic is the sum of its parts. In the last instance, we are the state, and the state is us.

The formation, maintenance, and expression of individual opinion, then, is the motive force of American life, for that opinion will—sooner or later, for good or for ill—manifest itself in the shape and substance of politics. The things we hope for can come to pass; the things we fear can hold us back. "What the tender poetic youth dreams, and prays, and paints today, but shuns the ridicule of saying aloud," wrote Emerson, "shall presently be the resolutions of public bodies, then shall be carried as grievance and bill of rights through conflict and war, and then shall be triumphant law and establishment for a hundred years, until it gives place, in turn, to new prayers and pictures."

Progress in America does not usually begin at the top and among the few, but from the bottom and among the many. It comes when the whispered hopes of those outside the mainstream rise in volume to reach the ears and hearts and minds of the powerful. Words attributed long afterward to Sojourner Truth, who spoke to a Woman's Rights Convention in Akron,

Ohio, in 1851, put the struggles of the day well: "I think that 'twixt the negroes of the South and the women at the North, all talking about rights, the white men will be in a fix pretty soon." And those voices carry the farthest when they call for fairness, not favors; for simple justice, not undue advantage. "We ask," Elizabeth Cady Stanton told the New York legislature in 1854, seeking equality for women, "for all that you have asked for yourselves in the progress of your development, since the **Mayflower** cast anchor [be]side Plymouth Rock; and simply on the ground that the rights of every human being are the same and identical." Arguing for black enfranchisement in 1867, Frederick Douglass said: "If black men have no rights in the eyes of white men, of course the whites can have none in the eyes of the blacks. The result is a war of races, and the annihilation of all proper human relations."

Sojourner Truth, Elizabeth Cady Stanton, Frederick Douglass: Their voices, articulating the feelings of innumerable others, ultimately prevailed in the causes of emancipation and of suffrage. It took presidential action to make things official—a Lincoln to free the slaves, a Wilson to support the women's suffrage amendment, a Lyndon Johnson to finish the fight against Jim Crow—but without the voices from afar, there would have been no chorus of liberty.

In a movement whose landmarks stretched from Seneca Falls in 1848 to the adoption of the women's suffrage amendment in 1920, Elizabeth Cady Stanton and Susan B. Anthony argued against slavery and for equal rights for women.

The lesson: The work of reformers—long, hard, almost unimaginably difficult work—can lead to progress and a broader understanding of who is included in the phrase "We, the People" that opened the Preamble of the Constitution. And that work unfolds still.

At Gettysburg in the spring of 1963, the centennial year of President Lincoln's address at the dedication of the cemetery there, Vice President Lyndon B. Johnson went to the Pennsylvania battlefield to speak at a Memorial Day commemoration. "One hundred years ago, the

Born into slavery in Ulster County, New York, in the last years of the eighteenth century, Sojourner Truth escaped from bondage and became a stirring advocate for abolition and for the rights of women.

slave was freed," Johnson said. "One hundred years later, the Negro remains in bondage to the color of his skin. The Negro today asks justice. We do not answer him—we do not answer those who lie beneath this soil—when we reply to the Negro by asking, 'Patience.'"

The country's fate, Johnson said, was intertwined with the country's sense of fairness. "Unless we are willing to yield up our destiny of greatness among civilizations of history, Americans—white and Negro together—must be about the business of resolving the challenge that confronts us now," he said. "Our nation found its soul of honor on these fields of Gettysburg one hundred years ago. We must not lose that soul in dishonor now on the fields of hate."

Five months and twenty-three days later, Vice President Johnson became President Johnson in a moment of tragedy and fear when John F. Kennedy, the president Johnson served, was shot to

Franklin D. Roosevelt and Lyndon B. Johnson in 1937, when LBJ was a young Texas congressman. Both believed in the transformative power of the presidency and sought to marshal federal power in the service of the excluded.

death in the streets of Dallas. On that autumn afternoon, in a crowded cabin aboard Air Force One at Love Field, with the fallen president in a coffin on board, Johnson took the oath of office and ordered the plane to take off for Washington. His mind whirring, the new president, always a man of action, did not believe he had a moment to waste.

The battle that Johnson chose in the bleak closing weeks of 1963 was among the most difficult in American history. It was the unfinished work of the Civil War. To understand how the forces of fear had kept equality at bay for a century, and how Lyndon Johnson, an American president thrust to authority by assassination, fulfilled long-unmet promises, we must begin the story not in Dallas nor in Washington but in a village in Virginia called Appomattox Court House.

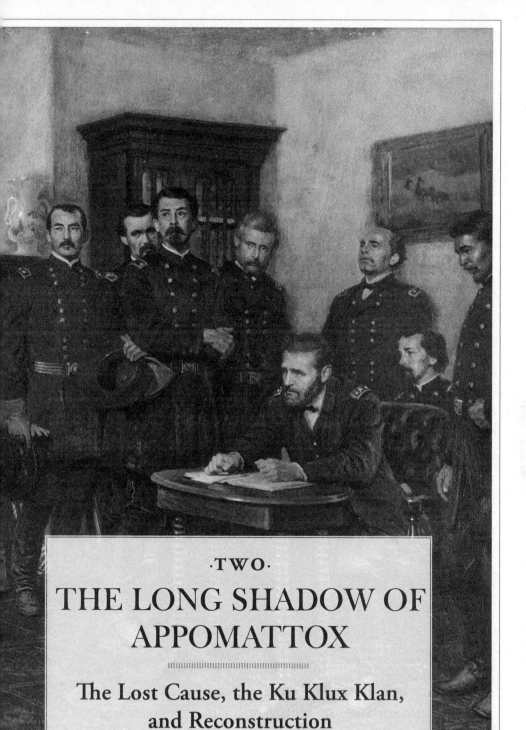

TWO

THE LONG SHADOW OF APPOMATTOX

The Lost Cause, the Ku Klux Klan,
and Reconstruction

It was, under the circumstances, the most cordial of encounters. On the afternoon of April 9, 1865—Palm Sunday, the beginning of Holy Week—Robert E. Lee, in an impeccable gray dress uniform, surrendered to Ulysses S. Grant at the village of Appomattox Court House in Virginia. With a handsome sword and a red sash, Lee met Grant, who wore only a private's blouse with muddied trousers and boots, in the first-floor parlor of a brick house belonging to Wilmer McLean. That morning Lee had mused about sacrificing himself to enemy fire rather than face the humiliation of capitulation. "How easily I could be rid of this, and be at rest!" he said at dawn on the day of his rendezvous with Grant.

"I have only to ride along the line and all will be over!" As the story is told, though, Lee mastered his despair. "But it is our duty to live," he said, reassuring himself and his comrades that they still had a mission. "What will become of the women and children of the South if we are not here to protect them?"

Grant, who arrived in the early afternoon to find Lee already inside McLean's house, had been suffering from a debilitating headache in the final days of the fighting. Relieved now—quietly "jubilant," he recalled, at the turn of events—the Union general chose to enter the parlor alone, leaving his officers outside for a moment. It was a small sign of respect, even of humility, on the part of the victor to the vanquished.

Taking Lee's hand, Grant spoke of their shared experience in the Mexican War. "I met you once before, General Lee," Grant said. "I have always remembered your appearance and I think I should have recognized you anywhere." They talked on for a bit; Grant was anxious to be gracious, and the past was a safer topic for the moment than the present. At last it fell to Lee to bring up the painful work at hand. "I suppose, General Grant, that the object of our present meeting is fully understood," Lee said. "I asked to see you to ascertain upon what terms you would receive the surrender of my army."

The business was handled with dispatch. Grant was magnanimous, allowing Lee's men to keep their horses so that the former Confederates could, Grant said, "put in a crop to carry themselves and their families through the next winter." Lee was pleased. "This will have the best possible effect upon the men," Lee told Grant. "It will be very gratifying, and will do much toward conciliating our people."

The occasion was muted, the generals gracious. These were soldiers, and they understood one another. In defeat Lee was stoic; in victory, Grant was sympathetic. "As he was a man of much dignity, with an impassable face," Grant recalled of Lee, "it was impossible to say whether he felt inwardly glad that the end had finally come, or felt sad over the result and was too manly to show it. Whatever his feelings they were entirely concealed from my observation; but my own feelings . . . were sad and depressed. I felt like anything rather than rejoicing at the downfall of a foe who had fought so long and valiantly, and had suffered so much for a cause, though that cause was, I believe, one of the worst for which a people ever fought."

Grant sent word to the Union troops: no gloating. "The war is over," he said. "The rebels are our countrymen again." As the two generals parted in the yard outside McLean's house,

Grant took off his hat as Lee rode by; Lee raised his own in mutual tribute.

Yet the comity of the commanders augured little about what was to come. The clash of arms was over, yes, but the battle between North and South, between Union and rebellion, between nothing less, really, than justice and injustice was not fully resolved in Mr. McLean's parlor. Far from it: What President Lincoln, who within a week of the surrender would be dead, the victim of an assassin's bullet, had called the "fiery trial" of the Civil War was only a chapter in the perennial contest between right and wrong in the nation's soul.

As things turned out, Appomattox was as much a beginning as an end. In the war's tragic wake we can see the possibilities of the American experiment and its all-too-persistent realities. As president, Grant fought against the Ku Klux Klan, but he was bracketed by Andrew Johnson, who attempted to obstruct many steps toward equality, and by Rutherford B. Hayes, who in 1877 agreed to remove federal troops from the South, effectively ending Reconstruction as part of a bargain to secure the presidency in a closely contested election. A number of the decisions made after Lincoln's assassination long delayed the "new birth of freedom" of which the president had spoken at Gettysburg.

For many, a new order in which blacks were

equal to whites was disorienting and had to be fought with ferocity. The battle was especially pitched for white Southerners, whose wartime crusade, they told themselves, had been righteous. In the creed of the Lost Cause, arguments over states' rights, not over slavery, had led to war. And now postbellum Southerners had to shift from military to political means in the battle for state power, which in practice meant the battle for white supremacy. Our history and our politics even now are unintelligible without first appreciating the roots of white Southern discontent about the verdict of the Civil War.

More than a century and a half on, the immensity of the Confederate defeat can be difficult to appreciate. Scholars estimate that between one in three and one in five Southern troops died during the conflict. Many, many more were injured either in body or mind. (A revealing, oft-cited detail: Mississippi earmarked 20 percent of its entire state budget in 1866 for wooden limbs.) In its attempt to make sense of the loss and to justify such staggering casualties, the South looked at once backward and, crucially, forward.

The years leading up to war had been fraught, even mad. Representative Preston Brooks of South Carolina nearly killed Senator Charles

Sumner with a cane on the floor of the Senate chamber. Virginia chose to hang John Brown after Harpers Ferry when, as Robert Penn Warren pointed out, he probably should have been committed to a mental institution. The decision to execute, Warren wrote, "thereby proved again what is never in much need of proof, that a crazy man is a large-scale menace only in a crazy society." James Petigru, a Union man from South Carolina, is reported to have observed that his state was "too small for a republic, but too large for an insane asylum."

The war had been about the most fundamental of things: slavery and freedom. William H. Seward had called the clash over chattel labor the "irrepressible conflict." As the years passed after Appomattox, however, more and more Southerners sought to diminish the role of slavery in bringing about the clash of arms. In his memoirs, Jefferson Davis said the Confederacy sought to preserve not slavery but "the inalienable right of a people to change their government . . . to withdraw from a Union into which they had, as sovereign communities, voluntarily entered," adding: "African servitude was in no wise the cause of the conflict, but only an incident." Though this view was to be echoed in sundry memorial addresses, tracts, sermons, and casual conversations down to the present day, it was unconvincing, not least because of what Southerners had said when the war itself was actually coming about.

In the month before Fort Sumter, Alexander H. Stephens, the vice president of the newly formed Confederate States of America, made his "Cornerstone Speech" in Savannah, Georgia. The crowd was raucous; feeling ran high. The Confederacy's "foundations are laid," Stephens said, "its cornerstone rests, upon the great truth that the negro is not equal to the white man; that slavery—subordination to the superior race—is his natural and normal condition. This, our new government, is the first, in the history of the world, based upon this great physical, philosophical, and moral truth."

To the North, on the banks of the Potomac, Abraham Lincoln set about rescuing the Union. The Republican Party's emergence in the mid-1850s had brought a fresh moral dimension to American politics. This is not to argue that the Party of Lincoln, as it was to become, was a perfect instrument. It is clearly the case, however, that restrictions on the expansion of slavery lay at the heart of the Republican claim to power.

"I am naturally anti-slavery," Lincoln was to write in April 1864. "If slavery is not wrong, nothing is wrong. I can not remember when I did not so think, and feel." As early as 1854, speaking in Peoria, Illinois, Lincoln had called slavery a "monstrous injustice," saying: "Let us re-adopt the Declaration of Independence, and with it, the practices, and policy, which harmonize with it. . . . If we do this, we shall not only have saved the Union; but we shall have so saved it, as to make, and to keep it, forever worthy of the saving."

He was less certain, though, about exactly how to design and implement this plan of salvation. "If all earthly power were given me, I should not know what to do, as to the existing institution," he said at Peoria, continuing:

My first impulse would be to free all the slaves, and send them to Liberia—to their own native land. But a moment's reflection would convince me, that whatever of high hope (as I think there is) there may be in this, in the long run, its sudden execution is impossible. . . . What then? Free them all, and keep them among us as underlings? Is it quite certain that this betters their condition? . . . Free them, and make them politically and socially, our equals? My own feelings will not admit of this; and if mine would, we well know that those of the great mass of white people will not. . . . A universal feeling, whether well or ill-founded, can not be safely disregarded. We can not, then, make them equals. It does seem to me that systems of gradual emancipation might be adopted; but for their tardiness in this, I will not undertake to judge our brethren of the south.

Intensely practical, attuned to the subtleties of public opinion, Lincoln was "always calculating, and always planning ahead," William Herndon, his law partner, remarked. "His ambition was a little engine that knew no rest."

What, then, as Lincoln came to the White House, were the objects of that ambition? For him it was, in the first instance, the rescue of the Union so long as slavery remained a Southern, not a Western, institution. He rejected any compromise in the Secession Winter of 1860–61 that would have expanded slavery. By the summer of 1862 it became evident to him that emancipation, even in a limited way, would be militarily wise and, in the abolitionist precincts of the North, politically beneficial—all while having the virtue, he believed, of being morally right.

To prepare public opinion for emancipation, Lincoln wrote the New York editor Horace Greeley in August 1862. "My paramount object in this struggle **is** to save the Union, and is **not** either to save or to destroy slavery," Lincoln wrote. "If I could save the Union without freeing **any** slave I would do it, and if I could save it by freeing **all** the slaves I would do it; and if I could save it by freeing some and leaving others alone I would also do that. . . . I have here stated my purpose according to my view of **official** duty; and I intend no modification of my oft-expressed **personal** wish that all men every where could be free."

By speaking of "freeing all the slaves," Lincoln was openly broaching the boldest of maneuvers—and, in the wake of the Confederate retreat from Antietam in September, he believed the time was right to strike. Lincoln told his cabinet that he had made a bargain with God: If the Union forces could prevail in Maryland, he, the president, would move on emancipation. Now victory had come, Lincoln said, and he was ready to act. He had drafted a proclamation and would entertain any minor editorial thoughts from the cabinet, but that was all he was interested in. He had, he told them, "resolved upon this step, and had not called them together to ask their advice, but to lay the subject-matter of a proclamation before them." The decision was the president's to make, and he had made it.

With the Preliminary Emancipation Proclamation of September 22, 1862, (which would free the slaves in Confederate states if those

With the Emancipation Proclamations (one in September 1862, the other in January 1863), Lincoln transformed the Civil War from one to preserve the Union to one that included the cause of liberty for the enslaved, a project realized, in legal terms, with the Thirteenth Amendment.

states did not end the rebellion by New Year's Day), and the Emancipation Proclamation of January 1, 1863 (which followed through on the warning issued in September), Lincoln gave the words that Julia Ward Howe had written earlier in the war, published as "The Battle Hymn of the Republic" in **The Atlantic Monthly**, newly urgent significance:

> As He died to make men holy, let us die to
>   make men free,
> While God is marching on.

Yet the war was not as morally dispositive as we tend—or like—to think. "The Union," the historian C. Vann Woodward wrote, "fought the Civil War on borrowed moral capital." To accept emancipation did not mean one favored equality. Lincoln himself was forever evolving on the question. "Your race are suffering, in my judgment, the greatest wrong inflicted on any people," Lincoln told a delegation of blacks in August 1862. "But even when you cease to be slaves, you are yet far removed from being placed on an equality with the white race. . . . I do not propose to discuss this, but to present it as a fact with which we have to deal. I cannot alter it if I would." One answer, Lincoln allowed, was the removal of blacks from the nation—colonization to Africa, perhaps. "But for your race among us there could not be war, although many men engaged on either side do not care for you one way or the other. . . . It is better for us both, therefore, to be separated."

Slavery had been conquered by the Union, but racism lived on across America. "When was it ever known that liberation from bondage was accompanied by a recognition of political equality?" the abolitionist William Lloyd Garrison wrote in 1864.

On Tuesday, April 11, 1865—two days after Lee's surrender—Lincoln made what would be his last public speech. That evening, from the North Portico of the White House, the president acknowledged both the magnitude of the Union victory and the coming agonies of Reconstruction. "We meet this evening, not in sorrow, but in gladness of heart," Lincoln told a large crowd that had gathered on an evening the journalist Noah Brooks described as "misty." The weather did not matter: The throngs of Washington were eager to hail their president. There were, Brooks wrote, "cheers upon cheers" and "wave after wave of applause."

As Tad Lincoln picked up the pages that fell away from Lincoln's hand, the president noted that the Confederate surrender had given the Union "hope of a righteous and speedy peace whose joyous expression cannot be restrained." Yet he worried about the work of reunion. "We simply must begin with, and mold from, disorganized and discordant elements," Lincoln said. "Nor is it a small additional embarrassment

that we, the loyal people, differ among ourselves as to the mode, manner, and measure of
reconstruction." In the chaos of the peace,
many Southern whites would find it possible to
carry on the war even after the guns had fallen
silent.

The Southern strategy to bring victory out of
defeat was articulated, among others, by
the Virginia Confederate and journalist Edward
Alfred Pollard. Born in 1832 in Nelson County,
Virginia, near Charlottesville, Pollard was a news-
paperman who had also served as clerk to the
House Judiciary Committee. Before Fort Sumter, Pollard defended slavery in an 1859 book
entitled **Black Diamonds Gathered in the
Darkey Homes of the South;** during the war,
he was captured by the Union navy while en
route to England and was held for a time as a
prisoner of war. In the wake of Appomattox,
Pollard produced a treatise on the meaning of
the war: **The Lost Cause: A New Southern History of the War of the Confederates,** published
in 1866. "No one can read aright the history of
America," he wrote, "unless in the light of a
North and a South: two political aliens existing
in a Union imperfectly defined as a confederation of States."

In Pollard's formulation, the Lost Cause was

both justified and enduring: It was not dead, but alive. The foe now was central authority and national will—Washington, D.C., writ large. "The people of the South have surrendered in the war what the war has conquered"—slavery and secession—"but they cannot be expected to give up what was not involved in the war, and voluntarily abandon their political schools for the dogma of Consolidation." Pollard declared that a " 'war of ideas,' " a new war that "the South wants and insists upon perpetrating," was under way. "The war has left the South its own memories, its own heroes, its own tears, its own dead," Pollard wrote. "Under these traditions, sons will grow to manhood, and lessons sink deep that are learned from the lips of widowed mothers."

It was a bold call to fight on in the face of loss. The war, Pollard wrote, "did not decide negro equality; it did not decide negro suffrage; it did not decide State Rights. . . . And these things which the war did not decide, the Southern people will still cling to, still claim, and still assert them in their rights and views."

He enlarged upon this thesis in another book, **The Lost Cause Regained**, published in 1868. Pollard wrote that he was "profoundly convinced that the true cause fought for in the late war has not been 'lost' immeasurably or irrevocably, but is yet in a condition to be 'regained' by the South on ultimate issues of the political contest." The question was no longer slavery, but white supremacy, which Pollard described as the "true cause of the war" and the "true hope of the South."

The reassertion of states' rights and the rejection of federal rule was a holy cause. Likening the lot of the Southerner to that of Christ himself, Pollard spoke in terms religiously inclined Southerners— which was to say most Southerners—could understand, calling on the defeated Confederates to be patient in the tribulation of Reconstruction. The South, Pollard wrote, "must wear the crown of thorns before she can assume that of victory."

The blood of their brothers and the faith of their fathers had consecrated a postwar Southern path. There was to be only limited accommodation to the will of the majority. Though the North had triumphed on the field of battle, the South, anxious about ceding control of their particular affairs to the federal government, settled in for the longest of sieges.

A Confederate general, Jubal A. Early, a veteran of Lee's Army of Northern Virginia, also heavily influenced the white Southern understanding of the war and of the Lost Cause. As the president of, and a longtime leading voice within, the Southern Historical Society, Early strove mightily to burnish the story of the war and its legacy, paying particular attention to the cultivation of the image of Robert E. Lee. By casting Lee as a model of virtue, who only reluctantly took up arms to defend his beloved Virginia and who sought reconciliation after the war, Early and his compatriots gave the Lost Cause narrative the greatest of heroes. When Lee died, in 1870, the praise was more than Frederick Douglass could bear. "We can scarcely take up a newspaper that is not filled with **nauseating** flatteries of the late Robert E. Lee," Douglass wrote. "It would seem from this that the soldier who kills the most men in battle, even in a bad cause, is the greatest Christian, and entitled to the highest place in heaven."

An article of faith in the Lost Cause creed was that the North had not outfought or outgeneraled the South. Victory had come to the Union, and defeat to the Confederacy, rather, because of the North's overwhelming advantages in manpower and industrial strength. By explaining away defeat as the result largely of brute force, the Lost Cause was comforting and utilitarian, for it gave Southerners a way both to think about the past and to act in the present. They had resisted Northern force in battle; now they would defy Northern authority in peace, fighting Pollard's "'war of ideas.'" Before Fort Sumter they had feared restrictions on slavery and had resorted to force of arms. After Appomattox they feared the imposition of the national consensus and would deploy political and paramilitary means to protect their way of life.

Old times there would not be forgotten. "The 'Lost Cause,'" Pollard wrote in 1868, "needs no war to regain it. We have taken up new hopes, new arms, new methods."

Vigilante violence was one such method. In the spring of 1866 in Pulaski, Tennessee, six former Confederates gathered in Thomas M. Jones's law office in a brick building in Giles County. They were bored, they recalled, and struck on the idea of founding a new organization. To be known as the Ku Klux Klan, the group's name was derived from **kuklos,** the Greek word for circle or band, and featured elaborate titles, costumes and hoods fashioned from bed linens, horseback rides through the night—and, soon enough, terror attacks against African Americans.

Southern accounts of the Klan's founding are sentimental. "Boys, let's start something to break the monotony and cheer up our mothers and girls," one of the organizers is alleged to have said. "Let's start a club of some kind." This version of the story, reported in Claude G. Bowers's 1929 book **The Tragic Era: The Revolution After Lincoln,** is blithely racist. When the white-sheeted Klansmen rode, Bowers wrote, "every one was merry for the moment—every one but the freedmen, who, being superstitious, thought they had seen ghosts from the near-by battlefields. Many of these, who had been idling, hurried back contritely and subdued to their old masters' fields. At first the whites laughed over the fears of the blacks, and then, noting an improvement among them, with more industry and less petty pilfering, the serious possibilities of the society were envisaged."

Not only envisaged, but acted upon. Spreading through the South, the Klan's night riders terrorized freed African Americans, many of whom were voting and holding office in the aftermath of the war, and the Klansmen undermined Reconstruction authorities—what the Southern writer and Nathan Bedford Forrest biographer Andrew Lytle called, without irony, "the Scalawag-Carpetbagger regime."

By the spring of 1867, at a gathering at the Maxwell House hotel in Nashville, the Klan was reorganized with a new "Prescript," a detailed hierarchical charter. Intrigued by what he was hearing about the Klan, Nathan Bedford Forrest, the former Confederate cavalry commander, came to Nashville, looked up an old officer of his, asked about joining, and was almost immediately elected "Grand Wizard of the Invisible Empire." Forrest was a legendary figure. "There will never be peace in Tennessee," Union general William T. Sherman had said during the war, "until Forrest is dead." And there was not peace—not really—even now.

The effectiveness of the presidency in the years after the war was underwhelming. Andrew Johnson, the Tennessee Democrat whom Lincoln had chosen as his vice presidential running mate to broaden the GOP's appeal during the 1864 election, proved untrue to Republican orthodoxy. There were, to be sure, landmark advances in the wake of Lincoln's assassination, but they largely came about in spite of Johnson, not because of him.

Therein lies a lesson: If sufficiently developed and organized, public sentiment, as manifested in Congress, can prevail over presidential intransigence. Lincoln offered a case study in the leadership of hope and progress; Andrew Johnson's is an unhappier story of willfulness and single-minded service to a favored constituency—in this case, to white Southerners.

Even the most obtuse chief executive, though, can be formidable without being indomitable. The Civil Rights Act of 1866 and Reconstruction legislation in 1867 that created military districts in the South and guaranteed black male suffrage were passed over Johnson's veto. The president also unsuccessfully opposed the Fourteenth Amendment, which granted citizenship to former slaves and guaranteed, at least on paper, equal protection. The amendment established the principle of birthright citizenship (thus overturning **Dred Scott** and making blacks citizens), and, with its equal protection clause, put the idea of equality into the Constitution for the first time, making the federal government, not the states, the protector of Americans' liberties.

There had been early hopes for Lincoln's successor. "Johnson, we have faith in you," Radical Republican senator Benjamin F. Wade told the new president. "By the Gods, there will be no trouble now in running the government." At first Johnson had seemed determined to punish the rebels. "I hold this: . . . **treason** is a crime, and **crime** must be punished," he said. Charles Sumner himself believed Johnson an ally. The new president, Sumner remarked, was "the sincere friend of the negro and ready to act for him decisively."

Sumner and his Radical Republican compatriots were, alas, wrong. The president from Tennessee sometimes said the right things, but in the end his view of Reconstruction favored a fast resolution of the outstanding issues with the conquered states—and the rights of black freedmen did not lend themselves to quick adjudication. "White men alone must manage the South," Johnson remarked in 1865. Two years later, in 1867, the president asserted that blacks were incapable of self-government. "No independent government of any form has ever been successful in their hands," Johnson wrote in his annual message. "On the contrary, wherever they have been left to their own devices they have shown a constant tendency to relapse into barbarism." It was, the historian Eric Foner observed, "probably the most blatantly racist pronouncement ever to appear in an official state paper of an American president."

Before his first year in office was out, Johnson had done much to return the Southern states to an antebellum footing. He had vetoed the 1866 civil rights bill and the Freedmen's Bureau bill, infuriating Radical Republicans; his civil rights veto message argued that "the distinction of race and color is by the bill made to operate in favor of the colored and against the white race." The presidency which under Lincoln had been a tool of transformation had become, under Johnson, a refuge from modernity.

Johnson was ultimately impeached but not removed from office—he escaped conviction in the Senate by one vote—by Radical Republicans who believed him to be hopelessly accommodating toward his native South. As he lost ground on Reconstruction, Johnson grew erratic, lashing out at opponents. He had, in fact, never seemed entirely stable: Johnson had had too much fortifying whiskey before delivering, or trying to deliver, his inaugural remarks on becoming vice president in 1865. "It must be said," the journalist Noah Brooks reported to his readers, "that upon that momentous and solemn occasion, where were assembled the good, the brave, the beautiful, the noble of our land, and the representatives of many foreign lands, Andrew Johnson, called to be Vice President of the United States, was in a state of manifest intoxication." Johnson rambled in remarks that were emotional, florid, and overlong; he "repeated inaudibly" the oath of office, superfluously adding in "I can say that with perfect propriety" at various points; and, once the oath was done, he started up again, aimlessly discoursing on the import of the occasion. (Defenders say he was fighting illness; sick or no, what people noticed was that he was drunk.)

On Washington's Birthday—Thursday, February 22, 1866—Johnson delivered an angry, self-pitying speech in the capital. "Who, I ask, has suffered more for the Union than I have?" Johnson said. (Lincoln, for one, comes to mind.) He attacked Radical Republicans, including Thaddeus Stevens, Charles Sumner, and Wendell Phillips, and asserted that federal steps toward equality amounted to a dangerous centralization of power—an argument in sync with Edward Pollard's.

Resentful and impassioned, Johnson also riled up the Washington's Birthday crowd with claims that his opponents were considering having him assassinated. Rather than offering reassurance to an anxious public, then, Johnson chose to foment chaos and promulgate fears of conspiracy. "If my blood is to be shed because I vindicate the Union and the preservation of this Government in its original purity and character," he said, "let it be shed; let an altar to the Union be erected, and then, if it is necessary, take me and lay me upon it, and the blood that now warms and animates my exis-

In the spring of 1871, President Grant went to Capitol Hill to seek legislative authority to take federal action to put down the Ku Klux Klan, personally writing out his call for laws to "secure life, liberty, and property."

tence shall be poured out as a fit libation to the Union of these States."

In the presidential contest of 1868, U. S. Grant won the White House as the nominee of the Republican Party, but he faced a complicated racial calculus. Northern opinion was divided between those who wished to force the white South to accept political equality for the freedmen and others who, sharing prevalent racial views of the time, were less interested in elevating blacks to the status of whites. The Union

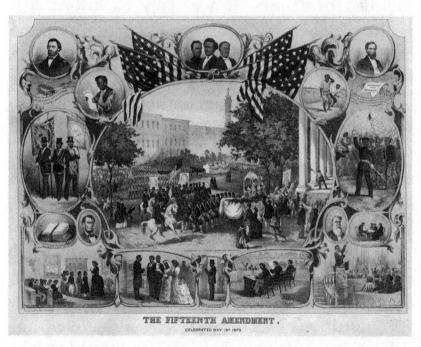

THE FIFTEENTH AMENDMENT.
CELEBRATED MAY 19ᵀ 1870

The amendment extending voting rights to black men, President Grant wrote, was a "measure of grander importance than any other one act of the kind from the foundation of our free Government to the present day."

general Thomas Ewing, Jr., a native of Ohio who served as the first chief justice of Kansas, articulated white fears about Reconstruction during the 1868 presidential campaign. He wanted to support Grant, he said, but worried about a rush to equality. "Blood is thicker than water," Ewing said, "and Northern whites will sympathize with Southern whites in their struggle to shake off the incubus of Negro rule."

As president from 1869 to 1877, Grant struggled to govern a majority-white nation along unionist principles in a racially backward age. Many Northern whites were largely uninterested in, if not outright hostile to, measures to bring equality to the races. And the South was the most confounding theater of the new war. "There has never been a moment since Lee surrendered," Grant said, "that I would not have gone more than halfway to meet the Southern people in a spirit of conciliation. But they have never responded to it. They have not forgotten the war."

Nor would they. "The principle for which we contended is bound to reassert itself," Jefferson Davis remarked after the Confederacy's fall, "though it may be at another time and in another form." Defeated on the battlefield, many Southerners, following Pollard, were determined to win the peace—and victory in the long shadow of Appomattox would be defined by the

extent to which the old Confederacy could sub-
jugate blacks.

Yet Grant, in contrast to Andrew Johnson,
appreciated the bigness of his office and of
the times. On Wednesday, March 30, 1870, to
commemorate the ratification of the Fifteenth
Amendment, with its constitutional extension of
voting rights to African American men, Grant
sent a special message to Congress. The amendment, he wrote, was "a measure of grander importance than any other one act of the kind from
the foundation of our free Government to the
present day." He took a broad view of the moment and its implications. "To the race more favored heretofore by our laws I would say,
Withhold no legal privilege of advancement to
the new citizen." Grant closed by affirming the
significance of the hour. "I repeat," he wrote,
"that the adoption of the fifteenth amendment
to the Constitution completes the greatest civil
change and constitutes the most important event
that has occurred since the nation came into life."

The amendment's ratification led to the passage of the Enforcement Act in May of that
year—a law that empowered federal authorities
to crack down on the Ku Klux Klan. (It was the
first of three such measures.) Still, the violence
and the terror continued. Force had to be met
with force. Senator John Sherman of Ohio,

younger brother of General William T. Sherman, articulated a fairly common Northern view: "If that is the only alternative," Sherman wrote, "I am willing to . . . again appeal to the power of the nation to crush, as we once before have done, this organized civil war."

At last, in the spring of 1871, President Grant intervened on Capitol Hill. He needed, he said, extraordinary powers to bring order to the chaos in the South. Writing in his own hand, he made the case for action. "A condition of affairs now exists in some of the States of the Union rendering life and property insecure and the carrying of the mails and the collection of the revenue dangerous." His conclusion: "Therefore I urgently recommend such legislation as in the judgment of Congress shall effectually secure life, liberty, and property, and the enforcement of law in all parts of the United States."

Congress agreed, and Grant was given the authority to suspend habeas corpus and to deploy military force to fight the Klan. The target of the bill: those who "conspire together, or go in disguise upon the public highway, or upon the premises of another for the purpose . . . of depriving any person or any class of persons of the equal protection of the laws."

The armies of the Lost Cause rallied against Grant and Congress. To the Mississippi **Clarion,** the law was "unconstitutional and hideously despotic." Congressman James M. Leach of North Carolina called it "an outrage upon the Constitution, an outrage upon liberty and free government, an outrage upon the good name of a noble State and a law-loving people."

The Grant-era maneuvers against the reign of terror in the South—which included prosecutions—had the desired effect, and the Klan dissipated as an active force. It was a moment of hope in the postbellum world, but it was a brief one. "Though rejoiced at the suppression of KuKluxery even in one neighborhood," Grant attorney general Amos T. Akerman wrote, "I feel greatly saddened by this business. It has revealed a perversion of moral sentiment among the Southern whites which bodes ill to that part of the country for this generation."

An economic depression, a series of racially reactionary Supreme Court decisions, and the withdrawal of federal forces from the Louisiana and South Carolina statehouses after the disputed 1876 presidential election—the price of Republican Rutherford B. Hayes's defeat of Democrat Samuel Tilden—essentially brought Reconstruction to a conclusion.

Fearing a Democratic victory, Hayes had written that a President Tilden would sacrifice the work of Lincoln and Grant. "I don't care for myself," Hayes said before the final outcome was known, "and the party, yes, and the country, too, can stand it; but I do care for the poor colored men of the South. . . . The result [of a Democratic presidency] will be that the Southern people will practically treat the constitutional amendments as nullities, and then the colored man's fate will be worse than when he was in slavery."

Yet it would be a President Hayes, not a President Tilden, who, in exchange for Southern support, would leave "the poor colored men of the South" without protection in hostile territory. "As to Southern affairs," Hayes wrote a friend from Texas, "'the let alone policy' seems now to be the true course." As for himself, Hayes said, he had "nothing but good will" for the South.

The post-1877 period was bleak. "The whole South—every state in the South—had got into the hands of the very men who held us as slaves," said a former slave. And violence, though more sporadic than in the Klan's heyday, remained a fact of life. The same year Hayes campaigned against Tilden, future South Carolina senator Ben Tillman was part of an attack on African American Republicans at Hamburg, South Carolina. "The purpose of our visit to Hamburg was to strike terror," Tillman recalled. "And the next morning when the Negroes who had fled to the swamp returned to the town, the ghastly sight . . . of seven dead Negroes lying stark and stiff certainly had its effect."

And so things would stand for years to come. "If," W.E.B. Du Bois wrote in 1935, "the Reconstruction of the Southern states, from slavery to free labor, and from aristocracy to industrial democracy, had been conceived as a major national program of America, whose accomplishment at any price was well worth the effort, we should be living today in a different world." But there had no such conception, or at least no such plausible conception given the political, cultural, and economic realities of the nation.

By the 1890s and into the first years of the twentieth century, Jim Crow laws were prevalent in the South, and black voters were systematically disenfranchised. The North, meanwhile, had its own pattern of de jure and de facto segregation. In 1894, Mississippi voted to include the Confederate battle emblem on its state flag. Two years later, in **Plessy v. Ferguson**, the Supreme Court sanctioned the racist principle of "separate but equal."

Justice John Marshall Harlan articulated a forward-leaning view, but his was the sole dissenting vote in **Plessy**. "The white race deems itself to be the dominant race in this country," Harlan wrote. "And so it is, in prestige, in achievements, in education, in wealth, and in power. . . . But in the view of the Constitution, in the eye of the law, there is in this country no superior, dominant, ruling class of citizens. There is no caste here. Our Constitution is color-blind, and neither knows nor tolerates classes among citizens. In respect of civil rights, all citizens are equal before the law. The humblest is the peer of the most powerful." However eloquent, Harlan was speaking against the overwhelming opinion of the time.

Whites reigned supreme. Within about three decades of Lee's surrender, angry and alienated Southern whites who had lost a war had successfully used terror and political inflexibility (a refusal to concede that the Civil War had altered the essential status of black people) to create a postbellum world of American apartheid. Many white Americans had feared a postslavery society in which emancipation might lead to equality, and they had successfully ensured that no such thing should come to pass, North or South. Lynchings, church burnings, and the denial of access to equal education and to the ballot box were the order of the decades. A succession of largely unmemorable presidents served after Grant; none successfully marshaled the power of the office to fight the Northern acquiescence to the South's imposition of Jim Crow.

"We fought," a Confederate veteran from Georgia remarked in 1890, "for the supremacy of the white race in America." That was a war they won—and, in a central American irony, they did so not alone but with the aid and comfort of many of their former foes on the field of battle.

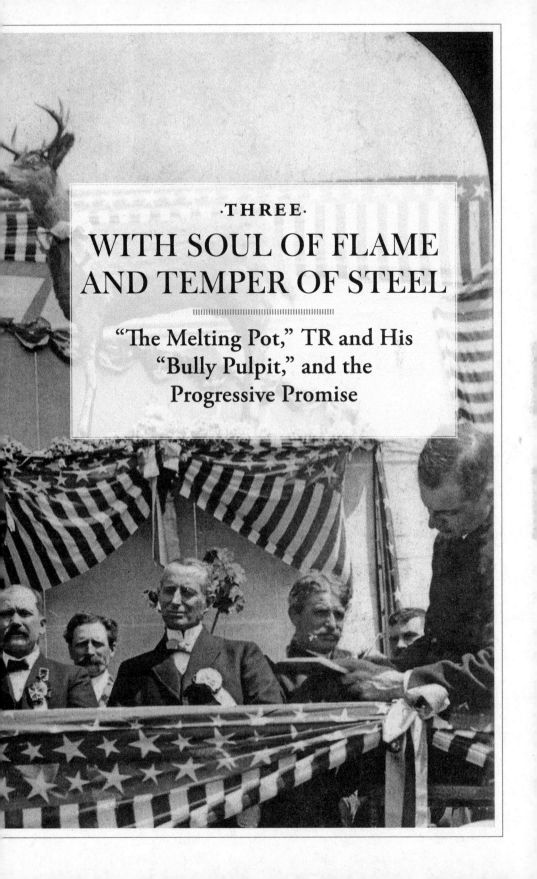

·THREE·

WITH SOUL OF FLAME AND TEMPER OF STEEL

"The Melting Pot," TR and His
"Bully Pulpit," and the
Progressive Promise

PREVIOUS PAGES: Theodore Roosevelt, his daughter Alice Roosevelt Longworth remarked, always wanted to be "the bride at every wedding, the corpse at every funeral"; a contemporary thought him "a dazzling . . . spectacle of a human engine driven at full speed."

FOR THE PRESIDENT, it was a quick half-mile trip from the White House to Washington's Columbia Theater on F Street between Eleventh and Twelfth streets Northwest. On the evening of Monday, October 5, 1908—a lovely early autumn day in the capital—Theodore Roosevelt, nearing the end of his time in office, left the executive mansion with his wife, Edith, to take in a play. TR wanted to make a night of it, and the president's party included three cabinet members and their wives—Elihu Root of State, Victor Metcalf of the Navy, and Oscar Straus of Commerce and Labor—as well as presidential secretary William Loeb and his wife.

The play was Israel Zangwill's **The Melting-Pot,** the story of a Jewish man who had fled

Israel Zangwill's 1908 play The Melting-Pot spoke of America as "God's Crucible." President Roosevelt approved. "It's great—it's a great play," he told Zangwill, who dedicated a published version to TR.

the deadly pogroms of Russia to make a new life in America. The action was set in the living room of a modest house in what Zangwill's stage directions called a "non-Jewish borough of New York" on a February afternoon in the first years of the twentieth century. The play's designers affixed a mezuzah—a tiny metal case to hold a parchment Hebrew scriptural passage—to a doorpost. An American flag was pinned on a wall; there were bookcases with "mouldering Hebrew books" and English-language volumes; pictures of Wagner, Columbus, and Lincoln hung in the room.

The protagonist, the Russian immigrant David Quixano, had reveled in America's openness to new arrivals and rhapsodized about the flow of refugees from the Old World through

New York Harbor. America, he said, was "God's Crucible, the great Melting-Pot, where all the races of Europe are melting and re-forming!" Roosevelt, who was seated next to Zangwill's wife, heartily approved. "Certain strong lines," **The New York Times** reported, "caused Mr. Roosevelt to lean forward in his box and say in a perfectly audible tone, 'That's all right!'"

A climactic speech of Quixano's prompted the president to lead an ovation. "There she lies, the great Melting-Pot. . . ." Quixano says.

> Ah, what a stirring and a seething! Celt and Latin, Slav and Teuton, Greek and Syrian . . . black and yellow . . . how the great Alchemist melts and fuses them with his purging flame! Here shall they all unite to build the Republic of Man and the Kingdom of God. . . . What is the glory of Rome and Jerusalem where all nations and races come to worship and look back, compared with the glory of America, where all races and nations come to labor and look forward!

Characteristically enthusiastic, Roosevelt was lavish in his praise. "It's great—it's a great play," TR told Zangwill. "I never was so stirred in all my life!" Zangwill was understandably thrilled; he had written the play, he recalled, so that audiences would see "that, in the crucible of love . . . the most violent antitheses of the past may be fused into a higher unity." Zangwill later dedicated a published version of **The Melting-Pot** to Roosevelt.

The play went on from Washington to Chicago and finally to Broadway. In 1915 the actor who had played Quixano on stage, Walker Whiteside, starred in a silent-film version, all of which helped popularize the image of the kind of nation that TR, before, during, and after his presidency, sought to sustain: one in which America was welcoming to certain groups if those groups put away their cultures of origin.

To Roosevelt, the sensible—and, in Rooseveltian terms, the **right**—position on the changing nature of the country was perfectly clear. "It is," TR said, "a base outrage to oppose a man because of his religion or birthplace, and all good citizens will hold any such effort in abhorrence."

That was, however, a sentiment more easily articulated than widely realized—even for Roosevelt himself. It would be a mistake to hold Roosevelt up as a forerunner or as a prophet of the racially and ethnically diverse America of the twenty-first century. His vision of the country was, as the title of Zangwill's play had it, of a melting pot, but for him the pot—to extend the metaphor—had been smelted from the achievements of the Anglo-Saxon conquerors of the American continent, and those who joined the American experience owed those conquerors their respect and fealty. "The rude, fierce settler who drives the savage from the land lays all civilized mankind under a debt to him," Roosevelt wrote in his multivolume **The Winning of the West.** He was largely uninterested in revisiting questions of justice about the white conquest of that which had belonged to Native Americans. "During the past century," Roosevelt wrote, "a good deal of sentimental nonsense has been talked about our taking the Indians' land."

TR's capacity on some occasions to stand for equality and for openness and in other contexts to argue that it was the destiny of the Anglo-Saxon peoples to rule the world was a particular example of a more universal American inconsistency. We believed in life and liberty for some; we simultaneously believed in imposing our will on the lives and liberties of others on the grounds that they were innately inferior. The tension between these visions of identity, of assimilation, and of power have long shaped American life, and rarely more so than in the Age of the first Roosevelt.

Born in a four-story brownstone on East Twentieth Street in New York City in 1858, a son of a prominent family, TR was a sickly child who suffered from terrible asthma attacks. "Nobody seemed to think I would live," he recalled. Finding solace in stories and poetry of adventure, of exploration, and of martial valor, he thought of books as "the greatest of companions." (As president of the United States he would read all the novels of Anthony Trollope.) Nicknamed "Teedie," the young Roosevelt fought through his illnesses. "There were all kinds of things of which I was afraid at first," he recalled, "ranging from grizzly bears to 'mean' horses and gun-fighters, but by acting as if I was not afraid I gradually ceased to be afraid." ("Most men," TR added, "can have the same experience if they choose.")

His imagination was filled with tales of strength and vigor. The Revolutionary soldiers of Valley Forge, for instance, were quite real to him, as were the soldiers of the Lost Cause of the Confederacy. His mother, Martha Bulloch Roosevelt, had grown up on a plantation in Georgia; his maternal uncles had fought against the Union. "My earliest training and principles were Southern," he once remarked. Martha Roosevelt, her son recalled, was "entirely 'unreconstructed' to the day of her death." TR had heard so many stories of the Old South from his mother that he knew his way around her family's mansion in Roswell, near Atlanta, on his very first visit—as president of the United States.

He always remembered, too, a visit in New York from his two Confederate uncles shortly after Appomattox. Traveling under assumed names, they would eventually make their homes in England. One, an admiral in the Confederate navy, had built the warship the **Alabama;** the other, TR proudly recalled, was a midshipman who had fired the last rounds from the **Alabama**'s guns in a battle against the Union's **Kearsarge.** The young Roosevelt adored "hearing of the feats performed by Southern forefathers and kinsfolk," tales that, together with his readings of history and heroic fiction, gave him with a love of adventure. "I felt a great admiration for men who were fearless and who could hold their own in the world," TR recalled, "and I had a great desire to be like them." As he remembered it, it was not until he was fourteen that these visions became anything more than "day-dreams."

A miserable stagecoach ride north changed him forever. "Teedie," trying to recover from an asthma attack, was en route to Moosehead Lake in Maine when two boys his age started bullying him. Roosevelt tried to fight back, but failed. He was too weak to defend himself. Humiliated, he decided then and there to do something about it. "The experience taught me what probably no amount of good advice could have taught me," TR recalled. "I made up my mind that I must try to learn so that I would not again be put in such a helpless position." He would take boxing lessons under the tutelage of John Long, a former prizefighter.

Teedie willed himself to strength, lifting weights at a gymnasium on Twenty-eighth Street and at home. He wrestled, rode horses, hunted, hiked, and climbed. As a national politician in an increasingly visual media age, he was shrewd about how he appeared to the masses. "You never saw a photograph of me playing tennis," Roosevelt wrote. "I'm careful about that. Photographs on horseback, yes. Tennis, no." His conception of himself was clear and certain. "Powerful, vigorous men of strong animal development must have some way in which their animal spirits can find vent," TR recalled, and he was surely such a man.

Once Roosevelt started, he never stopped. "Do you know the two most wonderful things I have seen in your country?" an English visitor said after talking with TR in the White House. "Niagara Falls and the President of the United States, both great wonders of nature!" To his daughter Alice Roosevelt Longworth, he was irrepressible. Her father, she said, always wanted to be "the bride at every wedding, and the corpse at every funeral." A contemporary of TR's was struck by the man's raw energy, and wrote that Roosevelt was "a dazzling, even appalling, spectacle of a human engine driven at full speed—the signals all properly set beforehand (and if they aren't, never mind!)." Watching him at a White House musicale, the investigative journalist Ida Tarbell thought the president might explode with energy. "I felt his clothes might not contain him," she recalled, "he was so steamed up, so ready to go, to attack anything, anywhere."

He relished public life. In remarks at Groton School when he was governor of New York, Roosevelt said, "If a man has courage, goodness, and brains, no limit can be placed on the greatness of the work he may accomplish. He is the man needed in politics today." One of his eager listeners was his young cousin, Franklin. In perhaps his most quoted speech, "Citizenship in a Republic," delivered at the Sorbonne in 1910, TR offered a brilliant vision of the virtues of action:

> It is not the critic who counts; not the man who points out how the strong man stumbles, or where the doer of deeds could have done them better. The credit belongs to the

man who is actually in the arena, whose face is marred by dust and sweat and blood; who strives valiantly; who errs, who comes short again and again, because there is no effort without error and shortcoming; but who does actually strive to do the deeds; who knows great enthusiasms, the great devotions; who spends himself in a worthy cause; who at the best knows in the end the triumph of high achievement, and who at the worst, if he fails, at least fails while daring greatly, so that his place shall never be with those cold and timid souls who neither know victory nor defeat.

What was the purpose of action for Roosevelt? Born to great privilege, he adopted the progressive passion for reform that grew out of revulsion at the capitalistic excesses of an industrializing America. Roosevelt targeted those whom he referred to as the "malefactors of great wealth" and argued that the Jeffersonian rights in the Declaration included "the rights of the worker to a living wage, to reasonable hours of labor, to decent working and living conditions, and to freedom of thought and speech and industrial representation—in short . . . in return for his arduous toil, to a worthy and decent life according to American standards." To him, "progress results not from the crowding out of the lower classes by the upper, but on the contrary from the steady rise of the lower classes to the level of the upper."

A rich New York woman once regaled TR with her horror at the progressive campaign against the wealthy and well connected. "What are we going to do, Mr. Roosevelt?"

"What do you mean **we**?" Roosevelt replied.

TR's father, whom the son venerated as "the best man I ever knew," laid the foundations for Roosevelt's engagement with reform. "I never knew anyone who got greater joy out of living than did my father," TR recalled, "or anyone who more whole-heartedly performed every duty"— two of the greatest tests of life in the Roosevelt universe. A bold driver of horses and a tender, attentive parent, the senior Roosevelt was also "interested in every social reform movement, and . . . did an immense amount of practical charitable work himself." In TR's memory, the father loomed large, strong, and generous. "He was a big, powerful man, with a leonine face," TR recalled, "and his heart filled with gentleness for those who needed help or protection, and with the possibility of much wrath against a bully or an oppressor." It's not difficult to see where the son first encountered what became the style and the substance of his own consequential life.

After graduating from Harvard College in 1880, Roosevelt won a seat in the New York assembly the next year. He spent the decade publishing a number of books, both about his adventures in the American West and on history. He adored Big Sky country; while in the Dakotas in the summer of 1886, he gave a Fourth of July address in Dickinson that weaved together his sundry passions. "Like all Americans," he said, "I like big things; big prairies, big forests and mountains, big wheat fields, railroads, and herds of cattle, too, big factories, steamboats and everything else. But we must keep steadily in mind that no people were ever yet benefitted by riches if their prosperity corrupted their virtue." Roosevelt lost a race for mayor of New York that year and became the U.S. Civil Service commissioner in 1889. Six years later, he accepted the post of commissioner of police in New York City.

His emerging convictions about helping the poor and the persecuted were strengthened by the publication, in 1890, of Jacob A. Riis's **How the Other Half Lives.** A pioneering urban journalist, Riis, himself an immigrant from Denmark, had taken powerful photographs of tenement life. "By this time . . . I was getting our social, industrial, and political needs into pretty fair perspective," Roosevelt recalled. He was, he said, "well awake to the need of making ours in good faith both an economic and an industrial as well as a political democracy."

Reading Riis in this state of mind, Roosevelt was profoundly moved by **How the Other Half Lives.** He thought it "an enlightenment and an inspiration." Describing garment sweatshops in "the Hebrew quarter" of the Lower East Side, Riis was struck, first, by the sounds of a crowded new America, by "the whir of a thousand sewing machines, worked at high pressure from earliest dawn till mind and muscle give out together. Every member of the family, from the youngest to the oldest, bears a hand, shut in the qualmy rooms, where the meals are cooked and clothing washed and dried besides, the live-long day. It is not unusual to find a dozen persons—men, women, and children—at work in a single small room."

TR went to see Riis at the offices of the New York **Evening Sun** downtown "to tell him how deeply impressed I was by the book, and that I wished to help him in any practical way to try to make things a little better." Riis was out; Roosevelt left his card with a note. "I have read your book," Roosevelt had written, "and I have come to help." To Riis, the words amounted to a solemn pledge. "It was like a man coming to enlist for a war because he believed in the cause," Riis said.

Riis, TR recalled, was to become "the man closest to me throughout my two years in the Police Department," and Roosevelt longed to take concrete steps. "I have always had a horror of words that are not translated into deeds, of speech that does not result in action," Roosevelt recalled. "I believe in realizable ideals and in realizing them, in preaching what can be practiced and then in practicing it."

Before he was done—after the police posting, after the governorship, after the vice presidency, after the presidency, and after his unsuccessful 1912 campaign to reclaim the White House on a third-party Progressive ticket—TR would fight against corrupt machine politics, against great business monopolies, and against abysmal working conditions. He would crusade, sometimes effectively, sometimes less so, for conservation of natural resources, for government regulation of railroads, for food safety, for women's suffrage, and for political reform.

In all of this TR anticipated the work of his cousin, Franklin, and of Harry Truman and Lyndon Johnson. "The Nation and Government," TR wrote, "within the range of fair play and a just administration of the law, must inevitably sympathize with the men who have nothing but their wages, with the men who are

A pioneering investigative urban journalist, Jacob Riis photographed tenement and sweatshop life. Riis's book **How the Other Half Lives** profoundly influenced Roosevelt.

struggling for a decent life, as opposed to men, however honorable, who are merely fighting for larger profits and autocratic control of big business."

Immigration, a dominant issue for TR's America, was an enduring source of political discontent. In 1798, John Adams, amid war fever about France, signed the Alien and Sedition Acts to protect, in his view, the national interest against internal dissent and outside agitation. Passed by a Federalist-controlled Congress, the legislation, among other things, increased the number of years applicants for citizenship had to wait and authorized the president to deport any foreigner he deemed dangerous to the country. "The Alien bill proposed in the Senate is a monster that must for ever disgrace its parents," James Madison wrote Thomas Jefferson in the spring of 1798. Madison was right: Adams's historical legacy has been tarnished by this un-republican grab for power. And in the short term, the acts had the unintended consequence of giving new force to Adams's opposition, led by Jefferson and Madison, who went on to defeat the Federalists in the 1800 election.

Writing in 1783, George Washington had articulated what we like to think of as the American way on such things: "The bosom of America is open to receive not only the opulent and respectable Stranger, but the oppressed and persecuted of all Nations and Religions." Yet fears about indiscriminate immigration are coeval with the Founding and the early republic. In 1802, Alexander Hamilton—himself an immigrant and, in the twenty-first century, an emblem of American mobility—had reservations: "The influx of foreigners must . . . tend to produce a heterogeneous compound; to change and corrupt the national spirit; to complicate and confound public opinion; to introduce foreign propensities." We've never been as open as we'd like to think, but at our best we've managed to remain truer to the spirit Washington expressed than to the one Hamilton did.

Anxiety about refugees and immigrants and the related desire of presidents to quell that unease were then—and have always been—an element in the American experience. The country often limited immigration in moments of fear, only to have those fears dissipate amid cooling emotions and a reinvigorated opposition. It had happened in 1798. It had happened in the mid-nineteenth century, when the Know-Nothings had sprung up in reaction to a wave of European immigration in the wake of the revolutions of 1848. And it had happened with the Chinese Exclusion Act under Chester Arthur, which was passed in reaction to fears of competing labor coming in from the Far East.

"Whatever business or trade they entered was, and is yet, absolutely doomed for the white laborer, as competition is simply impossible," the labor leaders Samuel Gompers and Herman Gutstadt wrote in a pamphlet entitled **Meat vs. Rice: American Manhood Against Asiatic Coolieism: Which Shall Survive?** "Not that the Chinese would not rather work for high wages than low, but in order to gain control he will work so cheaply as to bar all efforts of his competitor." The anxiety was pitched. "The negro slave of the South was housed and fed," Gompers and Gutstadt wrote, "but the white trash of California is placed beneath the Mongolian."

TR's era was imbued with ideas both of reform and of racial superiority. The movement for economic justice and improving workplace conditions, among other causes, was roughly simultaneous with the spread of eugenics and quasi-Darwinian notions, influenced by the work of Herbert Spencer, about white hegemony. (Spencer coined the phrase "survival of the fittest.") And there was a concomitant sense of destiny about Anglo-Saxon civilization. Captured in lectures such as John Fiske's 1879 "Manifest Destiny of the English Race" and Rudyard Kipling's

1899 poem "The White Man's Burden," the latter composed in honor of the American imperial enterprise in the Philippines, the ethos of the age celebrated the muscular virtues of those whom Winston Churchill later popularized as "the English-speaking peoples." Kipling sent TR a prepublication text of "The White Man's Burden," which Roosevelt passed along to his friend Henry Cabot Lodge with this note: "I send you an advance copy of a poem by Kipling which is rather poor poetry, but good sense from the expansionist viewpoint."

In his "Manifest Destiny" lecture, Fiske, a Harvard-educated historian and philosopher, spoke to the ambition of those who prayed that, in his phrase, "the language of Shakespeare may ultimately become the language of mankind." In this view, the march of white Anglo-Saxon civilization was inevitable, inevitably good, and universal. "Who can doubt," Fiske asked, "that within two or three centuries the African continent will be occupied by a mighty nation of English descent, and covered with populous cities and flourishing farms, with railroads and telegraphs and other devices of civilization as yet undreamed of?"

In his **The Winning of the West**, TR surveyed with pride the three hundred or so years that had elapsed between the reign of Elizabeth I and his own time. "During the past three centuries," he wrote, "the spread of the English-speaking peoples over the world's waste spaces has been not only the most striking feature in the world's history, but also the event of all others most far-reaching in its importance."

Such views were in keeping with the thought of the time. The eugenist and white supremacist Madison Grant worried that the rise of "the Slovak, the Italian, the Syrian, and the Jew" would soon displace what he argued had been the American strain from the "Teutonic part of the British Isles" that was "almost purely Nordic." According to Grant's book **The Passing of the Great Race,** immigrants from southern and eastern Europe, as well as from the Middle East, threatened to rise from the melting pot to new dominance. "The 'survival of the fittest,'" Grant wrote, "means the survival of the type best adapted to existing conditions of environment, which to-day are the tenement and factory, as in Colonial times they were the clearing of forests, fighting Indians, farming the fields, and sailing the Seven Seas."

New York was a source of particular concern to nativists. "Now we confront the melancholy spectacle of this pioneer breed being swamped and submerged by an overwhelming tide of late-comers from the old-world hive," the sociologist E. A. Ross wrote in 1914. He then italicized his alarm: "**Certainly never since the colonial era have the foreign-born and their children formed so large a proportion of the American people as at the present moment.**" From observation in New York's Union Square, Ross reported that he'd "scanned 368 persons as they passed me . . . at a time when the garment-workers of the Fifth Avenue lofts were returning to their homes. Only thirty-eight of these passers-by had the type of face one would find at a county fair in the West or the South."

That was a persistent view in the East. In the West, the fear of being overrun and outworked by the Chinese was a consuming one from the 1870s forward. "Either the Anglo-Saxon race will possess the Pacific slope or the Mongolians will possess it," Senator James G. Blaine of Maine said in February 1879. "You give them the start to-day . . . and it is entirely inevitable, if not demonstrable, that they will occupy that great space of country between the Sierras and the Pacific coast." Lest anyone miss his point, Blaine alliteratively added: "We have this day to choose whether we will have for the Pacific coast the civilization of Christ or the civilization of Confucius."

Roosevelt shared the dream of Anglo-Saxon imperialism; Longfellow's Nordic **Saga of King Olaf** was among his favorite poems. TR was redeemed to some extent, however, by a basic aversion to nativism. An emblem of a bustling, growing country that was open to those willing to adopt a creed of "Americanism," Roosevelt partially widened the understanding of the mainstream. "We freely extend the hand of welcome and of good-fellowship to every man, no matter what his creed or birthplace, who comes here honestly intent on becoming a good United States citizen like the rest of us," Roosevelt said in 1894, adding:

> Americanism is a question of spirit, conviction, and purpose, not of creed or birthplace. The politician who bids for the Irish or German vote, or the Irishman or German who votes as an Irishman or German, is despicable, for all citizens of this commonwealth should vote solely as Americans; but he is not a whit less despicable than the voter who votes against a good American, merely because that American happens to have been born in Ireland or Germany. . . . A Scandinavian, a German, or an Irishman who has really become an American has the right to stand on exactly the same footing as any native-born citizen in the land, and is just as much entitled to the friendship and support, social and political, of his neighbors.

Dinner was called for seven-thirty on the evening of Wednesday, October 16, 1901. The invitation to Booker T. Washington, the founder and president of the Tuskegee Institute in Alabama, had been dispatched that very day. Born a slave in 1856, Washington had risen to prominence in the long decades since. Now, at the beginning of a new century, a new president—Theodore Roosevelt had assumed the office after the assassination of William McKinley barely a month before, in September 1901—had asked Washington to become the first African American in history to dine formally at the White House.

TR knew Washington, and, according to his own recollection, had not given "very much thought" to the invitation. It seemed, Roosevelt said, "natural to ask him to dinner to talk over [his] work." Yet the president understood the implications of the evening, recalling, "the very fact that I felt a moment's qualm on inviting him because of his color made me ashamed of myself and made me hasten to send the invitation."

Reaction among white Southerners was swift. "There is a feeling of indignation among southern men, generally, that the President should, in the face of his declaration of friendliness toward the people of the south, take this early opportu-

DINNER GIVEN AT THE WHITE HOUSE BY PRESIDENT ROOSEVELT TO BOOKER T. WASHINGTON, OCTOBER 17th, 1901

In October 1901, Roosevelt invited Booker T. Washington to dine at the White House, provoking white outrage. On the facing page, Washington is also pictured speaking at a Lincoln commemoration in 1906; Mark Twain is seated behind him.

nity to show such a marked courtesy and distinction to a negro," **The Atlanta Constitution** wrote. The Memphis **Commercial Appeal** said, "President Roosevelt has committed a blunder that is worse than a crime, and no atonement or future act of his can remove the self-imprinted stigma." Alabama's **Geneva Reaper** was especially harsh. "Poor Roosevelt!" the paper wrote. "He might now just as well sleep with Booker Washington, for the scent of that coon will fol-

low him to the grave as far as the South is concerned."

Roosevelt knew the notices were rough. "As things have turned out I am very glad that I asked him," he wrote a correspondent after the Washington dinner, "for the clamor aroused by the act makes me feel as if the act was necessary." TR's reflections on the invitation tell us much about the era. Though asking Washington to dine was a pioneering act, the president was not a civil rights pioneer in the ways we, from a different century and in a different context, might hope to find. For his time, however, Roosevelt was closer to the side of the angels than many other Americans were. "I have not been able to think out any solution to the terrible problem offered by the presence of the negro on this continent," he wrote, "but of one thing I am sure, and that is that inasmuch as he is here and can neither be killed nor driven away, the only wise and honorable and Christian thing to do is to treat each black man and each white man strictly on his merits as a man, giving him no more and no less than he shows himself worthy to have," continuing:

> I say that I am "sure" this is the right solution. Of course I know that we see through a glass dimly, and, after all, it may be that I am wrong; but if I am, then all my thoughts and beliefs are wrong, and my whole way of looking at life is wrong. At any rate, while I am in public life, however short a time that may be, I am in honor bound to act up to my beliefs and convictions.

As a young political figure, Roosevelt had supported the nomination of an African American, John R. Lynch of Mississippi, to serve as temporary chair of the Republican National Convention in 1884. In a seconding speech, TR said that it was a "fitting thing for us to choose to preside over this convention one of that race whose right to sit within these walls is due to the blood and treasure so lavishly spent by the founders of the Republican Party."

In the White House, he backed Minnie M. Cox, the African American postmaster of Indianola, Mississippi, when whites demanded her removal in favor of a white candidate. He also refused to give in to opposition to his appointment of another African American, Dr. William Crum, as head of the customs house in Charleston, South Carolina. "I know of no people in the North so slavishly conventional, so slavishly afraid of expressing any opinion hostile to or different from that held by their neighbors, as is true of the southerners, and most especially of the Charleston aristocrats, on all vital questions." To a correspondent in South Carolina, Roosevelt said, "It seems to me that it is a good thing from every standpoint to let the colored man know that if he shows in marked degree the qualities of good citizenship—the qualities which in a white man we feel are entitled to reward—then he himself will not be cut off from all hope of similar reward."

At the same time, he could make racist remarks and observations, particularly about people of color abroad, and he worried that a white failure to reproduce sufficiently might lead to "race suicide," a popular theory in those days. "I am an optimist," Roosevelt wrote a sister in 1899, "but there are grave signs of deterioration in the English-speaking peoples." To William Howard Taft, who succeeded him in 1909, Roosevelt lamented a low birth rate among the "best people." "In spite of our enormous immigration," Roosevelt told Taft, "there is a good reason to fear that unless the present tendencies are checked your children and mine will see the day when our population is stationary, and so far as the native stock is concerned is dying out."

He could also be unfairly harsh about the conduct of black soldiers in the Spanish-American War, writing that they had flinched in battle and run to the rear. "Here again, I attributed the trouble to the superstition and fear of the darkey," TR wrote, "natural in those but one generation removed from slavery and but a few generations removed from the wildest savagery." Roosevelt was wrong: The troops he had thought were fleeing fire had in fact been following the orders of a white officer. Standing corrected, he said that he was "the last man in the world to say anything against the colored soldiers." The mistake was telling. "Roosevelt's frequent invocation of the idea of equal opportunity for all Americans regardless of race and his occasional efforts in behalf of blacks earned him a reputation among both his contemporaries and among many historians as a racial 'moderate,'" the scholar Thomas G. Dyer wrote. Still, Dyer added, "although Roosevelt may have been a moderating force in an age of high racism, he nevertheless harbored strong feelings about the inferiority of blacks, feelings which suggest the pervasiveness of racism and the harsh character of racial 'moderation' in turn-of-the-century America."

Most things in politics, in other words, are relative. To honor Lincoln's Birthday in 1905, shortly after he won a full presidential term on his own, Roosevelt gave a farsighted address to a Republican gathering in New York City:

> We of to-day, in dealing with all our fellow-citizens, white or colored, North or South, should strive to show just the qualities that Lincoln showed—his steadfastness in striving after the right, and his infinite patience and forbearance with those who saw that right less clearly than he did; his earnest endeavor to do what was best, and yet his readiness to accept the best that was practicable when the ideal best was unattainable; his unceasing effort to cure what was evil, coupled with his refusal to make a bad situation worse by any ill-judged or ill-timed effort to make it better.

TR nodded to the Lost Cause but made it clear that the right side had prevailed. Federal and Confederate troops, Roosevelt said, "fought with equal bravery and with equal sincerity of conviction, each striving for the light as it was given him to see the light; though it is now clear to all that the triumph of the cause of freedom and of the Union was essential to the welfare of mankind."

His words were eloquent, his tone gentle:

> Our effort should be to secure to each man, whatever his color, equality of opportunity, equality of treatment before the law. . . . Every generous impulse in us revolts at the thought of thrusting down instead of helping up such a man. To deny any man the fair treatment granted to others no better than he is to commit a wrong upon him—a wrong sure to react in the long run upon those guilty of such denial. The only safe principle upon which Americans can act is that of "all men up," not that of "some men down."

He knew it was not a matter of passing concern or quick solution. "The working out of this problem must necessarily be slow. . . . It is a problem demanding the best thought, the utmost patience, the most earnest effort, the broadest charity, of the statesman, the student, the philanthropist; of the leaders of thought in every department of our national life." He added:

> I believe in this country with all my heart and soul. I believe that our people will in the end rise level to every need, will in the end triumph over every difficulty that rises before them. I could not have such confident faith in the destiny of this mighty people if I had it merely as regards one portion of that people. Throughout our land things on the whole have grown better and not worse, and this is as true of one part of the country as it is of another. I believe in the Southerner as I believe in the Northerner. . . . For weal or for woe we are knit together, and we shall go up or go down together; and I believe that we shall go up and not down, that we shall go forward instead of halting and falling back, because I have an abiding faith in the generosity, the courage, the resolution, and the common sense of all my countrymen.

Like Jacob Riis, Jane Addams helped shape Roosevelt's vision of the emerging America of the twentieth century. The cofounder of Hull-House, a settlement house on the near west side

The cofounder of Chicago's Hull-House, Jane Addams was an important reformer, fighting for women's suffrage and civil rights and against child labor. She seconded TR's Bull Moose presidential nomination in 1912.

of Chicago, Addams was a critical figure in reform movements ranging from women's suffrage to civil rights to child labor. In 1913, TR opened his **Autobiography** with a meditation on the great democratic experiment of which Addams was a part. "Justice among the nations of mankind, and the uplifting of humanity, can be brought about only by those strong and daring men who with wisdom love peace, but who love righteousness more than peace," Roosevelt wrote. "There must be the keenest sense of duty, and with it must go the joy of living; there must be shame at the thought of shirking the hard work of the world, and at the same time delight in the many-sided beauty of life. With soul of flame and temper of steel we must act as our coolest judgment bids us."

Addams had that kind of soul. She was delighted with the platform of the Progressive Party, also known as the Bull Moose Party, which nominated Roosevelt for another presidential term in 1912. "The conscience of the people," the Progressive platform read, "in a time of grave national problems, has called into being a new party, born of the nation's sense of justice." TR took up the cause with typical ebullience, crying, "We fight in honorable fashion for the good of mankind; fearless of the future; unheeding of our individual fates; with unflinching hearts and undimmed eyes, we stand at Armageddon and we battle for the Lord!"

The platform endorsed women's suffrage, an issue TR embraced. It was, he wrote, "exactly as much a 'right' of women as of men to vote." By his own account he had believed so "only tepidly" until moved by the passion of Addams, among others. In a larger sense, Roosevelt argued that the vote was a weapon, not the war. "A vote is like a rifle: its usefulness depends upon the character of the user. . . . I believe in suffrage for women in America, because I think they are fit for it. I believe for women, as for men, more in the duty of fitting one's self to do well and wisely with the ballot than in the naked right to cast the ballot."

At the new party's convention in Chicago in August 1912, Addams seconded Roosevelt's nomination. She was doing so, she told the delegates, because "he is one of the few men in our public life who has been responsive to modern movement. Because of that, because the program will need a leader of invincible courage, of open mind, of democratic sympathies—one endowed with power to interpret the common man and to identify himself with the common lot, I heartily second the nomination." The crowd had greeted her appearance at the podium, a journalist wrote, with "a volcano of emotion and applause"; as she spoke, another reporter noted, "all noise ceased. The usual walking about . . . stopped. Everyone listened."

Addams saw the movement whole. "A great party has pledged itself to the protection of children, to the care of the aged, to the relief of overworked girls, to the safeguarding of burdened men," she said. "Committed to these humane undertakings, it is inevitable that such a party should appeal to women, should seek to draw upon the great reservoir of their moral energy, so long undesired and unutilized in practical politics. . . . The new party has become the American exponent of a world-wide movement toward juster social conditions, a movement which America, lagging behind other great nations, has been unaccountably slow to embody in political action."

Roosevelt thanked her profusely. "I prized your action not only because of what you are and stand for, but because of what it symbolized for the new movement," TR telegraphed Addams. "Our party stands for social and industrial justice, and we have a right to expect that women and men will work within the party for the cause with the same high sincerity of purpose and with like efficiency."

That same year, Israel Zangwill wrote Roosevelt to check in on the former president's views about the ideas of **The Melting-Pot.** An enthusiastic TR replied,

Now as a matter of fact that particular play I shall always count among the very strong and real influences upon my thought and my life. It has been in my mind continually, and on my lips often during the last three years. It not merely dealt with the "melting pot," with the fusing of all foreign nationalities into an American nationality, but it also dealt with the great ideals which it is just as essential for the native born as for the foreign to realize and uphold if the new nationality is to represent a real addition to the sum total of human achievement.

A speech saved his life. Leaving the Hotel Gilpatrick in Milwaukee on the evening of Monday, October 14, 1912, Roosevelt was shot in the chest by a deranged unemployed saloonkeeper who said the ghost of William McKinley had ordered him to kill Roosevelt. The bullet, a .38, was slowed by his metal glasses case, an army overcoat, and a fifty-page manuscript of the address the candidate was scheduled to deliver that night. "They wanted to rush me to the hospital," Roosevelt was recalled to have said. "It was nonsense; I had to make that speech! I knew that there were just two things that could happen: either I would die or I would recover. If I were to die, I specially wished to make the speech; if I were to recover, I might as well make it. And I have never thought of death as a calamity, as many do. It doesn't seem to me a thing to dread."

In the auditorium shortly thereafter, Roosevelt persevered. "At one time I promoted five men for gallantry on the field of battle," he told the crowd. "Afterward in making some inquiries about them I found that two of them were Protestants, two Catholic, and one a Jew. One Protestant came from Germany and one was born in Ireland. I did not promote them because of their religion. It just happened that way. If all five of them had been Jews I would have promoted them, or if all five of them had been Protestants I would have promoted them; or if they had been Catholics."

This, Roosevelt said, was the American way. "I ask in our civic life that we in the same way pay heed only to the man's quality of citizenship, to repudiate as the worst enemy that we can have whoever tries to get us to discriminate for or against any man because of his creed or birthplace."

He carried that bullet in his chest for the rest of his life. In 1919, two days before the seemingly unimaginable happened—the death of Theodore Roosevelt, at about four o'clock on the morning of Monday, January 6, from an embolism—the former president mused about the country. "There can be here no divided allegiance," he wrote in those final stages. "We have room for but one flag, the American flag; for but one language, the English language; for but one soul loyalty, and that is loyalty to the American people."

PRESID[E]
"This is the time

·FOUR·

A NEW AND GOOD THING IN THE WORLD

The Triumph of Women's Suffrage,
the Red Scare, and a New Klan

PREVIOUS PAGES: "Remember the Ladies," Abigail Adams had written her husband, John, in 1776. The long campaign for women's suffrage did not succeed until 1920, at the end of the Wilson years.

It was we, the people; not we, the white male citizens;
nor yet we, the male citizens; but we, the whole people,
who formed the Union.

—SUSAN B. ANTHONY, arguing for the equality
of women before the law, 1873

I would build a wall of steel, a wall as high as Heaven,
against the admission of a single one of those Southern
Europeans who never thought the thoughts or spoke the
language of a democracy in their lives.

—Georgia governor CLIFFORD WALKER, to the
Second Imperial Klonvokation of the Ku Klux Klan,
Kansas City, Missouri, 1924

THE PRESIDENT OF THE UNITED States typed the speech himself. It was, in a sense, the least Woodrow Wilson could do. Like many American men, he had hardly been an enthusiastic supporter of the decades-long struggle for a constitutional amendment on women's suffrage, but, in the middle of a world war, Wilson had changed his mind and was now, in the early autumn of 1918, ready to take the case to the Senate. After generations of activism—of appeals in the press, of marches and rallies, of vigils and hunger strikes—supporters of extending voting rights to women had at last convinced the most powerful man in the nation to stand up for them.

On Monday, September 30, 1918, Wilson went to Capitol Hill to deliver the speech he had composed on his typewriter. His mission: to urge lawmakers to approve the proposed Nineteenth Amendment to the Constitution granting women the vote. The war against the European imperial powers, Wilson told the Senate, was also a war for a more inclusive and enlightened era. The people of the world, he told the Senate, were "looking to the great, powerful, famous Democracy of the West to lead them to the new day for which they have so long waited; and they think . . . that democracy means that women shall play their part in affairs alongside men and upon an equal footing with them." Women had answered the call to service in war; they would soon be essential to the peace. "Without their counsellings," Wilson said, "we shall be only half wise."

Wilson had long been familiar with the energy driving the suffrage movement. On arriving in Washington for his first inauguration five years earlier, in March 1913, the president-elect wondered why there were so few well-wishers at Union Station or on the streets.

"Where," Wilson said, "are the people?"

"Oh," he was told, "they are out watching the suffrage parade."

The demonstration that day was enormous—

and chaotic. Angry men taunted the marchers and tried to break their ranks. The suffragists, the **Baltimore American** reported, "practically fought their way foot by foot up Pennsylvania Avenue, through a surging throng that completely defied Washington police." Only the arrival of cavalry troops from Fort Myer, the army base across the Potomac, brought a semblance of order to the day.

In a small meeting in the East Room later that month with Alice Paul, a leading advocate for suffrage, and seven of her colleagues, Wilson refused to take up their cause. The fact that the fight for the right to vote had been waged for seven decades—since, really, the founding convention of the movement at Seneca Falls, New York, in 1848—did not impress the president. "I do not care to enter into a discussion of that," Wilson told his visitors, ending the conversation.

It was not, then, an auspicious beginning. But the White House meeting was only that—a beginning. Alice Paul soon headquartered herself on Lafayette Square and launched a persistent campaign of protest at Wilson's doorstep. Born in 1885 to a distinguished Quaker family in New Jersey, Paul had been influenced by the more militant British suffrage movement during a stay in England from 1907 to 1910. There, under the leadership of Emmeline Pankhurst's Women's Social and Political Union, women moved from speechmaking to active street protest, including face-to-face challenges to lawmakers. If arrested, the suffragists, including the visiting Paul, would refuse food in jail, leading to highly publicized force-feedings. The gruesome details of prison officials jamming tubes carrying milk and mush through the protestors' nostrils to prevent starvation lent moral urgency to the suffragist cause. "The essence of the campaign of the suffragettes," Paul told American audiences on her return, "is opposition to the Government"—and a government that imprisoned and mistreated women for seeking the justice of the franchise was clearly worth opposing.

The roots of the long campaign to extend the vote and equal protection to women are older even than the Republic. A few months before the Second Continental Congress broke decisively with Great Britain, John Adams was at work in Philadelphia when he received an engaging letter from his wife, Abigail. "I long to hear that you have declared an independency—and by the way in the new Code of Laws which I suppose it will be necessary for you to make I desire you would Remember the Ladies, and be more generous and favorable to them than your ancestors," Mrs. Adams wrote. "Do not put such

Alice Paul, a leading suffragist,
headquartered herself on
Lafayette Square and focused
intense reform pressure on
President Wilson at the gates
of the White House.

unlimited power into the hands of the Husbands. Remember all Men would be tyrants if they could. If particular care and attention is not paid to the Ladies we are determined to foment a Rebellion, and will not hold ourselves bound by any Laws in which we have no voice, or Representation."

The July 1848 Seneca Falls women's rights convention—brought about by Elizabeth Cady Stanton and Lucretia Mott, among others—issued a "Declaration of Sentiments and Resolutions" that sanctified a movement's creed: "We hold these truths to be self-evident: that all men **and women** are created equal." The italics are mine; the vision the suffragists'. Susan B. Anthony, an essential figure, echoed the point down the years: "It was we, the people; not we, the white male citizens; nor yet we, the male citizens; but we, the whole people, who formed this Union," she said in 1873 after she illegally cast a ballot for U. S. Grant for president. "And we formed it, not to give the blessings of liberty, but to secure them; not to the half of ourselves and the half of our posterity, but to the whole people—women as well as men."

Through the years, by fits and starts and in good times and bad, the work went on. The climactic drama came in the Wilson years when Alice Paul, focused on the passage and ratification of the Nineteenth Amendment, kept the pressure on. Demonstrators known as "silent sentinels" stood outside the White House every day; when arrested (on charges of interfering with traffic), they, like their British counterparts, would refuse food in jail, leading to the dreaded force-feedings. During the 1916 State of the

Union, suffragists in the House gallery displayed a banner that read MR. WILSON, WHAT ARE YOU DOING FOR WOMEN'S SUFFRAGE? For "the first time in American history," the historian Jean H. Baker wrote, "an organized group of dissidents, not just a single individual like Thoreau, had employed passive resistance and civil disobedience in a direct confrontation with presidential authority."

And they prevailed when Wilson agreed to endorse the proposed amendment, which was ratified on Wednesday, August 18, 1920. "Will you take the opportunity to say to my fellow citizens that I deem it one of the greatest honors of my life that this great event, the ratification of this amendment, should have occurred during the period of my administration," he wrote the suffrage leader Carrie Chapman Catt in the summer of 1920. "Nothing has given me more pleasure than the privilege that has been mine to do what I could to advance the cause of ratification and to hasten the day when the womanhood of America would be recognized by the nation on the equal footing of citizenship that it deserves."

Catt herself wrote a letter to her staff on Thanksgiving Day 1920, a few weeks after women in all forty-eight states had the right to cast ballots for president for the first time under the Nineteenth

Amendment. "As I look back over the years," Catt wrote, "I realize that the greatest thing in the long campaign for us was not its crowning victory, but the discipline it gave us all. . . . It was a great crusade, the world has seen none more wonderful. . . . My admiration, love, and reverence go out to that band which fought and won a revolution . . . with congratulations that we were permitted to establish a new and good thing in the world."

Though he was slow to join the side of the angels, Wilson got suffrage right. The ratification of the Nineteenth Amendment was a landmark in American life, the result of nearly a century and a half—if we date things from Abigail Adams's admonition to her husband to "remember the ladies"—of toil. Leadership came from those without office; women resisted the suffocating opinion of generations to create new opinion, and new law, and a new nation.

And yet, and yet—there is always an "and yet" in American history. Taken all in all, Woodrow Wilson and his age are revealing examples of the battles between hope and fear. The era of the suffrage triumph, for instance, was also the age of segregation, of the suppression of free speech in wartime, of the Red Scare of 1919–20, and of the birth of a new Ku Klux Klan. The story of America is thus one of slow, often unsteady steps forward. If we expect the trumpets of a given era to sound unwavering notes, we will be disappointed, for the past tells us that politics is an uneven symphony.

In the autumn of 1914, Wilson was in mourning. Ellen, his beloved wife, had died in the White House, of Bright's disease, a kidney ailment, on Thursday, August 6. With Europe heading into war, Wilson labored under the weight of his grief and of his responsibilities. In that first season of the Great War, on Thursday, November 12, 1914, the president received a delegation of black leaders. In the 1912 campaign, Wilson had promised African Americans "absolute fair dealing," only to allow the segregation of federal departments. His callers were unhappy and weren't shy about speaking their minds.

Among the visitors, William Monroe Trotter of Boston, a prominent editor, was the most direct. With W.E.B. Du Bois, Trotter had founded the Niagara Movement, a forerunner of the National Association for the Advancement of Colored People. Niagara's guiding principles included this one: "We refuse to allow the impression to remain that the Negro-American assents to inferiority, is submissive under oppression and apologetic before insults."

In 1909, in the aftermath of a 1908 race riot in Springfield, Illinois, Oswald Garrison Villard, a grandson of the abolitionist William Lloyd Garrison, had written **The Call: A Lincoln Emancipation Conference to Discuss Means for Securing Political and Civil Equality for the Negro.** " 'A house divided against itself cannot stand,' " Villard wrote, and "this government cannot exist half-slave and half-free any better today than it could in 1861. Hence we call upon all the believers in democracy to join in a national conference for the discussion of present evils, the voicing of protests, and the renewal of the struggle for civil and political liberty." Issued on Lincoln's Birthday—it was the Great Emancipator's centennial—the statement, signed by whites and blacks, including Du Bois, led to the creation of the NAACP in 1909.

Three years later, in the 1912 presidential election, blacks faced what Du Bois called "desperate alternatives." Neither William Howard Taft, the Republican nominee, nor Theodore Roosevelt, the third-party Bull Moose candidate (despite his Lincoln Day rhetoric, his support for black appointees in the South, and the Booker T. Washington dinner) were thought to have enough to offer African Americans seeking to stride toward equality. Many gambled, then, on Wilson and the Democrats—to their great disappointment.

Opposition to the Wilson administration's segregationist policies offered twentieth-century America a glimpse of what would become decades of civil rights activism. Through reports, open letters, and mass meetings, the NAACP sought to dramatize the moral stakes in the hope that protest would fill the void left by the president. Equally significant, the organization, through its Legal Bureau, used the courts to fight segregation and discrimination.

In the November 1914 White House meeting with Wilson, Trotter was blunt. "Only two years ago you were heralded as perhaps the second Lincoln, and now the Afro-American leaders who supported you are hounded as false leaders and traitors to their race," Trotter told Wilson. "What a change segregation has wrought!"

Wilson replied that "it takes the world generations to outlive all its prejudices," yet Trotter pressed his point.

"We are not here as wards," Trotter said. "We are not here as dependents. We are here as full-fledged American citizens."

Trotter spoke heatedly, and Wilson snapped: "Let me say this, if you will, that if this organization wishes to approach me again, it must choose another spokesman. . . . You are an American citizen, as fully an American citizen as I am, but you are the only American citizen that has ever come into this office who has talked to me with

William Monroe Trotter, a founder of the Niagara Movement, challenged President Wilson on civil rights in a contentious White House meeting that ended with Wilson preemptorily dismissing Trotter's delegation.

a tone [and] with a background of passion that was evident."

"I am from a part of the people, Mr. President," Trotter replied.

"You have spoiled the whole cause for which you came," Wilson said, dismissing the delegation. (Wilson would later refer to Trotter as "that unspeakable fellow.")

From the president's perspective, the White House exchange was disastrous. (Given his experience with Alice Paul and her suffrage colleagues, Wilson did not have the best record with visiting delegations.) "I was damn fool enough to lose my temper and to point them to the door," Wilson remarked after the Trotter meeting. "What I ought to have done would have been to have listened, restrained my resentment, and, when they had finished, to have said to them that, of course, their petition would receive consideration. They would have withdrawn quietly and no more would have been heard about the matter. But I lost my temper and played the fool."

As a Democrat whose base included white Southerners, Wilson supported Jim Crow regulations within the government and, as his biographer John Milton Cooper, Jr., has written, "readily . . . accepted the customary racial inequalities and indignities of the time." In 1918, however, Wilson purged from the party two racist Democratic senators who opposed the administration—James K. Vardaman of Mississippi and Thomas Hardwick of Georgia—and strongly denounced lynching. The statement on lynching, Cooper writes, "gave a hint of what a powerful civil rights president he might have been if he had put his heart and mind into the cause. But they were not there. . . . His impatience with agitation over race from any quarter made him resemble northern whites of that time more than fellow southerners, but he had grown up despising abolitionists and regarding Reconstruction as an injustice." The freed slaves of the South, Wilson wrote in **The Atlantic Monthly** in 1901, had been "excited by a freedom they did not understand, exalted by false hopes; bewildered and without leaders, and yet insolent and aggressive; sick of work, covetous of pleasure—a host of dusky children untimely put out of school."

At the fiftieth anniversary of the Battle of Gettysburg, in the summer of 1913, Wilson had addressed a gathering of Union and Confederate veterans in terms Edward Alfred Pollard himself might have applauded, casting the war as one between men of goodwill. "These venerable men crowding here to this famous field have set us a great example of devotion and utter sacrifice," Wilson said. "They were willing to die that the people might live. . . . Their work is handed on to us, to be done in another way, but not in another spirit. Our day is not over; it is upon us in full tide."

Wilson was implicitly seeking support for his progressive agenda, one that included measures aimed at economic fairness. "Whom do I command?" he asked the crowd at Gettysburg. "The ghostly hosts who fought upon these battlefields long ago and are gone? These gallant gentlemen stricken in years whose fighting days are over, their glory won? . . . I have in my mind another host. . . . That host is the people themselves, the great and the small, without class or difference of kind or race or origin; and undivided in interest, if we have but the vision to guide and direct them and order their lives aright in what we do."

The duality of Wilson's Gettysburg speech—on the one hand ratifying the Lost Cause narrative of the Civil War while calling for vigorous public action, at the federal level, to reform basic elements of national life—reflected the duality inherent in many American hearts.

There was no more vivid manifestation of those lengthening shadows in the first decades of the twentieth century than the new Ku Klux Klan. A trilogy of novels by Thomas W. Dixon, Jr., a Lost Cause devotee, helped lead to the Klan's rebirth. Born in 1864 in North Carolina, Dixon published **The Leopard's Spots: A Romance of the White Man's Burden—1865–1900** in 1902 and followed it with **The Clansman: An Historical Romance of the Ku Klux Klan** in 1905 and **The Traitor: A Story of the Fall of the Invisible Empire** in 1907. The books were widely read, and Dixon, who became a popular figure, went on the lecture circuit to spread his message of white superiority. "My object is to teach the north, the young north, what it has never known—the awful suffering of the white man during the dreadful reconstruction period," Dixon said, for "the white man must and shall be supreme." He adapted **The Clansman** for the stage, and, in 1914, joined forces with the filmmaker D. W. Griffith to make a movie of

D. W. Griffith's 1915 movie **The Birth of a Nation,** a cinematic celebration of white supremacy based on a novel by Thomas W. Dixon, Jr., helped inspire a new Ku Klux Klan.

it. The film's ultimate title: **The Birth of a Nation,** a celebration of white supremacy and a sustained attack on African Americans.

Dixon, who understood that the rise of cinema opened a world of possibilities in terms of reaching the public, was ecstatic about the movie project. "The whole problem of swift universal education of public opinion is thus solved by this invention," Dixon said of motion pictures. "Civilization will be saved if we can stir and teach the slumbering millions behind the politician. By this device we can reach them. We can make them see things happen before their eyes until they cry in anguish. . . . Its scenes will be vivid realities, not cold works on printed pages, but scenes wet with tears and winged with hope."

At a running time of 187 minutes, Griffith's film, which featured Lillian Gish, was grand spectacle—and immensely profitable. The title cards included a version of a pro-Klan quotation from Woodrow Wilson from his scholarly days: "The white men were roused by a mere instinct of self-preservation . . . until at last there had sprung into existence a great Ku Klux Klan, a veritable empire of the South, to protect the Southern country."

Wilson and Dixon had overlapped for a time at Johns Hopkins University, and Dixon reached out to the president in the effort to publicize the film. Wilson agreed to host a screening. On Thursday, February 18, 1915, in the East Room, the president watched the movie. He offered little visible reaction to what he saw. An alleged remark—"It is like writing history with lightning. And my only regret is that it is all so ter-ribly true"—was almost certainly manufactured. Yet word of the presidential viewing offered a tacit endorsement that the film's promoters were more than happy to have.

The Birth of a Nation provoked protests in several cities, including Boston and New York, and offered the nascent NAACP an opportu-nity to organize and make the case for fairness in the public square. During a demonstration against the film in Boston at the Tremont The-atre, an African American observer noted, "As I looked over that vast crowd of Negro men and women, this thought came to me: this is a united people, though in the minority, and they are going to win." The NAACP's **Crisis**, the magazine edited by W.E.B. Du Bois, hailed the efforts against Griffith's movie. "It is gratifying to know that in this work," **The Crisis** noted, "we have the cooperation of all elements of col-ored people."

The reaction to the film as racist propaganda was compelling enough that President Wilson distanced himself from the entire enterprise. "It is true that 'The Birth of a Nation' was produced before the President and his family at the White House, but the President was entirely unaware of the character of [the film] before it was pre-sented and has at no time expressed his approbation of it," Wilson wrote in a third-person statement. "Its exhibition at the White House was a courtesy extended to an old acquaintance."

Whatever his prejudices and however strong he believed the constraints of the age on racial justice, the president was conscientious enough to know that there was something wrong with the familiar narrative of white supremacy.

Yet the film and its broader influence could not be contained. After **The Birth of a Nation,** a small group of men met on Stone Mountain, near Atlanta, on Thursday, November 25, 1915. Led by William J. Simmons, an Alabamaborn, circuit-riding minister and veteran of the Spanish-American War, the gathering burned a cross and founded a new Ku Klux Klan. Simmons claimed his father, a doctor and mill owner in Harpersville, Alabama, about thirty miles southeast of Birmingham, had been "an officer of the old Klan" in the 1860s. The son's imagination was fired by the stories of former days. "On horseback in their white robes they rode across the wall in front of me," Simmons said, describing an alleged childhood vision. "As the picture faded out I got down on my knees and swore that I would found a fraternal organization that would be a memorial to the Ku Klux Klan."

Simmons's choice of venue for the re-founding of the Klan in 1915 was rich in significance, for the Atlanta United Daughters of the Confederacy were campaigning for the creation of a Confederate memorial at Stone Mountain. "**The Birth of a Nation** will give us a percentage of the next Monday's matinee," the project's leader, Mrs. C. Helen Plane, wrote. "Since seeing this wonderful and beautiful picture of Reconstruction in the South, I feel that it is due to the Ku Klux Klan which saved us from Negro domination and carpet-bag rule, [to] be immortalized on Stone Mountain. Why not represent a small group of them in their nightly uniform approaching in the distance?" (In the end, the memorial—which was begun by Gutzon Borglum, the sculptor who would later carve Mount Rushmore—featured only Lee, Davis, and Stonewall Jackson.)

What began on that November night at Stone Mountain spread across white America. Forty-eight states—which is to say, **every** state in the Union at the time—had a Klan presence by 1924. Indiana was a stronghold; so were Oregon, Colorado, and Kansas. A combination of factors created a climate conducive to the Klan's rebirth. There was the wide influence of **The Birth of a Nation,** unease about crime, worry about anarchists, fear of immigrants flooding in from a Europe desolated by war, and, beginning in 1917, anxiety about Communism and subversion in the New World after the Bolshevik Revolution.

From afar it can be difficult to grasp the second Klan's reach. Nativism was prevalent; the new Klansmen hated blacks, Roman Catholics, and Jews alike. During a Klan meeting in Georgia, Simmons dramatically drove a bowie knife into a table between two handguns and announced: "Now let the Niggers, Catholics, Jews, and all others who disdain my imperial wizardry, come on." Simmons hired a pair of public relations experts, Mary Elizabeth Tyler and Edward Young Clarke, to promote the Klan nationally, and the enterprise was financed by a ten-dollar initiation fee known as a "Klectoken" that was split among Simmons, Tyler, Clarke, and the local "King Kleagles," lower-ranking "Kleagles," and "Grand Goblins" who recruited new members. Money—including revenue from selling robes and hoods—poured in.

At a time when industrialization and urbanization were transforming the old agrarian world, the Klan promised racial solidarity and cultural certitude. "The Klan offered structure, position, and brotherhood to many restive or disoriented men from small towns and big cities in the America of the 1920s," the historian

David H. Bennett wrote. "It was a movement so remarkably suited to its time and place that its growth matched the boom of the larger nation." Klansmen held governorships (eleven) and U.S. Senate seats (sixteen); scholars believe "scores" of U.S. House members also belonged to the KKK. (The Klan itself put the House figure at seventy-five in 1923.) In Alabama, Hugo Black, a future justice of the U.S. Supreme Court, joined the Klan. In 1922 in Independence, Missouri, a young Harry Truman, then seeking office as eastern judge of Jackson County, nearly joined the Klan but declined when he was told he would be expected to keep Roman Catholics out of county jobs.

During the Great War, which America entered in 1917, Wilson and the Congress had restricted freedom of expression in the name of national security. There was legislation to protect the military draft from interference or protest. The Espionage Act of 1917 and the Sedition Act of 1918 criminalized dissent in wartime. And Wilson's Justice Department targeted the Industrial Workers of the World with indictments and trials.

Speech itself was under siege. It was illegal, according to the 1918 legislation, to "utter, print, write, or publish any disloyal, profane, scurrilous,

The Red Scare era was marked by numerous bombings around the country, including this one on Wall Street in 1920.

or abusive language about the form of government of the United States, or the Constitution of the United States, or the military or naval forces of the United States." Under Wilson and through the direct offices of Postmaster General Albert Sidney Burleson of Texas, the post office became an enthusiastic and thoroughgoing censor, refusing to distribute publications it deemed unpatriotic. Among numerous other examples—as many as four hundred publications were censored—the suppression of **The Masses** magazine, edited by the leading radical Max Eastman, was particularly galling to the antiwar community. "I spent the whole winter trying to think up the worst possible consequences of our going to war, and advertise them in the public press," Eastman said, "but I never succeeded in thinking up anything half so bad as this."

On the afternoon of Sunday, June 16, 1918, at Nimisilla Park in Canton, Ohio, the Socialist Party leader Eugene V. Debs, a frequent presidential candidate, delivered an antiwar speech. He took the view—a common one in radical circles of the day—that the Great War was being fought to sustain capitalistic hegemony and imperialism. "And here let me emphasize the fact—and it cannot be repeated too often—that the working class who fight all the battles, the working class who make the supreme sacrifices, the working class who freely shed their blood and furnish the corpses, have never yet had a voice in either declaring war or making peace," Debs said. "It is the ruling class that invariably does both. They alone declare war and they alone make peace."

In the fever of wartime, Debs's words were taken as a violation of Wilson's Espionage Act, and the Socialist lion was arrested, tried, convicted, and sentenced to ten years in prison. "I have been accused of obstructing the war," Debs told the jury at his trial. "I admit it. Gentlemen, I abhor war. I would oppose it if I stood alone." With Oliver Wendell Holmes, Jr., writing the

opinion, the Supreme Court unanimously upheld the conviction; Debs dismissed the justices
as "begowned, bewhiskered, bepowdered old fos-
sils." President Wilson refused to intervene on
Debs's behalf, and it fell to President Warren G.
Harding, Wilson's Republican successor, to pardon him.

On Monday, June 2, 1919, an anarchist's
bomb exploded at the Washington home of
Attorney General A. Mitchell Palmer on R Street
Northwest. The terrorist accidentally blew himself up; bits and pieces of carnage were scattered
on the lawn. Assistant Secretary of the Navy
Franklin D. Roosevelt, a neighbor of Palmer's,
had just arrived home after a dinner party. After
checking on his son James, who was home to
study for his entrance tests for Groton, Roosevelt
rushed over to help. His cousin, TR's daughter
Alice, soon arrived with her husband, Congressman Nicholas Longworth of Ohio. "As we walked
across [R Street] it was difficult to avoid stepping
on bloody hunks of human being," Mrs. Longworth recalled. "The man had been torn apart,
fairly blown to butcher's meat." Eleanor wrote
her mother-in-law, Sara: "Now we are roped off,
and the police haven't yet allowed the gore to be
wiped up on our steps and James glories in every
bone found!"

Understandably furious, Palmer launched an

organized campaign against what he saw as the radical threat to the nation. Seven other bombings around the country took place on the same night. "My information showed that Communism in this country was an organization of thousands of aliens . . . direct allies of Trotsky, aliens of the same misshapen caste of mind and indecencies of character," Palmer wrote.

He later recalled the fear of the moment: "The blaze of Revolution was sweeping over every American institution of law and order . . . eating its way into the homes of the American workman, its sharp tongues of revolutionary heat . . . licking at the altars of the churches, leaping into the belfry of the school bell, crawling into the sacred corners of American homes, seeking to replace marriage vows with libertine laws, burning up the foundations of society." His action officer as he raided suspected Reds and fought dissent was a young John Edgar Hoover. Much of the press approved. "There is no time to waste on hairsplitting over infringement of liberty," **The Washington Post** wrote amid a series of January 1920 raids.

Palmer's assault came at a time when support for the idea of "100 Percent Americanism," a phrase championed by a collection of national organizations (including the Klan), was on the rise. "Innumerable patriotic societies had sprung up

President Woodrow Wilson and attorney general
A. Mitchell Palmer. Palmer—whose Washington
house was bombed in 1919 by an anarchist who
accidentally blew himself up while carrying out
the attack—curbed civil liberties in an attempt
to suppress dissent.

each with its executive secretary, and executive
secretaries must live, and therefore must conjure
up new and ever greater menaces," wrote the journalist and historian Frederick Lewis Allen. "Innumerable other gentlemen now discovered that
they could defeat whatever they wanted to defeat
by tarring it conspicuously with the Bolshevist
brush. Big-navy men, believers in compulsory
military service, drys, anti-cigarette campaigners,
anti-evolution Fundamentalists, defenders of the
moral order, book censors, Jew-haters, Negro-

haters, landlords, manufacturers, utility executives, upholders of every sort of cause, good, bad, and indifferent, all wrapped themselves in Old Glory and the mantle of the Founding Fathers and allied their opponents with Lenin."

It was the age of Sinclair Lewis's George Babbitt. Conformity, the order of the day, required open avowals of fidelity to America as defined by jingoists and sloganeers. In **Harper's,** the writer Katharine Fullerton Gerould observed: "America is no longer a free country, in the old sense; and liberty is, increasingly, a mere rhetorical figure. . . . The only way in which an American citizen who is really interested in all the social and political problems of his country can preserve any freedom of expression, is to choose the mob that is most sympathetic to him, and abide under the shadow of that mob."

Palmer, who craved the presidency for himself in the 1920 election, capitalized on the moment. His raids were numerous, opportunistic, and often unjustified. The attorney general was able to take advantage of the vacuum created after President Wilson suffered a debilitating stroke in early October 1919. Though the president remained in office, he was largely a convalescent in the White House. ("He looked as if he were dead," Ike Hoover, the chief White House usher, recalled of Wilson in the immediate aftermath of the stroke.) Palmer thus had a freer hand than he might otherwise have had, and the president failed to rein in the Justice Department as it attacked radical threats both real and imagined.

Reason, however, prevailed. The system worked: The fervid public atmosphere was unsustainable, and activists and the courts stepped in where a more engaged president might have done. Opinion turned in part after the New York state legislature voted in January 1920 to bar five duly elected lawmakers who were members of the Socialist Party—they'd been elected from districts in Manhattan, the Bronx, and Brooklyn—on the grounds that the Socialist platform was "absolutely inimical to the best interests of the State of New York and of the United States." One assemblyman, the historian Robert K. Murray reported, "suggested they ought to be shot" rather than simply expelled.

Watching the drama from England, George Bernard Shaw remarked, "Americans are savages still; that the primitive communities prosecute opinion [is] a matter of course." The Schenectady **Citizen** wrote, "Even the Czar of Russia in his palmiest days permitted Socialists to sit in the Duma." Writing on behalf of the New York Bar Association, Charles Evans Hughes, the former Supreme Court justice (and future chief justice) and 1916 Republican nominee for president, described the assembly's moves as undemocratic and un-American.

"Is it not clear," Hughes asked, "that the Government cannot be saved at the cost of its own principles?" In Massachusetts, the **Springfield Republican** raised the largest of questions: "And where will it all end? Shall we sometime see Republicans excluding Democrats and Democrats excluding Republicans from our law-making bodies, on the ground that the other party's principles are 'inimical to the best interests' of the United States? Every party has always thought that of its rivals, but it is something new in America for parties to translate the idea into action."

The fever was breaking. "The action of the New York assembly more than any other event underscored for the entire nation the dangerous effect of continued hysterical fear, and the grotesque spectacle of New York solons being frightened by five mild Socialists made many Americans laugh," Robert K. Murray wrote in a history of the era. "Citizens could now see their own exaggerated fears mirrored in those of the New York legislators and the reflection appeared ridiculous."

Albany was a skirmish in a larger war, and the forces of proportion were making progress on different fronts. Signed by future Supreme Court justice Felix Frankfurter, among others, a sixty-seven-page document entitled **To the American People: Report Upon the Illegal Practices of the U.S. Department of Justice** drew attention to Palmer's excesses. "Talk about Americanization!" a Massachusetts judge said. "What we need is the Americanization of the people who carry out such proceedings as these." Arthur Garfield Hays, the lawyer and ACLU general counsel, later summed up the view that was slowly but steadily coming back into vogue after the Red Scare: "I hate," Hays remarked, "to see people pushed around."

W.E.B. Du Bois understood what was happening. "In 1918, in order to win the war, we had to make Germans into Huns," he wrote. "In order to win, the South had to make Negroes into thieves, monsters, and idiots. Tomorrow, we must make Latins, South-eastern Europeans, Turks and other Asiatics into actual 'lesser breeds without the law'"—a quotation from Rudyard Kipling's 1897 imperial poem "Recessional." "Some," Du Bois wrote, "seem to see today anti-Christ in Catholicism; and in Jews, international plotters of the Protocol; and in 'the rising tide of color,' a threat to all civilization and human culture."

The "rising tide of color" was an allusion to a 1920 book by Lothrop Stoddard that laid out, in the words of his subtitle, "The Threat Against

White World-Supremacy." In 1925's **The Great Gatsby**, in a sign of how such views were in circulation among the affluent in America, F. Scott Fitzgerald had Tom Buchanan endorse Stoddard's views. "Well, it's a fine book, and everybody ought to read it," Buchanan says. "The idea is if we don't look out the white race will be—will be utterly submerged. It's all scientific stuff; it's been proved."

An 1892 poem by Thomas Bailey Aldrich, "The Unguarded Gates," had captured the ethos two decades before:

Wide open and unguarded stand our
gates,
And through them presses a wild motley
throng—
Men from the Volga and the Tartar steppes,
Featureless figures of the Hoang-Ho,
Malayan, Scythian, Teuton, Kelt, and Slav,
Flying the Old World's poverty and scorn;
These bringing with them unknown gods
and rites,—
Those, tiger passions, here to stretch their
claws.
In street and alley what strange tongues are
loud,
Accents of menace alien to our air,
Voices that once the Tower of Babel knew!

O Liberty, white Goddess! is it well
To leave the gates unguarded? On thy breast
Fold Sorrow's children, soothe the hurts of
    fate,
Lift the down-trodden, but with hand of steel
Stay those who to thy sacred portals come
To waste the gifts of freedom. Have a care
Lest from thy brow the clustered stars be torn
And trampled in the dust. For so of old
The thronging Goth and Vandal trampled
    Rome,
And where the temples of the Cæsars stood
The lean wolf unmolested made her lair.

Nine years earlier, in 1883, Emma Lazarus had written a sonnet that struck radically different notes; she composed it in order to raise funds for the completion of the Statue of Liberty in New York Harbor. (Her poem would be included at the site in 1903.)

Not like the brazen giant of Greek fame,
With conquering limbs astride from land to
    land;
Here at our sea-washed, sunset gates shall
    stand
A mighty woman with a torch, whose flame
Is the imprisoned lightning, and her name
Mother of Exiles. From her beacon-hand

Glows world-wide welcome; her mild eyes
  command
The air-bridged harbor that twin cities frame.
"Keep, ancient lands, your storied pomp!" cries
  she
With silent lips. "Give me your tired, your
  poor,
Your huddled masses yearning to breathe free,
The wretched refuse of your teeming shore.
Send these, the homeless, tempest-tost to me,
I lift my lamp beside the golden door!

The second Ku Klux Klan was thriving on Aldrich's sentiments, not Lazarus's. "Millions of Americans are in arduous quest of leadership toward better government, adequate law-enforcement, the elevation of society and a more perfect national patriotism," the then–imperial wizard, Hiram Wesley Evans, a dentist by trade, told a national meeting in 1924. "The Klan, alone, supplies this leadership. . . . The blood which produces human leadership must be protected from inferior blood. . . . **You are of this superior blood. You are more—you are leaders in the only movement in the world, at present, which exists solely to establish a civilization that will insure these things. Klansmen and Klanswomen are verily 'the salt of the earth,' upon whom depends the future of civilization."**

Anxiety about the new, about the unknown, was pervasive. "We are a movement of the plain people, very weak in the matter of culture, intellectual support and trained leadership," Evans once said. "We demand a return of power into the hands of the everyday, not highly cultured, not overly intellectualized but entirely unspoiled and not de-Americanized average citizens of the old stock."

Reliable numbers are hard to come by, but the best scholarly estimates put Klan membership at two million or so in the mid-1920s. Others fix it between three and six million. In explaining the economic and technological anxiety that leads to collective political action—of which the Klan of the 1920s was a towering example—the sociologist Rory McVeigh offered a revealing analogy. "If I am the only person in town who is willing to mow the lawn for the wealthy widow at the end of the block, I can demand a sizable reward for my services," McVeigh wrote in a study of the Klan's political influence. "My purchasing power would undergo devaluation if (a) the new kid on the block made his services available to her, or (b) the widow becomes tired of dealing with the lawn and replaces it with Astroturf." It is a useful way of thinking about why the Klan opposed immigration (which brought a bunch of new kids to the block who might mow the lawn for less money) and was anxious about technological change in general (the move from agrarian life to industrialized economy and then the attendant march of automation in factories meant jobs would become ever more difficult to come by).

The Zangwill-TR "melting pot" of immigration and assimilation, Hiram Evans said, was therefore among the "superficial doctrines" and "fallacious arguments" destroying the country. "The Klan believes in the upbuilding of the American nation—founded, as history emphatically declares, on the supremacy of the white race, the genius of the Nordic and Anglo-Saxon peoples, and the free private interpretation of God's word," Evans said. ("Jesus was a Protestant," was a Klan byword.)

The Klan of the 1920s gave its adherents a social and political program that spoke to both the practical fears of the moment and to a mythology of identity. In a speech entitled "Americanism Applied," the governor of Georgia, Clifford Walker, addressed the "Second Imperial Klonvokation," held in Kansas City over three days in September 1924. A Phi Beta Kappa graduate of the University of Georgia and a former attorney general of the state, Walker had lost an earlier gubernatorial election when his opponent, Thomas Hardwick, had courted the Klan. Learning his lesson, Walker joined the organization and became an enthusiastic advocate for the Klan.

Speaking in Kansas City of the need for education, for roads and highways, and for extending healthcare, Walker offered a platform for white working-class voters while enumerating the dangers foreign immigration posed to the destiny of his listeners. "What good will it do, I ask you, to train and develop the minds and hearts and bodies of our boys and our girls, what good will it do if we build a bridge across their chasm and at the end of the highway of youth—at the maturity of the boy and the girl—there is a darkened and a poisoned and a decadent nation for them to live in?"

There was more. "I would build a wall of steel," Walker said, "a wall as high as Heaven, against the admission of a single one of those Southern Europeans who never thought the thoughts or spoke the language of a democracy in their lives."

It became known, mordantly, as the "Klanbake." Inside Madison Square Garden from June 24 to July 9, 1924, the floor of the Democratic National Convention was the scene of platform battles and ballot after ballot after ballot—103 in all—to nominate a presidential candidate to stand against Republican Calvin Coolidge, who had succeeded Warren G. Harding after Harding's death the previous summer. The delegates included an estimated 343 Klansmen, and the "Invisible Empire" was all too evident on the convention floor. Their main mission in New York: the defeat of the Irish-Catholic governor of New York, Alfred E. Smith.

With the imperial wizard and his team headquartered at the Hotel McAlpin at Herald Square and at the Great Northern on Fifty-seventh Street, the Klan also fought an anti-KKK platform plank, and the struggle revealed a sad but inescapable political reality: The organization was big enough, and dispersed enough, to make many in the mainstream of the party fearful of opposing a movement with such support. "Outnumbering the anti-Klan members . . . will be those who are either in sympathy with the Knights or who deem it politically expedient to be neutral," the Klan newspaper **The Fiery Cross** wrote. "The delegates from the west and south, where the Klan is powerful and exercises great power, do not want to go to the voters of their states with a platform that says thumbs down to the millions of Klansmen throughout the nation."

A contentious fight ensued over the plank, which read:

> We condemn political secret societies of all kinds as opposed to the exercise of free gov-

ernment and contrary to the spirit of the Constitution of the United States. We pledge the Democratic Party to oppose any effort on the part of the Ku Klux Klan or any organization to interfere with the religious liberty or political freedom of any citizen, or to limit the civic rights of any citizen or body of citizens because of religion, birthplace, or racial origin.

The anti-Klan delegates were eloquent, but given the KKK's power—and the politicians' fear of its power, which of course multiplied its influence—the vote was certain to be close. "If you are opposed to the Ku Klux Klan," Bainbridge Colby, a former Wilson secretary of state, told the convention, "for God's sake, say so." It was, he added, "this un-American, this poisonous, this alien thing in our midst, abhorrent to every American, hateful to the genius of our institutions, in conflict and at variance with every throb in the precepts of Americanism that have come down to us through the decades from the fathers of our Country." Edmund Moore of Ohio said that "if 343 members of the Klan who are members of this Convention can control the action of the other eight hundred, if the Imperial Wizard has got us all in his pocket, I, for one, am going to crawl out."

William R. Pattangall of Maine also argued for explicitly denouncing the Klan. "I say to you," Pattangall told the delegates, "that there is need to be sent over the whole wide United States a message . . . that our party hates bigotry, hates intolerance; opposes bigotry and opposes intolerance; and because it hates them and hates hypocrisy and opposes them, it therefore calls bigotry and intolerance and hypocrisy by their right names when it speaks of them."

Pattangall then yielded to Mrs. Carroll Miller of Pennsylvania. "What would you, my friends, think of a home in America where the little children shuddered nightly in terrorizing fear of the hooded Ku Klux Klan?" she asked. "Oh, there are such places, hundreds of them . . . where a foreign-born is discriminated against by the shopkeeper, places where the wife waiting for her husband to return from the mine, the field or the factory never feels sure that he will not be mobbed or beaten to death before he returns to her and his family."

She called on her fellow newly enfranchised women to join her in opposing the Klan. "If the men are afraid to face this issue, I beg you women to cast aside your trepidation and deceit," Miller said. "We who are accustomed to suffer the pains of childbirth that the race may go on should not be afraid to uphold a great principle that our children may live in happiness and security. We who are accustomed to wait and fight in the lonely watches of the night for the life of the child when death is hovering over the crib should not be the ones to flinch now."

Rising in opposition, Governor Cameron Morrison of North Carolina urged the delegates to drop the reference to the Klan. "Are we, without trial and without evidence . . . to try, condemn, and execute more than a million men who are professed followers of the Lord Jesus Christ?" To attack the Klan directly, Morrison said, "will make half a million Ku Klux in the next ten days, in my judgment." Jared Y. Sanders of Louisiana was subtler, trying to cast the Klan as a victim of the proposed platform language. "And remember one thing more," Sanders said. "You cannot fight intolerance with intolerance. You cannot fight the devil with fire. He is an expert in that line."

Finally, William Jennings Bryan, the grand old man of the party, rose. To name the Klan specifically in the platform, he said, was not worth the political cost. It would divide the party, and for Bryan there were larger battles to be waged. "I call you back in the name of our God; I call you back in the name of our party; I call you back in the name of the Son of God and Savior of the world," Bryan told the delegates.

"Christians, stop fighting, and let us get together and save the world from the materialism that robs life of its spiritual values."

In a victory for the Klan, the plank was defeated, but only by the narrowest of margins. And while the Klan helped deny Al Smith the nomination, it also failed to carry its frontrunner, former secretary of the treasury (and Woodrow Wilson son-in-law) William G. McAdoo, to victory. At Madison Square Garden, Smith supporters, who opposed Prohibition, which the Klan favored, attacked with the cry of "Ku, Ku, McAdoo!" McAdoo's backers replied with: "Booze! Booze! Booze!" The convention was left with a compromise nominee in John W. Davis, a former congressman, solicitor general, and ambassador to the Court of St. James's.

After the 103rd ballot, a California delegate turned to a colleague on the floor and asked, "Is it really over?"

"Yes," his colleague said.

"Amen!"

In August 1925, on a day of occasional rain showers, thirty thousand Klansmen (some estimates say fifty thousand) converged on Washington for a huge march on the National Mall. "The parade was grander and gaudier, by far, than anything the wizards had prophesied," the journalist H. L. Mencken wrote. "It was longer, it was thicker, it was higher in tone. I stood in front of the Treasury for two hours watching the legions pass. They marched in lines of eighteen or twenty, solidly shoulder to shoulder. I retired for refreshment and was gone an hour." Returning, Mencken was struck by the continuity of the scene. "When I got back Pennsylvania Avenue was still a mass of white from the Treasury down to the foot of Capitol Hill—a full mile of Klansmen and their ladies."

The demonstration—in full regalia—took place at a time when long-standing cultural buoys seemed in danger of being swept away by a hostile modernity. The Scopes Trial in Dayton, Tennessee, in the summer of 1925 was emblematic of the struggles of the day. Bible-believing Southerners opposed the teaching of evolution in public schools, prompting a celebrated contest between William Jennings Bryan and Clarence Darrow in a rural East Tennessee county. A sign hung outside the courthouse urging people to READ YOUR BIBLE—as if that were the last word on the subject.

Which, for many believers, it was. Testifying about the literalism of the Bible—whether the whale in fact swallowed Jonah, for example—Bryan grew flustered. "I do not think about things I don't think about," he said at one point.

In August 1925, thirty thousand Ku Klux Klansmen (some estimates put it at fifty thousand) staged a massive demonstration on a day of occasional rain showers in Washington, D.C.

Darrow pounced. "Do you think about things you do think about?" he asked.

Eloquent, acerbic, and controversial (as well as, in the views of some of his contemporaries and in diary entries published after his death, anti-Semitic), Mencken came south from Baltimore to cover the trial. "Such obscenities as the forthcoming trial of the Tennessee evolutionist . . . call attention dramatically to the fact that enlightenment, among mankind, is very narrowly dispersed," Mencken wrote. "It is common to assume that human progress affects everyone—that even the dullest man, in these bright days, knows more than any man of, say, the Eighteenth Century, and is far more civilized. . . . But the great masses of men, even in this inspired republic, are precisely where the mob was at the dawn of history. . . . They know little if anything that is worth knowing, and there is not the slightest sign of a natural desire among them to increase their knowledge."

Mencken's brilliant, if ungenerous, caricature of Bryan, the former politician, captured the essence of a great man in decline. During a powerful speech by Darrow, Mencken wrote that Bryan "sat tight-lipped and unmoved. There is, of course, no reason why it should have shaken him. He has those hillbillies locked up in his pen and he knows it. . . . These are his people. They understand him when he speaks in tongues. The same dark face that is in his own eyes is in theirs, too. They feel with him, and they relish him."

And they exulted in his victory for their cause: The jury sided with Bryan, convicting Scopes of violating the Tennessee statute against the teaching of evolution. (Scopes was fined $100.) At the conclusion of the trial, Darrow predicted, rightly, that the events at Dayton would endure. "I think this case will be remembered because it

is the first case of this sort since we stopped trying people in America for witchcraft," Darrow
said. "We have done our best to turn the tide . . .
of testing every fact of science by a religious doctrine." One legacy of Dayton was that religion
and science had joined race and ethnicity as a
theater of war in the fight within the American
soul.

What of the Klan? "No arguments you may
use, no facts you may present, no logic
you may array will in the slightest affect these
people," the Kansas editor William Allen White,
who opposed the Klan in an unsuccessful race
for governor, wrote. "They have no capacity for
receiving arguments, no minds for retaining or
sifting facts and no mental processes that will
hold logic. If they had any of these they would
not be Kluxers."

Fortunately, White was being hyperbolic. The
story of the Klan in the 1920s suggests that arguments, facts, and logic, steadily presented, can
help shed light when darkness threatens to prevail. By 1928 or so, the Klan, like its Reconstruction predecessor in the early 1870s, was
ebbing. And just in time: A Klan with substantial strength in the tumult of the 1930s might
have increased the chances of America falling
into the totalitarianism that consumed some

European nations in the same years. "The Ku Klux Klan," the Reverend Charles Jefferson, the pro-Klan author of **Roman Catholicism and the Ku Klux Klan,** said, "is the Mussolini of America."

Despite the Klan's political power, American institutions designed to check and balance popular passion struck blows against the Invisible Empire. The courts, the press, and two presidents (Warren G. Harding and Calvin Coolidge) took stands, however limited, against the politics of fear.

In 1928, the U.S. Supreme Court upheld a New York law requiring the Klan to file membership lists with state authorities on the grounds that, as the appellate court in the case wrote, "It is a matter of common knowledge that the association or organization"—the Klan—"exercises activities tending to the prejudice and intimidation of sundry classes of our citizens."

In the opinion of the court, authored by Justice Willis Van Devanter, an appointee of President Taft's, the Klan "was conducting a crusade against Catholics, Jews, and negroes, and stimulating hurtful religious and race prejudices. . . . It was striving for political power, and assuming a sort of guardianship over the administration of local, state, and national affairs; and . . . at times it was taking into its own hands the punishment of what some of its members conceived to be crimes." Three years earlier, in 1925, a unanimous Supreme Court had declared a Klan-supported Oregon law targeted at Roman Catholic schools unconstitutional. The Klan and its allies had passed a statute to force all children to attend public schools, thus shuttering Catholic institutions; the court was unimpressed and struck it down.

Voices of reason in the popular press did what they could. Like William Allen White—and like the justices of the Supreme Court—many editors saw the Klan as potentially fatal to the yet-unrealized but nevertheless real promise of the country. The New York **World** had led the way, publishing a landmark investigative series on the Klan in 1921; its reporting on the organization's violence was particularly vivid. In the short run, though, the press's opposition had the perverse effect of boosting the Klan rather than undercutting it. In a dynamic that's familiar in our own time, hostility from the journalists of the East convinced a number of middle Americans that a cause under such assault must have something to recommend it.

"It wasn't until the newspapers began to attack the Klan that it really grew," William Simmons recalled. When the House Rules Committee, prodded by the **World** series, held brief hearings into the Klan, it, too, inadvertently fed the flames, at least for a time. "Certain newspapers also aided us by inducing Congress to investigate us," Simmons recalled. "The result was that Congress gave us the best advertising we ever got."

The work of combatting broadly held views like those of the Klansmen of the 1920s is almost never easy or quick. It requires years of persistent witness and of standing firm in protest when it would be more convenient to give in and move on. In the case of the Klan, journalists had to repeat the same points over and over at the risk of boring readers—and, truth be told, themselves, for one reason many people go into journalism is a love of novelty, of shifting narratives, changing scenes, new characters, and fresh contests. The case against the Klan, though (like the case against segregation, and, later, the case against Senator Joe McCarthy), required a willingness to return again and again to the argument that decency and the Klan could not coexist. "Wearing masks, practicing sacrilege in burning fiery crosses, appealing to race and religious hatreds is so thoroughly un-American and so contemptible that we are surprised that any intelligent person would engage in such perfidy for even one performance," **The Dalton Citizen**, a newspaper in North Georgia, wrote in 1925.

The presidency also played a role in suggesting that America should be above Klan-like extremism. In October 1921, President Harding, a Republican, went to the heart of Democratic Dixie for the fiftieth anniversary celebration of the founding of Birmingham, Alabama. Harding had supported anti-lynching laws—a strong civil rights position in that time—and took the occasion on this hot Wednesday in Birmingham's Capitol Park to deliver an unusual speech on race. He spoke of political equality ("I would say let the black man vote when he is fit to vote; prohibit the white man voting when he is unfit to vote") and of equality of opportunity in terms of economics and education. ("Partnership of the races in developing the highest aims of all humanity there must be if humanity . . . is to achieve the ends which we have set for it.")

Harding, however, approvingly cited the assertions of hereditary inferiority in Stoddard's **Rising Tide of Color** and insisted that he did not envision social equality or what he called "amalgamation."

"There are many who do not agree with [Harding] as to political equality," **The New York Times** reported after the speech, "but what he said about the impossibility of 'social equality' more than offset anything he said on other lines." That wasn't quite the case. "If the President's theory is carried to its ultimate conclusion," Senator Pat Harrison, Democrat of Mississippi, remarked, "then that means that the black man can strive to become President of the United States."

W.E.B. Du Bois gave Harding limited credit. It was, Du Bois said, "a braver, clearer utterance than Theodore Roosevelt ever dared to make or than William Taft or William McKinley ever dreamed of."

That said, Du Bois then eviscerated the president's Stoddard-inspired white-supremacist views. The "pseudo-science to which the President unhappily referred," Du Bois wrote, was "vain, wrong and hypocritical." For Du Bois the right path forward lay with those who shared the view of the Pan-African Congress, which Du Bois had helped found: **"The absolute equality of races—physical, political and social—is the founding stone of world peace and human advancement. No one denies great differences of gift, capacity and attainment among individuals of all races, but the voice of science, religion and practical politics is one in denying the God-appointed existence of superior races, or of races naturally and inevitably and eternally inferior."** For Du Bois, "To deny this fact is to throw open the door of the world to a future of hatred, war and murder such as never yet has staggered a bowed and crucified humanity."

William Edward Burghardt Du Bois (1868–1963) was a scholar, historian, and activist—as well as an editor and a poet—whose penetrating writings and devotion to the cause of equality made him one of the nation's most important voices through decades of tumult and progress.

At Birmingham, Harding obliquely spoke out against the Klan and its extra-legal vigilantism. "The nation which withstood internecine conflict, so heroically fought as was the Civil War, will tolerate the threat of no minority which challenges the supremacy of law or endangers our common welfare," Harding said. "There will never come the day when the rights of any minority are denied [and] . . . no minority shall ever challenge the supremacy of the rule of law."

The president was more direct on the Klan question in the third week of May 1923 when he dedicated a statue of Alexander Hamilton at the Treasury Department. "We have our factions which seek to promote this or that interest, without regard to the relationship to others, and without regard for the common weal," Harding said. "We have the factions of hatred and prejudice and violence. . . . Hamilton warned us that 'however such combinations or associations may now and then answer popular ends, they are likely themselves to usurp the reins of government, destroying afterward the very engines which have lifted them to unjust dominion.'" **The New York Times**'s headline on its story about the event made it clear that no one doubted what Harding was talking about: "Harding Deplores Growth of Factions and Strikes at Klan." He made the same case to the Imperial Grand Council of the Ancient Order of the Nobles of the Mystic Shrine in June of that year. Of "menacing organizations," Harding said, "This isn't fraternity, this is conspiracy."

In attempts to hurt Harding with racially minded white voters in the Jim Crow era, his political opponents had long trafficked in rumors that he had black ancestry. In the 1920 presidential campaign, a professor at the College of Wooster in Ohio, William E. Chancellor, produced inflammatory pamphlets on the subject. "By means of a fake family tree and a number of worthless affidavits," the historian Robert K. Murray wrote, "Chancellor's circulars showed that no fewer than four separate and converging lines of Harding ancestors possessed Negro blood." Harding chose to meet the allegations with a dignified public silence, as did his wife, Florence. "I want you to know I have known about these miserable attacks," Mrs. Harding wrote a friend, "but more than that, I want you to be assured, and absolutely certain that I am not in the least disturbed by them. . . . We are unafraid, undismayed, and undisturbed."

In private, Harding acknowledged that the facts of the matter were a mystery to him. "How do I know, Jim?" Harding privately said to James Faulkner of the **Cincinnati Enquirer.** "One of my ancestors may have jumped the fence." (In 2015, DNA testing disproved the speculation.)

There were other rumors, too. After Harding's death in 1923, the Klan put out the word that Harding had, as president, secretly joined its ranks while in office. "We have 227 in the House of Representatives and 27 in the United States Senate," Basil E. Newton of the Klan's Imperial Council exaggeratedly claimed, "and we held one initiation in the dining room of the White House. You know what that means." The Coolidge administration said the reports were "too ridiculous to discuss."

Coolidge, the new president, had been at his boyhood home in Vermont when the news about Harding's death came, and he took the oath of office in the middle of the night from his father, a notary public. Taciturn and enigmatic, an embodiment of New England rectitude, frugality, and learning, President Coolidge was a more interesting man than either many of his contemporaries or most historians have thought him. Though he, like Harding, refrained from taking the Klan on by name, Coolidge offered the country some glimpses of its better self.

In the general election campaign of 1924, Coolidge's running mate, Charles G. Dawes, denounced the Klan in a speech in Augusta, Maine. "Government cannot last if that way, the way of the Ku Klux Klan, is the way to enforce the law in this country," Dawes said that August. "Lawlessness cannot be met with lawlessness if civilization is to be maintained." Dawes tried to soften his attack, though, adding, as The New York Times put it, that "many join it in the interest of law and order." The speech, the Times reported, had "confound[ed the] party in Maine" and left the "audience unresponsive."

After conferring with Coolidge, Dawes dropped the subject. It was apparently the president's judgment that the less said about the Klan the better. "He was probably fearful that a direct attack on the Klan by name would detract from addressing the pressing issues of postwar reconstruction then demanding the attention of the

American people, as well as sow the seeds of discord among them at the very moment when national unity was essential for moving forward," the Coolidge scholar Jerry L. Wallace wrote. "In addition, such an attack would provide the Klan with a goldmine of publicity and likely bring it renewed vigor"—which, as Simmons had pointed out, had happened when Congress had investigated the Klan in 1921.

"Moreover," Wallace wrote, "the President undoubtedly realized from his study of history that hate groups like the Klan had historically come and gone, and that this Klan would be no different. Thus, it was best to let the Klan burn itself out, which, indeed, it did." Still, Coolidge's reticence had a price. "One political consequence was that black leaders, especially the younger ones, began to question their historic relationship with the Republican Party," Wallace wrote, "and urban Democrat politicians like [Al] Smith moved to take advantage of this."

On Saturday, August 9, 1924, Coolidge did make himself plain. A correspondent had written the president to express outrage at news that a black man was considering seeking the Republican nomination for a congressional seat from New York. "It is of some concern," the man had written, "whether a Negro is allowed to run for Congress anywhere, at any time, in any party, in this, a white man's country." Coolidge replied that he was "amazed" at the letter. Citing the service of half a million black men in the U.S. armed forces during the Great War, the president wrote:

The suggestion of denying any measure of their full political rights to such a great group of our population as the colored people is one which, however it might be received in some other quarters, could not possibly be permitted by one who feels a responsibility for living up to the traditions and maintaining the principles of the Republican Party. Our Constitution guarantees equal rights to all our citizens, without discrimination on account of race or color, I have taken my oath to support that Constitution. It is the source of your rights and my rights. I propose to regard it, and administer it, as the source of the rights of all the people, whatever their belief or race.

The African American Chicago **Defender** published Coolidge's letter under the headline "Cal Coolidge Tells Kluxer When to Stop."

Words like these set a proper tone, but the causes of the Klan's fall were complex.

Americans did not wake up one morning and decide to be a better people. For one thing, restrictive immigration law in the 1920s, particularly the National Origins Act of 1924, which set limiting quotas, defused the passion around the issue; there were fewer targets as the years went by. (The 805,228 immigrants arriving in 1921, for instance, fell to 164,000 by the end of the decade.) Economic growth—the much-heralded prosperity of the decade, which put the "roar" in the Roaring Twenties—also reduced tensions. As more people came to have a stake in the nation's success, and as that success became ever more linked to a widening opportunity, fewer of them were vulnerable to the Klan's creed. Commerce was culture; relative security in wages and employment undercut the potency of the politics of fear.

The Klan sabotaged itself, too, as when one of its key leaders, David Curtis Stephenson of Indiana, was arrested for the kidnapping, rape, and murder of a young woman on whom he had gnawed in a gruesome crime. (He was convicted of second-degree murder.) "I'm a nobody from nowhere, really—but I've got the biggest brains," he had said during his rise to power. "I'm going to be the biggest man in the United States!" As historians of the KKK phenomenon have noted, the revelation of depravity and of hypocrisy at the pinnacle of the Klan undercut the organization's self-righteous claims to be an irreproachable knighthood.

For his part, Coolidge urged the country to move beyond the forces that had fueled the rise of the second Klan. Addressing a convention of the American Legion in Omaha, Nebraska, on Tuesday, October 6, 1925, Coolidge was broad-gauged. "Whether one traces his Americanism back three centuries to the **Mayflower,** or three years of the steerage, is not half so important as whether his Americanism of to-day is real and genuine," Coolidge said. "No matter by what various crafts we came here, we are all now in the same boat."

He spoke of tolerance and of liberalism. "Granting first the essentials of loyalty to our country and to our fundamental institutions, we may not only overlook but we may encourage differences of opinion as to other things," Coolidge said. "For differences of this kind will certainly be elements of strength rather than of weakness. They will give variety to our tastes and interests. They will broaden our vision, strengthen our understanding, encourage the true humanities, and enrich our whole mode and conception of life." In an indirect but unmistakable allusion to the Klan and its "100 percent Americanism" platform, Coolidge told the veterans: "I recognize the full and complete necessity of 100 percent American-ism, but 100 percent Americanism may be made up of many various elements." Coolidge added:

> If we are to have . . . that union of spirit which is the foundation of real national ge-nius and national progress, we must all real-ize that there are true Americans who did not happen to be born in our section of the coun-try, who do not attend our place of religious worship, who are not of our racial stock, or who are not proficient in our language. If we are to create on this continent a free Republic and an enlightened civilization that will be capable of reflecting the true greatness and glory of mankind, it will be necessary to re-gard these differences as accidental and unes-sential. We shall have to look beyond the outward manifestations of race and creed. Divine Providence has not bestowed upon any race a monopoly of patriotism and char-acter.

Afterward, Henry Hugh Proctor, a graduate of Nashville's Fisk College and of the Yale Di-vinity School, a friend of W.E.B. Du Bois, and pastor of the First Congregational Church in Atlanta, and, later, the Nazarene Congrega-tional Church in Brooklyn, reflected on Coolidge's message. "Particularly do we want to thank you for that great word you spoke at Omaha, the bravest word spoken by any Executive in threescore years," Proctor said. "It sounds like Lincoln."

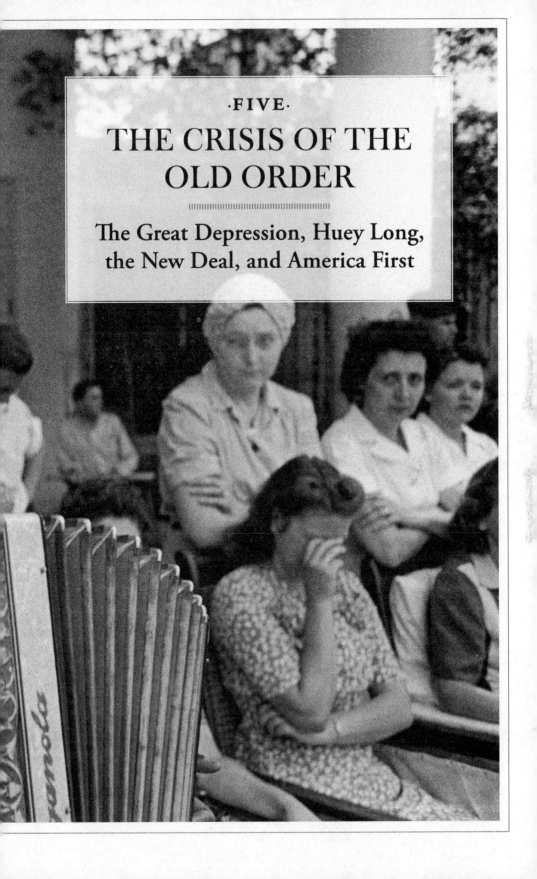

FIVE

THE CRISIS OF THE OLD ORDER

The Great Depression, Huey Long,
the New Deal, and America First

PREVIOUS PAGES: Navy Chief Petty Officer Graham Jackson, shedding tears of grief, plays as FDR's body is taken from the Warm Springs Foundation in Warm Springs, Georgia, April 1945.

We must drive the Jewish international bankers out of
Wall Street! We must destroy the Bolshevik labor unions!
We must purge our country of all the alien elements and
ideas that now infest her! America for Americans!

—The fictional former president Shagpoke Whipple,
in Nathanael West's 1934 novel, **A Cool Million**

The only limit to our realization of tomorrow will be
our doubts of today. Let us move forward with
strong and active faith.

—Franklin D. Roosevelt, undelivered
Jefferson Day Address, April 1945

O N C H R I S T M A S E V E 1 9 2 9 , not
quite two months after the disastrous
stock market crash, dessert was being
served to President Herbert Hoover and his holiday guests in the State Dining Room when
word came that the West Wing was in flames.
The Oval Office itself, installed by President Taft
during a 1909 renovation, was burning. According to published reports, the president, dressed
in a dinner jacket and smoking a cigar, excused
himself to inspect the fire. "At times it seemed as
if the flames were subdued," **The New York
Times** wrote, "but there were occasional bursts
of blaze through the roof, and the firemen had
great difficulty in getting control of the situa-

tion." In the main part of the mansion, the First Lady tried to distract the guests by asking the Marine Band to play on.

Metaphors don't come much more apropos: The Hoover White House, at the onset of the Great Depression, subject to the destructive whims of an uncontrollable force. "Those parts which had not been actually destroyed," the **Times** noted of the West Wing, "were gutted and water-soaked." Something seemingly invincible, impervious to destruction, was proving vulnerable.

The same would soon be said of America itself. By 1932–33, the Great Depression was consuming the United States, creating public anxiety and eroding trust in the most basic of institutions. In his trilogy on Roosevelt and the New Deal, published between 1957 and 1960, the historian Arthur Schlesinger, Jr., referred to the 1920s and early '30s as "The Crisis of the Old Order." America seemed on the cusp of a violent break from the ancien régime of democratic capitalism. Would the nation save itself or, like Italy and, as the '30s unfolded, Germany, seek comfort in totalitarianism? Or might it choose the path of the Soviet Union, casting its lot with Communism?

The questions were not academic. When the financier Bernard M. Baruch said the nation was facing a situation "worse than war," there was,

Time reported, "widespread agreement." Nearly 20 percent of the workforce, or one out of five people, was jobless. "The country had never before known unemployment of these magnitudes or of this duration," the historian David M. Kennedy wrote. "It had in place no mechanism with which to combat mass destitution on this scale." Mobs of hungry youths were loose in the countryside. Armed standoffs roiled placid places such as Sioux City, Iowa. A Senate committee was told hard truths: "There are many signs that if the lawfully constituted leadership does not soon substitute action for words, a new leadership, perhaps unlawfully constituted, will arise and act."

Hoover's successor knew all this. In the summer of 1932, Governor Franklin D. Roosevelt of New York had told an adviser that the two most dangerous men in America were Huey Long of Louisiana and Douglas MacArthur, the army chief of staff. Long, the powerful Louisiana "Kingfish," could conceivably orchestrate a coup from the populist left, and MacArthur might manage the same feat from the right. The general had already led a disastrous U.S. Army attack on veterans gathered in Washington seeking a promised pension bonus. ("MacArthur has decided to go into active command in the field," said MacArthur, speaking, as was his wont, in the third person. "There is incipient revolution in the air.")

The loudest cheers during Roosevelt's inaugural address on Saturday, March 4, 1933, did not come from his assurance that the only thing Americans had to fear was fear itself. No, as Eleanor Roosevelt noted, the greatest ovation greeted the new president's assertion that the present emergency might require him to assume extended wartime executive powers.

It was a mad, and maddening, time. In the middle of February 1933, Roosevelt, then the president-elect, was nearly killed in a park in Miami when an armed assailant, Giuseppe Zangara, opened fire from about ten yards away. FDR had stopped off in the city while on a fishing cruise aboard the **Nourmahal**, a yacht owned by his friend Vincent Astor. When Roosevelt disembarked, Astor, seeing the huge crowds, had a strange premonition. "It would be easy," the millionaire remarked, "for an assassin to do his work and escape."

Within half an hour, armed with an eight-dollar pearl-handled .32 revolver, Zangara got off five shots but missed Roosevelt, instead wounding the mayor of Chicago, Anton Cermak, who was standing near the president-elect. The news was yet another blow to the country's fragile sense of stability. "People seemed to feel that their faith in the future was also the assassin's target," **Time** wrote. Attending to the mayor, FDR, for his part, was preternaturally calm. "I'm all right," he called out. "Roosevelt was simply himself—easy, confident, poised, to all appearances unmoved," Roosevelt adviser Raymond Moley recalled. That night, safely back on the **Nourmahal,** Roosevelt drank a glass of whiskey and went to bed.

The assassination attempt exacerbated a fraught season. Asked whether history had ever seen anything like the Depression, John Maynard Keynes replied: "Yes. It was called the Dark Ages, and it lasted four hundred years." In 1930, testifying before Congress, Father Charles Coughlin, the popular, often incendiary, radio priest, said: "I think by 1933, unless something is done, you will see a revolution in this country." Describing the plight of the unemployed, the historian William Manchester wrote: "Although millions were trapped in a great tragedy for which there could plainly be no individual responsibility, social workers repeatedly observed that the jobless were suffering from feelings of guilt. 'I haven't had a steady job in more than two years,' a man facing eviction told a New York **Daily News** reporter in February 1932. 'Sometimes I feel like a murderer. What's wrong with me, that I can't protect my children?' "

A small group of rich Wall Streeters also tried their hand at conceiving and launching a plot to supplant FDR as president by attempting to convince the retired Marine major general Smedley Butler, a respected veteran, to raise an army, march on Washington, and take the capital. Fearful of Roosevelt and his reforms, the "Wall Street Putsch" conspirators were planning to impose a fascist state. (The episode was also known as the "Business Plot.") Butler was an unwilling traitor. "If you get 500,000 soldiers advocating anything smelling of Fascism," Butler told one of the plotters who approached him, "I am going to get 500,000 more and lick the hell out of you, and we will have a real war right at home." The retired general told FBI director J. Edgar Hoover about the conspiracy. Reports about the Wall Street cabal's machinations soon leaked, and the threat fell apart.

In late 1934, secret congressional hearings, highlights of which were reported in the press, detailed what the plotters had been planning. Twice awarded the Congressional Medal of Honor, Butler testified before a House panel led by Congressmen John McCormack of Massachusetts and Samuel Dickstein of New York. "May I preface my remarks by saying, sir," Butler told McCormack, who co-chaired the committee, "that I have one interest in all of this, and that is to try to do my best to see that a democracy is maintained in this country?"

"Nobody who has either read about or known about General Butler would have anything but that understanding," McCormack replied. The retired general then offered his side of the story of being approached by well-funded intermediaries to lead a military takeover of Roosevelt's Washington. "Gen. Butler Bares 'Fascist Plot' To Seize Government By Force," read the front-page headline in **The New York Times** on Wednesday, November 21, 1934.

"If General Butler had not been the patriot he was, and if they had been able to maintain secrecy, the plot certainly might very well have succeeded, having in mind the conditions existing at that time," McCormack recalled to the author Jules Archer nearly four decades later. "No one can say for sure, of course, but when times are desperate and people are frustrated, anything like that could happen. . . . If the plotters had got rid of Roosevelt, there's no telling what might have taken place. . . . A well-organized minority can always outmaneuver an unorganized majority, as Adolf Hitler did. . . . The same thing could have happened here."

McCormack had little patience for skepticism about the gravity of the possible coup. "The people were in a very confused state of mind, making the nation weak and ripe for some drastic kind of extremist reaction," McCormack said. "Mass frustration could bring about anything."

General Butler, McCormack added, "regarded the plot very gravely indeed. He knew that this was a threat to our very way of government by a bunch of rich men who wanted fascism."

Sinclair Lewis's 1935 novel **It Can't Happen Here** told the story of the rise of an authoritarian state in an America riven by economic and cultural chaos. Lewis's book painted a disturbing portrait of a United States that abandoned liberal democracy and sought stability in fascism. "Why, there's no country in the world," a fictional editor remarks in the novel, "that can get more hysterical—yes, or more obsequious—than America." The editor's sad rhetorical query: "Where in all history has there ever been a people so ripe for a dictatorship as ours!"

Across the Atlantic, Winston Churchill took note of Lewis's book. "I was reading the other day a recent American novel by Sinclair Lewis—**It Can't Happen Here,**" Churchill wrote in August 1936. "Such books render a public service to the English-speaking world. When we see what has happened in Germany, Italy and Russia we cannot neglect their warning."

Less well known than Lewis's work is a small novel by Nathanael West, **A Cool Million,** a **Candide**–Horatio Alger parody. Published a year before **It Can't Happen Here, A Cool Million** includes the tale of the rise of a fascist politician.

In it, a former American president, Shagpoke Whipple, takes advantage of the Depression to demagogue his way back to power. Here is West's portrait of a Whipple rally:

> "I'm a simple man," he said with great simplicity, "and I want to talk to you about simple things. You'll get no highfalutin' talk from me.
>
> "First of all, you people want jobs. Isn't that so? . . .
>
> "Well, that's the only and prime purpose of the National Revolutionary Party—to get jobs for everyone. . . .
>
> "This is our country and we must fight to keep it so. If America is ever again to be great, it can only be through the triumph of the revolutionary middle class.
>
> "We must drive the Jewish international bankers out of Wall Street! We must destroy the Bolshevik labor unions! We must purge our country of all the alien elements and ideas that now infest her!
>
> "America for Americans! Back to the principles of Andy Jackson and Abe Lincoln!"

West was writing fiction, but only just. Perhaps the most consequential figure of the day, aside from FDR himself, was Huey Long, the former Louisiana governor who went to the U.S. Senate in 1932. Charismatic, wily, ambitious, and able, Long had a deep connection to poor voters who felt marginalized and to middle-class people who felt threatened. At lunch one day at Hyde Park, the Roosevelt family seat, the flamboyant Long arrived in a loud suit and a colorful tie. "Who is that awful man sitting to my son's right?" Sara Delano Roosevelt asked.

Long was strikingly effective on the campaign trail. After watching him charm the farmers of the West and the Plains, five Democratic state chairmen sent word back to headquarters: "If you have any doubtful state," they wrote party chief James Farley, "send Huey Long to it." When Roosevelt lost the vote in Pennsylvania to Hoover in November 1932, Farley realized his mistake in failing to deploy Long to the depressed mining regions. "We never again underrated him," Farley recalled.

Change—revolutionary change—was at hand, Long believed, and he saw himself as the tribune of the people. "A mob is coming here in six months to hang the other ninety-five of you damned scoundrels," Long told a fellow senator, "and I'm undecided whether to stick here with you or go out and lead them." Before a meeting with the president-elect himself, Long told reporters, ominously: "I'm going to ask him did you mean it, or didn't you mean it?" By "it," Long meant his own vision of the redistribution of wealth, which he believed key to saving capitalism itself. "Certainly we are facing communism in America," Long said. "The country has been going toward communism ever since the wealth of this country began to get into the hands of a few people."

In an April 1932 speech to the Senate called "The Doom of America's Dream," Long argued that both Democrats and Republicans had failed the country at one time or another. Power was concentrated in the hands of a self-serving financial and political elite. Only radical change, brought about by dynamic, unconventional leaders—leaders like Long—could make the nation the property of the people once more:

> The great and grand dream of America that all men are created free and equal, endowed with the inalienable right of life and liberty and the pursuit of happiness—this great dream of America, this great light, and this great hope—has almost gone out of sight in this day and time, and everybody knows it; and there is a mere candle flicker here and yonder to take the place of what the great dream of America was supposed to be. . . .

Unless we provide for the redistribution of wealth in this country, the country is doomed; there is going to be no country left here very long. That may sound a little bit extravagant, but I tell you that we are not going to have this good little America here long if we do not take to redistribute the wealth of this country.

He focused not only on the poor. "Where is the middle class today?" Long asked in 1933. "Where is the corner groceryman, about whom President Roosevelt speaks? He is gone or going. Where is the corner druggist? He is gone or going. Where is the banker of moderate means? He is vanishing. . . . The middle class today cannot pay the debts they owe and come out alive. In other words, the middle class is no more."

Long was a master at generating headlines. "He delighted in starting a fight," his biographer T. Harry Williams wrote. "Things are awfully quiet around here," Long would say to his secretary, Earle Christenberry. "What have you got in your files that we can liven them up with?" A Democratic colleague said: "Frankly, we are afraid of him. He is unscrupulous beyond belief. He might say anything about me, something entirely untrue, but it would ruin me in my state. . . . It's like challenging a buzz saw. He will go to the limit. It is safer for me and the rest of us to leave him alone."

One day in the Senate, much to the delight of the spectators in the galleries, Long was baiting Tennessee senator Kenneth McKellar. The presiding officer tried to calm the crowd when Senator Alben Barkley of Kentucky spoke up. "When the people go to a circus," Barkley said, alluding to Long, "they ought to be allowed to laugh at the monkey."

Writing in **The Nation** in 1935, the journalist and broadcaster Raymond Gram Swing took Long's measure as candidate for the presidency. "He will be direct, picturesque, and amusing, a relief after the attenuated vagueness of most of the national speaking today," Swing wrote. As long as Americans trusted FDR and believed in the New Deal, Swing wrote, all would be well. But if that faith were to collapse, Long might well be the man of that troubled hour. "Huey's chances depend on those sands of hope and trust running out," Swing wrote. "He is no menace if the President produces reform and recovery. But if in two years, even six, misery and fear are not abated in America the field is free to the same kind of promise-mongers who swept away Democratic leaders in Italy and Germany."

As his "Share Our Wealth" message spread, taking political form in grassroots clubs, Long grew in popularity. A banker from Montana wrote to Roosevelt saying that Long was "the man we thought you were when we voted for you." Louis Howe, FDR's political adviser, told the president that "it is symptoms like this I think we should watch very carefully."

There was much to keep an eye on. Lawrence Dennis, a native of Georgia and a former foreign service officer, wrote a pair of books in the thirties: **Is Capitalism Doomed?** and **The Coming American Fascism.** "I am in favor of a middle-class revolution," Dennis wrote, arguing that the media of the age made Americans susceptible to suggestion. "We have perfected techniques in propaganda and press and radio control which should make the United States the easiest country in the world to indoctrinate with any set of ideas, and to control for any physically possible ends." Diversity—political, racial, religious, ethnic—was the enemy. Talk of equality for women or for racial and ethnic minorities would give the fascist movement room to run. To Dennis, "undoubtedly the easiest way to unite and animate large numbers in political association for action is to exploit the dynamic forces of hatred and fear."

While Long politicked and Dennis wrote, Charles Coughlin, a Roman Catholic priest who built a broadcasting kingdom on earth from the Royal Oak suburb of Detroit, was an influential

Huey Long of Louisiana and Father
Charles Coughlin of Royal Oak,
Michigan, were influential voices of
populist discontent in the turbulence
of the Great Depression.

"His impulse," Winston Churchill had
written of FDR in the mid-1930s, "is one
which makes toward the fuller life of the
masses of the people in every land."

voice over the airwaves. Coughlin started out as
anti-Communist in the late 1920s; his populist
message would morph through the years, set-
tling mainly on a platform of anti-Semitism. In
broadcasts, when Alexander Hamilton, the first
secretary of the treasury, came up, Coughlin
would say, as if in passing, "whose original name
was Alexander Levine."

To Lawrence Dennis, the Coughlin-Long
flocks were the perfect vehicles for revolution. "I
hail these movements and pressure groups," Dennis wrote in 1935, "not because their members
are as yet fascists or friends of fascism, but be-

cause they are making fascism the alternative to chaos and national disintegration."

Hugh S. Johnson, a retired general and former head of Roosevelt's National Recovery Administration, lashed out at the president's foes in March 1935. "You can laugh at Father Coughlin—you can snort at Huey Long—but this country was never under a greater menace," Johnson said. President Roosevelt, Johnson told the nation, was "our sole hope."

That hope, the man chosen to rescue the nation from the abyss, Franklin Roosevelt, was hardly seen in a heroic light in the shadows of 1932. According to **The New Republic,** the New York governor was "not a man of great intellectual force or supreme moral stamina." Walter Lippmann, the most important columnist of the time, wrote: "Franklin D. Roosevelt is no crusader. He is no tribune of the people. He is no enemy of entrenched privilege. He is a pleasant man who, without any important qualifications for the office, would very much like to be President." Oswald Garrison Villard, the NAACP cofounder, was harsh about the gentleman from Hyde Park. "He has spoken of the 'forgotten man,'" Villard wrote of Roosevelt, "but nowhere is there a real, passionate, ringing exposition of just what it is that the forgotten man has been deprived of or what should be done for him. . . . We can see in him no leader, and no evidence anywhere that he can rise to the needs of this extraordinary hour."

Charming, cagey, and courageous, FDR would spend the next dozen or so years winning four White House terms and trying, with varying degrees of success, to prove his critics wrong. Americans in his time were questioning the very viability of the constitutional order and of capitalism itself. In his speech accepting the presidential nomination at the Democratic National Convention in Chicago in July 1932, he addressed himself to the future. "Wild radicalism has made few converts, and the greatest tribute that I can pay to my countrymen is that in these days of crushing want there persists an orderly and hopeful spirit on the part of the millions of our people who have suffered so much," Roosevelt said. "To fail to offer them a new chance is not only to betray their hopes but to misunderstand their patience."

The forces of progress, Roosevelt believed, were not to cower or to lash out, but to engage. "To meet by reaction that danger of radicalism is to invite disaster," he said. "Reaction is no barrier to the radical. It is a challenge, a provocation. The way to meet that danger is to offer a workable program of reconstruction, and the party to offer it is the party with clean hands." He then introduced a crucial phrase: "I pledge you, I pledge myself," FDR said, "to a New Deal for the American people." The crisis was existential. "His impulse," Winston Churchill wrote of FDR in the mid-1930s, "is one which makes toward the fuller life of the masses of the people in every land, and which, as it glows the brighter, may well eclipse both the lurid flames of German Nordic self-assertion and the baleful unnatural lights which are diffused from Soviet Russia."

Roosevelt was, it is true, an unlikely revolutionary. Born into enveloping privilege at Springwood, his family's house at Hyde Park in New York's Hudson Valley, Roosevelt was educated at home, at Endicott Peabody's Groton School, at Harvard, and at Columbia law school. His mother adored him with an all-consuming, even suffocating, love ("Mama left this morning," he wrote his father at age eight and a half, "and I am to have my bath alone!"). Theodore Roosevelt was his hero and role model. He married TR's favorite niece, Eleanor, served in the New York State Senate, and went to Washington as assistant secretary of the navy (a post TR had also held) under Wilson. His marriage survived the discovery of a love affair with Lucy Mercer, his wife's social secretary, in 1918, and he was nominated for vice president on the Democratic ticket with James M. Cox of Ohio in 1920.

It was by any measure a dazzling life—and then, in August 1921, at his family's summer retreat at Campobello Island on the Bay of Fundy, Franklin Roosevelt was stricken with infantile paralysis. He would never walk unaided again. He was thirty-nine years old. A quarter of a century later, after Roosevelt died at Warm Springs, Georgia, in the spring of 1945, Churchill, his wartime ally, rose in the House of Commons to pay tribute to the fallen American chief. An astute biographer and a discerning statesman, Churchill, who said that FDR's death had struck him with the force of "a physical blow," spoke about the great, if largely unmentioned, fact about the American president. "President Roosevelt's physical affliction," Churchill said, "lay heavily upon him."

A man of courage, Churchill appreciated it when he detected courage in others, and he had seen it, intimately, in Franklin Roosevelt. "It was a marvel that he bore up against it through all the many years of tumult and storm," Churchill said of FDR's paralysis. "Not one man in ten millions, stricken and crippled as he was, would have attempted to plunge into a life of physical and mental exertion and of hard, ceaseless political controversy. Not one in ten millions would have tried, not one in a generation would have succeeded, not only in entering this sphere, not only in acting vehemently in it, but in becoming indisputable master of the scene."

Lyndon Johnson wept when he heard the news from Warm Springs. "He was just like a daddy to me always," Johnson, then a congressman from Texas, said. "He was the one person I ever knew, anywhere, who was never afraid. God, God—how he could take it for us all!" **The New York Times** wrote: "Men will thank God on their knees, a hundred years from now, that Franklin D. Roosevelt was in the White House, in a position to give leadership to the thought of the American people and direction to the activities of their government, in that dark hour when a powerful and ruthless barbarism threatened to overrun the civilization of the Western World."

How did he do it? How did the man scorned in the beginning die a hero, bringing innumerable ordinary citizens to tears in the streets and on the farms of the country he loved? How did he salvage what seemed unsalvageable, rising to lead a nation through depression and world war?

One answer—and there are more than a few; such is the complexity of history—lies in FDR's sense of hope, a spirit of optimism forged in his own experience. For it is not too much to say that a man who had personally survived cataclysm and overcome paralysis was well equipped—perhaps uniquely so—to prevail over national cataclysm and political paralysis.

"This great Nation will endure as it has endured, will revive and will prosper," Roosevelt told the country at his first inauguration. "So, first of all, let me assert my firm belief that the only thing we have to fear is fear itself—nameless, unreasoning, unjustified terror which paralyzes needed efforts to convert retreat into advance. In every dark hour of our national life a leadership of frankness and vigor has met with that understanding and support of the people themselves which is essential to victory. I am convinced that you will again give that support to leadership in these critical days."

By one account, FDR had drawn on his own reading for the most historically memorable line of the address—"The only thing we have to fear is fear itself." Eleanor told Roosevelt adviser Samuel Rosenman that a friend of hers had given the president-elect a volume of the writings of Henry David Thoreau not long before the inauguration. "Nothing is so much to be feared as fear," Thoreau had written in his journal entry for September 7, 1851. FDR had the book with him during his pre-inaugural stay in Suite 776 of the Mayflower Hotel. "Roosevelt frequently picked up a book at his bedside for brief reading

before turning out the lights," Rosenman recalled. "It may be that in this way he came across
the phrase, it stuck in his mind, and found its
way into the speech."

To Roosevelt, faith—powerful, resilient faith—
was key. "We do not distrust the future of essential democracy," Roosevelt said in closing his first
inaugural. "The people of the United States have
not failed. In their need they have registered a
mandate that they want direct, vigorous action.
They have asked for discipline and direction
under leadership. They have made me the present
instrument of their wishes. In the spirit of the gift
I take it."

In that spirit he carried on. Privately he wondered if all would come out right. A friend told
him he might well be remembered as the greatest
of presidents if he succeeded, but that he would
go down as the worst if he failed. "If I fail," Roosevelt replied, "I shall be the last one." Publicly,
though, he never wavered. Conservatives hated
him; radicals thought him a milquetoast opportunist; liberals weren't sure, from moment to
moment, quite what to make of him.

Just as he had to balance himself with steel
braces on his legs, a cane in one hand and an
aide—often one of his sons—on his other side
simply to force himself forward when he rose
from his wheelchair (he called it "stumping"),

Roosevelt maneuvered with care through the storms of the decade. "It was part of his conception of his role," adviser Rexford Tugwell said, "that he should never show exhaustion, boredom, or irritation." Or extremism of any kind. He had told Americans what to expect from him. Running for president in 1932, Roosevelt said:

> Say that civilization is a tree which, as it grows, continually produces rot and dead wood. The radical says: "Cut it down." The conservative says: "Don't touch it." The liberal compromises: "Let's prune, so that we lose neither the old trunk nor the new branches." This campaign is waged to teach the country to march upon its appointed course, the way of change, in an orderly march, avoiding alike the revolution of radicalism and the revolution of conservatism.

As one might expect, this course failed to please the loudest voices in the sundry camps of American politics. "Franklin, darling, why is everyone opposed to so much of your program?" his mother once asked him. "A number of people have told me that they don't think it will work."

"Mummy, I think I know who you have been

talking with, and if I'm right, they are people who don't understand the first thing about government, never having served in it, nor have they the slightest conception of the great problems facing the nation," FDR replied. "Their only worry is that they might find themselves having to get along with two automobiles instead of three, but they don't give a hoot for the man who not only can't afford a car but is unable to feed and clothe his family. These are the people I'm concerned about and if I succeed in raising their standard of living, I won't lose any sleep over some of our friends who are opposed to my Administration."

Disappointed liberals lobbied the president to move more quickly on social and economic issues. "You'll never be a good politician," FDR once told Eleanor, who frequently presented such pleas to her husband. "You are too impatient." At a White House meeting, Roosevelt parried a questioner with a lesson in practical politics. Lincoln, Roosevelt said, "was a sad man because he couldn't get it all at once. And nobody can. Maybe you would make a much better President than I have. Maybe you will, someday. If you ever sit here, you will learn that you cannot, just by shouting from the housetops, get what you want all the time." He sometimes turned to sports to make his point. "I have no expectation of making a hit every time I come to bat," Roosevelt remarked. "What I seek is the highest possible batting average."

He argued that leadership, even his own, was imperfect. A wise public, Roosevelt believed, would give a well-meaning, forward-leaning president the benefit of the doubt. "The country needs and, unless I mistake its temper, the country demands bold, persistent experimentation," Roosevelt said in 1932. "It is common sense to take a method and try it: If it fails, admit it frankly and try another. But above all, try something. . . . We need enthusiasm, imagination and the ability to face facts, even unpleasant ones, bravely."

His headmaster from Groton, Endicott Peabody, grasped the essence of his old pupil. "At the time Franklin Roosevelt became President," Peabody said, "things were in the worst kind of doldrums owing to the inefficiency of Mr. Hoover as President. Change of a drastic nature was called for, and Franklin answered the call. Some of his policies have been mistaken. He prophesied that they would be. . . . Many have in my judgment contributed to the benefit of the people at large and have saved this country from the serious attacks made upon it by extreme radicals."

The Rector, as Peabody was known, held a special place in Roosevelt's heart and mind. "It is a

great thing for our country," Peabody wrote Roosevelt, "to have before it the leadership of a man
who cares primarily for spiritual things." (This was
a common view among those who loved Roosevelt. "You and I are for Roosevelt because he's a
great spiritual figure, because he's an idealist,"
FDR confidant Harry Hopkins once remarked to
the playwright and speechwriter Robert E. Sherwood. "Oh—he sometimes tries to appear tough
and cynical and flippant, but that's an act he likes
to put on.") For all the exigencies of political life,
Roosevelt had been shaped by, and drew suste-
nance from, the message of hope that Peabody
had taught him.

Sustained by this view of progress, Roosevelt
urged the nation onward. "We shall strive for
perfection," Roosevelt said. "We shall not achieve
it immediately—but we still shall strive. We may
make mistakes—but they must never be mistakes which result from faintness of heart or
abandonment of moral principle. . . . Our Constitution of 1787 was not a perfect instrument;
it is not perfect yet. But it provided a firm base
upon which all manner of men, of all races and
colors and creeds, could build our solid structure of democracy."

The salience of hope, the dangers of fear, and
the need for open American hearts were familiar
Roosevelt themes throughout his presidency.

When FDR died, Harry Hopkins called Robert Sherwood. "You and I have got something great that we can take with us all the rest of our lives," Hopkins said, continuing:

> It's a great realization. Because we know it's true what so many people believed about him and what made them love him. The President never let them down. That's what you and I can remember. Oh, we all know he could be exasperating, and he could seem to be temporizing and delaying, and he'd get us all worked up when we thought he was making too many concessions to expediency. But all of that was in the little things, the unimportant things—and he knew exactly how little and how unimportant they really were. But in the big things—all of the things that were of real, permanent importance—he never let the people down.

Reporting from North Carolina in 1934, the journalist Martha Gellhorn wrote that she had found Roosevelt's portrait in house after house after house. The president, she wrote, was "at once God and their intimate friend; he knows them all by name, knows their little town and mill, their little lives and problems. . . . He is there, and will not let them down." The novelist Sherwood Anderson affirmed the point. "More than any man who has been President within the memory of any of us now living," Anderson wrote, "he has made us feel close to him."

Through the vagaries of the thirties, Roosevelt tacked this way and that, sometimes under-reaching with the New Deal, sometimes over-reaching. "The New Deal is simply the effort of a lot of half-baked Socialists to save capitalism for the dumb capitalists," a "shrewd liberal" re-marked to the journalist John Gunther. Roo-sevelt's initial two years in office were focused largely on rescuing the American system, includ-ing banks and basic economic confidence.

Beginning in 1935, in what was known as the Second New Deal, the president blunted much of Long's redistributive platform with the Social Security Act, the Wagner Act (guaranteeing col-lective bargaining), and programs that put mil-lions to work on infrastructure and other public projects. In a pre-1936 campaign conversation with his adviser Samuel Rosenman, Roosevelt sketched out how he would oppose himself if he were running as a Republican in the coming race for reelection: "I would say: 'I am for social security, work relief, etc., etc. But the Demo-crats cannot be entrusted with the administra-tion of these fine ideals.' I would cite chapter and verse on WPA inefficiency—and there's plenty of it—as there is bound to be in such a vast, emergency program. You know . . . the more I think about it, the more I think I could lick myself."

But no one else could. The threat from Huey Long ended with the Kingfish's assassination in the fall of 1935: Long had lived, and died, violently. Thunderously reelected in 1936—he lost only Maine and Vermont—Roosevelt read too much into his mandate and attempted to alter the makeup of the Supreme Court, which had blocked a number of New Deal measures. There was a backlash against the plan, which, along with a recession, brought the overconfident FDR back into balance. Arthur Krock of **The New York Times** evoked the era well with this observation about the president:

> The Republicans say officially that the President is an impulsive, uninformed opportunist, lacking policy or stability, wasteful, reckless, unreliable in act and contract. . . . Mr. Roosevelt seeks to supervene the constitutional processes of government, dominate Congress and the Supreme Court by illegal means and regiment the country to his shifting and current ideas—a perilous egomaniac.
>
> The Democrats say officially that the

President is the greatest practical humanitarian who ever averted social upheaval, the wisest economic mechanician who ever modernized a government . . . savior and protector of the American way—including the capitalist system—and rebuilder of the nation. . . . Mr. Roosevelt has constructed, with daring and fortitude, a sound bridge from the perilous past to the secure future.

He is not wholly either, and he is certainly something of both. In the opinion of this writer he is much more of the latter than the former.

The telephone in the president's bedroom in the family quarters of the White House rang in the middle of the night as Thursday, August 31, 1939, became Friday, September 1, 1939. Adolf Hitler's Wehr-macht, executing a war plan code-named Case White, had struck Poland. World War II had begun in earnest. William Bullitt, Roosevelt's ambassador to France, got the word and called the president, who took the call in bed. "Well, Bill," Roosevelt said, "it's come at last. God help us all."

It was understandable that Roosevelt was thinking about the Almighty, for the problems the president faced seemed insuperable. The nation was strongly isolationist, and fear was a common theme—fear of entanglement, fear of sacrificing American blood and treasure for the advantage of others, fear of putting foreign demands ahead of national needs. The Depression was global in nature; if only we could put America first, the isolationists argued, then all might still be well.

This view was held widely and deeply. In 1936, a survey by George Gallup found that 95 percent of those polled believed America should stay out of any European war. Roosevelt was intuitively attuned to such political facts. "He is a gentleman in every sense of the word, well meaning and very ambitious," Sir Ronald Lindsay, the British ambassador to the United States, wrote the Foreign Office in London. "He has antennae and political sense to his very finger-tips. Instinctively he knows what the feeling of the moment is and what is politically possible."

He also performed the essential presidential function of looking ahead, beyond the moment, to what the world might bring. And the more he contemplated Germany's evident designs to expand—Hitler referred to it as the Reich's search for Lebensraum, or living space—the more Roosevelt sensed ultimate trouble. Constrained by neutrality legislation and by public opinion, the president nevertheless did the best he could to prepare for the possibility of war. His success can be gauged, in part, by the anti-Roosevelt views of the more fervent isolationists. Oswald Garrison Villard believed "the greatest safeguard would be having a man in the White House firmly and immovably resolved not to let the country get into war under any conditions whatsoever."

Roosevelt waged a steady but not overwhelming campaign to make the world appear relevant to a country battered by Depression and wary of foreign entanglements. That wariness was tangible. Congressman Louis Ludlow of Indiana even proposed a constitutional amendment that would have required a popular referendum to declare war (except in cases where the United States was attacked). The amendment came to a vote in the House in early 1938. Polling showed significant public support, with 73 percent favoring Ludlow's bill. In a letter to the Speaker of the House, Roosevelt wrote: "Our Government is conducted by the people through representatives of their own choosing. It was with singular unanimity that the founders of the Republic agreed upon such free and representative form of government as the only practical means of government by the people. Such an amendment to the Constitution as that proposed would cripple any President in his conduct of our foreign relations, and it would encourage other nations to believe that they could violate American rights with impunity." The House voted the measure down, 209 to 188.

Score one for Roosevelt, but he did not win them all. "We must not be misguided by this foreign propaganda that our frontiers lie in Europe," the aviator and isolationist leader Charles Lindbergh said. "What more could we ask than the Atlantic Ocean on the east, the Pacific on the west? An ocean is a formidable barrier, even for modern aircraft." Roosevelt's view was subtler: The fates of nations were interconnected.

In late July 1939 the president met with the congressional leadership seeking to revise neutrality laws in order to enable the United States to sell arms to Britain and France. Led by Senator William Borah of Idaho, the isolationists refused. "Well, Captain, we may as well face the facts," Vice President John Nance Garner told Roosevelt. "You haven't got the votes, and that's all there is to it."

Then, in a matter of weeks, Hitler invaded Poland. In a broadcast two weeks after the invasion, Charles Lindbergh argued for leaving the Old World to its own devices. "Now that war has broken out again, we in America have a decision to make on which the destiny of our nation depends," Lindbergh said, adding: "In making our decision, this point should be clear:

these wars in Europe are not wars in which our civilization is defending itself against some Asiatic intruder. There is no Genghis Khan or Xerxes marching against our Western nations. This is not a question of banding together to defend the White race against foreign invasion. This is simply one more of those age-old quarrels within our own family of nations."

Roosevelt disagreed. In his own address to the nation in the first days of September 1939, FDR summed up the reality of the modern world. "Passionately though we may desire detachment," the president said, "we are forced to realize that every word that comes through the air, every ship that sails the sea, every battle that is fought, does affect the American future."

From the fall of 1939 through 1940 and into 1941, Roosevelt carefully but surely signaled his opposition to Germany. As he sought a third term, running against the Republican Wendell Willkie, himself an interventionist, the president conceded this much to isolationist sentiment, announcing in Boston: "And while I am talking to you mothers and fathers, I give you one more assurance. I have said this before, but I shall say it again and again and again: your boys are not going to be sent into any foreign wars." Listening on the radio, Willkie said, "That hypocritical son of a bitch! This is going to beat me."

Roosevelt's deeds did not comport with his remarks in Boston. He had already won repeal of
the embargo on arms sales overseas. He had
worked out an agreement with Britain to exchange old American destroyers for basing rights.
He waged an undeclared naval war in the Atlantic. And at the beginning of 1941, he proposed a
broad plan, called Lend-Lease, to supply the Allies.

The idea had come to him during a holiday
fishing trip aboard the USS **Tuscaloosa** in the
Caribbean with Harry Hopkins. A seaplane had
brought Roosevelt an impassioned letter from
Prime Minister Winston Churchill, who was
pleading for material aid to keep Hitler at bay.

Six months earlier, writing on the evening
of Saturday, June 15, 1940, Churchill, standing
virtually alone against Hitler, had begged Roosevelt for help. "Although the present government and I personally would never fail to send
the Fleet across the Atlantic if resistance was
beaten down here, a point may be reached in the
struggle where the present ministers no longer
have control of affairs and when very easy terms
could be obtained for the British Islands by their
becoming a vassal state of the Hitler empire,"
Churchill had said. "A pro-German Government would certainly be called into being to
make peace and might present to a shattered or

a starving nation an almost irresistible case for entire submission to the Nazi will."

In the bleak days of May and June, Churchill was ready to die, if necessary, for the cause of Britain; as he had told his cabinet on Tuesday, May 28, "We shall go on and we shall fight it out, here or elsewhere, and if at last the long story is to end, it were better it should end, not through surrender, but only when we are rolling senseless on the ground."

Now, in the closing weeks of 1940, Churchill sought aid from Roosevelt, who read the letter in the sunshine aboard the **Tuscaloosa**. "Unless we can establish our ability to feed this Island," Churchill wrote, "to import the munitions of all kinds which we need, unless we can move our armies to the various theatres where Hitler and his confederate, Mussolini, must be met, and maintain them there, and do all this with the assurance of being able to carry it on till the spirit of the Continental Dictators is broken, we may fall by the way, and the time needed by the United States to complete her defensive preparations may not be forthcoming."

Churchill's appeal worked. The president proposed Lend-Lease, a program to supply the British without becoming more directly involved in the war. Returning to Washington, Roosevelt used his State of the Union address, delivered to

Congress on Monday, January 6, 1941, to link his vision of life at home with his understanding of America's interests abroad: "Today, thinking of our children and of their children, we oppose enforced isolation for ourselves or for any other part of the Americas." He continued:

> Every realist knows that the democratic way of life is at this moment being directly assailed in every part of the world—assailed either by arms or by secret spreading of poisonous propaganda by those who seek to destroy unity and promote discord in nations that are still at peace. . . .
>
> As men do not live by bread alone, they do not fight by armaments alone. Those who man our defenses, and those behind them who build our defenses, must have the stamina and the courage which come from unshakable belief in the manner of life which they are defending. The mighty action that we are calling for cannot be based on a disregard of all things worth fighting for.

And what were the democracies fighting for? "In the future days, which we seek to make secure, we look forward to a world founded upon four essential human freedoms," he said.

The first is freedom of speech and expression—everywhere in the world. The second is freedom of every person to worship God in his own way—everywhere in the world. The third is freedom from want—which, translated into world terms, means economic understandings which will secure to every nation a healthy peacetime life for its inhabitants—everywhere in the world. The fourth is freedom from fear—which, translated into world terms, means a world-wide reduction of armaments to such a point and in such a thorough fashion that no nation will be in a position to commit an act of physical aggression against any neighbor—anywhere in the world.

He closed on a note of realistic hope. "That is no vision of a distant millennium," Roosevelt said. "It is a definite basis for a kind of world attainable in our own time and generation."

On Thursday, September 11, 1941, Charles Lindbergh stepped to the microphones at an America First Committee rally in Des Moines. Founded by law students at Yale University, America First was devoted to the principle that "American democracy can be preserved only by keeping out of the European war" and that " 'Aid short of war' weakens national defense at home and threatens to involve America in war abroad." In late 1940, so many Americans were signing up for America First that **Time** said the group's "organization drive . . . was going like a house afire." By one estimate sixty thousand people had joined eleven different chapters.

Lindbergh had taken it upon himself to speak, as he put it elsewhere, for "that silent majority of Americans who have no newspaper, or newsreel, or radio station at their command." Now it was time, he had decided, to make himself very clear on what he saw as a critical issue facing the nation as it debated whether to go to war against Hitler: the role of American Jews.

"It is not difficult to understand why Jewish people desire the overthrow of Nazi Germany," Lindbergh said in Des Moines. "The persecution they suffered in Germany would be sufficient to make bitter enemies of any race. No person with a sense of the dignity of mankind can condone the persecution of the Jewish race in Germany. But"—and the **but** here is epochal— "no person of honesty and vision can look on their pro-war policy here today without seeing the dangers involved in such a policy, both for us and for them. . . . Their greatest danger to this country lies in their large ownership and influence in our motion pictures, our press, our radio, and our Government." The British and the Jews, Lindbergh continued, "for reasons which are not American . . . wish to involve us in the war. We cannot blame them for looking out for what they believe to be their own interests, but we must also look out for ours."

Roosevelt had turned on Lindbergh long before. The previous year, after another isolationist plea to the country from the aviator, the president had told Secretary of the Treasury Henry Morgenthau, Jr.: "If I should die tomorrow, I want you to know this. I am absolutely convinced that Lindbergh is a Nazi."

The Lindbergh remarks in Des Moines on the role of Jewish opinion worried more than a few of his fellow isolationists. "Lindbergh's anti-Jewish speech is, of course, all wrong," Herbert Hoover wrote. "And I fear it will hurt all of us who are opposed to war." Norman Thomas, the Socialist leader, declined to speak further on behalf of America First. "Not all Jews are for war," Thomas said, "and Jews have a right to agitate for war if we have a right to agitate against it." John T. Flynn, a journalist and America Firster, sent a plaintive message to the committee's leaders after Des Moines. "It seems incredible to me that Col. Lindbergh without consulting anyone literally committed the America First movement to an open attack upon the Jews."

Anti-Semitism was a fact of life in America. In the Red Scare years, Henry Ford's **Dearborn Independent,** a Michigan newspaper, chronicled the alleged Jewish influence in American life and published **The Protocols of the Elders of Zion,** a fabricated anti-Semitic text that provided haters a false narrative of Jewish conspiracy.

"When we get through with the Jews in America," Father Coughlin told an audience, "they'll think the treatment they received in Germany was nothing." The German-American Bund, led by Fritz Kuhn, had held a twenty-thousand-strong gathering at Madison Square Garden in February 1939 that featured cries of "Heil Hitler." "The principles of the Bund and the principles of the Klan are the same," a Bund leader said while appearing with Arthur Bell, the grand dragon of the New Jersey Klan. In 1940, fearing a third Roosevelt term, the Third Reich had sought to influence the presidential election by placing newspaper ads and paying for isolationist congressmen to attend the Republican National Convention.

Even after Pearl Harbor and Hitler's declaration of war on the United States in December 1941, there were those who peddled a toxic blend of anti-Semitism (which came to include Holocaust denial), virulent anti-Communism, and Nazi ideology. Gerald L. K. Smith, a former ally of the late Huey Long, was a leading Hitlerite who ran for president in 1944 and published an alt-right forerunner, **The Cross and the Flag.** In later years, Smith advocated a form of Christian nationalism. "The Christian Nationalist Crusade," he wrote, "is a nationwide political movement dedicated to the mobilization of citizens who respect American tradition and whose idealism is founded on Christian principle. . . . We believe that the destiny of America in relationship to its governing authority must be in the hands of our own people. We must never be governed by aliens. We must keep control of our own money and our own blood."

Americans, FDR noted in 1941, would "rather die on our feet than live on our knees," and the passion for freedom, for justice, and for the rule of law was not limited to the world beyond the seas. After news of the June 1940 lynching of Elbert Williams, the secretary of his local NAACP branch in western Tennessee, **The Pittsburgh Courier** wrote: "There is something definitely wrong about a so-called democratic government that froths at the mouth about . . . terrorism abroad, yet has not a mumble of condemnation for the same sort of thing at home."

Eleanor Roosevelt was in many ways the conscience of the White House. "My impression of

The tireless Eleanor Roosevelt pressed FDR on anti-lynching legislation and resigned from the Daughters of the American Revolution when the group refused to allow Marian Anderson to perform at Constitution Hall.

both him and Mrs. Roosevelt," H. G. Wells wrote of the president and the First Lady, "is that they are unlimited people, entirely modern in the openness of their minds and the logic of their actions." As a younger woman she had shared the anti-Semitism of the age, once describing Felix Frankfurter as "an interesting little man but very Jew." As she grew older, her perspective widened. When **The New York Times** published a dispatch from Warm Springs on the twenty-fifth anniversary of FDR's death, it quoted a white Southerner: "Mrs. Roosevelt? Well, she was what you'd

"For gosh sakes, here comes Mrs. Roosevelt!"

call a Negro lover, wasn't she?" Roy Wilkins, of the NAACP, said: "The personal touch and the personal fight against discrimination were Mrs. Roosevelt's. That attached to Roosevelt also—he couldn't hardly get away from it—and he reaped the political benefit from it."

Lynchings of blacks by whites had still occurred with depressing regularity into the thirties. According to contemporary reports, there had been 3,500 such attacks since 1900 but only 67 indictments and 12 convictions. In December 1933, in a speech to the Federal Council of Churches of Christ in America, FDR spoke out against such racially motivated violence. "We know that it is murder, and a deliberate and definite disobedience of the Commandment, 'Thou shalt not kill,'" the president said. "We do not excuse those in high places or in low who condone lynch law."

Fine words, but the president felt constrained by the abiding problem of the Democratic Party: the appeasement of its segregationist Southern wing. Mrs. Roosevelt and the NAACP pressed the president to take a firm stand on federal anti-lynching measures only to find him consumed with other matters. "If I come out for the anti-lynching bill now, they will block every bill I ask Congress to pass to keep America from collapsing," Roosevelt told NAACP leader Walter White. "I just can't take the risk." He would not spend political capital on civil rights, but when Mrs. Roosevelt asked if she might speak her mind on the lynching question, the president said, "You can say anything you want. I can always say, 'Well, that is my wife; I can't do anything about her."

In the end, FDR supported such a measure, though it failed in Congress: The president sacrificed the legislation to ensure support for other New Deal programs. "I am so sorry about the bill," Eleanor wrote White. "Of course, all of us are going on fighting, and the only thing we can do is hope we will have better luck next time." A small sign of the structural nature of racist sentiment came when a young aide, Will Alexander, was leaving the administration in June 1940. "Will, don't you think the New Deal is undertaking to do too much for the Negro?" asked Henry Wallace, the secretary of agriculture who joined FDR's ticket as vice president later that summer.

On the symbolic front, Mrs. Roosevelt resigned from the Daughters of the American Revolution in 1939 when the group refused to allow Marian Anderson, the African American singer, to perform at the DAR's Constitution Hall near the White House. From Groton, Endicott Peabody wrote approvingly, telling Eleanor that the DAR's discrimination was "in line with the prejudice, I might say cruelty, with which we have dealt with the negro people. Your courage in taking this definite stand called for my admiration."

Anderson was instead invited to sing at the Lincoln Memorial to a vast Easter Sunday afternoon audience on the Mall. She opened with "My Country 'Tis of Thee" and closed with "Nobody Knows the Trouble I've Seen." Harold Ickes, the secretary of the interior, wrote that he had "never heard such a voice" and that "the whole setting was unique, majestic, and impressive." Walter White called the concert "one of the most thrilling experiences of our time."

The NAACP, among others, had been long at work battling discrimination in employment, education, housing, voting, and public accommodations. It was the slowest of goings, but the warriors for equality fought on, year in and year out, court case after court case, flashpoint after flashpoint. In early 1941, A. Philip Randolph, the leader of the Brotherhood of Sleeping Car Porters, decided that a mass march on Washington would be the best way to draw attention to segregation in the nation's burgeoning defense industries. Writing the NAACP's Walter White, Randolph argued that "something dramatic has got to be done to shake official Washington and the white industrialists and labor forces of America to the realization of the fact that the Negroes mean business about getting their rights as American citizens under national defense." The First Lady was also urging integration within the armed forces themselves and the promotion of blacks within the military. In his diary, Henry Stimson, the secretary of war, lamented "Mrs. Roosevelt's intrusive and impulsive folly."

When he heard about Randolph's proposed July 1941 march, Roosevelt dispatched his wife to New York to try to talk the African American leadership out of it. "You know where I stand," Mrs. Roosevelt told Randolph and White. "But the attitude of the Washington police, most of them Southerners, and the general feeling of Washington itself are such that I fear that there may be trouble if the march occurs." The reward for calling off the demonstration was Executive Order 8802, banning discrimination in military industries and creating the Fair Employment Practices Committee to enforce the new directive. "I hope from this first step," Mrs. Roosevelt wrote Randolph, "we may go on to others."

Roosevelt's greatest concession to fear, the internment of Japanese Americans after Pearl Harbor, was also arguably his greatest failure as president. Beginning in 1942, about 117,000 Americans of Japanese descent were rounded up and consigned to concentration camps for the duration of the war. The shameful episode had all the hallmarks of a fevered era of fear run amok. There was racial prejudice, anxiety about espionage, and a lost sense of justice. "Japs live like rats, breed like rats, and act like rats," said the governor of Idaho, Chase Clark. The attorney general of California, Earl Warren, argued in favor of internment.

On Thursday, February 12, 1942, Walter Lippmann wrote that while he understood "the unwillingness of Washington to adopt a policy of mass evacuation and mass internment," there was no real choice in the matter. "The Pacific Coast is officially a combat zone: some part of it may at any moment be a battlefield," Lippmann wrote. "Nobody's constitutional rights include the right to reside and do business on a battlefield."

Seven days later Roosevelt issued Executive Order 9066, giving legal sanction to the internment, in typically desperate conditions, of American citizens. It was a decision of a nation in panic, of a government that had lost its bearings, of a president who had chosen to forsake his duty to the spirit and to the letter of the Constitution. The ACLU challenged the program in court, writing Roosevelt: "Enforcing this on the Japanese alone approximates the totalitarian theory of justice practiced by the Nazis in their treatment of the Jews."

A majority of the Supreme Court upheld the essence of Roosevelt's order in several cases, deciding, coldly, that "Hardships are part of war, and war is an aggregation of hardships." The author of the opinion: Hugo Black.

The military did allow the creation of an all–Japanese American unit, the 442nd Regimental Combat Team, which fought bravely and well. In December 1945, General Joseph W. Stilwell, the American commander in the Far East known as "Vinegar Joe," flew to the farmlands of Orange County, California. On the porch of a frame shack, Stilwell presented Mary Masuda with the

Distinguished Service Cross. Masuda and her parents had been detained under Executive Order 9066; her brother Kazuo had served in the 442nd, performing nobly under fire in Europe, including a twelve-hour lone mortar barrage on German positions. He was killed in action.

There were some show business figures in Stilwell's entourage on his trip to the Masuda homestead. One of the party had this to say: "Blood that has soaked into the sands of a beach is all of one color. America stands unique in the world: the only country not founded on race but on a way, an ideal. Not in spite of but because of our

Japanese American children wave from a train window in Seattle en route to an internment camp in March 1942—the result of FDR's Executive Order 9066.

polyglot background, we have had all the strength in the world. That is the American way."

Eloquent words, and Ronald Reagan, then a thirty-four-year-old movie star and liberal activist, spoke them well. More than four decades later, Reagan, in his final year as president of the United States, quoted a newspaper clipping about the presentation at the Masudas' as he prepared to sign the Civil Liberties Act of 1988. The bill—numbered 442 in honor of the 442nd—authorized compensation for the detained families and, perhaps more important, apologized to the victims of Roosevelt's internment policy. "For here," Reagan said, "we admit a wrong; here we reaffirm our commitment as a nation to equal justice under the law."

As President Reagan's apology suggests, there was no real debate about the moral content of internment. The same cannot be said, however, of Roosevelt's response to the tragedy of the Holocaust, the systematic murder of six million Jews and others the Third Reich deemed less than human. Scholars continue to argue over the president and the Final Solution: Did Roosevelt do enough to save Jewish lives from being lost in the Shoah?

On Thursday, April 12, 1945, Edward R. Murrow of CBS—perhaps the most famous man in broadcast journalism—visited Buchenwald, a Nazi concentration camp where nearly sixty thousand people had died. The prisoners Murrow saw were too weak to rise from their cots; he told listeners that he watched a man fall over dead. Inmates showed Murrow the numbers tattooed on their arms. "There were two rows of bodies stacked up like cordwood," Murrow said, describing a room with a concrete floor. "They were thin and very white. Some of the bodies were terribly bruised, though there seemed to be little flesh to bruise. Some had been shot through the head, but they bled but little."

Three days later, Dwight Eisenhower, the Supreme Allied commander, wrote of his own tour of a death camp. "The things I saw beggar description," he said. "The visual evidence and the verbal testimony of starvation, cruelty and bestiality were so overpowering as to leave me a bit sick. . . . I made the visit deliberately, in order to be in a position to give first-hand evidence of these things if ever, in the future, there develops a tendency to charge these allegations merely to 'propaganda.'"

Hitler had come to power in Germany on Monday, January 30, 1933. "For us, it is a problem of whether our nation can ever recover its health, whether the Jewish spirit can ever really be eradicated," Hitler said as early as 1920.

"Don't be misled into thinking you can fight a disease without killing the carrier, without destroying the bacillus. Don't think you can fight racial tuberculosis without taking care to rid the nation of the carrier of that racial tuberculosis. This Jewish contamination will not subside, this poisoning of the nation will not end, until the carrier himself, the Jew, has been banished from our midst." The Nuremberg Laws of 1935 and Kristallnacht in November 1938 should have left no doubts about the evils of Nazi ideology even before World War II.

President Roosevelt responded, in a fashion, to the crisis even before Kristallnacht. As the scholars Richard Breitman and Allan J. Lichtman wrote, the president had two ideas, both politically risky—and he was not a man who undertook political risks lightly. First, after Hitler took over Austria, Roosevelt combined the Austrian and Germany immigration quotas to increase the number of refugees who could be accepted into the United States. His second idea, one that led to a not entirely successful international conference in Évian, France, was that the nations of the world would accept a certain number of refugees, thus—Roosevelt hoped—moving them out of harm's way.

After a time, however, Roosevelt slowed his efforts to increase the flow of refugees out of the Nazi sphere. Why? Because the 1940 election was approaching. Henry Morgenthau, Jr., the secretary of the treasury and a Hudson Valley neighbor of Roosevelt's, believed that Roosevelt began thinking of a third term as 1938 wore on—which led the president to return to safer political form. As Breitman and Lichtman wrote: "The more Roosevelt risked on initiatives for Jews, the less he thought he could carry Congress and the public with him on broad issues of foreign policy." And so ended the prewar Roosevelt story on Jewish questions.

As the global conflict grew, Roosevelt believed, strongly, that the best course was to focus on first preparing for total war and second on waging it. The fastest way to save the Jews, the president argued (and Churchill agreed) was to defeat Germany. That was the core conviction. On Thursday, December 17, 1942, the United States, Great Britain, and other Allied governments issued a declaration:

> The German authorities, not content with denying to persons of Jewish race in all the territories over which their barbarous rule has been extended, the most elementary human rights, are now carrying into effect Hitler's oft-repeated intention to exterminate the Jewish people in Europe.
>
> From all the occupied countries Jews are being transported in conditions of appall-

ing horror and brutality to Eastern Europe. In Poland, which has been made the principal Nazi slaughterhouse, the ghettos established by the German invader are being systematically emptied of all Jews except a few highly skilled workers required for war industries. None of those taken away are ever heard of again. The able-bodied are slowly worked to death in labor camps. The infirm are left to die of exposure and starvation or are deliberately massacred in mass executions. The number of victims of these bloody cruelties is reckoned in many hundreds of thousands of entirely innocent men, women and children.

Still, Roosevelt resisted turning the war into one to save the Jews, or to save any single group, and specific issues of rescue or of refugees tended to be put to the periphery.

Then, in early 1944, pressed by Treasury Secretary Henry Morgenthau, Roosevelt established the War Refugee Board in order to deal with as many such issues as possible. It was an imperfect solution, but it was a step forward. In 1998, the historian Gerhard L. Weinberg concluded:

Every single life counts, and every individual saved counts. There cannot be the slightest doubt that more efforts could have been made by an earlier establishment of the War Refugee Board and by any number of other steps and actions. The general picture in terms of overall statistics would not have been very different; but the record of the Allies would have been brighter, and each person saved could have lived out a decent life. The exertions of the Allies in World War II saved not only themselves but also the majority of the world's Jews. But the shadow of doubt whether enough was done will always remain, even if there really were not many things that could have been done.

One wishes for a better outcome, for wiser heads, for a more compassionate public. Yet one wishes in vain. The only comfort, if we can call it that, is that a knowledge of our past failings may equip us to confront evil without delay when evil comes again. For it will.

Eleanor Roosevelt brought her husband word of the opening of Operation Overlord, the Allied assault on Hitler's Fortress Europe on the northern coast of France. "On D-Day, about three o'clock in the morning, I was called by the White House switchboard and told to awaken the President, that the War Department wanted him on the telephone—General Marshall was speaking himself," Mrs. Roosevelt recalled of Tuesday, June 6, 1944. "I went in and wakened my husband. He sat up in bed and put on his sweater, and from then on was on the telephone."

Overlord was a vital turning point. Churchill called the landings at Normandy "the most difficult and complicated operation that has ever taken place." In his bedroom in the White House, Roosevelt "was tense waiting for news," Eleanor recalled, and his mind was on the fates of the men who were hitting the beaches and scaling the cliffs. "I wonder how Linaka will come out," Mrs. Roosevelt recalled the president saying. Russell Linaka, a World War I veteran, had worked on FDR's tree plantations at Hyde Park and was now commanding a landing craft. (He made it through.)

The president, who loved the King James Version of the Bible and the Episcopal Book of Common Prayer, was to broadcast a prayer that evening. His daughter, Anna, and son-in-law, John Boettiger, had helped him draft it during a weekend stay at Kenwood, his aide Edwin "Pa" Watson's estate in the shadow of Monticello. The White House released the text of the prayer to the afternoon newspapers. That night, with an estimated audience of one hundred million Americans, FDR recited his words in what was one of the largest mass prayers in human history:

Almighty God: Our sons, pride of our Nation, this day have set upon a mighty endeavor, a struggle to preserve our Republic, our religion, and our civilization, and to set free a suffering humanity.

Lead them straight and true; give strength to their arms, stoutness to their hearts, steadfastness in their faith.

They will be sore tried, by night and by day, without rest—until the victory is won. The darkness will be rent by noise and flame. Men's souls will be shaken with the violences of war.

For these men are lately drawn from the ways of peace. They fight not for the lust of conquest. They fight to end conquest. They fight to liberate. They fight to let justice arise, and tolerance and good will among all Thy people. They yearn but for the end of battle, for their return to the haven of home. . . .

With Thy blessing, we shall prevail over the unholy forces of our enemy. Help us to conquer the apostles of greed and racial arrogancies. Lead us to the saving of our country, and with our sister Nations into a

world unity that will spell a sure peace—
a peace invulnerable to the schemings of
unworthy men. And a peace that will let
all of men live in freedom, reaping the just
rewards of their honest toil.

Thy will be done, Almighty God.

Amen.

Listening to the broadcast, FDR's cousin Margaret "Daisy" Suckley wrote that the prayer had been "beautifully read by the P. this evening. It is wonderful, in these days, to find the head of this huge nation lead the people in prayer."

When news came of Roosevelt's death, Robert Sherwood could not fathom the reports. "I couldn't believe it when somebody told me he was dead," Sherwood recalled. "Like everybody else, I listened and listened to the radio, waiting for the announcement—probably in his own gaily reassuring voice—that it had all been a big mistake . . . and everything was going to be 'fine—grand—perfectly bully.' "

But it was true. "It finally crushed him," Sherwood thought. "He couldn't stand up under it any longer. . . . The fears and the hopes of hundreds of millions of human beings throughout the world had been bearing down on the mind of one man, until the pressure was more than mortal tissue could stand."

In his cottage at Warm Springs—where a porch had been designed to resemble the prow of a ship, giving the paralyzed president the illusion of movement, of freedom—Roosevelt left the draft of a speech he had been scheduled to deliver on Saturday, April 13, 1945, on the occasion of the birthday of Thomas Jefferson. "Today, science has brought all the different quarters of the globe so close together that it is impossible to isolate them one from another," Roosevelt was to have said. "Today we are faced with the preeminent fact that, if civilization is to survive, we must cultivate the science of human relationships— the ability of all peoples, of all kinds, to live together and work together, in the same world, at peace. . . . The only limit to our realization of tomorrow will be our doubts of today. Let us move forward with strong and active faith."

They were, in a way, his last words.

·SIX·

HAVE YOU NO SENSE OF DECENCY?

||||||||||||||||||||||||||||||||||||||||||||||||||||||||||||

"Making Everyone Middle Class," the GI Bill, McCarthyism, and Modern Media

The fact that we have a well-informed so-called
middle class in this country is what makes it
the greatest republic the sun has ever shone upon,
or ever will shine upon again.

—HARRY S. TRUMAN, 1948

He was impatient, overly aggressive, overly dramatic.
He acted on impulse. He tended to sensationalize
the evidence he had. . . . He would neglect to do
important homework and consequently would,
on occasion, make challengeable statements.

—New York lawyer ROY M. COHN,
on Senator Joseph R. McCarthy

The president, as usual, was up early. At eight o'clock on the morning of Thursday, October 30, 1952, Harry S. Truman stepped out on the rear platform of his train at Muskegon, Michigan. He was doing what he loved: conducting a whistle-stop tour of the country, delivering fiery campaign remarks. Four years earlier, in 1948, as an underdog in the contest to win a full term of his own, Truman had made the barnstorming train stop a political hallmark. Now he was out there again, this time for Adlai Stevenson, the Democratic nominee who was facing Republican Dwight D. Eisenhower.

Truman had been reading a recent issue of **Business Week,** a newsmagazine that was hardly a friend to the administration. The cover story was about John Jay Hopkins, the head of General Dynamics, and the defense contractor's mission to build an atomic submarine. But Truman was, for the moment, more interested in a story headlined "Making Everyone Middle Class."

"It used to be true," the magazine said, "as the old saying goes, that the rich got richer and the poor had children. But for the past 50 years at least, the U.S. economy has been making nonsense out of the adage. The poor have had children all right. But the children, by and large, have got richer."

Armed with the piece, Truman cheerfully addressed the crowd in Muskegon. "The Democratic Party has done great things for the people of this country in the past twenty years," Truman said. "We gave you social security, minimum wage laws, sound farm programs, and full employment. That is what the New Deal and the Fair Deal mean to you. Try to think of one thing the Republican Party has done to advance your interests. You will have a hard time finding it."

Truman then turned to **Business Week.** "The article points out that ten percent of the people at the very top of the economic scale get a smaller proportion of the national income than they used to, and the other ninety percent of the people get more of it," the president said. "This means that most of the people are better off than ever before. And the magazine points out that this is due to the things your Government has been doing." He quoted the piece: " 'High levels of employment have put millions of jobless onto somebody's payroll, cut unemployment to rock bottom. In addition, the number of women workers has jumped sharply, giving many low-income families a double paycheck. Farm prosperity has lifted a whole economic class out of the bottom brackets and into the middle class.' "

Truman was pleased. "Now there you have it," he said. "There you have it—in the words of an opposition magazine. That is what the Democratic Party means to you. So, my friends, when you go to the polls on Tuesday, think of the welfare of this great country of yours. The welfare of this United States, the greatest and the most powerful Republic in the history of the world is at stake."

The product of both government action and of market forces, the creation of the post–World War II middle class was one of the great achievements in history. When the historian James T. Patterson, writing a volume on the America of 1945 to 1974 for the Oxford History of the United

States, sat down to lay out the statistics for growth in the postwar years, he gave his chapter on the subject a simple but telling title: "Booms." America's economy in the quarter century after World War II, the former British prime minister Edward Heath observed, was "the greatest prosperity the world has ever known."

By 1945, average weekly earnings had nearly doubled since December 1941, and Americans had saved about $136 billion during the war—a staggering sum. By 1949 per-capita income in the United States handily outpaced that of the nearest global contenders. Birth and employment rates, college educations, home ownership, life expectancy—by just about every measure, many Americans in the years after V-E and V-J Days were enjoying unparalleled good fortune.

The engines of prosperity propelled millions into the broad middle class—an economic, cultural, and political ethos in which these millions of people had stakes in the present and future of the nation. "Of the three classes," Euripides had written, "it is the middle that saves the country." Rhapsodizing about the New World, J. Hector St. John de Crèvecoeur observed, "Here individuals of all nations are melted into a new race of men, whose labors and posterity will one day cause great changes in the world. Americans are the western pilgrims. . . . Here the rewards of his industry follow with equal steps the progress of his labor; his labor is founded on the basis of nature, **self-interest**; can it want a stronger allurement?" To Walt Whitman, "The most valuable class in any community is the middle class."

Theodore Roosevelt appears to have been the first president to use the term "middle class" in a state paper. In 1906, in his Sixth Annual Message to Congress, TR wrote approvingly of the bourgeois, observing, "The best Americanism is that which aims for stability and permanency of prosperous citizenship, rather than immediate returns on large masses of capital." Two years later, in his speech accepting the Republican presidential nomination, William Howard Taft said that the "farming" and "middle" classes tended "to build up a conservative, self-respecting community, capable of self-government." In 1948, in an address on healthcare, President Truman said, "The fact that we have a well-informed so-called middle class in this country is what makes it the greatest republic the sun has ever shone upon, or ever will shine upon again." In 1955, speaking to the AFL-CIO, President Eisenhower brought the architect of Communism into the conversation, saying, "The Class Struggle Doctrine of Marx was the invention of a lonely refugee scribbling in a dark recess of the British Museum. He abhorred and detested the middle class. He did not foresee that, in America, labor, respected and prosperous, would constitute—with the farmer and businessman—his hated middle class."

The middle mattered—and as the middle grew, it mattered ever more. As long ago as the American Founding, it was an accepted truth that an economic unit that was neither very rich nor very poor offered a republic vital political stability. Definitions of **middle-class** are elusive and elastic. The scholar Ganesh Sitaraman holds with one offered by **The Economist** magazine (the journal edited by Walter Bagehot, of the "dignified" and "efficient" construct of constitutions): "To be middle class," Sitaraman wrote, summarizing the magazine's criteria, "means that you have enough spending money to provide for yourself and your family without living hand to mouth, but not enough to guarantee their future." Nothing, in other words, can be taken for granted, for there's always the risk that your prosperity might fall victim to time and chance.

Whatever one's class status, there's a tendency for many to think that they're a Horatio Alger hero—an emblem of rugged individualism and singular success. The American ideal of what Henry Clay had called "self-made men" in 1832 is so central to the national mythology that there's often a missing character in the story Americans like to tell about American prosperity: government, which frequently helped create the conditions for the making of those men.

Many Americans have never liked acknowledging that the public sector has always been integral to making the private sector successful. We often approve of government's role when we benefit from it and disapprove when others seem to be getting something we aren't. Given the American Revolution's origins as a rebellion against taxation and distant authority, such skepticism is understandable, even if it's not well-founded. We have long proved ourselves quite capable of living with this contradiction, using Hamiltonian means (centralized decision-making) while speaking in Jeffersonian rhetorical terms (that government is best which governs least).

The Pacific Railroad and Homestead acts, signed by Lincoln, used the power of government to settle the West. The railway legislation gave federal support to the creation of a transcontinental railroad, a vast project that played a key role in making the United States an economic and cultural whole. Once the Golden Spike had joined the rails of East and West, the danger and duration of stagecoach rides gave way to the muscle and speed of locomotives—able to carry dreamers west, ship crops east, and shrink the psychic distance of the continent.

The Homestead measures enabled settlers to claim small parcels of farmland, making new lives (and livelihoods) possible. The Morrill Act created land-grant universities, opening higher education to many throughout the country. The legislation of the Progressive Era brought a measure of humanity to the rigors of the industrial age and a democratization of power through women's suffrage, the rise of primaries, and the direct election of senators. And when the prosperity of the Roaring Twenties proved short-lived, the New Deal and particularly Social Security redefined the individual's relationship to the state, knitting the public and private sectors together much more closely. While it took World War II to put a true end to the Great Depression, the work of the New Deal had already added a new and permanent dimension to the American experiment in the mid-twentieth century: the expectation that government could play a more direct role in individual lives.

That expectation was met in World War II and its aftermath. First came immense defense spending that truly transformed the United States into what FDR, in 1940, had called "the great arsenal of democracy." Then, while the war was still under way, the GI Bill of Rights, formally called the Servicemen's Readjustment Act of 1944, would eventually help lift millions into previously unreachable economic and cultural spheres.

Championed by the American Legion, the legislation provided veterans with college tuition, guaranteed home loans, and offered other benefits. It is not a coincidence that it was a prosperous white America, which, in the mid-1960s, became more open, however belatedly and reluctantly and incompletely, to people of color, women, and immigrants (after a 1965 law ended the quotas that had governed entry into the country since the 1920s). A sense of comfort and of economic security helped create a climate of hope—and that sense of comfort and of economic security was the result of public and private investment in a broad range of Americans.

President Eisenhower, a Republican, continued the work of his two Democratic predecessors, spending billions on Cold War defense and on the interstate highway system. Criticized by conservatives for failing to dismantle the New Deal and the Fair Deal—a dream of the right during the two-decade-long reigns of Roosevelt and Truman—Eisenhower resisted reflexive partisanship. "Now it is true that I believe this country is following a dangerous trend when it permits too great a degree of centralization of governmental functions," Eisenhower wrote one

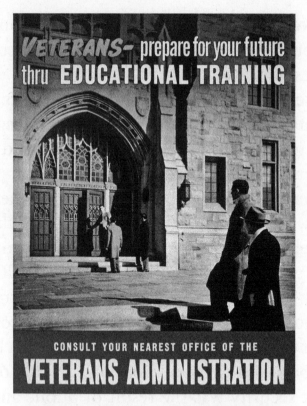

Officially the Servicemen's Readjustment Act of 1944, the G.I. Bill helped
create a thriving middle class by providing tuition, guaranteeing home
loans, and offering other benefits to
returning World War II veterans.

of his brothers in 1954. "I oppose this—in some
instances the fight is a rather desperate one. But
to attain any success it is quite clear that the
Federal government cannot avoid or escape responsibilities which the mass of the people firmly
believe should be undertaken by it. . . . Should
any political party attempt to abolish social se-

curity, unemployment insurance, and eliminate labor laws and farm programs, you would not hear of that party again in our political history."

Eisenhower's essential acceptance of the existing political order was wise governance, but, as ever, fear could not be totally conquered. In the same years Truman and Eisenhower were using the presidency to improve the infrastructure of prosperity, anxieties about foreign influence and subversion were growing. "There was an atmosphere throughout the land [in the early 1950s] of suspicion, intolerance, and fear that puzzled me," William L. Shirer, who had covered Nazi Germany, wrote on returning home. "I had seen these poisons grow into ugly witch hunting and worse in the totalitarian lands abroad, but I was not prepared to find them taking root in our own splendid democracy." Yet here they were.

In the closing weeks of 1954, during a long drive down the Hudson Valley to New York City, the conversation among the four passengers in the car—all friends—turned, as it usually did, to politics. One of their number: Robert Welch, a conservative candy manufacturer based in Massachusetts. (Two of his most popular products: the caramel "Sugar Daddy" and the chocolate "Tar Baby.") Welch believed, and told his friends, that President Eisenhower was to blame for the Republicans' loss of both the House and the Senate in the November 1954 midterm elections. The president, Welch said, had engaged in a "double-crossing" of his own party, refusing to campaign for candidates after promising to do so. The Congress had been "moved a few notches further left by the defeat of several conservatives," he said, adding that "this effect was probably intentional" on Eisenhower's part.

His friends expressed surprise, and Welch recalled that he then explained how Eisenhower—lifetime soldier, conqueror of Hitler, former supreme commander of NATO, and now president of the United States—was an "agent" of a "Communist conspiracy" to undermine and take over America. With a rising worry about domestic subversion in recent years, Welch said, there had been some hope that the country was coming to understand the threat from Moscow. "The American people," Welch later wrote, "had begun to wake up to the extent of Communist infiltration into our government and into every segment of our public life."

Eisenhower, Welch claimed, had changed all that. "The sad truth is that this tyranny was actually saved, in this period of great vulnerability, by just one thing: by the inauguration, on January 20, 1953, of Dwight David Eisenhower as

President of the United States," Welch wrote. "Subtly, cleverly, always proclaiming otherwise and finding specious excuses for what were really pro-Communist actions, these Communist influences made [Eisenhower] put the whole diplomatic power, economic power, and recognized leadership of this country to work, on the side of Russia and the Communists, in connection with every problem and trouble spot in their empire."

Eisenhower—whom Welch asserted was guilty of "a very sinister and hated word": treason— was not a lonely subversive or a solitary dupe. There were, Welch believed, plenty of others. One was Franklin Roosevelt, who, Welch wrote, had been "swept along and **used by** Communist forces . . . avid for the glory and the power of being a wartime president and of tossing around millions of men and billions of dollars with a nod of his head." Another was the former army chief of staff and Truman secretary of defense and of state George Marshall, whom Welch said was "a conscious, deliberate, dedicated agent of the Soviet conspiracy." To Welch, John Foster Dulles, Eisenhower's secretary of state, was yet another "Communist agent."

There was no evidence for such fevered assertions. A classic conspiracy theorist, Welch fell back on a dictum of Daniel Webster's: "There is nothing so powerful as truth, and often nothing so strange." Where the naked eye and the rational brain saw Eisenhower as a patriot seeking to govern in a nuclear age, Welch, his vision and perception warped by a fear of Communism, detected treason.

Four years after his ride along the Hudson, at a meeting in Indianapolis, Welch founded the John Birch Society. Named in honor of a soldier killed by Chinese Communists, the society believed itself to be engaged in an end-times struggle between good and evil. Of Birch, Welch wrote: "With his death and in his death the battle lines were drawn in a struggle from which either communism or Christian-style civilization must emerge with one completely triumphant and the other completely destroyed."

It was language made familiar in postwar America in part by Senator Joseph R. McCarthy, the hard-drinking provocateur from Wisconsin. "Today we are engaged in a final, all-out battle between communistic atheism and Christianity," McCarthy told the Ohio County Republican Women's Club in Wheeling, West Virginia, on Thursday, February 9, 1950. "The modern champions of communism have selected this as the time. And, ladies and gentlemen, the chips are down—they are truly down."

Concern about subversion was hardly novel.

The House of Representatives, for instance, had formed a Committee on Un-American Activities, under the chairmanship of Congressman Martin Dies, a Democrat from Texas, in 1938. In 1940 Congress passed the Smith Act, which made it a crime for anyone to "knowingly or willfully advocate, abet, advise, or teach the duty, necessity, desirability or propriety of overthrowing or destroying any government in the United States by force or violence." The bill was wildly popular. "The mood of the House is such that if you brought in the Ten Commandments today and asked for their repeal and attached to that request an alien law," a congressman said, "you could get it."

McCarthy, though, was something new in modern political life: a freelance performer who grasped what many ordinary Americans feared and who had direct access to the media of the day. He exploited the privileges of power and prominence without regard to its responsibilities; to him politics was not about the substantive but the sensational. The country feared Communism, and McCarthy knew it, and he fed those fears with years of headlines and hearings. A master of false charges, of conspiracy-tinged rhetoric, and of calculated disrespect for conventional figures (from Truman and Eisenhower to Marshall), McCarthy could distract the public, play the press, and change the subject—all while keeping himself at center stage.

Showcasing largely unfounded accusations of Communist subversion, McCarthyism was about exaggerated threats at a time of real danger. Abroad, evidence of the Soviets' post–World War II ambitions was genuine and growing. By 1949 Moscow had a successful atomic program. In response, the Manchester **Union-Leader,** a conservative New Hampshire newspaper edited by William Loeb, suggested a preemptive nuclear attack: "We cannot sit idle and wait for Armageddon and destruction. We must forestall such a catastrophe and the only way is to strike a proposed aggressor before he is ready to strike."

The arrests of Klaus Fuchs and Julius and Ethel Rosenberg for passing nuclear secrets to the Soviets—Fuchs in Great Britain, the Rosenbergs in the United States—terrified the West. China, meanwhile, fell into Communist hands, and the Korean War began. At home there was the celebrated case of Alger Hiss, the urbane New Deal lawyer and diplomat pursued by Congressman Richard Nixon—a member of the House Un-American Activities Committee—and convicted of perjury after denying knowing Whittaker Chambers, a confessed former spy for the Russians who had become a fervent Cold Warrior. And politically, the Republican Party was eager to win seats in the House and Senate elections of

1950. Domestic fears of Communist influence were potent—and might just make a powerful midterm issue.

It was in this climate that McCarthy delivered what **The Wheeling Intelligencer** described as an "intimate" and "homey" address to the 275 guests gathered in the Colonnade Room of the McLure Hotel at the corner of Market and Twelfth streets in Wheeling. "While I cannot take the time to name all of the men in the State Department who have been named as active members of the Communist Party and members of a spy ring," McCarthy said, "I have here in my hand a list of 205 that were made known to the Secretary of State as being members of the Communist Party and who, nevertheless, are still working and shaping the policy in the State Department."

The number of McCarthy's alleged Communists was a moving target; his charges were constantly shifting. (In the fullness of time, the 205 figure he offered at Wheeling wandered down to 57.) He thrived on a dangerous, but politically alluring, combination: hyperbole and imprecision. "Talking to Joe was like putting your hands in a bowl of mush," recalled George Reedy, a wire-service reporter who became an aide to President Lyndon B. Johnson.

McCarthy was an opportunist, uncommitted to much beyond his own fame and influence. His own lawyer, the young New Yorker Roy M. Cohn, could not discern any great ideological conviction in the junior senator from Wisconsin. "Joe McCarthy bought Communism in much the same way as other people purchase a new automobile," Cohn recalled. "The salesman showed him the model; he looked at it with interest, examined it more closely, kicked at the tires, sat at the wheel, squiggled in the seat, asked some questions, and bought. It was just as cold as that."

As Cohn tells the story, in late 1949 McCarthy was given an FBI report detailing allegations of Communist infiltration within the federal government, particularly in the Department of State. It was not new information: A copy had been on file at State since at least 1947. In truth, the Soviets had made strides in penetrating Washington in the 1930s and early '40s, but a loyalty program had rolled up many of the agents. Now, in the waning hours of the decade, Cold War ultra-hawks wanted to press the case, even though most observers believed the matter largely closed.

McCarthy was in; he said he was "buying the package." Why? Roy Cohn offered two reasons. "The first was patriotic," Cohn recalled. "He was worried about the threat to the country posed by the Communist conspiracy, and he decided to do what he could to expose it." The second?

McCarthy, Cohn said, "saw the dramatic political opportunities connected with a fight on Communism. McCarthy was gifted with a sense of political timing. Sometimes he misjudged, but on balance his sense of what made drama and headlines was uncommonly good. . . . He had found, he thought, a politically attractive issue he could sink his teeth into."

A few days after the Wheeling speech, a trio of Wisconsin journalists sat down with McCarthy at Moy Toy's, a Chinese restaurant on Third Street in Milwaukee.

"Joe, I don't believe you've got a goddamn thing to prove the things you've been saying," one of the reporters recalled saying. "It's all a lot of political hogwash."

"Listen, you bastards," McCarthy replied. "I'm not going to tell you anything. I just want you to know that I've got a pailful of shit and I'm going to use it where it does me the most good."

Thoughtful people correctly gauged the McCarthy threat. "McCarthy's methods, to me, look like Hitler's," Eleanor Roosevelt remarked. In a private letter, President Truman agreed with a correspondent who posited that "there is no difference in kind between Hitlerism and McCarthyism, both being the same form of bacteriological warfare against the minds and souls

"I think the greatest asset that the Kremlin has is Senator McCarthy," President Truman told a press conference in Key West, Florida, in March 1950.

of men." Winston Churchill, in office for a second term as prime minister, added a paragraph to Elizabeth II's Coronation Address, delivered from Buckingham Palace on the evening of the June 1953 ceremony at Westminster Abbey, implicitly defending the Anglo-American tradition of fair play from McCarthyite incursions. "Parliamentary institutions," the queen said, "with their free speech and respect for the rights of minorities, and the inspiration of a broad tolerance in thought and expression—all this we conceive to be a precious part of our way of life and outlook."

The Eisenhower-Nixon ticket was successful
in 1952, but the new president, who governed
from the center, alienated many on the right
who'd hoped for a wholesale repeal of
FDR-Truman programs.

On Thursday, March 30, 1950, at a press conference at his Florida retreat in Key West—where
Truman could indulge his fondness for Hawai-
ian shirts, bourbon, and poker—the president
told the assembled journalists exactly what he
believed. "I think the greatest asset that the
Kremlin has is Senator McCarthy," Truman said.
(The reporters knew they had news. "Brother,"
one exclaimed, "will that hit page one tomorrow!") Truman reminded them that he had instituted a loyalty program as the Cold War took
shape in 1947 to identify potential subversives.

The administration had found the ranks of the disloyal to be "an infinitesimal part of 1 percent."

The GOP, Truman said, was more interested in partisan advantage than in national security. "For political background, the Republicans have been trying vainly to find an issue on which to make a bid for the control of the Congress for next year," the president told reporters. "They tried 'statism.' They tried 'welfare state.' They tried 'socialism.' And there are a certain number of members of the Republican Party who are trying to dig up that old malodorous dead horse called 'isolationism.' And in order to do that, they are perfectly willing to sabotage the bipartisan foreign policy of the United States."

In his commonsense vernacular, Truman added: "Now, if anybody really felt that there were disloyal people in the employ of the Government, the proper and the honorable way to handle the situation would be to come to the President of the United States and say, 'This man is a disloyal person. He is in such and such a department.' We will investigate him immediately, and if he were a disloyal person he would be immediately fired. That is not what they want. They are trying to create an issue." The net effect of the McCarthyite campaign, Truman said, was to undermine confidence in the country in a time of cold war. "To try to sabotage the foreign policy of the United States," he said, "is just as bad in this cold war as it would be to shoot our soldiers in the back in a hot war."

Not every Republican signed on for McCarthy's machinations. On Thursday, June 1, 1950— fewer than four months after Wheeling—Senator Margaret Chase Smith, a Republican from Maine, issued what she called a "Declaration of Conscience" against McCarthy's methods. "Joe began to get publicity-crazy," Smith recalled in an interview with the historian David M. Oshinsky. "And the other senators were now afraid to speak their minds, to take issue with him. It got to the point where some of us refused to be seen with people he disapproved of. A wave of fear had struck Washington."

As Smith recalled it, she ran into McCarthy, who had flattered her in the past with the suggestion that she would be a fine vice presidential nominee for the Republicans in 1952, on her way to the floor.

"Margaret," McCarthy said, "you look very serious. Are you going to make a speech?"

"Yes," Smith replied, "and you will not like it."

"Is it about me?"

"Yes," Smith said, "but I am not going to mention your name."

A frowning McCarthy, Smith recalled, then said: "Remember, Margaret, I control Wisconsin's twenty-seven convention votes."

"For what?" Smith said, pushing on.

She rose a few moments later on the Senate floor. "I would like to speak briefly and simply about a serious national condition," Smith said. "It is a national feeling of fear and frustration that could result in national suicide and the end of everything that we Americans hold dear." She continued:

> I speak as a Republican. I speak as a woman. I speak as a United States Senator. I speak as an American. . . .
>
> I think that it is high time that we remembered that we have sworn to uphold and defend the Constitution. I think that it is high time that we remembered that the Constitution, as amended, speaks not only of the freedom of speech but also of trial by jury instead of trial by accusation. . . .
>
> Those of us who shout the loudest about Americanism in making character assassinations are all too frequently those who, by our own words and acts, ignore some of the basic principles of Americanism:
>
> The right to criticize;
>
> The right to hold unpopular beliefs;

The right to protest;
The right of independent thought.

Too few heeded Smith's warning; she was
about four years ahead of most of her colleagues.
While she did convince six other senators to
join her "Declaration"—a defiant McCarthy
dismissed them as "Snow White and the Six
Dwarfs"—the Republicans were open to seeing
where McCarthy's act might lead. "Joe, you're a
real SOB," Senator John Bricker, a Republican
from Ohio, told McCarthy, "but sometimes it's
useful to have SOBs around to do the dirty
work."

McCarthy's popular appeal was clear. "He's
unbeatable now," Milwaukee mayor Frank Zeid-
ler said in the spring of 1950. "He's a Northern
Huey Long."

His followers loved his style; his foes feared it.
"From a distance, McCarthy may have
looked, by some odd reversal of optical principles, larger than life and of greater consequence
than he ever really was," Richard H. Rovere of
The New Yorker wrote at the close of the fifties.
"But he was large and consequential enough in
those years. . . . He was the first American ever
to be actively hated and feared by foreigners in
large numbers." In 1953, Eleanor Roosevelt, on
a trip to Japan, found herself facing questions

Senator Margaret Chase Smith, a Republican from Maine, was an early opponent of McCarthy's. Her "Declaration of Conscience" called for decency and fair play amid anti-Communist hysteria.

On CBS's See It Now on Tuesday, March 9, 1954, the legendary broadcaster Edward R. Murrow took McCarthy on. "We must not confuse dissent with disloyalty," Murrow said.

Roy M. Cohn, who served as McCarthy's chief counsel, recalled the senator "saw the dramatic political opportunities connected with a fight on Communism."

about McCarthyism. "Will you please explain these attitudes?" a Japanese businessman asked the former First Lady. "We are unable to understand why these things happen in a great democratic nation like the United States."

Part of the answer lies in the nature of democracy itself: Millions of Americans approved of McCarthy no matter what the elites might say or do. And McCarthy was not without support and connections in sophisticated quarters. He was friendly with the Kennedys, hiring Robert Kennedy as a staff lawyer for his committee in 1953 and taking two of the Kennedy sisters on dates. As an anti-Communist Roman Catholic, McCarthy was popular in Massachusetts, and a hospitalized Senator John F. Kennedy would miss the McCarthy censure vote in 1954.

JFK, though he privately recoiled at McCarthy's tactics and manner, chose to remain silent on censure, upsetting the liberal wing of the Democratic Party—including Mrs. Roosevelt—who long saw his failure to stand up to McCarthy as a sign of opportunism and weakness. They weren't far wrong: JFK wanted to keep the anti-Communist Massachusetts delegation united behind him in his hopes to become Adlai Stevenson's vice presidential running mate in 1956 and, failing a step to higher office in the meantime, he did not want a McCarthyite challenge in his 1958 bid for reelection to the Senate. Challenged a decade or so later about his work for McCarthy, Robert Kennedy replied, "Well, at the time, I thought there was a serious internal security threat to the United States . . . and Joe McCarthy was the only one doing anything about it." (But, RFK admitted, "I was wrong.")

In the early 1950s legions of people were entranced by McCarthy's Manichaean vision of life. He spoke in the starkest of terms, savoring superlatives. Everything was dramatic, contentious, **perilous**: So few things, McCarthy implied, stood between American freedom and Communist slavery. But one of those things—perhaps the most important of them—was McCarthy himself, who quoted John Paul Jones: "I have just begun to fight."

How he loved the story of himself as the brave

warrior, a story that dominated the newspapers of the day. McCarthy needed the press, and the press came to need McCarthy. He was fantastic copy, a real-life serial. The twists and turns of the McCarthy saga meant more bylines for the reporters, more exciting headlines for the editors, and, given the subject matter—alleged infiltration of the government of the United States by a fatal foe—more copies sold for the owners. Radio and television amplified McCarthy's impact.

As Richard Hofstadter, the Columbia University historian, wrote at the time, the "growth of the mass media of communication and their use in politics have brought politics closer to the people than ever before and have made politics a form of entertainment in which the spectators feel themselves involved. Thus it has become, more than ever before, an arena into which private emotions and personal problems can be readily projected. Mass communications have made it possible to keep the mass man in an almost constant state of political mobilization."

McCarthy understood the media's ways and means. "Things have to be done by a certain time," recalled George Reedy. "And Joe somewhat instinctively picked up the absolutely vital course of the cycle. He knew that every wire service man had to have a lead by eleven o'clock [for the afternoon newspapers]. There just wasn't any question about it; you had to have a lead." The senator learned to make sensational charges at just the right moment, forcing reporters to write quick stories that surged across the country by wire, reaching millions of readers before sundown.

The New Yorker's Richard Rovere reconstructed the rhythms of the age. McCarthy, Rovere wrote, "invented the morning press conference called for the purpose of announcing an afternoon press conference." Rovere continued:

> The reporters would come in—they were beginning, in this period, to respond to his summonses like Pavlov's dogs at the clang of a bell—and McCarthy would say that he just wanted to give them the word that he expected to be ready with a shattering announcement later in the day, for use in the papers the following morning. This would gain him a headline in the afternoon papers: "NEW MCCARTHY REVELATIONS AWAITED IN CAPITAL." Afternoon would come, and if McCarthy had something, he would give it out, but often enough he had nothing, and this was a matter of slight concern. He would simply say that he wasn't quite ready, that he was having difficulty in getting some of the "documents" he needed or that a "witness" was proving elusive. Morning headlines: "DELAY SEEN

IN NEW MCCARTHY CASE—MYSTERY WITNESS BEING SOUGHT." He had no cause for concern if the whole thing turned out to be nothing, as so often happened. He had the headlines; "MCCARTHY" was becoming a more and more familiar arrangement of type and was engraved more and more deeply on the American mind.

His office produced weekly phonograph albums to send to Wisconsin stations that dutifully aired them. As described by the journalist Edwin R. Bayley, who obtained some of these recordings, interviewers posing as journalists would ask McCarthy congenial questions that led to senatorial disquisitions on the iniquities of the mainstream press, the Democrats, the Communists—anybody, really, who had had anything negative to say about McCarthy and his methods that week.

Television offered him ever expanding reach. The number of TV sets in America quintupled during McCarthy's heyday, rising from 5 million in 1950 to 26 million in 1954. To McCarthy, the new medium created nearly unlimited possibilities to dominate the public consciousness, and he valued performance over substance. "People aren't going to remember the things we say on the issues here, our logic, our common sense, our facts," he remarked to Roy Cohn before the televised army hearings. "They're only going to remember the impressions."

The senator inhabited his own curious world, moving around Washington and around the nation with a coterie of aides, investigators, and reporters. He was good company. A showman at heart, McCarthy attacked the press in public but drank and schmoozed with journalists in private. Amid hearings in the capital, he would adjourn for lunch at a corner table in the Carroll Arms Hotel where he would take off his suit coat, have a Manhattan, eat a slab of lamb, order coffee, and muse about the action.

McCarthy's headline hunting also benefitted from the culture of journalism at midcentury: that the job of a journalist was to report the content of a statement, not to assess its validity. "My own impression was that Joe was a demagogue," one journalist of the era observed. "But what could I do? I had to report—quote—McCarthy. How do you say in the middle of your story, 'This is a lie'? The press is supposedly neutral. You write what the man says." Walter Lippmann defended the press in similar terms. "McCarthy's charges . . . are news which cannot be suppressed or ignored," Lippmann wrote. "They come from a United States senator and a politician . . . in good standing at the headquarters of the Republican Party. When he makes such attacks against the State Department . . . it is news which has to be published."

Palmer Hoyt, the editor and publisher of **The Denver Post,** thought McCarthyism required a new way of reporting. In a memorandum to his staff, Hoyt suggested that neutrality was not the highest virtue—truth was. Reporters should "apply any reasonable doubt they [might] have to the treatment of the story." In other words, if a McCarthy statement was demonstrably false, the journalists should feel free to say so—in print. "It seems obvious that many charges made by reckless or impulsive public officials cannot and should not be ignored," Hoyt wrote, "but it seems to me that news stories and headlines can be presented in such a manner that the reading public will be able to measure the real worth or value and the true meaning of the stories."

Hoyt believed steady and informed reporting on McCarthy was the best antidote to the fever of the time. "Believe me, there is nothing wrong with this country that repeated strong dosages of the facts will not correct," Hoyt told other editors at a Tucson, Arizona, meeting in November 1954. "Even McCarthyism will melt away before this treatment."

When he read coverage he disliked, McCarthy did not keep quiet—he went on the offensive, singling out specific publications and particular journalists, sometimes at rallies. He particularly hated **The Milwaukee Journal**. "Keep in mind that when you send checks over to the **Journal**," McCarthy told business audiences, "you are contributing to bringing the Communist Party line into the homes of Wisconsin." To a **Journal** reporter, McCarthy confided: "Off the record, I don't know that I can cut [the **Journal**'s] profits at all. . . . But if you show a newspaper as unfriendly and having a reason for being antagonistic, you can take the sting out of what it says about you. I think I can convince a lot of people that they can't believe what they read in the **Journal**."

The **Washington Post** had assigned the reporter Murrey Marder to cover McCarthy after Wheeling. On Election Night 1952, the paper's publisher, Philip Graham, told Marder that Eisenhower's victory over Adlai Stevenson would cost Marder his beat. According to David Halberstam, who interviewed Marder about the moment, "Graham was sure that Ike's presidency would eventually mean McCarthy's isolation; now that the Republicans had the White House, they would not need McCarthy any longer. But Marder understood McCarthy's recklessness and his hatred of authority. Party loyalty was not even an issue with the senator—it would not matter who was in the White House. No, Marder speculated, his beat was not finished; instead they would now need two people to cover the senator." Halberstam's verdict: "They were both right."

The **Post** expected much from Eisenhower. "It is this newspaper's hope and belief," the **Post** editorialized in March 1952, "that McCarthyism would disappear overnight if Eisenhower were elected." That was not to be. One sign of trouble: Eisenhower had flinched in taking McCarthy on during the presidential campaign. The senator had accused George Marshall of treason the year before, telling the Senate that Marshall was part of "a conspiracy of infamy so black that, when it is finally exposed, its principals shall be forever deserving of the maledictions of all honest men."

In the text of a speech he was to deliver in Milwaukee on Friday, October 3, 1952, Eisenhower was slated to defend Marshall in no uncertain terms. "I know that charges of disloyalty have, in the past, been leveled against General George C. Marshall," Eisenhower was to have said. "I have been privileged for thirty-five years to know General Marshall personally. I know him, as a man and as a soldier, to be dedicated with singular selflessness and the profoundest patriotism to the service of America. And this episode is a sobering lesson in the way freedom must **not** defend itself."

Ike never uttered the words. Talked out of it by political advisers who thought it unwise to antagonize McCarthy and his supporters (the voices included Wisconsin governor Walter J. Kohler, Jr., and New Hampshire governor Sherman Adams, the future White House chief of staff), Eisenhower always regretted his failure to say what he thought, and he hated that the world knew what had happened, for word of the dropped paragraph leaked to **The New York Times**. ("It turned my stomach," General Omar Bradley wrote of the Eisenhower-Marshall-McCarthy episode.)

Unlike Truman, who openly denounced McCarthy, Eisenhower was patient and reticent. "Nothing will be so effective in combating his particular kind of trouble-making as to ignore him," the new president wrote in 1953. "This he cannot stand."

The strategy was less dramatic—and less heroic—than one could have hoped for from Eisenhower. But it was his strategy, and he stuck to it. "I had made up my mind how I was going to handle McCarthy," Eisenhower recalled. "This was to ignore him. . . . I would give him no satisfaction. I'd never defend anything. I don't care what he called me, or mentioned, or put in the papers. I'd just ignore him."

"Getting in the gutter" with McCarthy, a phrase Eisenhower often used, would be counterproductive. "I would not have you believe that I have acquiesced in, or by any means approve, the methods he uses," Eisenhower wrote. "I despise them. . . . But I am quite sure that the people who want me to stand up and publicly label McCarthy with derogatory titles are mistaken."

Still, he did speak out occasionally. In 1953, McCarthy deplored the contents of libraries at American installations overseas. Cohn and David Schine, a hotel heir, took a highly publicized European trip, a kind of grand tour of censorship. Among other titles, the senator's staff targeted **The Maltese Falcon** and **The Thin Man,** on the grounds that the writer Dashiell Hammett, who supported left-wing causes, had posted bail for a group with Communist ties in 1951, and refused to name names in Red-hunting hearings. They also complained that the libraries failed to subscribe to **American Legion Monthly.** The European newspapers, Benjamin C. Bradlee, then the press attaché at the American embassy in Paris, recalled, were aghast. "What is America becoming to allow these people to go around and represent it?" was a typical comment.

At Dartmouth College in 1953, Eisenhower alluded to the controversy. "Don't join the book burners," he said. "Don't think you are going to conceal faults by concealing evidence that they ever existed. Don't be afraid to go into your library and read every book, as long as that document does not offend our own ideas of decency.

That should be the only censorship. How will we defeat communism unless we know what it is, and what it teaches, and why does it have such appeal for men, why are so many people swearing allegiance to it?"

At ten-thirty on the evening of Tuesday, March 9, 1954, CBS broadcast an episode of Edward R. Murrow's **See It Now.** Its subject: Senator McCarthy. Its means of storytelling: images and recordings of McCarthy's own words. At the conclusion of the report, Murrow spoke more in sorrow than in anger. "We must not confuse dissent with disloyalty," he said. "We must remember always that accusation is not proof and that conviction depends upon evidence and due process of law. We will not walk in fear, one of another. We will not be driven by fear into an age of unreason if we dig deep in our history and our doctrine, and remember that we are not descended from fearful men— not from men who feared to write, to speak, to associate and to defend causes that were, for the moment, unpopular."

Then came Murrow's final words. "The actions of the junior Senator from Wisconsin have caused alarm and dismay amongst our allies abroad, and given considerable comfort to our enemies," Murrow said. "And whose fault is that? Not really his. He didn't create this situation of fear; he merely exploited it—and rather successfully. Cassius was right. 'The fault, dear Brutus, is not in our stars, but in ourselves.' Good night, and good luck."

A few weeks later, on the evening of Monday, April 5, 1954, President Eisenhower walked down to the Broadcast Room in the White House basement. Featuring a handsome desk, special lights, and large prompters, the studio offered the president a convenient venue from which to address the nation. He had decided to try something new: a more casual speech, without a full text. There would be cue cards with a few notes— that was all. He would be seated on the edge of the desk and look directly into the camera—a Fireside Chat for the television age. His theme was fear—and how America should fight it.

Eisenhower is usually remembered for two rhetorical moments. The first dates from June 1944, when he drafted a letter accepting full responsibility in the event of the failure of the D-Day landings against Hitler's Fortress Europe. The second came in his January 1961 Farewell Address warning about the "military-industrial complex." His April 1954 speech about fear, which falls about midway between these landmarks, appears, at first glance, to be a forgettable presidential address—or at least a routine one.

The remarks repay consideration, however, for in them Eisenhower described the disposition necessary to survive life in an age of strain and uncertainty. "We are worried about Communist penetration of our own country," he said, "and we are worried about the possibility of depression and the loss of jobs among us here at home." He continued:

> Now, the greater any of these apprehensions, the greater is the need that we look at them clearly, face to face, without fear, like honest, straightforward Americans, so we do not develop the jitters or any other kind of panic, that we do not fall prey to hysterical thinking.
>
> Sometimes you feel, almost, that we can be excused for getting a little bit hysterical, because these dangers come from so many angles, and they are of such different kinds, and no matter what we do they still seem to exist. . . .
>
> It is the American belief in decency and justice and progress, and the value of individual liberty, because of the rights conferred upon each of us by our Creator, that will carry us through. . . . There must be something in the heart as well as in the head.

The end for McCarthy came in the months following the Murrow broadcast and the Eisenhower speech on fear, when hearings into McCarthy and the U.S. Army opened in the Senate. Behind the scenes, the president had maneuvered to detail the pressure that McCarthy and Roy Cohn had exerted to secure favors for David Schine, an intimate of Cohn's who had been drafted. The report of this influence—with its implication of an illicit relationship between Cohn and Schine, always denied by Cohn—drove the hearings. Day by day and week by week, McCarthy performed poorly before large television audiences, coming across as more gadfly than crusader.

In an iconic moment, the counsel for the army, Joseph N. Welch, attacked the senator, who had clumsily attempted to impugn the loyalty of a young lawyer on Welch's team. "Until this moment, Senator, I think I never really gauged your cruelty or your recklessness," Welch told McCarthy. "Little did I dream you would be so reckless and cruel as to do an injury to that lad. . . . I fear he shall always bear a scar needlessly inflicted by you. If it were in my power to forgive you for your reckless cruelty I would do so. I like to think than I am a gentle man, but your forgiveness will have to come from someone other than me."

McCarthy blundered forward and took up

the theme again. Welch was ready and struck with force. "Let us not assassinate this lad further, Senator," Welch said. "You have done enough. Have you no sense of decency, sir, at long last? Have you left no sense of decency?"

Yet a good bit of McCarthy's base of support remained loyal. After the Welch drama, Gallup found that while McCarthy's favorability ratings were falling, 34 percent of the country still backed the senator, a formidable-enough number. "Unless we can get rid of [McCarthy]," an Eisenhower Republican senator remarked to Cohn, "he's going to be a mighty big thorn in our side." That 34 percent figure was the problem. The Republicans, Cohn believed, were worried that McCarthy could bolt the GOP, form a "right-wing third party ticket," and attract enough support to throw the 1956 presidential election to the Democrats.

By the end of the year the threat evaporated when the Senate censured McCarthy. The move to condemn him by resolution was the result of much of the Senate's revulsion against his reckless methods. Senator Ralph Flanders, Republican of Vermont, led the charge. "This matter is indeed a serious one," Flanders said. "The senator [McCarthy] has an habitual contempt for people. . . . Unrebuked, his behavior casts a blot upon the reputation of the Senate itself."

The senior senator from Connecticut, Prescott Bush, spoke out in favor of censure. It was not the first time that Bush, a patrician with a strong New England moral code and sense of fair play, had taken on McCarthyism. Two years earlier, while sharing a stage with McCarthy in Bridgeport, Connecticut, during the 1952 campaign, Bush had criticized his Wisconsin colleague's methods in front of a raucously pro-McCarthy crowd. Now, with the censure resolution pending, Bush told the Senate that McCarthy "has caused dangerous divisions among the American people because of his attitude, and the attitude he has encouraged among his followers, that there can be no honest differences of opinion with him. Either you must follow Senator McCarthy blindly, not daring to express any doubts or disagreements about any of his actions, or in his eyes you must be a Communist, a Communist sympathizer, or a fool who has been duped by the Communist line." The resolution passed by a vote of 67 to 22. (Twenty-two of the Senate's 44 Republicans voted to condemn.)

Once feared as indomitable, McCarthy was finished politically. He continued to drink heavily, and his health deteriorated. He died of acute hepatitis—his liver was inflamed, almost certainly because of his drinking—in 1957, at the age of forty-eight.

The conventional view of McCarthy's fall turns on his erratic performance during the army hearings. But Roy Cohn believed something deeper was also at work. "Undoubtedly the hearings were a setback," Cohn recalled. "But there were other perhaps more fundamental reasons for his decline. By the time the hearings ended, McCarthy had been the center of the national and world spotlight for three and a half years. He had an urgent universal message, and people, whether they idolized or hated him, listened. Almost everything he said or did was chronicled."

That surfeit of attention, Cohn argued, itself contributed to McCarthy's decline. "Human nature being what it is, any outstanding actor on the stage of public affairs—and especially a holder of high office—cannot remain indefinitely at the center of controversy," Cohn recalled. "The public must eventually lose interest in him and his cause. And Joe McCarthy had nothing to offer but more of the same. The public sought new thrills. . . . The surprise, the drama, were gone."

To everything, in other words, there is a season, and McCarthy's hubris hastened the end of his hour upon the stage. "I was fully aware of McCarthy's faults, which were neither few nor minor," Cohn recalled. "He was impatient, overly aggressive, overly dramatic. He acted on impulse. He tended to sensationalize the evidence he had—in order to draw attention to the rock-bottom seriousness of the situation. He would neglect to do important homework and consequently would, on occasion, make challengeable statements."

The urge to overstate, to overdramatize, to dominate the news, could be costly, and so it proved to be for McCarthy. The Wisconsin senator, Cohn said, was essentially a salesman. "He was selling the story of America's peril," Cohn recalled. "He knew that he could never hope to convince anybody by delivering a dry, general-accounting-office type of presentation. In consequence, he stepped up circumstances a notch or two"—and in so doing he opened himself to attacks that proved fatal. He oversold, and the customers—the public—tired of the pitch, and the pitchman.

By the end of 1954, McCarthy may have been spent, but the forces he represented—popular anxiety about the fate of the nation—would never completely subside. Like McCarthy, right-wing figures such as the John Birch Society's Robert Welch cast Eisenhower in the role of villain. The old general's moderate domestic views and pragmatic foreign policy made him anathema to conservatives who, longing for a crusader, instead found themselves living with a conciliator.

But we ought not to paint the rise of post–World War II movement conservatism—a movement that reached its apotheosis with the election of one of its early enthusiasts, Ronald Reagan, to the presidency in 1980—with too broad a brush. It is true that, as William A. Rusher, the publisher of William F. Buckley, Jr.'s **National Review,** the conservative magazine founded in 1955, recalled, "modern American conservatism largely organized itself during, and in explicit opposition to, the Eisenhower Administration." For most of those conservatives, however, Eisenhower was too moderate, not too Red. Writing in the inaugural issue of the magazine, Buckley, then twenty-nine years old, argued that the conservative mission was to stand "athwart history, yelling Stop"—history in this instance being understood as the flow of power to the state, which Buckley called "the dominant social feature of this century." Buckley's respectable conservatism was based not on paranoia but on a reasonable critique of the assumptions of midcentury liberalism.

Buckley, in fact, was a critical figure in moving the Birchers out of the mainstream conservative movement. In January 1961, during a meeting at the Breakers in Palm Beach with a handful of conservatives that included Barry Goldwater, Buckley agreed to take on the far right by attacking what he called the "Birch fallacy."

"How would you define the Birch fallacy?" Buckley was asked.

"The fallacy," Buckley replied, "is the assumption that you can infer subjective intention from objective consequence: we lost China to the Communists, therefore the President of the United States and the Secretary of State wished China to go to the Communists."

"I like that," Goldwater said.

In **National Review,** Buckley wrote: "How can the John Birch Society be an effective political instrument while it is led by a man whose views on current affairs are, at so many critical points . . . so far removed from common sense? That dilemma weighs on conservatives across America. . . . The underlying problem is whether conservatives can continue to acquiesce quietly in a rendition of the causes of the decline of the Republic and the entire Western world which is false, and, besides that, crucially different in practical emphasis from their own."

The Birchers represented a persistent type of political belief. In the spring of 1954, shortly before McCarthy's fall, Richard Hofstadter delivered a lecture as part of the American Civilization Program at Barnard College. Later published in **The American Scholar** as "The Pseudo-Conservative Revolt," this piece of Hofstadter's, while less celebrated than the essay on the "paranoid style in American politics," is equally incisive. In it, Hofstadter argued that the right was now animated not by a classical understanding of conservatism (a recognition of the limits of human reform and a skepticism about far-reaching public initiatives) but by a mindset that was, in its way, as expansive as the liberal hope of progress. He called this strain "pseudo-conservatism," writing:

> Who is the pseudo-conservative, and what does he want? It is impossible to identify him by social class, for the pseudo-conservative impulse can be found in practically all classes in society, although its power probably rests largely upon its appeal to the less educated members of the middle classes. The ideology of pseudo-conservatism can be characterized but not defined, because the pseudo-conservative tends to be more than ordinarily incoherent about politics. The lady who, when General Eisenhower's victory over Senator [Robert A.] Taft [for the Republican presidential nomination] had finally become official in 1952, stalked out of the Hilton Hotel declaiming, "This means eight more years of socialism" was probably a fairly good representative of the pseudo-conservative mentality. . . .
>
> The restlessness, suspicion and fear shown in various phases of the pseudo-conservative revolt give evidence of the real

suffering which the pseudo-conservative experiences in his capacity as a citizen. He believes himself to be living in a world in which he is spied upon, plotted against, betrayed, and very likely destined for total ruin. He feels that his liberties have been arbitrarily and outrageously invaded.

A key Hofstadter insight had to do with motivation. Politics was not a high-minded philosophical contest between competing visions of reality; it was, rather, a messy struggle that often defied easy categorization. As Hofstadter wrote:

> Political life is not simply an arena in which the conflicting interests of various social groups in concrete material gains are fought out; it is also an arena into which status aspirations and frustrations are, as the psychologists would say, projected. It is at this point that the issues of politics, or the pretended issues of politics, become interwoven with and dependent upon the personal problems of individuals. We have, at all times, two kinds of processes going on in inextricable connection with each other: **interest politics**, the clash of material aims and needs among various groups and blocs; and **status politics**, the clash of various projective rationalizations arising from status aspirations and other personal motives.

When Joe McCarthy died at Bethesda Naval Hospital on Thursday, May 2, 1957, he was once more the center of attention. "Years will pass before the results of his work can be objectively evaluated," Vice President Nixon said, "but his friends and many of his critics will not question his devotion to what he considered to be the best interests of his country."

Many others did not believe a distance of years was required to offer their verdict. His home-state **Milwaukee Journal** wrote, "The harmful influence of McCarthy and McCarthyism was felt far beyond the world of politics. It injured American prestige in the eyes of the world. . . . Future generations are likely to find this period as fantastic, and harmful to the American spirit, as that of the Salem witch hunts, the post–Civil War Reconstruction or the Ku Klux Klan."

The Louisville **Courier-Journal** took the longest of views:

> There is an element almost of classical tragedy in the life and death of Joseph McCarthy. His rise to fame had the sudden, spectacular violence of a rocket splitting the night sky with unhealthy brilliance. With equal speed the glare faded and the spent stick came racing downward. Now it has struck earth. McCarthy, the meteoric, the defiant, the

proud is now dead. In the classic form, true tragedy derives only from a man of great qualities who is destroyed by one fatal flaw of character. It would be hard to make a case for greatness in the Senator from Wisconsin.

At a requiem mass at St. Matthew's Cathedral, Monsignor John Cartwright said that McCarthy would "take his place among those colleagues of the hall of fame, each one of whom is great in memory because at one time or another he had the fortitude to stand alone." McCarthy's casket was borne from the church to the Capitol for a brief state funeral—customary for sitting senators—attended by Vice President Nixon, 32 of 49 Senate Democrats, and 38 of 46 Senate Republicans. House Speaker Sam Rayburn, Alice Roosevelt Longworth, and Roy Cohn were there, too.

A notable fixer, Cohn thrived at the nexus of law, politics, media, and society. "I don't want to know what the law is," he'd say of a case. "I want to know who the judge is." One of his more celebrated clients in afteryears was a young real-estate developer who was looking to move into Manhattan from his family's base in Queens. And Roy Cohn was always there for Donald Trump.

WHAT THE HELL IS THE PRESIDENCY FOR?

"Segregation Forever," King's Crusade,
and LBJ in the Crucible

PREVIOUS PAGES: King and Johnson, pictured here in the Oval Office in December 1963, found themselves sharing history's stage as the country confronted the unfinished business of the Civil War.

Nigguhs hate whites, and whites hate nigguhs.
Everybody knows that deep down.
—Governor GEORGE C. WALLACE of Alabama

At the moment when I was hit on the bridge and began
to fall, I really thought it was my last protest, my last
march. I thought I saw death, and I thought, "It's okay,
it's all right—I am doing what I am supposed to do."
—JOHN LEWIS, who was beaten at the foot of the Edmund
Pettus Bridge in Selma, Alabama, on Sunday, March 7, 1965

Lyndon Johnson couldn't sleep. As Friday, November 22, 1963, turned into Saturday the twenty-third, the new president of the United States—he had taken the oath of office some eight hours before, in Dallas, in the wake of the assassination of his predecessor, John F. Kennedy—wanted to **move.** "Very frankly, Mr. Speaker," Johnson told House Speaker John McCormack of Massachusetts in these difficult days, "I can't sit still. I've got to keep the government going." "Lyndon acts as if there is never going to be a tomorrow," his wife, Lady Bird, once observed, and on this long Friday evening, her husband, wearing his pajamas in the Johnsons' house in Spring Valley in northwest Washington, gave orders about everything he could think of. There was so much to do—a president to bury; a sudden, tragic transition to manage; a Cold War world to master.

To his aides who sat by his bedside, taking notes, Johnson seemed calm in the madness of the hour. "Lyndon," Lady Bird remarked that night, "is a good man to have in a crisis." No president had been assassinated since William McKinley, and the horror in Dallas marked the first unexpected transfer of American power in the Nuclear Age. Johnson was already thinking beyond the moment. "Well, I'm going to tell you," he said, "I'm going to pass the civil rights bill and not change one word of it. I'm not going to cavil, and I'm not going to compromise. I'm going to fix it so everyone can vote, so everyone can get all the education they can get." Fate had given him ultimate power, and he intended to use it.

President Kennedy had left a proposed civil rights act in the Congress. Martin Luther King, Jr.'s eight-year-old daughter Yolanda was distraught on the afternoon of the assassination. "Oh, Daddy," she said, "now we will never get our freedom!" King was reassuring. "Now don't you worry, baby," he said. "It's going to be all right."

It was a crowded moment. In June, Governor George Wallace had tried to prevent the integration of the University of Alabama in Tuscaloosa. The next day, Medgar Evers, the field director of the NAACP in Mississippi, had been assassinated in his driveway. In August the country had watched King address the March on Washington. In September had come the brutal deaths of four little girls on a Sunday morning when Klansmen bombed the Sixteenth Street Baptist Church in Birmingham, Alabama. And yet, as King well knew, the American attention span was notoriously brief. "We're still a ten-day nation, Walter," King said to his colleague the Reverend Walter Fauntroy, who recalled the remark to the writer Nick Kotz. King, according to Kotz, had a "sense that the country seemed unable to focus on a single issue such as civil rights for more than ten days."

A Southerner in a Democratic Party divided between liberals based in the Northeast and segregationists in the Old Confederacy, Johnson faced the worst of all political worlds on civil rights. Yet he knew, too, that it was a task for the ages—a task for great and good men who, if they overcame the tyranny of the present, would bask in the warm light of history. As Johnson gathered himself to press ahead with the Kennedy administration's civil rights legislation—in his first address to Congress as president LBJ would frame the fight as the most fitting possible tribute to JFK—he was advised to go slow and to play it safe, at least until after the 1964 presidential election. As political a man as ever drew breath, Johnson, however, dismissed such counsel with a penetrating rhetorical question: "Well, what the hell is the presidency for?" he asked, if not to do the big things lesser men might not?

Johnson had hardly been a progressive in his pre–White House years. A Texan with an astute sense of politics and a consuming ambition, he had erred on the side of appeasing his segregationist constituents. While he had declined (along with Tennessee senators Albert Gore, Sr., and Estes Kefauver) to sign the 1956 Southern Manifesto, a declaration pledging resistance to the Warren Court's groundbreaking school-integration decisions, Johnson had also weakened civil rights bills in the Senate. (Though he would point out that at least they passed, in some form.)

His commitment to the cause after Dallas forms one of the great chapters of personal transformation and of political courage in the history of the presidency—one akin to Lincoln's move from tolerance of slavery in 1861 to emancipation in 1862–63. "I've never felt freer in my life," LBJ remarked in January 1964. In the story of Johnson and civil rights we can see the difference a singular president can make when the circumstances are right—and when the voices of protest are steady and brave.

He had begun this journey as vice president. He was stirred by the fact of his national election, even if he were the understudy on the ticket.

"I wasn't a crusader," LBJ recalled of his days on Capitol Hill. "I represented a southern state, and if I got out too far ahead of my voters they'd have sent me right back to Johnson City where I couldn't have done anything for anybody, white or Negro." John Kennedy's death had changed everything. "Now I represent the whole country, and I can do what the whole country thinks is right," Johnson said. "Or ought to."

As he prepared for his first major speech as president, an address to Congress on Wednesday, November 27, 1963, Johnson received a piece of advice from Whitney Young of the National Urban League. "Let me make a quick suggestion," Young told Johnson. "I think you've just got to . . . point out that . . . with the death of President Kennedy . . . that hate anywhere that goes unchecked doesn't stop just for the week. And the killing at Birmingham [the Sixteenth Street Baptist Church bombing]—the people feel that they can react with violence when they dissent."

Johnson agreed. "I dictated a whole page on hate—hate international—hate domestically—and just say that this hate that produces inequality, this hate that produces poverty, that's why we've got to have a tax bill—the hate that produces injustice—that's why we've got to have a civil rights bill," he told Young. "It's a cancer that just eats out our national existence."

Three years before, right-wing demonstrators in Dallas had spit at Lady Bird Johnson on a day when protestors had greeted the Johnsons with placards reading TEXAS TRAITOR. JUDAS JOHNSON: TURNCOAT TEXAN. LET'S BEAT JUDAS. In October 1963 a similar crowd had attacked Adlai Stevenson, the ambassador to the United Nations, also spitting on him, striking him on the head with a sign, and denouncing him with cries of "TRAITOR!" One protestor shouted: "Kennedy will get his reward in hell. Stevenson is going to die. His heart will stop, stop, stop. And he will burn, burn, burn." Pulling away from the chaos in his car, cleaning the spit from his face, Stevenson murmured, "Are these human beings or animals?"

In his November 1963 appearance before the Congress, Johnson said: "John Kennedy's death commands what his life conveyed—that America must move forward. Let us turn away from the fanatics of the far left and the far right, from the apostles of bitterness and bigotry, from those defiant of law, and those who pour venom into our Nation's bloodstream."

In the South in particular—as ever—national characteristics were magnified to the point of absurdity during the Cold War. Race—also as ever—was the flashpoint. "We know that if we protest we will be called 'bad niggers,'" the novelist Richard Wright wrote in his 1941 book **Twelve Million Black Voices.** "The Lords of the Land will preach the doctrine of 'white supremacy' to the poor whites who are eager to form mobs. In the midst of general hysteria they will seize one of us—it does not matter who, the innocent or guilty—and, as a token, a naked and bleeding body will be dragged through the dusty streets." Such hysteria was fomented, Wright noted, by appeals to poor whites for whom color was everything since they had nothing else.

In 1948, when Hubert H. Humphrey, then the mayor of Minneapolis, called on the Democratic National Convention in Philadelphia to "get out of the shadow of states' rights and walk forthrightly into the bright sunshine of human rights," supporters of Strom Thurmond and his segregationist worldview marched out of the convention, went south, and met at Birmingham to form the Dixiecrat ticket. Worried about Communists and civil rights—President Truman had integrated the military the same month of the Dixiecrat rebellion—the disaffected began to carry Confederate battle flags to rallies, seeking to link their cause with the Lost one. After the school-integration rulings of 1954 and 1955, defiance grew. IMPEACH EARL WARREN signs appeared across the South. Georgia incorporated the battle emblem into its flag in 1956. South Carolina hoisted the Confederate colors over its capitol in 1962 as part of the centennial commemoration of the war. And George Wallace ordered the flag to be flown above the state capitol dome on the day Attorney General Robert Kennedy called on him in Montgomery.

In her memoir, **I Know Why the Caged Bird Sings**, Maya Angelou recalled a childhood spent in the universe of the rural Jim Crow South. She and her brother, who were three and four, had been put on a train to travel—alone—from Long Beach, California, to Stamps, Arkansas, where their grandmother ran a country store. One evening, Angelou recalled hearing the hoofbeats of the sheriff's horse in the yard. "His twang," she wrote, "jogged in the brittle air." He warned of a planned Klan night ride. Angelou's uncle Willie, the sheriff said, " 'better lay low tonight.' " A black man had apparently " 'messed with a white lady today. Some of the boys'll be coming over here later.' "

Listening from the side of the store, Angelou reflected on the Klansmen. "The 'boys'? Those cement faces and eyes of hate that burned the clothes off you if they happened to see you lounging on the main street downtown on Saturday. Boys? It seemed youth had never happened to them. Boys? No, rather men who were covered with graves' dust and age without beauty or learning. The ugliness and rottenness of old abominations."

In a way, Angelou was just as furious about the sheriff's condescension, the blithe evil of warning the innocent to "lay low." "If on Judgment Day I were summoned by St. Peter to give testimony to the used-to-be sheriff's act of kindness, I would be unable to say anything in his behalf," she wrote. "His confidence that my uncle and every other Black man who heard of the Klan's coming ride would scurry under their houses to hide in chicken droppings was too humiliating to hear."

Yet her uncle hid. What choice did he have? Angelou, her brother and her grandmother covered him in potatoes and vegetables inside the store's storage bins. The night passed without incident—the Klansmen did not call—but if they had, Angelou wrote, "they would have surely found Uncle Willie and just as surely lynched him."

Robert Penn Warren had come from the world Angelou was describing. A native of Guthrie, Kentucky, who had been educated at Vanderbilt University and was a Rhodes Scholar at Oxford, Warren began his academic career at Louisiana State University and at what was then known as Southwestern, a university in Memphis, before moving north to Yale. In the wake of the school-integration decisions, Warren—novelist, poet, critic, professor—accepted an assignment from **Life** magazine to travel from Connecticut to his native South, where enraged white Southerners were carrying signs that read KEEP OUR SCHOOLS WHITE. A Southern-born friend of Warren's in New York told him: "I'm glad it's you going, and not me."

He knew what she meant. He didn't really want to do it, but he knew he had to. Bearing witness, seeking to understand, confronting past and present in their complexity and pain: It was all part of what Warren had called "the awful responsibility of Time" in his 1946 novel **All the King's Men.** The result of Warren's journey was his 1956 book **Segregation: The Inner Conflict in the South.** Warren, who had written sympathetically of segregation in a 1930 essay he now repudiated, sought out the voices of African Americans and white supremacists, of ministers and teachers, of businessmen and farmers.

In the South there was suspicion of "the New York press," with one resident of the Old Confederacy telling Warren: "Well, by God, it's just a fact, it's not in them not to load the dice in a news story!" There was a tragic sense that full reconciliation was impossible. "You hear some white men say they know Negroes," a black teacher in Louisiana told Warren. "Understand Negroes. But it's not true. No white man ever born ever understood what a Negro is thinking. What he's feeling." And there was the making of common cause with neo-Nazis and anti-Semites. One segregationist mused to Warren about Gerald L. K. Smith, the prominent white nationalist. "Lord, that man's mailing list would be worth a million dollars!"

A few years later, on the occasion of the centennial of Fort Sumter, Warren wrote a small book, **The Legacy of the Civil War.** In it he posited that the war had given the South the "Great Alibi" and the North a "Treasury of Virtue." The Great Alibi "explains, condones, and transmutes everything." Evil became good; the inexcusable explicable, pardonable. "Even now, any common lyncher becomes a defender of the Southern tradition, and any rabble-rouser the gallant leader of a thin gray line of heroes, his hat on saberpoint to provide reference by which to hold formation in the charge," Warren wrote. "Even if the Southerner prays to feel different, he may still feel that to change his attitude would be a treachery—to that City of the Soul which the historical Confederacy became, to blood spilled in hopeless valor, to the dead fathers, and even to the self. He is trapped in history."

Did the Southern "man who, in the relative safety of mob anonymity, stands howling vituperation at a little Negro girl being conducted into a school building," Warren asked, "ever consider the possibility that whatever degree of dignity and success a Negro achieves actually enriches, in the end, the life of the white man and enlarges his own worth as a human being?"

The answer was no. The Southerner who stood howling, or who voted for those who instigated and benefitted from that howling, was being governed by a fear that, having lost the war of 1861–65, he was now being asked to suffer yet another defeat—the loss of a way of life in which whites were supreme.

To Warren, though, there was also fault among the victors. "The Treasury of Virtue, which is the psychological heritage left to the North by the Civil War, may not be as comic or vicious as the Great Alibi, but it is equally unlovely," he wrote. "It may even be, in the end, equally corrosive of national, and personal, integrity. If the Southerner, with his Great Alibi, feels trapped by history, the Northerner, with his Treasury of Virtue, feels redeemed by history, automatically redeemed. He has in his pocket, not a Papal indulgence peddled by some wandering pardoner of the Middle Ages, but an indulgence, a plenary indulgence, for all sins past, present, and future, freely given by the hand of history."

The sins of the North, past and present, had been paid off from the Treasury of Virtue. "In the happy contemplation of the Treasury of Virtue it is forgotten that the Republican platform of 1860 pledged protection to the institution of slavery where it existed, and that the Republicans were ready, in 1861, to guarantee slavery in the South, as bait for a return to the Union," Warren wrote. "It is forgotten that racism and Abolitionism might, and often did, go hand in hand." After Appomattox, Warren argued, the North fell victim to self-righteousness. "The crusaders themselves, back from the wars, seemed to feel that they had finished the work of virtue," he wrote. "Their efforts had, indeed, been almost superhuman, but they themselves were, after all, human."

In the closing pages of **Segregation,** the earlier book, Warren mused about the path forward for both North and South. "We have to deal with the problem our historical moment proposes, the burden of our time," he wrote. "We all live with a thousand unsolved problems of justice all the time. . . . All we can do for posterity is to try to plug along in a way to make them think we— the old folks—did the best we could for justice, as we could understand it."

A noble, high-minded view. The reality on the ground in the America into which Warren was publishing his books, though, could be neither noble nor high-minded—or even mindful at all. "Nigguhs hate whites, and whites hate nigguhs," George Corley Wallace once drawled. "Everybody knows that deep down."

Born in 1919, a native of Barbour County, Alabama, Wallace had not always been a race-baiter. Just after World War II, as a young man, he'd expressed progressive thoughts. "You know, we just can't keep the colored folks down like we been doin' around here for years and years," Wallace told a Sunday school teacher at his church. "We got to quit. We got to start treatin' 'em right. They just like everybody else." He veered between hard-line segregation and a (relatively) more moderate stance for the next decade or so. In 1948 he sought election as an alternate delegate to the Democratic National Convention with the slogan: "Unalterably opposed to nominating Harry S. Truman and the so-called Civil Rights Program." Yet in 1958, in a race for governor against fellow Democrat John Patterson, Wallace denounced the Ku Klux Klan while Patterson ran right. Never again. "John Patterson out-nigguhed me," Wallace was reputed to have remarked to a group of pols at Montgomery's Jefferson Davis Hotel after he lost. "And boys, I'm not goin' to be out-nigguhed again." (Wallace denied this oft-repeated anecdote ever afterward.) "He used to be anything but a racist," an old political associate recalled, "but with all his chattering, he managed to talk himself into it."

Elected governor in 1962, Wallace was inaugurated at the state capitol on Monday, January 14, 1963, at the site where Jefferson Davis had taken the oath as president of the Confederate States of America; Dexter Avenue Baptist Church, where Martin Luther King, Jr., had been pastor from 1954 to 1960, sat a block away. Speaking from what he proudly called "this Cradle of the Confederacy, this very Heart of the Great Anglo-Saxon Southland," Wallace cried: "In the name of the greatest people that have ever trod this earth, I draw the line in the dust and toss the gauntlet before the feet of tyranny and I say . . . segregation now . . . segregation tomorrow . . . segregation forever."

The crowd erupted. Wallace took a moment to wipe his nose in the winter cold, then plunged on. He knew what he was doing. "I'm gonna make race the basis of politics in this state," Wallace said before the inaugural, "and I'm gonna make it the basis of politics in this country." Wallace brought something intriguing to the modern politics of fear in America: a visceral connection to his crowds, an appeal that confounded elites but which gave him a durable base. The cigar-chewing bantam figure with slicked-back hair (he privately admired Robert Kennedy's tousled look) was "simply more alive than all the others," a female journalist told the writer Marshall Frady. Alluding to a Wallace speech in New Hampshire, the woman continued: "You saw those people in that auditorium when he was speaking—you saw their eyes. He made those people feel something **real** for once in their lives. You can't help but respond to him. Me—my heart was pounding. I couldn't take my eyes off him, there were all those people screaming. You almost **love** him, though you know what a little gremlin he actually is."

He provoked devotion and rage. Many adored him, revering him as a new savior; many others despaired of a future under his rule. Educated people in Alabama were said to be reading books about Nazi Germany, particularly William L. Shirer's **The Rise and Fall of the Third Reich**, searching for parallels. One woman whom Frady described as "a gentle, bespectacled, exquisitely civilized Montgomery dowager" could not contain herself: "I wish he were dead. I wish someone would kill him. He ought to die. He's awful, terrible. I would kill him myself if I just had the chance—I would."

In Wallace the Lost Cause found new relevance. In the months after his inauguration, the crisis came: A federal court ordered the integration of the University of Alabama. Wallace had pledged to stand in the schoolhouse door—as the popular phrase had it—to prevent just such a thing. He savored the hour, however hopeless it was. The very hopelessness of it all was in fact part of the appeal of defiance, for Southerners loved tragic stands against the inevitable. Wallace reminded Marshall Frady of William Faulkner's Reverend Hightower in **Light in August,** "whose gray head, as he sits by his window at dusk, is filled with the flash and roar of the old glorious doomed charges, the lifted sabers and bugles and grimy howling faces above gaunt, galloping horses." It was more than sentiment about a distant past; it was tangible, present, **unfolding**.

So ran the line from the polemics of Edward Alfred Pollard to the politics of George Corley Wallace—a line connecting the Civil War to the Cold War, the 1860s to the 1960s, a distant America to the contemporary one. The federal government was the villain. States' rights were the salvation of the Founders' vision. White supremacy was to be protected by whatever means possible.

Yet Wallace failed. The Kennedy Justice Department enforced the court order, and the university was integrated. On the evening of the day federal officials compelled Wallace to stand aside, President Kennedy spoke to the nation.

"Today," the president said, "we are committed to a worldwide struggle to promote and protect the rights of all who wish to be free."

Kennedy's language was straightforward, his tone reasonable. "This is not a sectional issue," he said. "Difficulties over segregation and discrimination exist in every city, in every State of the Union, producing in many cities a rising tide of discontent that threatens the public safety. Nor is this a partisan issue. . . . We are confronted primarily with a moral issue. It is as old as the Scriptures and is as clear as the American Constitution."

An elegant formulation, but Kennedy continued to speak in concrete terms, making the issue as tangible as he could: "If an American, because his skin is dark, cannot eat lunch in a restaurant open to the public, if he cannot send his children to the best public school available, if he cannot vote for the public officials who represent him, if, in short, he cannot enjoy the full and free life which all of us want, then who among us would be content to have the color of his skin changed and stand in his place?"

Wallace was forced to step aside at Tuscaloosa ("Now you sonuvabitches are on the other side, ain't you?" he joked to the federalized Alabama National Guard, now under presidential orders to enforce the law against their governor), and his stand in Tuscaloosa in the early summer of

1963 helped push Kennedy to introduce a wide-ranging civil rights measure—the legislation that was still pending when the president was killed in November. Kennedy had carried the day against Wallace, but it was just that—the day, not eternity.

Title II of the proposed bill outlawed segregation in public accommodations. One day in the Senate, Johnson, still the vice president, called over John Stennis of Mississippi, a fellow Democrat. As a Senate Democratic aide recalled the moment:

> Johnson said, "How do you like that Title II of the civil rights bill, John?"
> Stennis said, "Oh, Lyndon, well, you know, our people just can't take that kind of thing. It's just impossible. I mean, I believe a man ought to have the right to—if he owns a store or owns a café—he ought to have the right to serve whom he wants to serve. Our people will just never take it."
> Lyndon said, "Then you don't think you'll support it."
> "Oh, no, Lyndon, I don't think I'll support it at all."
> Johnson said, "Well, you know, John, the other day a sad thing happened. Helen

Williams and her husband, Gene, who [are African Americans and] have been working for me for many years, drove my official car from Washington down to Texas, the Cadillac limousine of the vice-president of the United States. They drove through your state, and when they got hungry, they stopped at grocery stores on the edge of town in colored areas and bought Vienna sausage and beans and ate them with a plastic spoon. And when they had to go to the bathroom, they would stop, pull off on a side road, and Helen Williams, an employee of the vice-president of the United States, would squat in the road to pee. And you know, John, that's just bad. That's wrong. And there ought to be something to change that. And it seems to me that if people in Mississippi don't change it voluntarily, that it's just going to be necessary to change it by law."

"Well, Lyndon, I'm sure that there were nice places where . . ."

Then the vice-president just said, "Uh-huh, uh-huh," and sort of looked away vacantly and said, "Well, thank you, John." And Stennis left. Johnson turned around to me and winked. It represented, as I say, the first time I had ever really had the feeling that the comprehension of the simple indignity of discrimination was deep in Johnson.

On the evening of Kennedy's funeral in Washington, Johnson tracked King down in New York City. King, who was staying at the Waldorf Astoria on Park Avenue, had issued a supportive statement the day after the assassination, and Johnson was grateful. "President Johnson will follow the path charted by President Kennedy in civil rights," King had said. "It does not at all mean a setback."

"We know what a difficult period this is," King said to Johnson on the telephone.

"It's just an impossible period," Johnson said. "We've got a budget coming out that's practically already made, and we've got a civil rights bill. . . . We've got to just not give up on any of them."

"Well, this is mighty fine," King said. "I think one of the great tributes we can pay in memory of President Kennedy is to try to enact some of the great progressive policies that he sought to initiate."

"I'm going to support 'em all and you can count on that," Johnson said. "And I'm going to do my best to get other men to do likewise and I'll have to have you-all's help. I never needed it more'n I do now."

Providence—or fate, depending on one's worldview—had brought King to the center of the great domestic drama of the American Century. A scion of the African American ecclesiastical elite—his father, Martin Luther King, Sr., was a leading preacher, the pastor of Atlanta's Ebenezer Baptist Church—the younger King was educated at Morehouse College in Atlanta, Crozer Theological Seminary in Pennsylvania, and Boston University. He was called to the pulpit of Dexter Avenue Baptist Church in Montgomery in 1954. In December 1955, when Rosa Parks, a seamstress, was arrested after declining to surrender her seat on a Montgomery city bus to a white passenger, organizers needed a place to meet to explore a boycott of public transportation. E. D. Nixon, the president of the local NAACP, called King. Nixon wanted to hold the gathering at Dexter.

Geography, as Napoleon is sometimes said to have remarked, was destiny. Dexter's "central location made the church convenient for people working in downtown offices," wrote King biographer Taylor Branch. Yes, of course, King told Nixon.

On the night he first spoke to a mass meeting on the boycott, in a scene vividly described by Branch, King sensed the possibilities of the moment—not least because there were so many people flocking to the gathering that his car could not get near the building. "This," King remarked to a friend, "could turn into something big."

"We are here this evening—for serious business," King told the huge crowd on Monday, December 5, 1955. "We are here in a general sense, because first and foremost—we are American citizens—and we are determined to apply our citizenship—to the fullness of its meaning."

He saluted Rosa Parks's courage, then offered a trilogy of sentences that transported his audience and set the keynote for the next dozen years of his now-public life. "And you know, my friends," King said, "there comes a time when people get tired of being trampled over by the iron feet of oppression. There comes a time, my friends, when people get tired of being plunged across the abyss of humiliation, where they experience the bleakness of nagging despair. There comes a time when people get tired of being pushed out of the glittering sunlight of life's July, and left standing amid the piercing chill of an Alpine November."

As the ecstatic crowd calmed, he said again: "We are here—we are here this evening because we are tired now."

And at last, at last: "And we are determined here in Montgomery—to work and fight until justice runs down like water and righteousness like a mighty stream!"

From that moment until his assassination on the balcony of a Memphis motel in April 1968, King would lead a complex movement of nonviolent protest against segregation and for economic justice. His house in Montgomery was bombed within two months of his debut boycott sermon. "Nigger, we are tired of you and your mess now," a caller told King on the telephone after the attack. "If you aren't out of this town in three days, we're going to blow your brains out and blow up your house." In the face of such hate, King's faith sustained him. "Lord, I'm down here trying to do what's right," he prayed after the call. "But Lord I must confess that I'm weak now. I'm faltering, I'm losing my courage."

As King recalled it, "I could hear an inner voice saying to me: 'Martin Luther, stand up for righteousness. Stand up for justice. Stand up for truth. And, lo, I will be with you even until the end of the world.' I heard Jesus saying still to fight on. He promised never to leave me, never to leave me alone."

By making a nonviolent case against segregation, King and innumerable others appealed to the nation's conscience in memorable campaigns—from sit-ins to Freedom Rides to Mississippi's

Freedom Summer to the Children's Crusade in Birmingham. Protest and high politics—the crucial forces that history usually requires to make great changes—intersected most notably, perhaps, on Wednesday, August 28, 1963, at the March on Washington for Jobs and Freedom.

King's address to the march that afternoon was not going well, or at least not as well as he had hoped. The day had been long; the crowds massed before the Lincoln Memorial were ready for some rhetorical adrenaline, some true poetry. King's task was to lift his speech from the ordinary to the historic, from the mundane to the sacred. He was standing before the greatest audience of his life. Yet with the television networks broadcasting live and President Kennedy watching from the White House, King was struggling with a text that had been drafted by too many hands late the previous night at the Willard Hotel. One sentence he was about to deliver was particularly awkward: "And so today, let us go back to our communities as members of the international association for the advancement of creative dissatisfaction." King was on the verge of letting the hour pass him by.

Then, as on Easter morning at the tomb of the crucified Jesus, there was the sound of a woman's voice. King had already begun to extemporize when the singer Mahalia Jackson spoke up. "Tell 'em about the dream, Martin," said Jackson, who was standing nearby. King left his text altogether at this point—a departure that put him on a path to speaking words of American scripture, words as essential to the nation's destiny in their way as those of Lincoln, before whose memorial King stood, and those of Jefferson, whose monument lay to the preacher's right, toward the Potomac. The moments of ensuing oratory lifted King above the tumult of history and made him a figure of history—a "new founding father," in Taylor Branch's apt phrase.

"I say to you today, my friends . . . even though we face the difficulties of today and tomorrow, I still have a dream," King said. "It is a dream deeply rooted in the American Dream"—a dream that had been best captured in the promise of words written in a distant summer in Philadelphia by Jefferson. "I have a dream," King continued, "that one day this nation will rise up, live out the true meaning of its creed: 'We hold these truths to be self-evident, that all men are created equal.'"

Drawing on the Bible and "My Country, 'Tis of Thee," on the Emancipation Proclamation and the Constitution, King projected an ideal vision of an exceptional nation. In King's imagined country, hope triumphed over the fear. In doing so, King defined the best of the nation as surely as Jefferson did in Philadelphia in 1776 or Lincoln did at Gettysburg in 1863.

> I have a dream that one day on the red hills of Georgia, sons of former slaves and the sons of former slave owners will be able to sit down together at the table of brotherhood.
>
> I have a dream that one day even the state of Mississippi, a state sweltering with the heat of injustice, sweltering with the heat of oppression, will be transformed into an oasis of freedom and justice.
>
> I have a dream that my four little children will one day live in a nation where they will not be judged by the color of their skin but by the content of their character. . . .
>
> I have a dream today.

Like our more familiar founders (Washington, Adams, Hamilton, Jefferson), King was a practical idealist, a man who could articulate the perfect but knew that human progress, while sometimes intoxicatingly rapid, tends to be provisional. The march was but a step. Nineteen sixty-three, King said that day, was "not an end but a beginning."

It's tempting to romanticize the words King

spoke before the Lincoln Memorial. To do so, however, cheapens the courage of the nonviolent soldiers of freedom who faced—and too often paid—the ultimate price for daring America to live up to the implications of the Declaration of Independence and become a country in which liberty was innate and universal, not particular to station, creed, or color. In Washington to demand legislative action, King spoke as a minister of the Lord, invoking the meaning of the Sermon on the Mount in a city more often interested in the mechanics of the Congress.

White Washington had expected mayhem. Few bureaucrats or lawyers who worked downtown in the capital showed up for work on the day of the march. That many blacks? In one place? Who knew what might happen? Even the ordinarily liberal **New York Times** was wary. "There was great fear there would be rioting," recalled **The New York Times**'s Russell Baker, who was assigned a front-page feature on the march, "so the **Times** chartered a chopper." Boarding the helicopter early in the day, Baker grew so bored by the peaceable spectacle that he asked the pilot to fly over his house so he could check on the condition of his roof. "Finally," said Baker, "I had him land at National Airport and went to the Lincoln Memorial."

It was, it turned out, not only orderly but also

integrated. Bob Dylan, Charlton Heston, and Marlon Brando were there; Baker took note of the series of speeches and songs, including Mahalia Jackson's "I Been 'Buked and I Been Scorned," a spiritual delivered with such power that Baker reported Jackson's voice seemed to echo off the far-off Capitol. Speaker after speaker—the young John Lewis, the aged A. Philip Randolph—made the case for racial justice. "For many, the day seemed an adventure, a long outing in the late summer sun—part liberation from home, part Sunday School picnic, part political convention, and part fish-fry," James Reston wrote in his piece for the **Times** the next day.

In the White House, "JFK heard some of the speeches and chants through an open window of the third-floor White House Solarium," the historian Michael Beschloss wrote. "Gripping the windowsill, he told the Mansion's courtly black doorman, Preston Bruce, 'Oh, Bruce, I wish I were out there with them!'" But not enough to risk appearing at an event that Kennedy believed would alienate many white voters.

The president watched King's speech on television, listened with appreciation, then readied for a meeting with the march's leadership to discuss pushing legislation through a Congress still dominated by white-segregationist Democrats. The conversation did not produce much in the way of progress. Kennedy feared moving too quickly, and, as they had said again and again all afternoon, the civil rights delegates from the Mall believed the time for action was at hand.

King had anticipated Kennedy's temporizing. The pilgrimage would be long, he had told his listeners, and the pilgrims had to maintain the moral high ground they had so effectively claimed through nonviolence. "In the process of gaining our rightful place, we must not be guilty of wrongful deeds," King had told the crowd. "We must forever conduct our struggle on the high plane of dignity and discipline." If the politicians were too slow, well, that meant there had to be yet more dignity and yet more discipline.

The **Times**'s Reston, a reliable molder and barometer of Establishment opinion, however, believed the day had in fact accomplished something, even if JFK was less than enthusiastic during the White House meeting late that afternoon. "The demonstration impressed political Washington because it combined a number of things no politician can ignore," Reston wrote. "It had the force of numbers. It had the melodies of both the church and the theater. And it was able to invoke the principles of the founding fathers to rebuke the inequalities and hypocrisies of modern American life."

On that August Wednesday, on the steps of

the Lincoln Memorial—the spot on which he stood is marked there now, a sacred slab hidden in plain sight in the middle of the American capital—King drew from scripture as he joined the ranks of the founders. In the beginning of the Republic, men dreamed big but failed to include everyone in that dream, limiting liberty largely to white men. Speaking in 1963, King brilliantly argued for the expansion of the founders' vision—nothing more, but surely nothing less. In so doing, a preacher from the South summoned a nation to justice and won his place in the American pantheon. "I have a dream that one day every valley shall be exalted, every hill and every mountain shall be made low," King said. "The rough places will be made plain, and the crooked places will be made straight. And the glory of the Lord shall be revealed, and all flesh shall see it together." He paused, then pressed on: "This is our hope. This is the faith that I go back to the South with. With this faith we will be able to hew out of the mountain of despair a stone of hope." Transforming that hope into history remained the work of King's days.

And of Lyndon Johnson's. In the months after the Kennedy assassination, the new president pressed his old colleagues on Capitol Hill to give the civil rights bill a full and fair trial.

President Johnson asked King to come see him in the Oval Office on Tuesday, December 3, 1963. LBJ spoke of the minutiae of reform—he needed to force the legislation out of the Southern-controlled Rules Committee in the House with a "discharge petition," a device that would put the bill on the floor for a vote. Johnson was understandably consumed with the maneuver. Without it the bill would die a procedural death; with it progress was possible. "He made it very clear he wants the civil rights bill out of the Rules Committee before Christmas," King told reporters afterward. "He means business. I think we can expect even more from him than we have had up to now."

The day before his meeting with King, Johnson had also made himself clear in a telephone conversation with **Washington Post** publisher Katharine Graham. "Now every person that doesn't sign that petition has got to be fairly regarded as being anti–civil rights," Johnson had said. "I don't care if he votes against the bill after he gets a chance to vote on it. . . . But I don't think any American can say that he won't let 'em have a hearing either in the committee or on the floor. That is worse than Hitler did. So we've got to get ready for that and we've got to get ready every day. Front page. In and out. Individuals. Why—are—you—a-gainst—a—hearing? And point 'em out and have their pictures and have editorials and have everything else that is in a dignified way for a hearing on the floor."

Johnson went to work on members of the House and, after victory there in January (when the Rules Committee forwarded the bill to the full House) and in February (when the House passed the legislation), he shifted his energies to his former colleagues in the Senate. He needed sixty-seven votes in the upper chamber to invoke cloture and cut off the Southern-led filibuster.

"They tell [this] story [about] the difference between Kennedy as president and Johnson as president," recalled James H. Rowe, Jr., an old FDR hand:

A senator would come to Kennedy and say, "I'd love to go along with you, Mr. President, but it would give me serious trouble back home." Kennedy would always say, "I understand." Now Johnson knew damn well the senator was going to tell him that, and he never let the senator get to the point of his troubles back home. He would tell him about the flag, and by God, the story of the country, and he'd get them by the lapels and they were out the door. That's why he got so much done so fast. Roosevelt would do that, too. He would do it, let's say, with more charm than Johnson, but they'd get the same results. They'd get what they wanted.

Richard Russell, Jr., of Georgia, a segregationist and a Johnson mentor, appreciated his apprentice's gifts—so much so that he feared defeat for the Southern way of life at the hands of a Southern president. "I have no doubt that the president intends to throw the full weight of his powerful office and the full force of his personality—both of which are considerable—to secure the passage of this program," Russell said in January 1964.

From the White House, Johnson wheedled and cajoled, pressing the case again and again (rightly, as it turned out) that history would reward those who voted with him. "I made my position unmistakably clear: We are not prepared to compromise in any way," Johnson recalled. "'So far as this administration is concerned,' I told a press conference, 'its position is firm.' I wanted absolutely no room for bargaining. . . . I knew that the slightest wavering on my part would give hope to the opposition's strategy of amending the bill to death."

The president would not bend. "Dick, you've got to get out of my way," Johnson told Russell. "If you don't, I'm going to roll over you. I don't intend to cavil or compromise"—a phrase Johnson had also used on the night of the assassination.

"You may do that," Russell said. "But it's going to cost you the South, and cost you the [1964 presidential] election."

"If that's the price I have to pay," Johnson said, "I'll pay it gladly."

Which was not strictly true—Johnson never found anything gladdening about political defeat. But it says much about his commitment to doing the right thing that he was willing even to entertain the possibility of sacrificing the presidency itself for the cause of a single bill.

He tasked Senator Hubert Humphrey of Minnesota with a great deal of management of the legislation. The Republican minority leader, Everett Dirksen of Illinois, was a key player. "Now you know that this bill can't pass unless you get Ev Dirksen," Johnson told Humphrey. "You and I are going to get him. You make up your mind now that you've got to spend time with Ev Dirksen. You've got to let him have a piece of the action. He's got to look good all the time." The president was emphatic: "You get in there to see Dirksen! You drink with Dirksen! You talk to Dirksen! You listen to Dirksen!"

Johnson and his allies never gave up. "We were well organized, very well organized," Humphrey recalled. "We issued a daily newsletter, I think for the first time in history, that reported what had happened the day before and gave our supporters answers to the arguments of the opposition. But the main thing was that we had complete liaison at all times with the White House, with the president himself, and he answered every question and so far as I can remember did everything we asked—and usually a lot more, too."

The president did not believe such a large legislative and cultural undertaking could be done on a partisan line vote. "Unless we have the Republicans joining us and helping us," Johnson told Humphrey, "we'll have a mutiny in this goddamn country, so we've got to make this an **American** bill and not just a Democratic bill." He used similar language in talking to Dirksen. "We don't want this to be a Democratic bill," Johnson told the Republican from Illinois. "We want it to be an American bill. It is going to be worthy of the 'Land of Lincoln,' and the man from Illinois is going to pass the bill, and I'm going to see that he gets proper credit."

Finally, in the early summer of 1964, Johnson won the cloture vote to shut down the segregationist filibuster of the civil rights bill in the Senate. "It's just a miracle," Robert Kennedy remarked to Johnson, but it wasn't, really—it was the result of incredibly intense work by the president to force the triumph of hope and history over political calculation and fear. "There was a glorious feeling about it, there really was," recalled Ramsey Clark, a Kennedy-Johnson Justice Department official. "It just seemed like there was immense generosity in the American people, and goodwill, and they were going to do something about this great wrong." One Southern member of the House, Congressman Charles Weltner, a Democrat from Atlanta, changed his initial nay to a yea on the final bill. "I would urge that we at home now move on to the unfinished task of building a new South," Weltner said. "We must not forever be bound to another lost cause." President Johnson could not have put it better.

He signed the Civil Rights Act of 1964 in the East Room on Thursday, July 2. Two days later, on the Fourth, Robert Kennedy called Johnson at the president's ranch. "Well, listen, we had a good day!" Kennedy said.

"Good," Johnson said.

"I think that the most significant thing is that the Chamber of Commerce in Jackson, Mississippi, voted last night to abide by the law," Kennedy said. "And the vote was sixteen to one."

"Good," said Johnson. "That's wonderful!"

"Yeah, and then . . . Savannah, Atlanta, and all these cities went along. Birmingham, Montgomery, and a lot of the cities went along very, very well."

Johnson was pleased, but he knew, too, that it was a battle, not the war. "I want you to write me the goddamndest, toughest voting rights act that you can devise," Johnson told Nicholas Katzenbach of the Justice Department. He made the same point to Hubert Humphrey, who would soon become Johnson's vice president. "He used to tell me, 'Yes, yes, Hubert, I want all those other things—buses, restaurants, all of that—but the right to vote with no ifs, ands, or buts, that's the key," Humphrey recalled of Johnson. "'When the Negroes get that, they'll have every politician, north and south, east and west, kissing their ass, begging for their support.'"

On the 1964 bill, Johnson had risen to the occasion created by the voices of protest—had, in fact, surpassed the occasion. And he knew that he and his party would pay a political price. "It is an important gain," Johnson told Bill Moyers after signing the 1964 law, "but I think we just delivered the South to the Republican Party for a long time to come."

In the hour of victory—he had done something of a scale no president since Lincoln had seriously attempted to do—Johnson suffered a fairly common fate: gloom amid the grandeur of achievement. ("Nothing except a battle lost," Wellington once remarked, "can be half so melancholy as a battle won.") He mused for a time about bowing out of the 1964 presidential campaign and retiring to Texas. "You are as brave a man as Harry Truman—or FDR—or Lincoln,"

Mrs. Johnson, addressing her husband as "**Beloved**," wrote him in this period. "You have been strong, patient, determined beyond any words of mine to express. I honor you for it. So does most of the country. To step out now would be wrong for your country, and I can see nothing but a lonely wasteland for your future."

Johnson remained in the fight. The presidency seemed to be everything (or close to it) to him, and he believed it could be everything (or close to it) for the nation as well. In the first week of June 1963, in a recorded telephone call with Kennedy counsel and speechwriter Theodore C. Sorensen, Johnson, then the vice president, had pressed Sorensen on the need for President Kennedy to make an explicit statement of support for civil rights—ideally in the South. Kennedy, Johnson told Sorensen, should say something like this:

> We're all Americans. We got a Golden Rule, "Do unto others as you would have them do unto you." Now I'm leader of this country. When I order men into battle I order the men without regard to color. They carry our flag into foxholes. The Negro can do that, the Mexican can do it, others can do it. We've got to do the same thing when we drive down the highway at places they eat. I'm going to

have to ask you all to do this thing. I'm going to have to ask the Congress to say that we'll all be treated without regard to our race.

Johnson said that he was certain such candor would be worth it. "I believe that he'd run some of the demagogues right in the hole," Johnson said of Kennedy. The key thing, LBJ believed, was to make the moral case for racial justice so self-evident that the country could not help but agree. "Then a man is put in the position almost where he's a bigot to be against the president," Johnson told Sorensen. "This aura, this thing, this halo around the President, everybody wants to believe in the President and the Commander in Chief. . . . The good people, the church people, I think have to come around to him, not the majority of them maybe, but a good many of them over the country. . . . I'm telling you they'd be out there by the hundreds of thousands."

Major civil rights progress was possible, Johnson said, and only the president could successfully press the message. "I think the presidency can get it for him," LBJ said, still referring to Kennedy. "I have spoken from Milwaukee to Chicago to New York to Los Angeles to Illinois last night, and Gettysburg and Dallas, and Johnson City, Texas, and I think that I know one thing, that the Negroes are tired of this patient stuff and tired of this piecemeal stuff and what they want more than anything else is not an executive order or legislation, they want a moral commitment that he's behind them."

Proud of his own remarks at Gettysburg, where he had spoken out in favor of civil rights the week before, on Memorial Day, the vice president recalled other encouraging moments on the road. "I've been in North Carolina this year. . . . I've been into Florida," Johnson said. "Neither place would they allow Negroes to come. I said, 'I'm going to come and I'm going to talk about their constitutional rights and I want them on the platform with me, and if you don't let them I'm not coming, period.' By God, they put them on both places, right on the platform and . . . eating with us."

Johnson was thinking about the uses of TR's "bully pulpit," returning to his argument for presidential leadership:

> The President is the cannon. You let him be on all the TV networks just speaking from his conscience, not at a rally in Harlem, but at a place in Mississippi, or Texas or Louisiana and just have the honor guard there with a few Negroes in it. Then let him reach over and point and say, "I have to order these boys into battle, in the foxholes carrying that flag. I

don't ask them what their name is, whether it's Gomez or Smith, or what color they got, what religion. If I can order them into battle I've got to make it possible for them to eat and sleep in this country." Then . . . everybody . . . goes home and asks his wife, "What's wrong with this?" and they go to searching their conscience. Every preacher starts preaching about it. We ought to recognize that and [keep] them busy.

In the 1964 general election campaign against Republican nominee Barry Goldwater, the conservative senator from Arizona, LBJ got the chance to act on the advice he had given Sorensen. In October, the president was due in New Orleans. His aide Bill Moyers passed along some advice by wire: "Several people in New Orleans, including our advance men, feel the President should not refer to 'civil rights.'" The preferred term, Johnson was told, was "constitutional rights."

The president had other ideas. At an evening banquet at the Jung Hotel in New Orleans, Johnson said, "If we are to heal our history and make this Nation whole, prosperity must know no Mason-Dixon line and opportunity must know no color line." He called for unity against the forces of fear. "Now, the people that would use us and destroy us first divide us. . . . If they divide us, they can make some hay. And all these years they have kept their foot on our necks by appealing to our animosities, and dividing us."

Now was the time, the president said, to rise above racism. "Whatever your views are, we have a Constitution and we have a Bill of Rights, and we have the law of the land, and two-thirds of the Democrats in the Senate voted for [the Civil Rights Bill of 1964] and three-fourths of the Republicans," Johnson said. "I signed it, and I am going to enforce it, and I am going to observe it, and I think any man that is worthy of the high office of President is going to do the same thing. . . . I am not going to let them build up the hate and try to buy my people by appealing to their prejudice."

In his memoirs, Johnson recalled that the "applause was less than overwhelming. But I was in it, and I had to continue. I wanted the whole nation to know how profoundly animosity and hatred waste the common effort and dissipate the common energy." He could, he recalled, "only say what I deeply believed. I spoke off the cuff and from the heart."

An old Democratic senator from the South, Johnson told the New Orleans audience, had been chatting one evening with Sam Rayburn, then a young congressman from Texas. (Though

Johnson did not name him in the speech, he was referring to Senator Joe Bailey, Sr., who was raised in Mississippi and represented Texas in the House and in the Senate.) "He was talking about how we had been at the mercy of certain economic interests, and how they had exploited us," Johnson recalled. And he said, "Sammy, . . . I would like to go back down there and make them one more Democratic speech. I just feel like I have one in me. The poor old State, they haven't heard a Democratic speech in 30 years. All they ever hear at election time is **Nigra, Nigra, Nigra!**"

The crowd was shocked—and then rose to give the president a prolonged ovation. "Many of his most acerbic critics have affirmed that this was Johnson's finest hour," the historian William E. Leuchtenburg wrote. "There was no way a northerner could have delivered that speech and had it carry the same meaning." Johnson had done what he had come to do. Determined to preach the gospel of inclusion in the segregated South, he had done so, he recalled, "not in New York or Chicago or Los Angeles, but in New Orleans—near home, in my own backyard."

In November LBJ won a full presidential term in his own right with 61.1 percent of the popular vote in a forty-four-state landslide; Goldwater took just six states. (Though, with the exception of Arizona, Goldwater's victories all came in the old Confederacy and included Louisiana, where Johnson had made his impassioned plea for civil rights.)

No matter the margin, Johnson could not remain still. "I've just been elected and right now we'll have a honeymoon with Congress," the president told his staff. "But after I make my recommendations, I'm going to start to lose the power and authority I have. . . . Every day that I'm in office and every day I push my program, I'll be losing part of my ability to be influential, because that's in the nature of what the President does. He uses up capital. Something is going to come up . . . something like the Vietnam War or something else where I will begin to lose all that I have now. So I want you guys to get off your asses and do everything possible to get everything in my program passed as soon as possible, before the aura and the halo that surround me disappear."

Just as he had wooed Dirksen the previous year, Johnson reached out to Congressman Gerald Ford of Michigan, the new House Republican leader. "I don't want to start out fighting with you, because I'm not running for re-election [a debatable proposition in 1965]," Johnson told Ford. "I'm just trying to make a good president and I want you to help me. I thought you could support me when you thought it was right and be proud of it."

King marked his thirty-sixth birthday on Friday, January 15, 1965, and the president of the United States called to wish him the best. Voting rights, which were routinely denied to blacks in the South, were top of mind for Johnson. "There is not going to be anything, Doctor, as effective as all [black citizens] voting," Johnson told King. "That will give you a message that all the eloquence in the world won't bring," for votes meant the powerful—and a candidate aspiring to power—"will be coming to you then, instead of you calling him."

King and his colleagues in the movement understood, and they had launched a voting-rights drive in Alabama in the first days of 1965. The flashpoint: Selma, Alabama, the seat of Dallas County. On Sunday, March 7, 1965, a voting-rights march from Selma to Montgomery had barely begun when Alabama state troopers charged a line of nonviolent demonstrators. Trapped between asphalt and his uniformed attackers at the foot of the Edmund Pettus Bridge, inhaling tear gas and reeling from two billy-club blows to his head, John Lewis, then twenty-five-years old, felt everything dimming. He could hear screams and racial slurs and the clop-clop-clop of the troopers' horses. His skull fractured, his vision blurred, Lewis believed the end had come. "People are going to die here," he said to himself. "I'm going to die here." Yet for Lewis there was, strangely, no sense of panic, no gasping, no thrashing, no fear. He was at peace.

The world around him on that day, though, was at war, and the television cameras were whirring. Images of the Alabama troopers' attack on Lewis and his fellow marchers ran that evening; ABC broke into the network broadcast premiere of **Judgment at Nuremberg** to show the footage. What had begun as an ordinary day in a small Southern city was soon to be known as Bloody Sunday, and the scene at the bridge became that rarest of things: a crossroads in the long story of civilization.

Lewis's was a vision of nonviolent social change that has more in common with the martyrs of old than with the politics of a given hour. "At the moment when I was hit on the bridge and began to fall," Lewis recalled, "I really thought it was my last protest, my last march. I thought I saw death, and I thought, 'It's okay, it's all right—I am doing what I am supposed to do.'" Which was to dramatize the injustice of segregation and to call white America to redemption—not through violence but through witness.

Born in 1940 to sharecropper parents, Lewis overcame a childhood stutter by preaching to chickens on the family farm in Pike County, Alabama. After the Montgomery bus boycott catapulted King to fame, Lewis sought out the emerging civil rights icon, became chairman of the Student Nonviolent Coordinating Committee, and began a fabled life in the movement. Lewis was beaten and arrested across the South, including on the epochal Freedom Rides; spoke at the March on Washington in 1963; and was leading the Selma-to-Montgomery voting-rights effort when he and Hosea Williams crested the Pettus Bridge and spotted the line of troopers on that March Sunday.

Lewis had prepared to be arrested. In his backpack he carried two books, an apple and an orange, and a toothbrush and toothpaste. Then he heard the commander's order: "Troopers, advance!" He has always remembered the enormity, the totality, of the reaction of his attackers: "The troopers and possemen swept forward as one, like a human wave, a blur of blue shirts and billy clubs and bullwhips," Lewis wrote in his affecting memoir of the movement, **Walking with the Wind.** "We had no chance to turn and retreat." The pain was to be endured. There was no help for it.

Lewis made it back to Brown Chapel AME,

the Selma church that served as the headquarters for the march, and was eventually persuaded to go to a local emergency room. He still remembers the ambient smell of tear gas from the clothes of the victims seeking medical attention.

For Lewis, the civil rights struggle always centered on whether the best of the American soul (the grace and the love, the godliness and the generosity) could finally win out over the worst (the racism and the hatred, the fear and the cruelty). In the end, after the marches and the beatings and the riots, the light has largely triumphed over the dark. "I always felt growing up that in the South there was evil but also good—so much good," Lewis said. "We are still in the process of becoming. I am very, very hopeful about the American South—I believe that we will lead America to what Dr. King called 'the beloved community.' I travel all the time, but when I come back to the South, I see such progress. In a real sense a great deal of the South has been redeemed. People feel freer, more complete, more whole, because of what happened in the movement."

He is a preacher still, one whose voice, trained so long ago in the farmyard, continues to captivate. "The march of 1965 injected something very special into the soul and the heart and the

Sunday, March 7, 1965, would become known as
"Bloody Sunday" after Alabama authorities attacked
nonviolent voting-rights marchers.

veins of America," Lewis said. "It said, in effect, that we must humanize our social and political and economic structure. When people
saw what happened on that bridge, there was a
sense of revulsion all over America."

Revulsion, then redemption: "In the final analysis, we are one people, one family, one house—
not just the house of black and white, but the
house of the South, the house of America," Lewis
said. "We can move ahead, we can move forward,
we can create a multiracial community, a truly
democratic society. I think we're on our way there.
There may be some setbacks. But we are going to

get there. We have to be hopeful. Never give up, never give in, keep moving on."

As images from the beatings at Selma spread around the nation, Johnson knew he needed to act. But he was careful. To lash out at Governor Wallace and the power structure in Alabama too hard might create more problems than it solved. "If I just send in federal troops with their big black boots, it will look like Reconstruction all over again," Johnson said privately. "I will lose every moderate, not just in Alabama but all over the South. Most southern people don't like this violence. They know deep in their hearts that things are going to change. . . . But not if it looks like the Civil War all over again!"

Working through his friend Buford Ellington, a once and future Tennessee governor, Johnson got Wallace to agree to come to the White House for a meeting. It was a classic LBJ encounter. The president seated Wallace on a couch in the Oval Office and then positioned himself in a taller rocking chair, dominating the smaller man. "I kept my eyes directly on the Governor's face the entire time," Johnson recalled. "I saw a nervous, aggressive man; a rough, shrewd politician who had managed to touch the deepest chords of pride as well as prejudice among his people."

"Segregation forever!" Governor George Wallace declared in his inaugural address in January 1963. That June he made a show of standing in the door of the University of Alabama to prevent its integration—but failed.

Wallace, the looming Johnson said, could take care of all this trouble in a heartbeat. "Why don't you just desegregate all your schools?" Johnson asked. "You and I go out there in front of those television cameras right now, and you announce you've decided to desegregate every school in Alabama."

"Oh, Mr. President, I can't do that," Wallace said. "You know, the schools have got school boards. They're locally run. I haven't got the political power to do that."

"Don't you shit me, George Wallace," Johnson said. Later, in the meeting, the president pressed a larger question.

"George, why are you doing this?" Johnson asked. "You came into office a liberal—you spent all your life trying to do things for the poor. Now, why are you working on this? Why are you off on this Negro thing? You ought to be down there calling for help for Aunt Susie in the nursing home."

He described the Great Society—the broad Johnson program on healthcare, education, and poverty. Everything seemed possible. Why not get on board?

"Now, listen, George, don't think about 1968," Johnson said. "Think about 1988. You and me, we'll be dead and gone then, George. . . . What do you want left after you, when you die? Do you want a great big marble monument that reads, 'George Wallace—He Built.' Or do you want a little piece of scrawny pine board lying across that harsh caliche soil that reads, 'George Wallace—He Hated.'"

Wallace surrendered. Under pressure from the president, the governor consented to maintain order when the march resumed. "Hell, if I'd stayed in there much longer," Wallace remarked, "he'd have had me coming out for civil rights." The marchers would be protected. The president of the United States had prevailed.

The meeting with Wallace was held at midday on Saturday, March 13, 1965. Two days later, on the evening of Monday, March 15, Lyndon Johnson entered the chamber of the House of Representatives with a purposeful stride. He did not pause to shake many hands as he walked to the well; he had work to do. Standing at the rostrum with Vice President Humphrey and Speaker of the House John McCormack behind him, the president opened a folder—the address had been written, on deadline, by Richard Goodwin—and began to speak. He did so slowly. Johnson's public cadences could be unctuous, even ponderous, as he sought to infuse his public rhetoric with solemnity. Tonight, the tone was just right. He seemed, for once for a public man, free from political calculation or pragmatic consideration. "I speak tonight for the dignity of man and the destiny of democracy," Johnson said. "I urge every member of both parties, Americans of all religions and of all colors, from every section of this country, to join me in that cause." He went on:

> At times history and fate meet at a single time in a single place to shape a turning point in man's unending search for freedom. So it was at Lexington and

Concord. So it was a century ago at Appomattox. So it was last week in Selma, Alabama. . . .

In our time we have come to live with moments of great crisis. Our lives have been marked with debate about great issues; issues of war and peace, issues of prosperity and depression. But rarely in any time does an issue lay bare the secret heart of America itself. Rarely are we met with a challenge, not to our growth or abundance, our welfare or our security, but rather to the values and the purposes and the meaning of our beloved Nation.

The issue of equal rights for American Negroes is such an issue. And should we defeat every enemy, should we double our wealth and conquer the stars, and still be unequal to this issue, then we will have failed as a people and as a nation.

For with a country as with a person, "What is a man profited, if he shall gain the whole world, and lose his own soul?"

Here, for the first time, the lawmakers and guests were moved from reverie to applause. The evocation of scripture—Johnson was quoting the words of Jesus from the Gospel of St. Mark—resonated. The president continued:

There is no Negro problem. There is no Southern problem. There is no Northern problem. There is only an American problem. And we are met here tonight as Americans—not as Democrats or Republicans—we are met here as Americans to solve that problem.

This was the first nation in the history of the world to be founded with a purpose. The great phrases of that purpose still sound in every American heart, North and South: "All men are created equal"—"government by consent of the governed"—"give me liberty or give me death." Well, those are not just clever words, or those are not just empty theories. . . .

Many of the issues of civil rights are very complex and most difficult. But about this there can and should be no argument. Every American citizen must have an equal right to vote. . . .

Yet the harsh fact is that in many places in this country men and women are kept from voting simply because they are Negroes.

Every device of which human ingenuity is capable has been used to deny this right. The Negro citizen may go to register only to be told that the day is wrong, or the hour is late, or the official in charge is absent. And if he persists, and if he manages to present himself to the registrar, he may be disqualified because he did not spell out his middle name or because he abbreviated a word on the application.

And if he manages to fill out an application he is given a test. The registrar is the sole judge of whether he passes this test. He may be asked to recite the entire Constitution, or explain the most complex provisions of State law. And even a college degree cannot be used to prove that he can read and write.

For the fact is that the only way to pass these barriers is to show a white skin. . . .

What happened in Selma is part of a far larger movement which reaches into every section and State of America. It is the effort of American Negroes to secure for themselves the full blessings of American life.

Their cause must be our cause too. Because it is not just Negroes, but really it is all of us, who must overcome the crippling legacy of bigotry and injustice.

And we shall overcome.

On the night of the speech to Congress, King called Johnson, who was back in the White House. "It is ironic, Mr. President," King said, "that after a century, a southern white President would help lead the way toward the salvation of the Negro."

"Thank you, Reverend," Johnson said. "You're the leader who is making it all possible. I'm just following along trying to do what's right."

"It is difficult to fight for freedom," Johnson said as he signed the Voting Rights Act of 1965 in August. "But I also know how difficult it can be to bend long years of habit and custom to grant it. There is no room for injustice anywhere in the American mansion. But there is always room for understanding toward those who see the old ways crumbling. And to them today I say simply this: It must come. It is right that it should come."

An echo of Lincoln, perhaps inadvertent but nonetheless telling. Lincoln had spoken of the tragedy of the Civil War ("And the war came"). Johnson now spoke of progress, of a brighter day ("It must come").

No one in the loop—including, almost surely, the man himself—knew whether he'd really do it. On Sunday, March 31, 1968, President Johnson was scheduled to address the nation about the Vietnam War at 9 P.M. He had a draft of a short section for the end of the speech announcing that he would not seek reelection in November. The president had talked about it with family and a few advisers, but the circle of

trust was small after more than four years of tumult and war, and Johnson wanted to keep his
options open.

At one point that Sunday, Johnson stopped in
his aide Marvin Watson's office to talk about the
race with Terry Sanford, the former North Carolina governor who had agreed to manage the
1968 campaign. "After spending all day at the
White House," Johnson adviser John P. Roche
recalled, "Terry Sanford left for the airport still
under the impression that he was the campaign
manager." Only a few hours later, on television,
Johnson withdrew, solemnly drawling, "I shall
not seek, and I will not accept, the nomination
of my party for another term as your President."
Roche couldn't believe it. "I had already put an
LBJ '68 bumper sticker on my car," he said, "and
I was wearing an LBJ '68 button. We were left
with 15,000 of the goddamn things."

The watershed of 1968 was that kind of year:
one of surprises and reversals, of blasted hopes
and rising fears, of scuttled plans and unexpected
new realities. The year began with Tet and cas-
caded into chaos: the deaths of King and of
Robert Kennedy, the riots that engulfed many
American cities, the calamitous Democratic National Convention in Chicago, and finally, wea-
rily, the election of Richard Nixon as the nation's
thirty-seventh president. More than half a mil-

lion U.S. troops were in Vietnam, and combat deaths occurred at a rate of about 46 U.S. troops a day, for a total of 16,899 that year. It was a period of disorienting violence, of disorder, of loss, of pervasive tragedy.

The setting was splendid, the congregation rapt, the preacher at ease. On the morning of the same day Johnson made his evening announcement about withdrawing from the 1968 campaign, Martin Luther King was in Washington to offer a Lenten sermon at the National Cathedral. Easter was two weeks away, but King's mind was more on the world beyond the cathedral's splendid stained glass than it was on the details of the Christian calendar. Standing in the ornate Canterbury pulpit, gazing out across the sprawling nave, King summoned his listeners to the hard work of the Gospel.

"We are tied together in the single garment of destiny, caught in an inescapable network of mutuality," King said. "And whatever affects one directly affects all indirectly. For some strange reason I can never be what I ought to be until you are what you ought to be. And you can never be what you ought to be until I am what I ought to be. This is the way God's universe is made; this is the way it is structured."

He would be dead before the week was out.

"Every man who occupies the position," LBJ said
of the presidency, "has to strain to the utmost
of his ability to fill it."

History was moving quickly as King preached
amid the hymns and the psalms of the Episcopal
liturgy. In the shadow of the hilltop cathedral,
Johnson was preparing for his evening address
to the nation. And by the time Sunday worship-
pers gathered again in the sacred space of the
National Cathedral, King would be martyred by
an assassin's bullet outside Room 306 at the Lorraine Motel in Memphis.

King's earthly journey thus ended as his public
life had begun back in Montgomery—at the uneasy but essential intersection of faith, politics,

"We are tied together in the single garment of destiny," King would preach around the country, "caught in an inescapable network of mutuality."

and history. His was a life lived between different, though sometimes overlapping, worlds: of black and white, of good and evil, of the kingdom of men and the kingdom of heaven. Buffeted by the demands of the present, King bore witness to a message that was, in Saint Augustine's phrase, "ever ancient, ever new": an insistence that the testimony of the prophets and the example of Christ could march from the past into what King called "the fierce urgency of now" in order to liberate the future.

King was not perfect, but then no man is. To

know him is to know American history. From the bus boycott in Montgomery to the show-downs in Birmingham; from the "I Have a Dream" speech to the struggle for voting rights in Selma; from his antipoverty Poor People's Campaign to his opposition to the Vietnam War, King spoke with the voice of a prophet, urging a nation to repent and return to righteousness.

The movement was about much more than King, but it's a recurrent fact of history that human beings seek apostles who embody widely shared creeds. And in the battle against Jim Crow and for economic justice in the 1950s and '60s, King was that apostle, and he will be a source of fascination and veneration as long as the American story is told.

In that last Sunday sermon in Washington in 1968, King spoke of America, and of her obligations. To whom much is given, the scriptures tell us, much is expected—of individuals and of nations. "One day we will have to stand before the God of history and we will talk in terms of things we've done," King preached. "Yes, we will be able to say we built gargantuan bridges to span the seas, we built gigantic buildings to kiss the skies. Yes, we made our submarines to penetrate oceanic depths. We brought into being many other things with our scientific and technological power."

It was a message that united politics and faith. King continued: "It seems that I can hear the God of history saying, 'That was not enough! But I was hungry, and ye fed me not. I was naked, and ye clothed me not. I was devoid of a decent sanitary house to live in, and ye provided no shelter for me. And consequently, you cannot enter the kingdom of greatness. If ye do it unto the least of these, my brethren, ye do it unto me.' That's the question facing America today."

By Thursday evening King was dead. When Johnson learned of King's assassination, he telephoned Coretta Scott King and appealed to the country for calm. The next day, Friday, April 5, the president attended a memorial service for the slain King at the National Cathedral. On returning to the White House, Johnson announced a national day of mourning. "The dream of Dr. Martin Luther King, Jr.," the president said, "has not died with him."

On the road in Indianapolis on the evening King was shot, Robert Kennedy, who was seeking the Democratic presidential nomination, learned about the assassination from R. W. Apple, Jr., of **The New York Times**. Wearing an overcoat that had belonged to his brother Jack,

RFK broke the news to an inner-city crowd. "What we need in the United States," he said, "is not division; what we need in the United States is not hatred; what we need in the United States is not violence and lawlessness; but is love and wisdom and compassion toward one another, and a feeling of justice toward those who still suffer within our country, whether they be white or whether they be black."

Even then the fates were not yet satisfied. In April, Jacqueline Kennedy had shared a premonition of disaster. "Do you know what I think will happen to Bobby?" she asked Arthur Schlesinger, Jr. "The same thing that happened to Jack. . . . There is so much hatred in this country." She was proved correct in June, when RFK was gunned down in the Ambassador Hotel in Los Angeles after winning the California primary. Back in the ballroom, a woman screamed, "No, God, no. It's happened again."

The fear that the world was out of balance helped Richard Nixon, who had only narrowly lost to John F. Kennedy eight years earlier, prevail, also narrowly, in November against Hubert Humphrey. The dynamics of the '68 campaign resonate still: Nixon—advised, among others, by Roger Ailes, who would go on to found the Fox News Channel—campaigned on a cultural populism, arguing that elites and implying that

minorities were undercutting American greatness. That November, running on a third-party
ticket, George Wallace carried 13.5 percent of the
popular vote nationally and won five states: Alabama, Louisiana, Georgia, Arkansas, and Mississippi, giving him forty-six electoral votes. It was
not a bad starting point for a subsequent populist
candidate who would tell voters that walls and
tariffs would bring back the America they thought
they had once known.

At noon on Monday, January 20, 1969,
Richard Nixon stood on the East Portico of
the Capitol to take the oath of office as the nation's thirty-seventh president. To the side, wea-
ried by an inconclusive war in Southeast Asia
and exhausted from the toil of seeking to build
a Great Society at home, Lyndon Johnson found
his mind ranging widely. "The magnitude of the
job dwarfs every man who aspires to it," Johnson recalled in his memoirs. "Every man who
occupies the position has to strain to the utmost
of his ability to fill it. I believe that every man
who ever occupied it, within his inner self, was
humble enough to realize that no living mortal
has ever possessed all the required qualifications."

Johnson had done the best he could, he recalled, the very best. "Scholars have been defin-

ing and refining the role of the President for almost two centuries," he recalled. "At the core of all those definitions one basic tenet remains: The job of the President is to set priorities for the nation, and he must set them according to his own judgment and his own conscience. . . . If the Presidency can be said to have been employed and to have been enjoyed, I had employed it to the utmost, and I had enjoyed it to the limit."

Though much of his presidency was consumed by the war in Vietnam, Johnson's domestic legacy is enormous. In addition to Medicare and the other legislation of the Great Society, he signed the landmark Immigration and Nationality Act on Liberty Island in 1965, eliminating the national-origins quotas in force since the early 1920s and opening the doors of the country more widely. And a single word in the 1964 Civil Rights Act—"sex"—included gender in the bill's protections. The addition of women to the legislation helped give the rising women's movement an important legislative victory as they fought for equality.

On the House floor on Wednesday, May 21, 1969, Representative Shirley Chisholm of New York spoke out in the spirit of the time to introduce the Equal Rights Amendment. (Which was first introduced in 1923, and would fail to be enacted despite years of activism.) "Mr. Speaker, when a young woman graduates from college and starts looking for a job, she is likely to have a frustrating and even demeaning experience ahead of her," Chisholm said. "If she walks into an office for an interview, the first question she will be asked is, 'Do you type?'" Chisholm continued:

As a black person, I am no stranger to race prejudice. But the truth is that in the political world I have been far oftener discriminated against because I am a woman than because I am black.

Prejudice against blacks is becoming unacceptable although it will take years to eliminate it. But it is doomed because, slowly, white America is beginning to admit that it exists. Prejudice against women is still acceptable. There is very little understanding yet of the immorality involved in double pay scales and the classification of most of the better jobs as "for men only." . . .

What we need are laws to protect working people, to guarantee them fair pay, safe working conditions, protection against sickness and layoffs, and provision for dignified, comfortable retirement. Men and women need these things equally. That one sex needs protection more than the other is a male supremacist myth as ridiculous and unworthy of respect as the white supremacist myths that society is trying to cure itself of at this time.

Lyndon Johnson's last public appearance, in late 1972, very nearly didn't happen. The former president was scheduled to speak at a conference on civil rights on Tuesday, December 12, 1972, at the LBJ Presidential Library in Austin. The Hubert Humphreys were coming; so were the Earl Warrens. Congresswoman-elect Barbara Jordan of Houston was to be there, as was Congressman Henry Gonzalez of San Antonio, Vernon Jordan, and Julian Bond. Johnson was looking forward to it, but the night before the conference began, he was sick at his ranch sixty miles away in Stonewall. To make matters worse, a highly unusual winter storm had hit central Texas. The snow and the ice were so bad that the organizers in Austin were told the roads between Stonewall and Austin were impassable. "I was just heartsick at that," Harry Middleton, the director of the LBJ library, recalled.

But Johnson, predictably, wasn't interested in being told what couldn't be done. First, he overruled his doctors when they advised him that he was too ill to leave the ranch that morning. "For

Johnson," the journalist Hugh Sidey recalled, " the night was filled with pain and restlessness."

"I was determined that he wasn't going to attend that symposium, and the doctor insisted that he absolutely, positively could not go—but he went," Lady Bird said. "I now realize it was all right that he went, because he knew what he was spending and had a right to decide how he wanted to spend it." The willful former president, Sidey reported, "put on his dark-blue presidential suit and those flawlessly polished oxfords" and headed out into the stormy morning. Then, en route, Johnson grew frustrated with his driver and commandeered the wheel, pressing ahead through the snow and ice.

In his remarks at the library, Johnson—his hair longer now, his frame more stooped—spoke of how far the country had come, and how far it had to go. "The progress has been much too small," he said. "I'm kind of ashamed of myself that I had six years and couldn't do more. So let no one delude himself that his work is done. To be black or brown in a white society is not to stand on equal ground."

As Nick Kotz, who covered the event for **The Washington Post**, reported, two members of the audience jumped up to call for the conference to denounce President Nixon. Johnson returned to the podium and offered some final political counsel to the country. Here was the Johnson of old. "The fatigue of the night before seemed to drop away, the old adrenaline machine pumping back into action," Sidey wrote. "Going to the microphone with his hands molding the air, he delivered one of his sermons on brotherhood and reason."

Back at center stage, if only for a moment, Johnson said, "Let's try to get our folks reasoning together and reasoning with Congress and with the Cabinet! Reason with the leadership and with the President! . . . And you don't need to start off by saying he is terrible—because **he** doesn't think he's terrible. Start talking about how you believe that he wants to do what's right and how you believe **this** is right, and you'll be surprised how many who want to do what's right will try to help you."

It was a word of pragmatic hope from a man who had seen the best and the worst of a nation he knew was capable, however dark the hour, of doing the right thing. He had seen it. He had **done** it. And he died, three weeks into the new year, believing it could always be done again.

On Sunday, June 29, 1947, at the Lincoln Memorial,
Harry S. Truman became the first president to address a meeting
of the NAACP. "I'm everybody's President," he told one white
Southerner who challenged his civil rights program.

THE FIRST DUTY OF AN AMERICAN CITIZEN

||||||||||||||||||||||||||||||||||||||||||||||||||||||||

The people have often made mistakes, but given time
and the facts, they will make the corrections.
—HARRY S. TRUMAN

Begin with the little thing, and do not expect to
accomplish anything without an effort.
—THEODORE ROOSEVELT

Great leaders we have had, but we could not have had
great leaders unless they had a great people to follow.
You cannot be a great leader unless the people are great.
—ELEANOR ROOSEVELT

||||||||||||||||||||||||||||||||||||||||||||||||||||||||

HARRY TRUMAN KNEW there'd be hell
to pay, but he went ahead anyway. In the
first months of 1948 he dispatched his
ten-point civil rights program to Congress. It
was a revolutionary call for a new day of fairness
and equality, and the president framed his pro-
posals as part and parcel of what Truman called
"our American faith."

To be sure, like many of his countrymen, Truman was no saint on matters of race. Truman
used racial slurs in private, and in 1911, while

courting his future wife, Bess, he wrote her that he was "strongly of the opinion that negroes ought to be in Africa, yellow men in Asia and white men in Europe and America." A child of border state Missouri, he was the descendant of slave owners who loved Robert E. Lee and hated Abraham Lincoln. And after his White House years Truman at times sounded reactionary, dismissing the March on Washington as "silly" and speculating that demonstrations against Jim Crow were inspired by Communists.

But as president of the United States, he saw his duty whole. Truman's work on civil rights, including his focus on lynching and his decision to integrate the American military, was in part driven by his horror over brutal attacks like one in South Carolina, where a severe police beating to the face of a newly discharged black soldier had blinded the man. "My God!" Truman said. "I had no idea it was as terrible as that! We've got to do something!" In his public capacity he transcended the limitations of his personal background. "My forebears were Confederates. . . . But my very stomach turned over when I learned that Negro soldiers, just back from overseas, were being dumped out of Army trucks in Mississippi and being beaten," he told Democratic leaders. "Whatever my inclinations as a native of Missouri might have been, as President I know this is bad. I shall fight to end evils like this."

In his 1948 message on civil rights Truman was doing just that. "We believe that all men are created equal and that they have the right to equal justice under law," the president wrote to Congress. "We believe that all men have the right to freedom of thought and of expression and the right to worship as they please. We believe that all men are entitled to equal opportunities for jobs, for homes, for good health and for education. We believe that all men should have a voice in their government and that government should protect, not usurp, the rights of the people."

Hence the need for federal action to fulfill the nation's promise on voting, employment, housing, criminal justice, and public accommodations. Southerners, in particular, were aghast; the Speaker of the Mississippi House of Representatives, Walter Sillers, said Truman was proposing "damnable, communistic, unconstitutional, anti-American, anti-Southern legislation." At a White House luncheon for the executive committee of the Democratic National Committee, a committeewoman from Alabama, Mrs. Leonard Thomas, confronted the president.

"I want to take a message back to the South," Mrs. Thomas said to Truman. "Can I tell them you're not ramming miscegenation down our throats? That you're for all the people, not just the North?"

The president thought the moment right for a history lesson. Then and there, in front of the leaders of his party in a contentious time just ahead of a closely fought presidential election, Truman reached for American scripture—the Bill of Rights.

Taking a copy of the Constitution from his pocket, the president, in his flat Missouri accent, began to read. " 'Congress shall make no law respecting an establishment of religion, or prohibiting the free exercise thereof; or abridging the freedom of speech, or of the press; or the right of the people peaceably to assemble, and to petition the Government for a redress of grievances,' " Truman said, then moved on from amendment to amendment, enumerating the liberties of the people—**all** of the people. When he finished, he declared himself immovable on civil rights.

"I'm everybody's president," Truman told Mrs. Thomas. "I take back nothing of what I propose and make no excuses for it." A White House waiter, an African American, was said to have become so animated by the tense exchange that he inadvertently knocked a cup of coffee out of Truman's hands.

"Those—the Bill of Rights—applies to every-

body in this country," Truman said, still addressing his visitor from Alabama, and "don't you
ever forget it." Recalling the moment years later,
Truman laughed. "I was just thinking of that
old woman's face when I started reading her the
Bill of Rights," he said. "It was quite a sight. . . .
But you know something? It's not a bad idea to
read those ten amendments every once in a
while. Not enough people do, and that's one of
the reasons we're in the trouble we're in."

In his long retirement in Independence—he
lived for nearly twenty years after leaving the
White House—Truman often mused about history and the presidency. Dictating to his secretary or to his wife or daughter and in scribbled
notes to himself, the thirty-third president was
characteristically plainspoken. "You never can
tell what's going to happen to a man until he gets
to a place of responsibility," Truman observed.
"You just can't tell in advance, whether you're
talking about a general in the field in a military
situation or the manager of a large farm or a bank
officer or a president. . . . You've just got to pick
the man you **think** is best on the basis of his past
history and the views he expresses on present
events and situations, and then you sit around
and do a lot of hoping and if you're inclined that
way, a certain amount of praying."

You just can't tell. Sobering words, but we still have to try, or else the whole democratic enterprise becomes even less intelligible than it already is. History—which is all we have to go on—suggests that a president's vices and his virtues matter enormously, for politics is a human, not a clinical, undertaking. So, too, do the vices and virtues of the people at large, for leadership is the art of the possible, and possibility is determined by whether generosity can triumph over selfishness in the American soul.

It's easy to be cynical about, and dismissive of, such a view. But if natives and newcomers alike can live up to the American idea of inclusion, then our best instincts will carry the day against our worst. To think this angle of vision hokey fails to take the common sense of our history into account. As a matter of observable fact, the United States, through its sporadic adherence to its finest aspirations, is the most durable experiment in pluralistic republicanism the world has known. Other national revolutions have descended into dictatorship and persecution; ours has produced enviable, if fragile, democratic institutions.

In the main, the America of the twenty-first century is, for all its shortcomings, freer and more accepting than it has ever been. If that weren't the case, right-wing populist attacks on immigrants and the widening mainstream wouldn't be so ferocious. A tragic element of history is that every advance must contend with forces of reaction. In the years after Lincoln, the America that emancipated its enslaved population endured an uneven Reconstruction and a century of regional revanchism. Under Theodore Roosevelt and Woodrow Wilson, the America that was rapidly industrializing and embracing many progressive reforms was plagued by theories of racial superiority and fears of the "other" that kept us from acting on the implications of the promise of the country. In the age of Franklin Roosevelt and of Harry Truman, the America that rescued capitalism, redefined the role of the state to lift up the weakest among us, and defeated fascism fell victim to racial hysteria and interned innocent Americans of Japanese descent. Truman and Eisenhower played critical roles in building an America of broadening wealth, and there was the beginning of progress on civil rights, in roughly the same years the country was roiled by McCarthyism and right-wing conspiracy theories.

The only way to make sense of this eternal struggle is to understand that it is just that: an eternal struggle. And the only way to come to that understanding is by knowing the history that's shaped us. "The next generation never learns anything from the previous one until it's brought home with a hammer," Truman once said. "I've wondered why the next generation can't profit from the generation before but they never do until they get knocked in the head by experience."

So what can we, in our time, learn from the past, even while we're getting knocked in the head? That the perfect should not be the enemy of the good. That compromise is the oxygen of democracy. And that we learn the most from those who came before not by gazing up at them uncritically or down on them condescendingly but by looking them in the eye and taking their true measure as human beings, not as gods.

Which brings us to the moral utility of history. It is tempting to feel superior to the past. But as Arthur Schlesinger, Jr., once said, "Righteousness is easy, also cheap, in retrospect." When we condemn posterity for slavery, or for Native American removal, or for denying women their full role in the life of the nation, we ought to pause and think: What injustices are we perpetuating even now that will one day face the harshest of verdicts by those who come after us? One of the points of reflecting on the past is to prepare us for action in the present.

As Truman knew—and the visiting Southerner, to her discomfort, learned at that White House luncheon—the presidency offers possibilities for such action that are both dazzling and daunting. "The President," Woodrow Wilson wrote, "is at liberty, both in law and conscience, to be as big a man as he can." In an echo of that point, in his speech at American University in June 1963 proposing a ban on nuclear testing, JFK said, "Man can be as big as he wants."

Or as small. One risk we always face can grow out of the anger of crowds—literal and, in our own time, also virtual—of the alienated and the emboldened. In 1935, W.E.B. Du Bois plumbed the mind and motives of the Ku Klux Klan, and indeed of mobs and mass movements driven by fear in all times and at all places. "The method of force which hides itself in secrecy is a method as old as humanity," Du Bois wrote. "The kind of thing that men are afraid or ashamed to do openly, and by day, they accomplish secretly, masked, and at night. . . . How is it that men who want certain things done by brute force can so often depend upon the mob?"

The better presidents do not cater to such forces; they conquer them with a breadth of vision that speaks to the best parts of our soul. None of these men was without fault. For generations Democrats provided many of the most strident segregationists, particularly from the South, a political home, and for the past half century or so, too many Republicans have used coded racial appeals to win votes. Still, they—and we—have also had the ability to rise above their baser impulses.

A masterful performer, Ronald Reagan came to power during what his predecessor, Jimmy Carter, called a "crisis of confidence" in a country suffering from high inflation and interest rates at home and worries about weakness abroad. Reagan had spent his pre-political days as a radio sportscaster and as a movie actor and had a remarkable ability to capture great and elusive truths. In a 1985 speech honoring the memory of John F. Kennedy, Reagan let his vivid imagination take flight in describing life in the White House. "Sometimes I want to say to those who are still in school, and who sometimes think that history is a dry thing that lives in a book: Nothing is ever lost in that great house; some music plays on," Reagan said.

I've even been told that late at night when the clouds are still and the moon is high, you can just about hear the sound of certain memories brushing by. You can almost hear, if you listen close, the whir of a wheelchair rolling by and the sound of a voice calling out, "And another thing, Eleanor!" Turn down a hall and you hear the brisk strut of a

fellow saying, "Bully! Absolutely ripping!"
Walk softly now and you're drawn to the soft
notes of a piano and a brilliant gathering in
the East Room, where a crowd surrounds a
bright young president who is full of hope
and laughter. I don't know if this is true, but
it's a story I've been told. And it's not a bad
one, because it reminds us that history is a
living thing that never dies.

In his Farewell Address in January 1989, Reagan addressed himself to America's generosity of
spirit in his evocation of John Winthrop's "city
upon a hill"—an image, in a sign of some con-
sistency of thought among those who have led
the nation, that John Kennedy had cited in his
1961 speech to the Massachusetts legislature as
he prepared to leave for his inauguration in
Washington. "I've spoken of the shining city all
my political life," Reagan said, "but I don't know
if I ever quite communicated what I saw when I
said it." He went on:

> But in my mind it was a tall, proud city
> built on rocks stronger than oceans, wind-
> swept, God-blessed, and teeming with people
> of all kinds living in harmony and peace; a
> city with free ports that hummed with com-
> merce and creativity. And if there had to be

city walls, the walls had doors and the doors were open to anyone with the will and the heart to get here. That's how I saw it, and see it still. . . . And she's still a beacon, still a magnet for all who must have freedom, for all the pilgrims from all the lost places who are hurtling through the darkness, toward home.

In 1995, when Timothy McVeigh, darkly inspired by anti-Semitism, white nationalism, and antigovernment sentiment, bombed the federal building in Oklahoma City, killing 168, including 19 children in the facility's day-care center, leaders of both major parties said and did the right things. "Let us let our own children know that we will stand against the forces of fear," President Clinton told mourners in Oklahoma City. "When there is talk of hatred, let us stand up and talk against it. When there is talk of violence, let us stand up and talk against it. In the face of death, let us honor life. As St. Paul admonished us, Let us 'not be overcome by evil, but overcome evil with good.'"

In those terrible weeks, the National Rifle Association dispatched a fund-raising letter that targeted not the murderers of innocents but federal agents whom the gun lobby's leadership derided as "jackbooted thugs." Reading the missive, former president George H. W. Bush, a life member, resigned from the group. "To attack Secret Service agents or A.T.F. people or any government law enforcement people as 'wearing Nazi bucket helmets and black storm trooper uniforms' wanting to 'attack law abiding citizens' is a vicious slander on good people," Bush wrote, adding that "your broadside against Federal agents deeply offends my own sense of decency and honor; and it offends my concept of service to country." The forty-first president asked that his name be permanently removed from the rolls of the NRA.

Clinton and Bush: There, from two men of different generations, different philosophies, different temperaments, came unambiguous words of denunciation in a time of national crisis over hate and extremism. The same spirit animated George W. Bush when, six years later, he insisted that America's war on terror was not a war against all of Islam. "The terrorists are traitors to their own faith, trying, in effect, to hijack Islam itself," Bush 43 said. "The enemy of America is not our many Muslim friends; it is not our many Arab friends. Our enemy is a radical network of terrorists, and every government that supports them."

Three days after the terrorist attacks of Tuesday, September 11, 2001, with thousands dead and many missing, never to be found, Bush climbed the steps of the lectern at Washington's

National Cathedral to speak of America's resolve. But he was pastoral, too, acknowledging
the loss of the hour and summoning the forces
of love. "Our purpose as a nation is firm," Bush
said, continuing:

> Yet, our wounds as a people are recent and
> unhealed and lead us to pray. In many of our
> prayers this week, there is a searching and an
> honesty. At St. Patrick's Cathedral in New
> York on Tuesday, a woman said, "I prayed to
> God to give us a sign that He is still here." . . .
> There are prayers that help us last through
> the day or endure the night. There are prayers
> of friends and strangers that give us strength
> for the journey. And there are prayers that
> yield our will to a will greater than our own.

A pause, and then Bush said: "This world He
created is of moral design. Grief and tragedy and
hatred are only for a time. Goodness, remem-
brance, and love have no end. And the Lord of
life holds all who die and all who mourn."

In Charleston, South Carolina, in 2015, late in
the presidency of Barack Obama, a young white
supremacist armed with a .45-caliber Glock pis-
tol murdered nine innocents during a Bible study
group at the Emanuel African Methodist Episcopal Church. As the president eulogized one of

For Robert and John Kennedy, both martyred in the turbulent 1960s, politics was at once the most pragmatic and idealistic of undertakings. Here, a photographer captured an image of the brothers outside the Oval Office on the eve of the Cuban Missile Crisis in October 1962.

the victims, the Reverend Clementa Pinckney, Obama spoke of hope and hate and history.

"According to the Christian tradition, grace is not earned," the president said. "Grace is not merited. It's not something we deserve. Rather, grace is the free and benevolent favor of God as manifested in the salvation of sinners and the bestowal of blessings. Grace—as a nation, out of this terrible tragedy, God has visited grace upon us for he has allowed us to see where we've been blind. He has given us the chance, where we've been lost, to find our best selves."

Action had to follow words. "For too long, we've been blind to the way past injustices continue to shape the present," Obama said. "Perhaps we see that now. Perhaps this tragedy causes us to ask some tough questions about how we can permit so many of our children to languish in poverty or attend dilapidated schools or grow up without prospects for a job or for a career. Perhaps it causes us to examine what we're doing to cause some of our children to hate."

Suddenly, unexpectedly, Obama began to sing the old hymn:

Amazing grace! How sweet the sound,
That saved a wretch; like me!
I once was lost, but now am found,
Was blind, but now I see.

Progress—redemption, even—was possible in this hour of grief. "We may not have earned it, this grace, with our rancor and complacency and short-sightedness and fear of each other, but we got it all the same," Obama said. "He gave it to us anyway. He's once more given us grace. But it is up to us now to make the most of it, to receive it with gratitude and to prove ourselves worthy of this gift."

Even by the standards of the presidency, the

day Obama spoke in Charleston was a full one. That morning, before he had gone to South Carolina, he had received word that the Supreme Court had ruled in favor of same-sex marriage. "Our nation was founded on a bedrock principle that we are all created equal," Obama said in the Rose Garden. "The project of each generation is to bridge the meaning of those founding words with the realities of changing times—a never-ending quest to ensure those words ring true for every single American. Progress on this journey often comes in small increments, sometimes two steps forward, one step back, propelled by the persistent effort of dedicated citizens. And then sometimes, there are days like this when that slow, steady effort is rewarded with justice that arrives like a thunderbolt." The ruling, he said, "reaffirmed that all Americans are entitled to the equal protection of the law . . . regardless of who they are or who they love."

It was a watershed. "I know change for many of our LGBT brothers and sisters must have seemed so slow for so long," Obama said, adding:

But compared to so many other issues, America's shift has been so quick. I know that Americans of goodwill continue to hold a wide range of views on this issue. Opposition in some cases has been based on sincere and deeply held beliefs. All of us who welcome today's news should be mindful of that fact; recognize different viewpoints; revere our deep commitment to religious freedom. But today should also give us hope that on the many issues with which we grapple, often painfully, real change is possible. Shifts in hearts and minds is possible.

In his postpresidential notes, Harry Truman was candid about the tricky nature of democracy. Yes, much of the nation's fate lies in the hands of the president, but the voters have the ultimate authority. "The country has to awaken every now and then to the fact that the people are responsible for the government they get," Truman wrote. "And when they elect a man to the presidency who doesn't take care of the job, they've got nobody to blame but themselves."

As usual, the old man was on to something. Truman had immense regard for FDR's longtime adviser Harry Hopkins, who also believed the followers mattered as much as the leader. "God damn it," Hopkins had told Robert Sherwood on the day of FDR's White House funeral, "now we've got to get to work on our own. This is where we've really got to begin. We've had it too easy all this time, because we knew he was there, and we had the privilege of being able to get to him. . . . Well—he isn't here now, and we've got to find a way to do things by ourselves."

Hopkins and Sherwood, though, were working in a national context of hope; FDR and Truman came out of the best of the American tradition of leadership. To those presidents the nation was rising, not falling. It was already great, and could be made greater.

In our own moment, fears of American decline are pervasive. But the imminence of chaos, of a nation torn asunder, of a country irretrievably lost is a long-standing political trope. "Commerce, luxury, and avarice have destroyed every republican government," John Adams wrote in 1808. "We mortals cannot work miracles; we struggle in vain against the . . . course of nature."

Every generation tends to think of itself as uniquely challenged and under siege. The questions of the present assume outsize and urgent importance, for they are, after all, the questions that shape and suffuse the lives of those living in the moment. Humankind seems to be forever coping with crisis. Strike the "seems": Humankind **is** forever coping with crisis, or believes it is, and will until what William Faulkner described as "the last red and dying evening."

We have managed, however, to survive the crises and vicissitudes of history. Our brightest hours are almost never as bright as we like to think; our glummest moments are rarely as irredeemable as they feel at the time. How, then, in an hour of anxiety about the future of the country, at a time when a president of the United States appears determined to undermine the rule of law, a free press, and the sense of hope essential to American life, can those with deep concerns about the nation's future enlist on the side of the angels?

Enter the Arena

The battle begins with political engagement itself. Theodore Roosevelt put it best: "The first duty of an American citizen, then, is that he shall work in politics; his second duty is that he shall do that work in a practical manner; and his third is that it shall be done in accord with the highest principles of honor and justice."

Those who disdain the arena are unilaterally disarming themselves in the great contests of the soul, for they are cutting themselves off, childishly, from what Oliver Wendell Holmes, Jr., called the "passion and action" of the age. Politicians will disappoint; that's inevitable. But they will also, from time to time, thrill. "Every man who has been in practical politics," TR remarked, "grows to realize that politicians, big and little, are no more all of them bad than they are all of them good." One need not become a candidate (though that's certainly an option worth considering) or a political addict hooked on every twist and every turn and every tweet. But the paying of attention, the expressing of opinion, and the casting of ballots are foundational to living up to the obligations of citizenship in a republic.

To believe something creates an obligation to make that belief known and to act upon it within the arena. Politicians are far more often mirrors of public sentiment than they are molders; that is the nature of things in a popular government and should be a source of hope for those who long for a change of presidents or of policy. In **The English Constitution**, Walter Bagehot defined public opinion as "the secret pervading disposition of society" that reveals itself in elections, and James Bryce, in **The American Commonwealth**, argued that "hereditary monarchs were strong because they reigned by a right of their own, not derived from the people. A President is strong for the exactly opposite reason, because his rights come straight from the people . . . Nowhere is the rule of public opinion so complete as in America, or so direct."

Skepticism about the incumbent authority of the moment is embedded in our character, for what was the American Revolution but one of history's largest and boldest acts of reform in the cause of progress? "The spirit of resistance to government is so valuable on certain occasions that I wish it to be always kept alive," Thomas Jefferson wrote Abigail Adams in the winter of 1787. "It will often be exercised when wrong, but better so than not to be exercised at all. I like a little rebellion now and then. It is like a storm in the Atmosphere." So long as the resistance was informed by fact and executed with integrity, Jefferson believed, all would be well.

Resist Tribalism

Engagement, especially at a time of heightened conflict, has its perils: Those motivated by what they see as extremism on the other side are likely to view politics not as a mediation of difference but as total warfare where no quarter can be given. The country works best, however, when we resist such tribal inclinations. "We know instinctively," Jane Addams wrote, "that if we grow contemptuous of our fellows and consciously limit our intercourse to certain kinds of people whom we have previously decided to respect, we not only tremendously circumscribe our range of life, but limit the scope of our ethics."

Ever practical, Eleanor Roosevelt offered a prescription to guard against tribal self-certitude. "It is not only important but mentally invigorating to discuss political matters with people whose opinions differ radically from one's own," she wrote. "For the same reason, I believe it is a sound idea to attend not only the meetings of one's own party but of the opposition. Find out what people are saying, what they are thinking, what they believe. This is an invaluable check on one's own ideas. . . . If we are to cope intelligently with a changing world, we must be flexible and willing to relinquish opinions that no longer have any bearing on existing conditions." If Mrs. Roosevelt were writing today, she might put it this way: Don't let any single cable network or Twitter feed tell you what to think.

Wisdom generally comes from a free exchange of ideas, and there can be no free exchange of ideas if everyone on your side already agrees with one another. "I have been fiercely partisan in politics and always militantly liberal," Harry Truman recalled. "I will be that way as long as I live. Yet I think we would lose something important to our political life if the conservatives were all in one party and the liberals all in the other. This would make us a nation divided either into two opposing and irreconcilable camps or into even smaller and more contentious groups."

RESPECT FACTS AND DEPLOY REASON

There is such a thing as discernible reality. Facts, as John Adams once said, are stubborn things, and yet too many Americans are locked into their particular vision of the world, choosing this view or that perspective based not on its grounding in fact but on whether it's a view or perspective endorsed by the leaders one follows. "The dictators of the world say that if you tell a lie often enough, why, people will believe it," Truman wrote. "Well, if you tell the truth often enough, they'll believe it and go along with you."

To reflexively resist one side or the other without weighing the merits of a given issue is all too common—and all too regrettable. By closing our minds to the even remote possibility that a political leader with whom we nearly always disagree might have a point about a particular matter is to preemptively surrender the capacity of the mind to shape our public lives. Of course, it may be that you believe, after consideration, that the other side is wrong—but at least take a minute to make sure. To expect to get everything you want simply because you want it is to invite frustration. Reform is slow work, and it is for neither the fainthearted nor the impatient.

FIND A CRITICAL BALANCE

"Wherever the people are well informed they can be trusted with their own government," Jefferson wrote in 1789, adding: "Whenever things get so far wrong as to attract their notice, they may be relied on to set them to rights." Being informed is more than knowing details and arguments. It also entails being humble enough to recognize that only on the rarest of occasions does any single camp have a monopoly on virtue or on wisdom.

American presidents are not mythic figures. They are human beings, with good days and bad days, flashes of genius and the occasional dumb idea, alternately articulate and tongue-tied. If we are sympathetic rather than blindly condemnatory or celebratory, we will, I believe, help create a more rational political climate. One evening in 1962, as part of a series of what the Kennedys called "Hickory Hill seminars" (they had started at RFK's house in McLean, Virginia) in which a small group of high-ranking officials would have dinner and listen to an informal lecture by a visiting scholar, the historian David Herbert Donald was chatting with President Kennedy and other guests in the Yellow Oval Room. The conversation turned to presidential rankings, and Kennedy burst out: "No one has a right to grade a President—even poor James Buchanan—who has not sat in his chair, examined the mail and information that came across his desk, and learned why he made his decisions."

Theodore H. White, the Time-Life writer who

helped create the modern genre of presidential campaign books in which the quest for the American presidency has Arthurian tones, once defined what he called "the politician's optic," in which the hostile language in any press story leaps off the page while the positive recedes. By the same token, even the slightest compliment to an opponent "swells to double-size capitals" in the politician's gaze. "This is an occupational disease of politicians," White wrote, "just as it is for authors and actors, who similarly live by public approval or distaste."

Fair enough, but this injunction of TR's remains resonant: "To announce that there must be no criticism of the president, or that we are to stand by the president, right or wrong, is not only unpatriotic and servile, but is morally treasonable to the American public." Even with their manifold failings, journalists who seek to report and to illuminate rather than to opine and to divide are critical to a democracy. "Publicity is the very soul of justice," the English philosopher Jeremy Bentham wrote. "It is the keenest spur to exertion, and the surest of all guards against impropriety. . . . Without publicity, all other checks are fruitless: in comparison with publicity, all other checks are of small account."

JFK, despite his defensiveness with Professor Donald about criticism of the presidents, understood this large truth. In a Christmastime 1962 "Conversation with the President" in the Oval Office with three television network interviewers, Kennedy acknowledged the importance of a free press:

> I think [the press] is invaluable, even though . . . it is never pleasant to be reading things that are not agreeable news. But I would say that it is an invaluable arm of the Presidency. . . . There is a terrific disadvantage [in] not having the abrasive quality of the press applied to you daily. . . . Even though we never like it, and even though we wish they didn't write it, and even though we disapprove, there isn't any doubt that we could not do the job at all in a free society without a very, very active press.

KEEP HISTORY IN MIND

A grasp of the past can be orienting. "When the mariner has been tossed for many days in thick weather, and on an unknown sea, he naturally avails himself of the first pause in the storm, the earliest glance of the sun, to take his latitude, and ascertain how far the elements have driven him from his true course," Senator Daniel Webster said in 1830. "Let us imitate this prudence, and before we float farther on the waves of this debate, refer to the point from which we departed, that we may at least be able to conjecture where we now are."

To remember Joe McCarthy, for instance, gives us a way to gauge demagoguery. Writing in 1959, five years after the senator's fall, Richard Rovere reflected on the meaning of McCarthy. "I cannot easily conceive of circumstances in which McCarthy, either faulted as he was or freed of his disabling weaknesses, could have become President of the United States or could have seized the reins of power on any terms," Rovere wrote. "To visualize him in the White House, one has, I think, to imagine a radical change in the national character and will and taste." There was, though, no guarantee against such a radical change. "But if I am right in thinking we have been, by and large, lucky," Rovere wrote, "there is no assurance that our luck will hold." And it didn't.

The past and the present tell us, too, that demagogues can only thrive when a substantial portion of the **demos**—the people—want him to. In **The American Commonwealth**, James Bryce warned of the dangers of a renegade president. Bryce's view was not that the individual himself, from the White House, could overthrow the Constitution. Disaster would come, Bryce believed, at the hands of a demagogic president with an enthusiastic public base. "A bold President who knew himself to be supported by a majority in the country, might be tempted to override the law, and deprive the minority of the protection which the law affords it," Bryce wrote. "He might be a tyrant, not against the masses, but with the masses." The cheering news is that hope is not lost. "The people have often made mistakes," Harry Truman said, "but given time and the facts, they will make the corrections."

Lincoln, who gave us the image of our better angels, should have the last word. "He was a president who understood people, and when it came time to make decisions, he was willing to take the responsibility and make those decisions no matter how difficult they were," Truman wrote. "He had a good head and a great brain and a kind heart. . . . He was the best kind of ordinary man, and when I say that he was an ordinary man, I mean that as high praise, not deprecation. That's the highest praise you can give a man, that he's one of the people and becomes distinguished in the service that he gives other people. I don't know of any higher compliment you can pay a man than that."

In the summer of 1864, the 166th Ohio Regiment called at the White House. The volunteer infantry had seen action some weeks before when Confederate general Jubal Early—the Jubal Early who would, after Appomattox, become one of the most influential defenders of the Lost Cause through the miserable years of Reconstruction—had moved against Washington. Headquartered at Silver Spring, Maryland, in the country house of Francis Preston Blair, Early was, he recalled, "in sight of the dome of the Capitol."

The Federal troops mounted a stand at Fort Stevens, in northwest Washington, and held their ground. Lincoln, who observed the battle firsthand, came under enemy fire; "a man," his secretary John Hay wrote, "was shot by his side." Lincoln never flinched. "He stood there with a long frock coat and plug hat on, making a very conspicuous figure," one observer recalled of the commander in chief. "Get down, you damn fool!" a young officer, Oliver Wendell Holmes, Jr., of the Twentieth Massachusetts, was reputed to have snapped at the president.

To the veterans returning to Ohio after the battle, Lincoln made some brief remarks as they prepared to go west. No one knew when the war would end; no one knew if Lincoln, who was facing reelection in November, would even be president in a matter of months. He spoke not with the poetry of Gettysburg, but his words on that August day said much about why the salvation of the Union would repay any price in blood and toil and treasure. The tall, tired president, his face heavily lined, his burdens unimaginable, was straightforward.

"It is," he said, "in order that each one of you may have, through this free government which we have enjoyed, an open field, and a fair chance for your industry, enterprise, and intelligence; that you may all have equal privileges in the race of life with all its desirable human aspirations—it is for this that the struggle should be maintained, that we may not lose our birthrights—not only for one, but for two or three years, if necessary." And, finally: "The nation is worth fighting for, to secure such an inestimable jewel."

For all of our darker impulses, for all of our shortcomings, and for all of the dreams denied and deferred, the experiment begun so long ago, carried out so imperfectly, is worth the fight. There is, in fact, no struggle more important, and none nobler, than the one we wage in the service of those better angels who, however besieged, are always ready for battle.

Author's Note and Acknowledgments

||||||||||||||||||||||||||||||||||||||||||||||||||

THE ROOTS OF THIS BOOK can be traced to a Sunday afternoon call I received from Nancy Gibbs, then the editor in chief of **Time,** who reached out to ask me if I had anything to say about the terrible events in Charlottesville, Virginia, in August 2017. As a Southerner who grew up on Missionary Ridge, the Civil War battlefield, I could still find minié balls in our yard as late as the 1970s and '80s. William Faulkner's observation in **Requiem for a Nun—** that "The past is never dead; it's not even past"— has always struck me as one of the great truths, and the American battles over power and race and history have proven Faulkner right with astonishing regularity.

The result of the call from Nancy was an essay that formed the genesis of this larger project. For **Time** that week, I explored several different eras in which a politics of fear seemed to triumph, at least temporarily, over hope. That tension is a defining one in American history, and I soon decided that the subject merited a fuller treatment.

For careful students of history, some of these stories may be familiar, but if we have learned anything in recent years—years in which the president of the United States has taken pride in his deliberate lack of acquaintance with the most essential historical elements of his office—it is that even the most basic facts of our common past repay attention. "Eternal vigilance," it has been long said, "is the price of liberty," and a consciousness about what has worked—and what hasn't—in previous eras is surely a useful form of such vigilance. Such is my goal here.

In addition to my work for **Time,** I have also drawn on a series of essays that I wrote for **The New York Times Book Review** on books that, while not fresh from the presses, seemed to me to speak to our current political and cultural moment, as well as **Times** op-ed columns. An interview I conducted with Congressman John Lewis for **Garden & Gun** magazine on the occasion of the fiftieth anniversary of Bloody Sunday at Selma, Alabama, was also helpful. I am grateful to my editors at these publications for the opportunities they have given me and for their permission to adapt that work for the present volume: Nancy Gibbs, Michael Duffy, Edward

Felsenthal, Pamela Paul, James Bennet, James Dao, Clay Risen, Radhika Jones, David DiBenedetto, and Susan Ellingwood.

A number of excellent historians, writers, and friends—the categories, I'm happy to say, are not mutually exclusive—generously took time to read the manuscript (or parts of it) and offer wise counsel: Annette Gordon-Reed, Eric Foner, David Oshinsky, John Milton Cooper, Jr., Walter Isaacson, Amity Shlaes, Tom Brokaw, Ken Burns, John Huey, Julia Reed, Jonathan Karp, Rushad Thomas, and Jerry L. Wallace. Thanks, too, to Corey Robin, whose **Fear: The History of a Political Idea,** was essential, and to Jeffrey Engel, Howard Fineman, and Ann McDaniel. I benefitted greatly from the observations of Nicholas S. Zeppos and John Geer of Vanderbilt University, both of whom had to listen to more of my musings about the project than I suspect either of them would have liked, but they never let on, for which I'm grateful. Lamar Alexander, who once taught a course on "The American Character and America's Government" at Harvard's Kennedy School of Government, kindly shared his work on the subject with me. I also owe an ancient debt to Charles Peters, and to the late Arthur Schlesinger, Jr. Their books and essays informed my argument at nearly every step of the way.

Michael Hill, my friend and colleague, is a master of the craft of research, and his energy, experience, and good cheer are at once enviable and unique. Jack Bales performed his usual bibliographic magic; Merrill Fabry fact-checked the manuscript with intelligence and insight; Abigail Abrams, the initial researcher on the original **Time** essay, provided invaluable assistance.

At Vanderbilt, where I am privileged to teach, I am indebted to David Eric Lewis, the chair of the Department of Political Science, and to Sam Girgus. For their grace in matters large and small, I am grateful to Amanda Urban, Will Byrd, Ratu Kamlani, Jean Becker, Freddy Ford, Barbara DiVittorio, Ann Patchett, Sally Quinn, Andrew Mead, Rachel Adler, Kate Childs, Jack Rose, Pamela Carter, Margaret Shannon, and Andy Brennan.

Random House has been my publishing home for two decades and seven books. Gina Centrello remains a force to be reckoned with, though I don't advise it; better, in my experience, to do as she says in the beginning, because she always prevails in the end. Which is a good thing, for her instincts and insights are spot-on. She is a matchless friend and leader.

Wise, gracious, and tireless, Kate Medina is the best. Most writers say this about their editors, but I know this: I would never want to publish without her. The same holds true of the larger Random House team: Tom Perry, Susan Kamil, Andy Ward, Benjamin Dreyer, Dennis Ambrose, Erica Gonzalez, Anna Pitoniak, Joe Perez, Simon Sullivan, Leigh Marchant, Andrea DeWerd, Sally Marvin, Barbara Fillon, Mary Moates, and Porscha Burke. I am also grateful to Carol Poticny and Fred Courtright. My copy editor, Michelle Daniel, was characteristically indispensable.

This book is dedicated to the most steadfast friends and counselors anyone could ever wish for: Evan Thomas and Michael Beschloss. They are reassuring, selfless, and kind; I owe them debts I cannot possibly repay. To them—and to Oscie and to Afsaneh—I can only offer my deepest thanks and endless affection.

And to Keith, of course, a final word of gratitude and of love. Our life with Sam, Mary, and Maggie is more than I could have imagined, and certainly more than I deserve.

Notes

||||||||||||||||||||||||||||||||||||||||||||||||||||||||

EPIGRAPHS

ix HISTORY, AS NEARLY NO ONE   James Baldwin, "The White Man's Guilt," **Ebony,** August 1965, 47. The essay appears in slightly different form under the title "Unnameable Objects, Unspeakable Crimes," in **The White Problem in America,** ed. The Editors of **Ebony** (Chicago, 1966), 174.

ix THE PRESIDENCY IS NOT MERELY   Anne O'Hare McCormick, "Roosevelt's View of the Big Job: The Presidency Is 'a Superb Opportunity for Applying the Simple Rules of Human Conduct,' Says the Democratic Candidate, Interviewed in the Midst of a Whirl of Varied Activity," **The New York Times (NYT),** September 11, 1932.

ix NOTHING MAKES A MAN   Lyndon Baines Johnson, **The Vantage Point: Perspectives of the Presidency, 1963–1969** (New York, 1971), 157.

INTRODUCTION · To Hope Rather Than to Fear

3 BACK OF THE WRITHING   W.E.B. Du Bois, **Black Reconstruction in America: An Essay**

Toward a History of the Part Which Black Folk Played in the Attempt to Reconstruct Democracy in America, 1860–1880 (New York, 1983), 678.

3 We are not enemies Abraham Lincoln: "Inaugural Address," March 4, 1861, American Presidency Project, University of California, Santa Barbara, http://www.presidency.ucsb.edu/ws/?pid=25818. See David Herbert Donald, **Lincoln** (New York, 1995), 283–84, for details about the drafting of the passage.

3 On the autumn evening "Local Crowd Cheers Thurmond Blasts at Truman and Dewey," Charlottesville **Daily Progress,** October 8, 1948. I drew on this scene in my essay "American Hate, a History," **Time,** August 17, 2017, and I am grateful to Abigail Abrams for her research assistance on details of the Thurmond visit to Cabell Hall.

4 Truman's civil rights program For Truman, civil rights, and the 1948 campaign, see Michael R. Gardner, **Harry Truman and Civil Rights: Moral Courage and Political Risks** (Carbondale, Ill., 2002), 87–146; and Patricia Sullivan, **Lift Every Voice: The NAACP and the Making of the Civil Rights Movement** (New York, 2009), 355–56. For his role in general, see William E. Leuchtenburg, **The White House Looks South: Franklin D. Roosevelt, Harry S. Truman, Lyndon B. Johnson** (Baton Rouge, La., 2005), 147–225; Gardner, **Harry Truman and Civil Rights,** and Raymond H. Geselbracht, ed.,

The Civil Rights Legacy of Harry S. Truman (Kirksville, Mo., 2007). "If we wish to inspire the peoples of the world whose freedom is in jeopardy . . . we must correct the remaining imperfections in our practice of democracy," Truman said in announcing the plan to Congress, framing the call for justice at home in Cold War terms. Sullivan, **Lift Every Voice,** 346; 355–56. See also Harry S. Truman, "Special Message to the Congress on Civil Rights," February 2, 1948, American Presidency Project, http://www.presidency.ucsb.edu/ws/?pid=13006.

4 SUCH MEASURES . . . "WOULD UNDERMINE" "Local Crowd Cheers Thurmond," **Daily Progress,** October 8, 1948.

4 INTERRUPTED BY APPLAUSE Ibid.

4 HAD BOLTED THE DEMOCRATIC NATIONAL CONVENTION See, for instance, Jack Bass and Marilyn W. Thompson, **Strom: The Complicated Personal and Political Life of Strom Thurmond** (New York, 2005), 114–19; Nadine Cohodas, **Strom Thurmond and the Politics of Southern Change** (New York, 1993), 140–92; Zachary Karabell, **The Last Campaign: How Harry Truman Won the 1948 Election** (New York, 2000), 164–75; Joseph Crespino, **Strom Thurmond's America** (New York, 2012), 62–84.

4 "I WANT TO TELL YOU" Bass and Thompson, **Strom,** 117. For an illuminating account of the Dixiecrat convention—with particular emphasis on the use of the Confederate battle emblem as a symbol of states' rights in the middle of the twen-

tieth century—see John M. Coski, **The Confed-erate Battle Flag: America's Most Embattled Emblem** (Cambridge, Mass., 2005), 98–109.

4   OFFERED "THE ONLY"   "Local Crowd Cheers Thurmond," **Daily Progress**, October 8, 1948.

4   CIVIL RIGHTS, THURMOND DECLARED   Ibid.

4   "ONLY THE STATES RIGHTS DEMOCRATS"   Ibid.

5   HEIRS TO THE DIXIECRATS' PLATFORM   See, for instance, Sheryl Gay Stolberg and Brian M. Rosenthal, "Man Charged After White Nationalist Rally Ends in Deadly Violence," **NYT**, August 12, 2017; "Charlottesville: 'Unite the Right' Rally, State of Emergency," **Time**, August 12, 2017.

5   A YOUNG COUNTER-PROTESTOR   Christina Caron, "Heather Heyer, Charlottesville Victim, Is Recalled as 'a Strong Woman,'" **NYT**, August 13, 2017.

5   TWO VIRGINIA STATE TROOPERS   Matthew Haag, "Death of 2 State Troopers Adds Another Layer of Tragedy in Charlottesville," **NYT**, August 14, 2017.

5   AN "EGREGIOUS DISPLAY"   See, for instance, Maggie Astor, Christina Caron, and Daniel Victor, "A Guide to the Charlottesville Aftermath," **NYT**, August 13, 2017; Jonathan Lemire, "Trump Blames 'Many Sides' After Violent White Supremacist Rally in Virginia," **Chicago Tribune**, August 12, 2017; Michael D. Shear and Maggie Haberman, "Trump Defends Initial Remarks on Charlottesville; Again Blames 'Both Sides,'" **NYT**, August 15, 2017.

5   TEND TO SPIKE   See, for instance, David H.

Bennett, **The Party of Fear: From Nativist Movements to the New Right in American History** (New York, 1995); Richard Hofstadter, **The Paranoid Style in American Politics, and Other Essays** (New York, 1965); Peter Schrag, **Not Fit for Our Society: Nativism and Immigration** (Berkeley, Calif., 2010); Arlie Russell Hochschild, **Strangers in Their Own Land: Anger and Mourning on the American Right** (New York, 2016); Alan Brinkley, **Voices of Protest: Huey Long, Father Coughlin, and the Great Depression** (New York, 1982).

5 LITTLE TRUST IN GOVERNMENT According to the Pew Research Center, as of May 2017, "Only 18% of Americans today say they can trust the government in Washington to do what is right 'just about always' (3%) or 'most of the time' (15%)," down from a high of 77 percent in October 1964. "Public Trust in Government, 1958–2017," Pew Research Center, May 3, 2017, http://www.people-press.org/2017/05/03/public-trust-in-government-1958-2017/.

5 HOUSEHOLD INCOMES LAG "Historical Income Tables: Households," https://www.census.gov/data/tables/time-series/demo/income-poverty/historical-income-households.html. According to a 2014 **USA Today** analysis, while a family of four requires $130,000 to live what Americans came to understand as a middle-class life, only about one in eight households earned that much in 2013, when the actual median figure was around $51,000. Howard R. Gold, "Price

tag for the American dream: $130K a year," **USA Today,** July 4, 2014, https://www.usatoday.com/story/money/personalfinance/2014/07/04/american-dream/11122015/.

6 "We are determined" "David Duke: Charlottesville Rally Part of Effort to 'Take Country Back,'" NBC News, August 12, 2017, https://www.nbcnews.com/video/david-duke-says-he-was-at-charlottesville-rally-to-fulfill-promise-of-trump-1023420483642.

7 a natural tendency For the perils of selective historical memory, see, for instance, Barbara W. Tuchman, **The March of Folly: From Troy to Vietnam** (New York, 1984), where she quoted Samuel Coleridge: "If men could learn from history, what lessons it might teach us! But passion and party blind our eyes, and the light which experience gives us is a lantern on the stern which shines only on the waves behind us." Yet Tuchman added, tellingly, "The image is beautiful but the message misleading, for the light on the waves we have passed through should enable us to infer the nature of the waves ahead." Ibid., 383. The key thing is to see the waves behind us clearly by the light of which Coleridge spoke. In Richard E. Neustadt and Ernest R. May, **Thinking in Time: The Uses of History for Decision Makers** (New York, 1986), the authors cited Thucydides, who observed that he wrote his histories for "those who want to understand clearly the events which happened in the past and which (human nature being what it is) will at some point or other and

in much the same ways be repeated in the future."
Ibid., 232. For a much more recent essay on the
question, see Corey Robin, "Forget About It,"
Harper's Magazine (April 2018): 5–7.

8   To speak of a soul   I am indebted to Stewart
Goetz and Charles Taliaferro, **A Brief History of
the Soul** (Hoboken, N.J., 2011); Richard Swinburne, **The Evolution of the Soul** (Oxford, 1986),
especially 174–312; Jacob Needleman, **The American Soul: Rediscovering the Wisdom of the
Founders** (New York, 2003); and Jim Cullen, **The
American Dream: A Short History of an Idea
That Shaped a Nation** (New York, 2003).

8   called the American Creed: Gunnar
Myrdal, **An American Dilemma: The Negro
Problem and Modern Democracy** (New York,
1962), 3–25. Myrdal quoted Ralph Bunche:
"Every man in the street, white, black, red, or yellow, knows that this is 'the land of the free,' the
'land of opportunity,' the 'cradle of liberty,' the
'home of democracy,' that the American flag sym-
bolizes the 'equality of all men' and guarantees us
all 'the protection of life, liberty and property,'
freedom of speech, freedom of religion and racial
tolerance." Ibid., 4.

Another way of thinking about the same theme
can be found in the American historian James
Truslow Adams's 1931 book **The Epic of America,** which popularized a term not yet in the general vernacular in those last years of the reigns of
Harding, Coolidge, and Hoover. Adams wrote
that his subject was "that American dream of a

better, richer, and happier life for all our citizens of every rank which is the greatest contribution we have as yet made to the thought and welfare of the world." It was not a new thing, this abiding belief that tomorrow would be better than today. "That dream or hope," Adams wrote, "has been present from the start." James Truslow Adams, **The Epic of America** (Boston, 1931), viii.

According to the historian Allan Nevins, Adams's thesis was that the American Dream "had contributed to the struggle for independence, and from the hour independence was won, every generation had witnessed some kind of uprising of the common folk to protect the dream from forces that seemed likely to overwhelm and dissipate it. 'Possibly the greatest of these struggles lies just ahead of us at the present time,' wrote Adams, who perceived that the hour was striking for drastic politico-economic changes." Allan Nevins, **James Truslow Adams: Historian of the American Dream** (Urbana, Ill., 1968), 68. See also my "Keeping the Dream Alive," **Time,** June 21, 2012.

9 "THE GENIUS OF AMERICA" Arthur M. Schlesinger, Jr., **The Disuniting of America** (New York, 1992), 142, 145.

10 "WHAT IS IT THAT" Hendrik Lorenz, "Ancient Theories of Soul," **The Stanford Encyclopedia of Philosophy,** ed. Edward N. Zalta, Summer 2009, https://plato.stanford.edu/archives/sum2009/entries/ancient-soul/.

10 "AND THE LORD GOD" Carl Schultz, "Soul," **Baker's Evangelical Dictionary of Biblical Theol-**

ogy, ed. Walter A. Elwell, https://www.bible studytools.com/dictionary/soul/. See also Goetz and Taliaferro, **Brief History of the Soul,** 30–32.

10 "GREATER LOVE HATH NO MAN" Schultz, "Soul," **Baker's Evangelical Dictionary.**

10 "AN ASSEMBLAGE OF" Saint Augustine of Hippo, **The City of God,** trans. Marcus Dods (New York, 1993), 706.

11 "JUST AND GENEROUS" Harold Holzer and Norton Garfinkle, **A Just and Generous Nation: Abraham Lincoln and the Fight for American Opportunity** (New York, 2015), 6. The remark came in a speech Lincoln delivered in Milwaukee on September 30, 1859.

11 TOO OFTEN, PEOPLE VIEW I am indebted to Professor Eric Foner for this insight.

11 THE SOUL OF THE COUNTRY My views on the nature of America have been informed by innumerable works, reportage, and conversations. In particular, but not exclusively, I owe much to Myrdal, **American Dilemma;** Gordon S. Wood, **The Idea of America: Reflections on the Birth of the United States** (New York, 2011); Schlesinger, **Disuniting of America;** Samuel P. Huntington, **American Politics and the Promise of Disharmony** (Cambridge, Mass., 1981), and Huntingdon, **Who Are We? The Challenges to America's National Identity** (New York, 2005); Seymour Martin Lipset, **American Exceptionalism: A Double-Edged Sword** (New York, 1996); Daniel J. Boorstin, **The Genius of American Politics** (Chicago, 1958); Michael Walzer, **What It Means**

to Be an American (New York, 1992); Howard Zinn, **A People's History of the United States** (New York, 1980); Alan Wolfe, **One Nation, After All: What Middle-Class Americans Really Think About God, Country, and Family, Racism, Welfare, Immigration, Homosexuality, Work, the Right, the Left and Each Other** (New York, 1998); Ganesh Sitaraman, **The Crisis of the Middle-Class Constitution: Why Economic Inequality Threatens Our Republic** (New York, 2017); Ibram X. Kendi, **Stamped from the Beginning: The Definitive History of Racist Ideas in America** (New York, 2016); Fareed Zakaria, **The Future of Freedom: Illiberal Democracy at Home and Abroad** (New York, 2007); Jonathan Bean, ed., **Race and Liberty in America: The Essential Reader** (Lexington, Ky., 2009); Philip Gorski, **American Covenant: A History of Civil Religion from the Puritans to the Present** (Princeton, N.J., 2017); Sacvan Bercovitch, **The American Jeremiad** (Madison, Wis., 1978); Robert N. Bellah and Phillip E. Hammond, **Varieties of Civil Religion** (San Francisco, 1980); Bellah, **The Broken Covenant: American Civil Religion in a Time of Trial** (Chicago, 1992); Martin E. Marty, **The One and the Many: America's Struggle for the Common Good** (Cambridge, Mass., 1997); Michael Warner, ed., **American Sermons: The Pilgrims to Martin Luther King Jr.** (New York, 1999); G. K. Chesterton, **What I Saw in America** (London, 1923); Eleanor Roosevelt, **Tomorrow Is Now** (New York, 2012); and **A Testament** of Hope: The Essential Writings and Speeches of **Martin Luther King, Jr.**, ed. James Melvin Washington (San Francisco, 2003).

12 "WE HAVE IT IN OUR POWER" Craig Nelson, **Thomas Paine: Enlightenment, Revolution, and the Birth of Modern Nations** (New York, 2007), 335.

12 "THINGS IN LIFE" Franklin D. Roosevelt, "Inaugural Address," January 20, 1945, American Presidency Project, http://www.presidency.ucsb .edu/ws/?pid=16607.

13 "I ALWAYS CONSIDER" John Adams, "Fragmentary Draft of a Dissertation on Canon and Feudal Law, February 1765," Founders Online, National Archives, https://founders.archives.gov/documents/ Adams/01-01-02-0009-0002.

13 A "MARCH OF CIVILIZATION" Thomas Jefferson to William Ludlow, September 6, 1824, Founders Online, National Archives, https://founders.ar chives.gov/documents/Jefferson/98-01-02-4523. Laws and institutions, Jefferson said elsewhere, "must go hand in hand with the progress of the human mind. As that becomes more developed, more enlightened, as new discoveries are made, new truths disclosed, and manners and opinions change with the change of circumstances, institutions must advance also, and keep pace with the times. We might as well require a man to wear still the coat which fitted him when a boy, as civilized society to remain ever under the regimen of their barbarous ancestors." Thomas Jefferson to "Henry Tompkinson" [Samuel Kercheval], July 12, 1816,

Founders Online, National Archives, https:// founders.archives.gov/documents/Jefferson/ 03-10-02-0128-0002.

13 "THE AMERICAN IDEA" Theodore Parker, "Discourses of Slavery," May 29, 1850.

14 "I KNOW OF NO SOIL BETTER" Frederick Douglass in **Let Nobody Turn Us Around: Voices of Resistance, Reform, and Renewal,** ed. Manning Marable and Leith Mullings, (Lanham, Md., 2003), 99.

14 "IT IS ESSENTIAL" Roosevelt, **Tomorrow Is Now,** 4.

14 "MAN'S CAPACITY FOR" Reinhold Niebuhr, **Major Works on Religion and Politics,** ed. Elisabeth Sifton (New York, 2015), 354.

15 "INTELLECTUALLY I KNOW" "Lewis Holds Books Do Not Prevent War," **NYT,** December 30, 1930.

16 IN THE 1790S James Rogers Sharp, **American Politics in the Early Republic: The New Nation in Crisis** (New Haven, Conn., 1993), 12.

18 "YOU CAN'T DIVIDE" Merle Miller, **Plain Speaking: An Oral Biography of Harry S. Truman** (New York, 1974), 252.

19 "THE PRESIDENCY IS NOT MERELY" McCormick, "Roosevelt's View of the Big Job," **NYT,** September 11, 1932.

19 "FOR ONLY THE PRESIDENT" John F. Kennedy, "The Presidency in 1960—National Press Club, Washington, D.C.," January 14, 1960, American Presidency Project, http://www.presidency.ucsb.edu/ws/?pid=25795.

19 THERE WAS NOTHING Johnson, **Vantage Point,** 157.

20 A PRESIDENT SETS A TONE   For the rhetorical and symbolic role of the presidency, I have learned much from Eric F. Goldman, "The Presidency as Moral Leadership," in **The Annals of the American Academy of Political and Social Science: Ethical Standards in American Public Life,** ed. Clarence N. Callender and James C. Charlesworth (Philadelphia, 1952), 37–45; Erwin C. Hargrove, **The President as Leader: Appealing to the Better Angels of Our Nature** (Lawrence, Kans., 1998); Vanessa B. Beasley, **You, the People: American National Identity in Presidential Rhetoric** (College Station, Tex., 2004), and Beasley, ed., **Who Belongs in America? Presidents, Rhetoric, and Immigration** (College Station, Tex., 2006); Roderick P. Hart, **The Political Pulpit** (West Lafayette, Ind., 1977); Michael Novak, **Choosing Presidents: Symbols of Political Leadership** (New Brunswick, N.J., 1992); James David Fairbanks, "The Priestly Functions of the Presidency: A Discussion of the Literature on Civil Religion and Its Implications for the Study of Presidential Leadership," **Presidential Studies Quarterly** 11, no. 2 (Spring 1981), 214–32; Richard Hofstadter, **The American Political Tradition and the Men Who Made It** (New York, 1948); Garth E. Pauley, **The Modern Presidency and Civil Rights: Rhetoric on Race from Roosevelt to Nixon** (College Station, Tex., 2001); Jeffrey K. Tulis, **The Rhetorical Presidency** (Princeton, N.J., 1987); James MacGregor Burns, **Leadership** (New York, 1978); and Burns, **Presidential Government: The Crucible of Leadership** (New York, 1965).

I share this view of Arthur Schlesinger, Jr.'s:

> In the end, a President of the United States must stand or fall by his instinct for the future as well as by his understanding of the past and his mastery of the present. Implanted within him, there must be an image, not necessarily—or even desirably—explicit or conscious, but profoundly rich, plastic, and capacious, of the kind of America he wants, of the vision of the American promise he is dedicated to realize, of the direction in which he believes the world is moving. Without such a sense, his Presidency will be static and uncreative. As Franklin Roosevelt's successor once put it, 'The President's got to set the sights.' This vision of the future becomes the source of his values; it justifies his strivings; it renews his hopes; it provides his life with its magnetic orientation. Arthur M. Schlesinger, Jr., **The Coming of the New Deal,** The Age of Roosevelt, vol. 2 (Boston, 1957), 587.

20 "AT THE FRONT"   Woodrow Wilson, **Constitutional Government in the United States** (New York, 1908), 33.

21 "HIS PERSON, COUNTENANCE"   John Adams, **The Works of John Adams, Second President of the U.S. With a Life of the Author, Notes and Illustrations, by his Grandson Charles Francis Adams** (Boston, 1851), 6:255–56. The observation came in his **Discourses on Davila,** published in 1790 and 1791.

21 "THE PEOPLE . . . OUGHT"   Ibid., 302.

21 "THE PEOPLE CANNOT"   Ibid.

21 "THE POWERS OF"   Henry Jones Ford, **The Rise and Growth of American Politics: A Sketch of Constitutional Development** (New York, 1967), 291.

21 "THIS GREAT OFFICE"   James Bryce, **The American Commonwealth**, vol. 1, **The National Government; The State Governments** (New York, 1911), 77. The quotation is from a chapter of Bryce's entitled "Why Great Men Are Not Chosen President." Ibid., 77–84.

21 "THE TRUTH IS"   Ford, **Rise and Growth of American Politics**, 293.

22 "ONE THING I BELIEVE"   Roosevelt, **Tomorrow Is Now**, 10.

22 "THE ARC OF"   Martin Luther King, Jr., "Remaining Awake Through a Great Revolution," March 31, 1968, **King Institute Encyclopedia**, Martin Luther King, Jr., and the Global Freedom Struggle, Martin Luther King, Jr., Research and Education Institute, Stanford University, http://kingencyclopedia.stanford.edu/encyclopedia/documentsentry/doc_remaining_awake_through_a_great_revolution.1.html. The quotation, which King used frequently, echoed words from Theodore Parker. See, for instance, "Theodore Parker And The 'Moral Universe,'" National Public Radio, September 2, 2010. https://www.npr.org/templates/story/story.php?storyId=129609461.

22 "SURELY, IN THE LIGHT OF HISTORY"   Eleanor

Roosevelt, **You Learn by Living: Eleven Keys for a More Fulfilling Life** (New York, 1960), 168.

22 THE HINGE OF   The writer Shelby Foote called the war the "cross-roads of our being." Shelby Foote in **The Civil War,** PBS documentary miniseries, Ken Burns director and producer, Sept. 23–27, 1990. In it, Foote added: "And it was a hell of a cross-roads." Ibid.

23 "THE PROBLEM OF"   W.E.B. Du Bois, **The Souls of Black Folk** (New York, 1993), 5.

23 FEAR, AS THE POLITICAL THEORIST COREY ROBIN   Corey Robin, **Fear: The History of a Political Idea** (New York, 2004), was invaluable. "By political fear," Robin wrote, "I mean a people's felt apprehension of some harm to their collective well-being—the fear of terrorism, panic over crime, anxiety about moral decay—or the intimidation wielded over men and women by governmental groups. What makes both types of fear political rather than personal is that they emanate from society or have consequences for society." Ibid., 2. I also learned much from Robin, **The Reactionary Mind: Conservatism from Edmund Burke to Sarah Palin** (New York, 2011); Joanna Bourke, **Fear: A Cultural History** (Emeryville, Calif., 2006); Philip Perlmutter, **Legacy of Hate: A Short History of Ethnic, Religious, and Racial Prejudice in America** (Armonk, N.Y., 1990); and, for the other side of the spectrum, James W. Fraser, **A History of Hope: When Americans Have Dared to Dream of a Better Future** (New York, 2002).

24   UNDERSTOOD BY ROBIN AND MANY SCHOL-
ARS   Robin, **Fear,** 2. Throughout this book, I
am also indebted, as noted above, to Bennett,
Party of Fear, for its excellent treatment of fear in
a right-wing political context. "If there has been
political extremism of the Right in American history, it is found in large measure in . . . efforts to
combat peoples and ideas that were seen as alien
threats to a cherished but embattled American
'way of life,'" Bennett wrote. "The passionate
men and women who joined the right-wing
groups that sought to check various alien enemies
became extremists when they violated democratic
procedures and moved outside the norms of
democratic society. . . . They were the leaders and
members of the party of fear." Ibid., 3.

24   "POLITICAL FEAR"   Robin, **Fear,** 2.

24   CAN BE "SPARKED"   Ibid.

24   AND "MAY DICTATE"   Ibid.

24   WHO ONE BELIEVES POSE A THREAT   Ibid.

24   "IS CAUSED BY"   Aristotle, "Rhetorica," book 2,
sec. 5 in **The Works of Aristotle,** trans. W. D.
Ross (Oxford, 1928), 11:1382A.

24   THOMAS HOBBES BELIEVED   Mitchell Cohen
and Nicole Fermon, eds., **Princeton Readings in
Political Thought: Essential Texts Since Plato**
(Princeton, N.J., 1996), 208. The point is drawn
from Hobbes's 1651 **Leviathan.**

24   TO BE CONCERNED   My argument about fear
emphasizes its disorienting effects, but this is a
complex subject with many nuances. Corey Robin,
for example, has argued that "[P]olitical fear re-

flects the interests and reasoned judgments of the fearful about what is good for them, and responds to real dangers in the world: to genuine threats to the nation's security and well-being, to the coercive power wielded by elites and the lurking challenge the lower orders pose to those elites. . . . It is an affair of collusion, involving the grunt work of collaborators, the cooperation of victims, and aid from those bystanders who do nothing to protest fear's repressive hold." Robin, **Fear,** 162–63. He added, "It is fear's repressive consequences, not just the personal suffering it inflicts, that make it a toxic fact of life that must be opposed." Ibid., 164.

25 FEAR . . . DOES NOT STRIKE   Aristotle, "Rhetorica," 11:1383A.

25 "NO PASSION . . . SO EFFECTUALLY ROBS"   "Inquiry into the Sublime and Beautiful," pt. 2, sec. 2 in "Terror" from Edmund Burke, **Reflections on the Revolution in France, and Other Writings,** ed. Jesse Norman (New York, 2015), 55. I am indebted to my friend and teacher Dale Richardson for introducing me to Burke's literary criticism nearly thirty years ago, at the University of the South.

25 HOPE, DEFINED AS THE EXPECTATION   My analysis and its supporting quotations owe much to Claudia Bloeser and Titus Stahl, "Hope," **The Stanford Encyclopedia of Philosophy,** ed. Edward N. Zalta, Spring 2017, https://plato.stanford.edu/archives/spr2017/entries/hope/.

25 "THE COWARD, THEN, IS"   Ibid. In political life, fear, which can be hidden, often manifests

itself in detectable expressions of anger. Seneca noted that wise men had long said that anger "is a brief madness" and likened it to "a collapsing building that's reduced to rubble even as it crushes what it falls upon." Seneca, **Anger, Mercy, Revenge,** trans. Robert A. Kaster and Martha C. Nussbaum (Chicago, 2010), 14.

Anger is not something one can easily disguise: "As madmen exhibit specific symptoms—a bold and threatening expression, a knitted brow, a fierce set of the features, a quickened step, restless hands, a changed complexion, frequent, very forceful sighing—so do angry people show the same symptoms: their eyes blaze and flicker, their faces flush deeply as the blood surges up from the depths of the heart, their lips quiver and their teeth grind, their hair bristles and stands on end, their breathing is forced and ragged." Ibid. The bottom line: "Anger," Seneca wrote, "turns everything from what is best and most righteous to the opposite." Ibid., 15–16.

25 "THE LOSS OF WHAT WE LOVE"   "Question 40: Of the Irascible Passions—Of Hope and Despair, First Article, Obj. 3 with answer and Question 43": Whether Love Is the Cause of Fear? Obj. 3 from St. Thomas Aquinas and Reginaldo de Piperno, **The "Summa Theologica" of St. Thomas Aquinas** (London, 1914), 4:456. See also Peter Koritansky, "Thomas Aquinas: Political Philosophy," **Internet Encyclopedia of Philosophy,** http://www.iep.utm.edu/aqui-pol/.

26 "PROPERLY SPEAKING, HOPE REGARDS"

"Summa Theologica" of St. Thomas Aquinas, 4:487.

26 "THE DEVIL CAN" William Shakespeare, **The Merchant of Venice,** act 1, scene 3, http://shake speare.mit.edu/merchant/merchant.1.3.html.

26 "I DO NOT KNOW" Alexis de Tocqueville, **Democracy in America,** ed. J. P. Mayer and trans. George Lawrence (New York, 1969), 293. For all the perils of religion—among them the divine sanction a believer might feel for any course of action, however wrong, and the potential for the kinds of sectarian conflicts that had roiled the Old World—the first generation of the Republic's leaders, as well as their successors, have acknowledged the reality of religious belief and sought to deploy it for the good.

"And let us with caution indulge the supposition that morality can be maintained without religion," George Washington wrote. "Whatever may be conceded to the influence of refined education on minds of peculiar structure, reason and experience both forbid us to expect that national morality can prevail in exclusion of religious principle." George Washington, **Writings,** ed. John H. Rhodehamel (New York, 1997), 971.

A citizen (or a president) who is motivated by religiously informed impulses may undertake work that will make the lives of believers and of secularists better, just as a citizen (or a president) who is motivated by impulses that have nothing to do with religion may undertake work that will make the lives of secularists and of believers better. The motives can matter less than the means and the ends of action. "This is the first principle of democracy: that the essential things in men are the things they hold in common, not the things they hold separately," G. K. Chesterton once remarked, and experience shows us that America is at its best when we follow that counsel and turn our minds to that which unites us— chiefly the right to fair play and the love of liberty—rather than to the multitude of forces that divide us. G. K. Chesterton, **Orthodoxy** (New York, 2001), 43.

26 AS SUSCEPTIBLE TO HUMAN PASSIONS   "Why has government been instituted at all?" Alexander Hamilton asked in **The Federalist Papers**. "Because the passions of men will not conform to the dictates of reason and justice, without constraint." Alexander Hamilton, **Writings**, ed. Joanne B. Freeman (New York, 2001), 223.

27 IN A NOVEMBER 1963 LECTURE   Hofstadter, **Paranoid Style**, 3.

28 "THE PARANOID SPOKESMAN"   Ibid., 29–30.

28 DIVISIONS OF OPINION   Jon Meacham, **Thomas Jefferson: The Art of Power** (New York, 2012), 458–59. Jefferson expressed this view in an 1813 letter to John Adams. Ibid.

29 A PRESIDENT WHO, IN 1947   Sullivan, **Lift Every Voice**, 345. For the speech itself, see Harry S. Truman: "Address Before the National Association for the Advancement of Colored People," June 29, 1947. American Presidency Project, http://www.presidency.ucsb.edu/ws/?pid=12686.

29   HAD COMMISSIONED A REPORT   Sullivan, **Lift Every Voice**, 329–30; 352–56. The document itself repays consideration: Steven F. Lawson, ed., **To Secure These Rights: The Report of President Harry S Truman's Committee on Civil Rights** (New York, 2003). See also David McCullough, **Truman** (New York, 1992), 569–70; 586–90. The speech to the NAACP, McCullough wrote, was "the strongest statement on civil rights heard in Washington since the time of Lincoln." Ibid., 569.

29   TRUMAN'S MOTIVATIONS WERE   See, for instance, William Lee Miller, **Two Americans: Truman, Eisenhower, and a Dangerous World** (New York, 2012), 336–41.

29   "IT IS MY DEEP CONVICTION"   Truman, "Address Before the National Association for the Advancement of Colored People."

30   THE PRESIDENT HAD WRITTEN   Fourth draft, speech to NAACP, with corrections by Harry S. Truman, June 28, 1947, Papers of Harry S. Truman: President's Secretary's File, Harry S. Truman Presidential Library and Museum, https://www.trumanlibrary.org/flip_books/index.php?collectionid=ihow&groupid=3723&tldate=1947-06-28.

30   ON THE FOURTH OF JULY, 1947   Harry S. Truman, "Independence Day Address Delivered at the Home of Thomas Jefferson," July 4, 1947, American Presidency Project, http://www.presidency.ucsb.edu/ws/?pid=12694.

30   "WE HAVE LEARNED"   Ibid.

30   "SO LONG AS THE BASIC RIGHTS"   Ibid.

ONE · The Confidence of the Whole People

35 ENERGY IN THE EXECUTIVE   James Madison, Alexander Hamilton, and John Jay, **The Federalist Papers,** ed. Isaac Kramnick (New York, 1987), 402.

35 I THINK THAT   "Sojouner's Words and Music," Sojourner Truth Memorial Committee, http://sojournertruthmemorial.org/sojourner-truth/her-words/. Nell Irvin Painter, **Sojourner Truth: A Life, a Symbol** (New York, 1996), convincingly argues that this version of Truth's remarks, popularly in circulation as the "Ain't I a Woman?" speech, was a later invention. Truth was highly unlikely to have spoken in such a dialect; the legendary account was written by a fellow feminist, Frances Dana Gage, in 1863. At the time Gage was writing, she was in South Carolina, which probably influenced her decision to render Truth's speech in such a way. Ibid., 164–78.

35 DREAMS OF GOD AND OF GOLD   Charles W. Eliot, ed., **Harvard Classics,** vol. 43, **American Historical Documents** (New York, 1910), 51–61. For the details about the First Charter of Virginia, I also drew on my **American Gospel: God, the Founding Fathers, and the Making of a Nation** (New York, 2006), 41–42, and my essay "Keeping the Dream Alive," **Time,** June 21, 2012. See also James Horn, **A Land as God Made It: Jamestown and the Birth of America** (New York, 2005), and Ed Southern, ed., **The Jamestown Adventure: Accounts of the Vir-**

ginia Colony, 1605–1614 (Winston-Salem, N.C., 2004).

35 IN 1630, THE PURITAN JOHN WINTHROP Francis J. Bremer, **John Winthrop: America's Forgotten Founding Father** (New York, 2003), 180. The phrase "city upon a hill" is from the Gospel of Matthew, 5:14.

36 "A MODEL OF CHRISTIAN CHARITY" John Winthrop, **Winthrop Papers**, vol., 2, **1623–1630,** ed. Malcolm Freiburg (Boston, 1931), 282–95. See also **The Journal of John Winthrop, 1630–1649,** ed. Richard S. Dunn, James Savage, and Laetitia Yeadle (Cambridge, Mass., 1996), 1, 726.

36 RONALD REAGAN ADDED See, for instance, Ronald Reagan, "Farewell Address to the Nation," January 11, 1989, American Presidency Project, http://www.presidency.ucsb.edu/ws/?pid=29650.

36 IN 1619, A DUTCH "MAN OF WARRE" Kenneth M. Stampp, **The Peculiar Institution: Slavery in the Ante-Bellum South** (New York, 1956), 17–18.

36 EUROPEAN SETTLERS, MEANWHILE Francis Paul Prucha, **The Great Father: The United States Government and the American Indians** (Lincoln, Neb., 1984), is a foundational work. "The great distinguishing feature of English relations with the Indian groups was replacement of the Indians on the land by white settlers, not conversion and assimilation of the Indians into European colonial society." Ibid., 11.

36 THE VASTNESS OF THE CONTINENT The clas-

sic statement of this case is Frederick Jackson Turner's "The Significance of the Frontier in American History," delivered at the ninth annual meeting of the American Historical Association, Chicago, July 11–13, 1893, and reported in **The Annual Report of the American Historical Association,** 1894, 119–227.

37 "ENTERPRISING AND SELF-MADE MEN" Edward Pessen, **Riches, Class, and Power Before the Civil War** (New York, 1990), 77. See also Cullen, **American Dream,** 69.

37 APPOINTED ONE SUCH MAN Donald, **Lincoln,** 50. See also my **American Lion: Andrew Jackson in the White House** (New York, 2008), 247. Nearly three decades later, in late 1860, Lincoln would summon the spirit of Jackson in his own struggle against disunion. "The right of a state to secede is not an open or debatable question," Lincoln said. "It was fully discussed in Jackson's time, and denied . . . by him. . . . It is the duty of a President to execute the laws and maintain the existing government. He cannot entertain any proposition for dissolution or dismemberment. He was not elected for any such purpose." Meacham, **American Lion,** 355. The Union was essential. "The central pervading idea of this struggle," Lincoln told Congress on the Fourth of July, 1861, "is the necessity . . . of proving that popular government is not an absurdity. We must settle this question now, whether in a free government the minority have the right to break up the government whenever they choose." William J.

Cooper and John M. McCardell, eds., **In the Cause of Liberty: How the Civil War Redefined American Ideals** (Baton Rouge, La., 2009), 3.

37 "I HAPPEN, TEMPORARILY" Abraham Lincoln, "Address to the 166th Ohio Regiment," August 22, 1864, American Presidency Project, http://www.presidency.ucsb.edu/ws/?pid=88874.

38 GOVERNED BY THE WEAK ARTICLES For the road to the Constitutional Convention of 1787, see Richard Beeman, **Plain, Honest Men: The Making of the American Constitution** (New York, 2009), 3–21; Carol Berkin, **A Brilliant Solution: Inventing the American Constitution** (New York, 2002), 11–47; and David O. Stewart, **The Summer of 1787: The Men Who Invented the Constitution** (New York, 2007), 1–45. Jack N. Rakove, **Original Meanings: Politics and Ideas in the Making of the Constitution** (New York, 1997), is also invaluable on the story of the Constitution, as is Pauline Maier, **Ratification: The People Debate the Constitution, 1787–1788** (New York, 2010).

38 "FAST VERGING TO ANARCHY" George Washington to James Madison, November 5, 1786, Founders Online, National Archives, https://founders.archives.gov/documents/Washington/04-04-02-0299.

38 THOMAS PAINE HAD SUGGESTED William M. Goldsmith, **The Growth of Presidential Power: A Documented History** (New York, 1974), 3:88.

39 "BUT WHERE, SAY SOME" Ibid., 89.

39 "A NATIONAL EXECUTIVE" Ibid., 82.

40   TO BE ELECTED FOR LIFE   **Notes of Debates in the Federal Convention of 1787 Reported by James Madison** (Athens, Ohio, 1984), 136.

40   OTHERS FAVORED PLANS   Beeman, **Plain, Honest Men,** 299–305.

40   BECAUSE OF GEORGE WASHINGTON   Ibid., 128.

40   (THE DELEGATES DID PROVIDE)   Ibid., 301. "It was in some respects an odd decision, since several members of the Convention themselves had been born outside the United States, but it was dictated in large measure by the delegates' fears of the corrupting effects of European society." Ibid.

40   THE CREATION OF THE OFFICE   See, for instance, ibid., 124–43; Harlow Giles Unger, **"Mr. President": George Washington and the Making of the Nation's Highest Office** (Boston, 2013); Thomas E. Cronin, ed., **Inventing the American Presidency** (Lawrence, Kan., 1989); Sidney M. Milkis and Michael Nelson, **The American Presidency: Origins and Development, 1776–2007** (Washington, D.C., 2008); Charles W. Thach, Jr., **The Creation of the Presidency, 1775–1789: A Study in Constitutional History** (Farmington Hills, Mich., 2010). Arthur M. Schlesinger, Jr., **The Imperial Presidency** (New York, 2004), 1–34, is also illuminating.

41   "TOLD TOP AIDES"   Maggie Haberman, Glenn Thrush, and Peter Baker, "Inside Trump's Hour-by-Hour Battle for Self-Preservation," **NYT,** December 9, 2017.

41   A WAR OF ALL AGAINST ALL   Cohen and Fermon, **Princeton Readings in Political Thought,**

208. The precise line of Hobbes, who was describing what he called "the natural condition of mankind": "Hereby it is manifest, that during the time men live without a common power to keep them all in awe, they are in that condition which is called war; and such a war, as is of every man, against every man." Ibid., 207–8.

41 "First, those which excite" Walter Bagehot, **The English Constitution** (New York, 1967), 61.

41 "the dignified parts of government" Ibid.

41 "the head of the nation" Bryce, **American Commonwealth,** 3:36.

41 "The President has a position" Ibid., 3:68.

41 "As he has the ear" Ibid., 3:72. Bryce went on to delineate the constraints a president faced despite the power of the office.

42 "Every hope and" Harry S. Truman, **Mr. Citizen** (New York, 1960), 222.

42 "I knew that" Johnson, **Vantage Point,** 157.

43 published on Tuesday, March 18, 1788 Alexander Hamilton, "The Executive Department Further Considered," Avalon Project, Yale Law School Lillian Goldman Law Library, http://avalon .law.yale.edu/18th_century/fed70.asp.

43 "Energy in the Executive" Madison, Hamilton, and Jay, **Federalist Papers,** 402.

43 "The history of human conduct" Schlesinger, **Imperial Presidency,** xi. The quotation is from **Federalist** 75. Madison, Hamilton, and Jay, **Federalist Papers,** 424–28.

44 "As the first" George Washington to James Madison, May 5, 1789, Founders Online, National Archives, https://founders.archives.gov/documents/Washington/05-02-02-0157. See also, for instance, Glenn A. Phelps, "George Washington: Precedent Setter," in Cronin, **Inventing the American Presidency,** 259–82—an illuminating essay.

44 that "the President was" Ford, **Rise and Growth of American Politics,** 277.

44 In 1792, when farmers See, for instance, William Hogeland, **The Whiskey Rebellion: George Washington, Alexander Hamilton, and the Frontier Rebels Who Challenged America's Newfound Sovereignty** (New York, 2006).

44 "Moderation enough has been" Goldsmith, **Growth of Presidential Power,** 3:245. Hamilton also said: "The appearance of the President in the business will awaken the attention of a great number of persons . . . to the evil tendency of the conduct reprehended, who have not yet viewed it with due seriousness." Ibid.

44 "Whereas it is" Ibid., 244.

45 "In a government like ours" Thomas Jefferson to John Garland Jefferson, January 25, 1810, Founders Online, National Archives, https://founders.archives.gov/documents/Jefferson/03-02-02-0145.

45 Before Andrew Jackson, for example I drew, in part, on my **American Lion** for my treatment of Jackson here.

46 "the humble members" Andrew Jackson:

"Veto Message [Of the Re-authorization of Bank of the United States]," July 10, 1832, American Presidency Project, http://www.presidency.ucsb.edu/ws/?pid=67043. The veto marked a critical moment in the history of populism in America as well as in the development of the presidency itself.

46 "ONE GREAT FAMILY" Andrew Jackson, **The Papers of Andrew Jackson,** ed. Sam B. Smith et al., vol. 4, **1816–1820,** ed. Harold D. Moser et al. (Knoxville, 1994), 476.

47 JACKSON THUNDERED ON Meacham, **American Lion,** xv–xvii; 223–47.

47 JACKSON WAS STANDING James Parton, **Life of Andrew Jackson** (Boston, 1866), 3:466–67.

47 "WITH THE FEELINGS" Robert V. Remini, **Andrew Jackson and the Course of American Democracy, 1833–1845** (New York, 1984), 18. The phrase is included in notes Jackson made for Edward Livingston. Edward Livingston Papers, Manuscripts Division, Department of Rare Books and Special Collections, Princeton University Library.

47 WAS "INCOMPATIBLE WITH" Andrew Jackson: "Proclamation 43—Regarding the Nullifying Laws of South Carolina," December 10, 1832, American Presidency Project, http://www.presidency.ucsb.edu/ws/?pid=67078.

The final language in question read this way: "Fellow-citizens of my native State, let me not only admonish you, as the First Magistrate of our common country, not to incur the penalty of its laws, but use the influence that a father would over his children whom he saw rushing to certain ruin. In that paternal language, with that paternal feeling, let me tell you, my countrymen, that you are deluded by men who are either deceived themselves or wish to deceive you." Ibid.

47 HE WROTE SO QUICKLY Parton, **Life of Andrew Jackson,** 3:466. "A gentleman who came in when the President had written fifteen or twenty pages," the nineteenth-century Jackson biographer James Parton reported, "observed that three of them were glistening with wet ink at the same moment." Ibid. The pages were sent over to Secretary of State Edward Livingston, who had moved into Decatur House, on Lafayette Square, for the final drafting. Ibid.

48 "THE PRESIDENT," JACKSON WROTE Andrew Jackson: "Message to the Senate Protesting Censure Resolution," April 15, 1834, American Presidency Project, http://www.presidency.ucsb.edu/ws/?pid=67039.

48 THE CLAIM PROVOKED FURY **The Papers of John C. Calhoun,** ed. Robert L. Meriwether (Columbia, S.C., 1959–2003), 12:310.

48 "IF I CAN JUDGE" **Correspondence of Andrew Jackson: 1829–1832,** ed. John Spencer Bassett (Washington, D.C., 1929), 4:502.

48 IN THE PROCLAMATION Andrew Jackson: "Proclamation 43—Regarding the Nullifying Laws of South Carolina," December 10, 1832, American Presidency Project, http://www.presidency.ucsb.edu/ws/?pid=67078.

From the adoption of the Articles of Confederation to the formation and ratification of the Constitution to New England's Hartford Convention during the War of 1812 to the Missouri Compromise of 1820 to the crisis over nullification with South Carolina in 1832–33 to the cascading clashes of the 1850s, the country wrestled with federal authority and states' rights. Put roughly, the issue was whether the Union was formed from "We the People" or "We the States." As a matter of constitutional nuance, it was both. The framers, fearful of the power of passion, had carefully divided sovereignty not only among the central government and the states but among the branches of the federal establishment.

There was a respectable argument that nullification and even secession were implied rights in the Constitution. Calhoun in particular devoted years of intellectual and political labor to formulating just such a doctrine. In the battle over South Carolina's efforts to nullify a federal tariff, Senator Robert Hayne of South Carolina argued for Calhoun's vision: "Sir, I am one of those who believe that the very life of our system is the independence of the States, and that there is no evil more to be deprecated than the consolidation of this Government," Hayne told the Senate Tuesday, January 19, 1830. "It is only by a strict adherence to the limitations imposed by the constitution on the Federal Government that this system works well, and can answer the great ends for which it was instituted." Herman Belz, ed., **Webster-Hayne Debate on the Nature of the Union: Selected Documents** (Indianapolis, 2000), 10.

Among those listening to Hayne's speech was Senator Daniel Webster of Massachusetts, who took him on in what became a celebrated series of debates from Tuesday, January 19, to Wednesday, January 27, 1830. Meacham, **American Lion,** 127–30.

Webster executed a brilliant rhetorical feat, attacking the South Carolina doctrine and investing the Union with a power at once real and mystical. What, Webster asked, was the "origin of this government and the source of its power"? He answered:

Whose agent is it? Is it the creature of the State legislatures, or the creature of the people? If the government of the United States be the agent of the State governments, then they may control it, provided they can agree in the manner of controlling it; if it be the agent of the people, then the people alone can control it, restrain it, modify, or reform it. It is observable enough, that the doctrine for which the honorable gentleman contends leads him to the necessity of maintaining, not only that this general government is the creature of the States, but that it is the creature of each of the States severally, so that each may assert the power for itself of determining whether it acts

within the limits of its authority. It is the ser-
vant of four-and-twenty masters, of different
will and different purposes and yet bound to
obey all. This absurdity (for it seems no less)
arises from a misconception as to the origin of
this government and its true character. It is,
Sir, the people's Constitution, the people's
government, made for the people, made by
the people, and answerable to the people. The
people of the United States have declared that
the Constitution shall be the supreme law. We
must either admit the proposition, or dispute
their authority. Daniel Webster, "The Second
Reply to Hayne," http://www.dartmouth.edu/
~dwebster/speeches/hayne-speech.html.

In a stirring peroration, Webster offered a prose
poem to the virtues of Union:

While the Union lasts, we have high, exciting,
gratifying prospects spread out before us and
our children. Beyond that I seek not to penetrate the veil. God grant that in my day, at
least, that curtain may not rise! God grant that
on my vision never may be opened what lies
behind! When my eyes shall be turned to behold for the last time the sun in heaven, may I
not see him shining on the broken and dis-
honored fragments of a once glorious Union;
on States dissevered, discordant, belligerent;
on a land rent with civil feuds, or drenched, it
may be, in fraternal blood! Let their last feeble

and lingering glance rather behold the gorgeous ensign of the republic, now known and honored throughout the earth, still full high advanced, its arms and trophies streaming in their original lustre, not a stripe erased or polluted, not a single star obscured, bearing for its motto, no such miserable interrogatory as "What is all this worth?" nor those other words of delusion and folly, "Liberty first and Union afterwards"; but everywhere, spread all over in characters of living light, blazing on all it sample folds, as they float over the sea and over the land, and in every wind under the whole heavens, that other sentiment, dear to every true American heart—Liberty **and** Union, now and for ever, one and inseparable! Ibid.

In his eloquence, Webster had defined the notion of a perpetual union. Jackson was grateful, and he put the senator's oratory into action in late 1832 and early 1833.

50 THE INTERVAL BETWEEN JACKSON AND LINCOLN Goldsmith, **Growth of Presidential Power,** 1:597–721.

50 SERIES OF EXECUTIVE ACTIONS See, for instance, Schlesinger, **Imperial Presidency,** 58–67.

50 "CERTAIN PROCEEDINGS ARE" Ibid., 61. Lincoln was even blunter on another occasion, saying: "I think the Constitution invests its Commander-in-Chief with the law of war in the time of war." Goldsmith, **Growth of Presidential Power,** 2:964. Lord Bryce wrote, "In troublous

times . . . immense responsibility is then thrown on one who is both the commander-in-chief and the head of the civil executive. Abraham Lincoln wielded more authority than any single Englishman has done since Oliver Cromwell." Bryce, **American Commonwealth**, 1:65.

51 AT GETTYSBURG   For the Gettysburg Address's origins, development, and influence, see, for instance, Garry Wills, **Lincoln at Gettysburg: The Words That Remade America** (New York, 1992). For a thoughtful analysis of the speech and of Wills's argument, see Gary W. Gallagher, **The Union War** (Cambridge, Mass., 2011), 87–92.

51 "WITH MALICE TOWARD NONE"   Abraham Lincoln, "Inaugural Address," March 4, 1865, American Presidency Project, http://www.presi dency.ucsb.edu/ws/?pid=25819. Lincoln added: "Yet, if God wills that it continue until all the wealth piled by the bondsman's two hundred and fifty years of unrequited toil shall be sunk, and until every drop of blood drawn with the lash shall be paid by another drawn with the sword, as was said three thousand years ago, so still it must be said 'the judgments of the Lord are true and righteous altogether.'" Ibid.

The Biblical allusion was to Psalm 19, and Lincoln's point was stark. If the war went on, if more men had to die, then so be it, for such was the will of the Almighty. Lincoln believed the war a mysterious inevitability in the Jeffersonian course of human events. It was like the Fall of Man: It was something to be regretted but endured. For Lincoln, the fact of the matter was straightforward— not simple, but straightforward: that because of slavery, the war came.

52 LINCOLN RECEIVED FREDERICK DOUGLASS Lucas E. Morel, **Lincoln's Sacred Effort: Defining Religion's Role in American Self-Government** (Lanham, Md., 2000), 163. See also Donald, **Lincoln**, 568.

52 HE HAD FEARLESSLY PRESSED LINCOLN Michael Burlingame, **Abraham Lincoln: A Life** (Baltimore, 2008), 2:522–23. "My whole interview with the President was gratifying and did much to assure me that slavery would not survive the War and that the country would survive both slavery and the War." Ibid., 523.

52 "MR. LINCOLN," DOUGLASS SAID Morel, **Lincoln's Sacred Effort**, 163.

53 IN APRIL 1876 Frederick Douglass, "Oration in Memory of Abraham Lincoln," April 14, 1876, TeachingAmericanHistory.org, http://teaching americanhistory.org/library/document/oration -in-memory-of-abraham-lincoln/.

53 TO BE KNOWN "Lincoln Park," National Park Service, https://www.nps.gov/nr/travel/wash/dc87 .htm.

53 "TRUTH IS PROPER" Douglass, "Oration in Memory of Abraham Lincoln."

55 "WHILE ABRAHAM LINCOLN" Ibid.

55 "OUR FAITH IN HIM" Ibid.

56 "HIS GREAT MISSION" Ibid.

57 AN ADHERENT OF ULTIMATELY DISCREDITED

THEORIES   See, for instance, Evan Thomas, **The War Lovers: Roosevelt, Lodge, Hearst, and the Rush to Empire, 1898** (New York, 2010), 43–44; Leroy G. Dorsey, **We Are All Americans, Pure and Simple: Theodore Roosevelt and the Myth of Americanism** (Tuscaloosa, Ala., 2007), 2, which offers a summary view; and Thomas G. Dyer, **Theodore Roosevelt and the Idea of Race** (Baton Rouge, La., 1980), 89–92.

57   A "BULLY PULPIT"   Edward S. Corwin, **The President, Office and Powers: History and Analysis of Practice and Opinion** (New York, 1941), 267.

57   USED THE PHRASE ONE EVENING   Lyman Abbott, "A Review of President Roosevelt's Administration IV: Its Influence on Patriotism and Public Service," **The Outlook,** February 27, 1909, 430.

57   AS A FRIEND RECALLED   Ibid.

57   TR RECALLED THE TYPICAL AMERICAN   Theodore Roosevelt, **The Rough Riders and An Autobiography,** ed. Louis Auchincloss (New York, 2004), 646–47.

58   "I DECLINED TO ADOPT"   Ibid., 614.

58   "EVERY SUN, EVERY PLANET"   Wilson, **Constitutional Government,** 55.

59   "THE TROUBLE WITH"   Ibid., 56–57.

59   FORTUNATELY, THE DEFINITIONS   Ibid., 57.

60   "HIS POSITION TAKES"   Ibid., 68.

60   THE TWO MEN CHATTED   Geoffrey C. Ward, **A First-Class Temperament: The Emergence of Franklin Roosevelt** (New York, 1989), xi–xiii.

Together with his volume **Before the Trumpet: Young Franklin Roosevelt, 1882–1905** (New York, 1985), Ward has, I believe, produced the most psychologically astute portrait of FDR to date. I also drew on my "What a President Needs to Know," **Time,** July 14, 2016, for this section.

61 "You know, his [Cousin] Ted"   Ward, **First-Class Temperament,** xiii.

61 "a second-class intellect"   Ibid. There is some debate about whether Justice Holmes, in rendering his "first-class temperament" verdict, was talking about Theodore rather than Franklin Roosevelt. See, for instance, Jonathan Alter, **The Defining Moment: FDR's Hundred Days and the Triumph of Hope** (New York, 2006), 234; 375.

61 Potter Stewart's definition of hardcore pornography   John P. MacKenzie, "Potter Stewart Is Dead at 70; Was on High Court 23 Years," **NYT,** December 8, 1985. The observation is found in Stewart's concurring opinion, handed down on June 22, 1964, in the case of **Jacobellis v. Ohio.** See "Jacobellis v. Ohio," Legal Information Institute, Cornell Law School, https://www.law.cornell.edu/supremecourt/text/378/184#writing-USSC_CR_0378_0184 _ZC1.

61 The word itself derives   **The Oxford English Dictionary,** 2nd ed., prepared by J. A. Simpson and E.S.C. Weiner (Oxford, 1989), 17:747.

61 Once, after watching   John Gunther, **Roosevelt in Retrospect: A Profile in History** (New

York, 1950), 62. For this section, I drew on my "Donald Trump and the Limits of the Reality-TV Presidency," originally published in **NYT**, December 30, 2017.

61 "You know, Orson" Gunther, **Roosevelt in Retrospect,** 62.

61 "I guess that" **Where the Buck Stops: The Personal and Private Writings of Harry S. Truman,** ed. Margaret Truman (New York, 1989), 363.

62 "I know . . . that" **F.D.R.: His Personal Letters, 1928–1945,** ed. Elliott Roosevelt (New York, 1950), 1:466.

62 "There is another thought" Ibid.

63 "band of brothers" William Shakespeare, **The Life of King Henry the Fifth,** act 4, scene 3, http://shakespeare.mit.edu/henryv/henryv .4.3.html.

63 "I keep telling you" Emmet John Hughes, **The Ordeal of Power: A Political Memoir of the Eisenhower Years** (New York, 1963), 131–32.

63 subject to "clamorous counsel" John F. Kennedy, "Foreword to Theodore C. Sorensen's 'Decision-Making in the White House,'" September 23, 1963, American Presidency Project, http://www.presidency.ucsb.edu/ws/?pid=9421.

64 "Now, look, I happen" Hughes, **Ordeal of Power,** 124.

64 Well, I have been President Theodore Roosevelt to Maria Longworth Storer, December 8, 1902, **The Letters of Theodore Roosevelt,** vol. 3, **The Square Deal, 1901–1903,** ed. Elting Morison (Cambridge, Mass., 1951), 391–92.

66 "VITAL CENTER OF ACTION" Kennedy, "The Presidency in 1960."

66 CHARACTER IS DESTINY The remark, also sometimes translated as "character is fate," is attributed to Heraclitus. See Richard G. Geldard, **Remembering Heraclitus** (Hudson, N.Y., 2000), 85.

66 "THE FORM OF GOVERNMENT" Ralph Waldo Emerson, **Essays and Lectures,** ed. Joel Porte (New York, 1983), 559.

66 THE "PURSUIT OF HAPPINESS" This section on the pursuit of happiness is drawn from my essay "Free to Be Happy," **Time,** June 27, 2013. See also Arthur M. Schlesinger, Sr., "The Lost Meaning of 'The Pursuit of Happiness,'" **William and Mary Quarterly** 21, no. 3 (July 1964): 325–27; James R. Rogers, "The Meaning of 'The Pursuit of Happiness,'" First Things, June 19, 2012, https://www.firstthings.com/web-exclusives/2012/06/the-meaning-of-the-pursuit-of-happiness; and A. J. Beitzinger, **A History of American Political Thought** (New York, 1972), 164–66.

66 HIS RENTED SECOND-FLOOR QUARTERS "Declaration House," National Park Service, https://www.nps.gov/inde/learn/historyculture/places-declarationhouse.htm.

66 "WHEN JEFFERSON SPOKE" Garry Wills, **Inventing America: Jefferson's Declaration of Independence** (Garden City, N.Y., 1978), 164.

67 "THE ELEMENTARY BOOKS" Ibid., 172.

67 HAPPINESS, HE WROTE Richard Kraut, "Aris-

totle's Ethics," **The Stanford Encyclopedia of Philosophy,** ed. Edward N. Zalta, Summer 2017, https://plato.stanford.edu/archives/sum2017/entries/aristotle-ethics/. See also "Aristotle's Definition of Happiness," The Pursuit of Happiness, http://www.pursuit-of-happiness.org/history-of-happiness/aristotle/.

The thinking about happiness came to American shores most directly from the work of John Locke and from Scottish-Irish philosopher Francis Hutcheson. During the Enlightenment, thinkers and politicians struggled with redefining the role of the individual in an ethos so long dominated by feudalism, autocratic religious establishments, and the divine rights of kings. A key insight of the age was that reason, not revelation, should have primacy in human affairs. That belief in the power of reason was leading Western thinkers to focus on the idea of happiness, which in Jefferson's hands—and in ours, down the ages—is better understood as the pursuit of individual excellence that shapes the life of a broader community.

Like, say, the newly emerging United States of America. Pre-Jefferson, the centrality of happiness was explicitly expressed in the Virginia Declaration of Rights, a document written by George Mason and very much on Jefferson's mind in the summer of 1776. Men, wrote Mason, "are by nature equally free and independent and have certain inherent rights . . . namely, the enjoyment of life and liberty, with the means of acquiring and possessing property, and pursuing and obtaining happiness and safety."

Property is often key to happiness, but Mason was thinking more broadly, drawing on the tradition of the ancients to articulate a larger scope for civic life. Much is often made of the fact that Jefferson inserted "the pursuit of happiness" in place of "property" from earlier formulations of fundamental rights. Yet property and prosperity are essential to the Jeffersonian pursuit, for economic progress has long proven a precursor of political and social liberty. As Jefferson's friend and neighbor James Madison would say, the test is one of balance and proportion. Meacham, "Free to Be Happy," **Time.**

67 EUDAIMONIA—THE GREEK WORD   Kraut, "Aristotle's Ethics." "Aristotle asks what the **ergon** ("function," "task," "work") of a human being is, and argues that it consists in activity of the rational part of the soul in accordance with virtue," Kraut wrote. Ibid.

67 A BROAD UNDERSTANDING   Schlesinger, "Lost Meaning," 326.

68 "FROM THE RAPID PROGRESS"   Robert A. Nisbet, **History of the Idea of Progress** (New York, 1980), 202.

68 THE IDEA THAT   Ibid., 4–9. I also owe much to Nisbet's "Idea of Progress: A Bibliographic Essay," Online Library of Liberty, http://oll.libertyfund .org/pages/idea-of-progress-a-bibliographical -essay-by-robert-nisbet. "Simply stated," Nisbet wrote in his **History,** "the idea of progress holds

that mankind has advanced in the past—from some aboriginal condition of primitiveness, barbarism, or even nullity—is now advancing, and will continue to advance through the foreseeable future. . . . The idea must not be thought the companion of mere caprice or accident; it must be thought a part of the very scheme of things in universe and society. Advance from the inferior to the superior must seem as real and certain as anything in the laws of nature." Nisbet, **History of the Idea of Progress**, 4–5.

69　("The gods did not reveal")　Ibid., 11.

69　the myth of Prometheus　Ibid., 18–21.

69　"The education of"　Ibid., 61. "The Greeks contributed the seminal conception of the natural growth in time of knowledge, and accordingly the natural advance of the human condition," Nisbet wrote.

This emphasis upon knowledge, upon the arts and sciences, is . . . very much a part of the Christian philosophy of history. . . . The Christian philosophers, starting with Eusebius and Tertullian and reaching masterful and lasting expression in St. Augustine, endowed the idea of progress with new attributes which were bound to give it a spiritual force unknown to their pagan predecessors. I refer to such attributes as the vision of the unity of all mankind, the role of historical necessity, the image of progress as the unfolding through long ages of a design present from the very beginning of man's history, and far from least, a confidence in the future that would become steadily greater and also more **this**-worldly in orientation as compared with **next**-worldly. Ibid., 47.

69 FOR THE AMERICAN FOUNDERS   Ibid., 193–206.

69 "THE WHOLE HUMAN RACE"   **Turgot on Progress, Sociology and Economics,** trans. Ronald L. Meek (Cambridge, 1973), 41.

69 "LIKE THE EBB AND FLOW"   Ibid., 44.

70 "AMERICA IS THE HOPE"   Nisbet, **History of the Idea of Progress,** 193.

71 "EVERY MAN, AS LONG"   Ibid., 191.

71 BY "PURSUING HIS"   Adam Smith, **An Inquiry into the Nature and Causes of the Wealth of Nations,** Library of Economics and Liberty, http://www.econlib.org/library/Smith/smWN13.html.

71 "HOW SELFISH SOEVER"   Adam Smith, **The Theory of Moral Sentiments,** ed. Ryan Patrick Hanley (New York, 2009), 13.

71 "MACHIAVELLI, DISCOURSING ON THESE MATTERS"   See, for instance, Alan Craig Houston, **Algernon Sidney and the Republican Heritage in England and America** (Princeton, N.J., 2014), 146. Expanding on the point, Houston characterized Sidney's view this way: "Only a republic could claim stability, strength, and the pursuit of the public interest, for only a republic was founded on obedience to the law, the defense of common interests, and the keeping of covenants." Ibid., 147.

72 "WHAT THE TENDER POETIC YOUTH" Emerson, **Essays and Lectures,** 560.

73 "I THINK THAT" "Sojouner's Words and Music," Sojourner Truth Memorial Committee. See also Painter, **Sojourner Truth,** 121–31; 164–78. For the complicated history of the reports of Truth's remarks, see, as noted above, ibid., 164–78.

73 "WE ASK," ELIZABETH CADY STANTON TOLD Elizabeth Cady Stanton, "Address to the Legislature of New York, 1854," "Women's Rights," National Park Service, https://www.nps.gov/wori/learn/historyculture/address-to-the-new-york-legislature-1854.htm.

73 "IF BLACK MEN" Frederick Douglass, "An Appeal to Congress for Impartial Suffrage," **The Atlantic Monthly,** January 1867.

74 "ONE HUNDRED YEARS AGO" "Remarks of Vice President Lyndon B. Johnson," May 30, 1963, http://www.usmemorialday.org/Speeches/President/may3063.txt.

75 "UNLESS WE ARE WILLING" Ibid.

TWO · The Long Shadow of Appomattox

81 THE PRINCIPLE FOR WHICH Edward A. Pollard, **The Lost Cause: A New Southern History of the War of the Confederates** (New York, 1866), 749.

81 WE MAY SAY THAT ONLY Robert Penn Warren, **The Legacy of the Civil War: Meditations on the Centennial** (New York, 1961), 15.

81 ON THE AFTERNOON OF APRIL 9, 1865 For

my account of the surrender, I drew on Shelby Foote, **The Civil War: A Narrative** (New York, 1958), 3:939–56; James M. McPherson, **Battle Cry of Freedom: The Civil War Era** (New York, 1988), 848–51; Douglas Southall Freeman, **R. E. Lee: A Biography** (New York, 1935), 4:115–48. Elizabeth R. Varon, **Appomattox: Victory, Defeat, and Freedom at the End of the Civil War** (New York, 2014) is an engaging and challenging study of how differing views of the surrender helped shape the conflicts of post-war America. "The two men represented competing visions of the peace," Varon wrote.

For Grant, the Union victory was one of right over wrong. He believed that his magnanimity, no less than his victory, vindicated free society and the Union's way of war. Grant's eyes were on the future—a future in which Southerners, chastened and repentant, would join their Northern brethren in the march towards moral and material progress. Lee, by contrast, believed that the Union victory was one of might over right. In his view, Southerners had nothing to repent of and had survived the war with their honor and principles intact. He was intent on restoration—on turning the clock back, as much as possible, to the days when Virginia led the nation and before sectional extremism alienated the North from the South. Ibid., 1–2.

81   WITH A HANDSOME SWORD   Foote, **Civil War,** 3:946.

81   LEE MET GRANT, WHO WORE ONLY   McPherson, **Battle Cry of Freedom,** 849.

81   THAT MORNING LEE HAD MUSED   Freeman, **R. E. Lee,** 4:121.

81   "HOW EASILY I COULD"   Ibid.

82   AS THE STORY IS TOLD   Ibid.

82   "BUT IT IS OUR DUTY"   Ibid.

82   "WHAT WILL BECOME"   Ibid.

82   GRANT, WHO ARRIVED   Ibid., 4:134–35.

82   A DEBILITATING HEADACHE   McPherson, **Battle Cry of Freedom,** 848.

82   QUIETLY "JUBILANT," HE RECALLED   Foote, **Civil War,** 3:946.

82   CHOSE TO ENTER THE PARLOR ALONE   Freeman, **R. E. Lee,** 4:135.

82   TAKING LEE'S HAND   Foote, **Civil War,** 3:946–47.

82   "I MET YOU ONCE"   Ibid. "I have always remembered your appearance and I think I should have recognized you anywhere," Grant said. "Yes, I know I met you on that occasion," Lee replied, "and I have often thought of it and tried to recollect how you looked. But I have never been able to recall a single feature." As Foote noted, drily: "If this was a snub Grant did not realize it, or else he let it pass." Ibid. See also Freeman, **R. E. Lee,** 4:135–36.

82   AT LAST IT FELL TO LEE   Foote, **Civil War,** 3:947.

82   "I SUPPOSE, GENERAL GRANT"   Ibid.

83   GRANT WAS MAGNANIMOUS   Ibid. See also
McPherson, **Battle Cry of Freedom**, 849.

83   "PUT IN A CROP"   McPherson, **Battle Cry of
Freedom**, 849.

83   "THIS WILL HAVE"   Ibid.

83   "AS HE WAS A MAN"   Foote, **Civil War**, 3:946.

83   "THE WAR IS OVER"   McPherson, **Battle Cry of
Freedom**, 850.

83   AS THE TWO GENERALS PARTED   Foote, **Civil
War**, 3:950.

84   THE "FIERY TRIAL"   Abraham Lincoln: "Second
Annual Message," December 1, 1862, American
Presidency Project, http://www.presidency.ucsb
.edu/ws/?pid=29503. Lincoln's peroration is among
the most memorable in the literature of the American presidency:

Fellow-citizens, we can not escape history. We
of this Congress and this Administration will
be remembered in spite of ourselves. No personal significance or insignificance can spare
one or another of us. The fiery trial through
which we pass will light us down in honor or
dishonor to the latest generation. We say we
are for the Union. The world will not forget
that we say this. We know how to save the
Union. The world knows we do know how to
save it. We, even we here, hold the power and
bear the responsibility. In giving freedom to
the slave we assure freedom to the free—
honorable alike in what we give and what we
preserve. We shall nobly save or meanly lose

the last best hope of earth. Other means may succeed; this could not fail. The way is plain, peaceful, generous, just—a way which if followed the world will forever applaud and God must forever bless." Ibid.

85   IN THE CREED OF THE LOST CAUSE   I learned much from the Edward Pollard books cited below, as well as from W. Fitzhugh Brundage, "Redeeming a Failed Revolution: Confederate Memory," in **In the Cause of Liberty**, ed. Cooper and McCardell, 126–35; David W. Blight, "Traced by Blood: African Americans and the Legacies of the Civil War," ibid., 136–53; Blight, **Race and Reunion: The Civil War in American Memory** (Cambridge, Mass., 2002), especially 255–99; Caroline E. Janney, **Remembering the Civil War: Reunion and the Limits of Reconciliation** (Chapel Hill, N.C., 2013) 133–96; Gary W. Gallagher and Alan T. Nolan, eds., **The Myth of the Lost Cause and Civil War History** (Bloomington, Ind., 2000); Thomas L. Connelly and Barbara L. Bellows, eds., **God and General Longstreet: The Lost Cause and the Southern Mind** (Baton Rouge, La., 1982); Connelly, **The Marble Man: Robert E. Lee and His Image in American Society** (Baton Rouge, La., 1977); Gaines M. Foster, **Ghosts of the Confederacy: Defeat, the Lost Cause, and the Emergence of the New South, 1865 to 1913** (New York, 1987); Charles Reagan Wilson, **Baptized in Blood: The Religion of the Lost Cause, 1865–1920** (Ath-

ens, Ga., 2009); and Varon, **Appomattox**, especially 208–43; 252–55.

85   BETWEEN ONE IN THREE AND ONE IN FIVE Brundage, "Redeeming a Failed Revolution," 127. For discussions of casualties in the war as a whole, see, for instance, Drew Gilpin Faust, **This Republic of Suffering: Death and the American Civil War** (New York, 2008), xi–xvii; Gallagher, **Union War**, 164–65; J. David Hacker, "A Census-Based Count of the Civil War Dead," **Civil War History** 57, no. 4, (December 2011): 307–48. The overall toll, North and South, military and civilian, was, James McPherson wrote, "as great as in all of the nation's other wars combined through Vietnam. Was the liberation of four million slaves and the preservation of the Union worth the cost? That question too will probably never cease to be debated—but in 1865 few black people and not many northerners doubted the answer." McPherson, **Battle Cry of Freedom**, 854. Faust wrote: "The American Civil War produced carnage that has often been thought reserved for the combination of technological proficiency and inhumanity characteristic of a later time." Faust, **This Republic of Suffering**, xii.

85   MISSISSIPPI EARMARKED 20 PERCENT Brundage, "Redeeming a Failed Revolution," 127. See also Richard White, **The Republic for Which It Stands: The United States During Reconstruction and the Gilded Age, 1865–1896** (New York, 2017), 28.

85   PRESTON BROOKS OF SOUTH CAROLINA Wil-

liamjames Hull Hoffer, **The Caning of Charles Sumner: Honor, Idealism, and the Origins of the Civil War** (Baltimore, 2010).

86 VIRGINIA CHOSE TO HANG JOHN BROWN   Warren, **Legacy of the Civil War,** 40.

86 "THEREBY PROVED AGAIN"   Ibid.

86 HIS STATE WAS "TOO SMALL"   Sean Wilentz, **The Rise of American Democracy: Jefferson to Lincoln** (New York, 2005), 769. See also Wilentz, "Why Did Southerners Secede?" in **In the Cause of Liberty,** 31.

86 THE "IRREPRESSIBLE CONFLICT"   "The Irrepressible Conflict.; History of Slavery as a Political Issue . . . Speech of Hon. William H. Seward in the Senate of the United States," **NYT**, March 1, 1860.

86 IN HIS MEMOIRS   James M. McPherson, "Southern Comfort," **New York Review of Books,** April 12, 2001.

86 "AFRICAN SERVITUDE WAS"   Ibid.

87 HIS "CORNERSTONE SPEECH" IN SAVANNAH   Alexander H. Stephens, " 'Corner Stone' Speech," March 21, 1861, TeachingAmericanHistory.org, http://teachingamericanhistory.org/library/document/cornerstone-speech/.

87 THE REPUBLICAN PARTY'S EMERGENCE   Eric Foner, "The Ideology of the Republican Party" in **The Birth of the Grand Old Party: The Republicans' First Generation,** ed. Robert F. Engs and Randall M. Miller (Philadelphia, 2002), 8–28; Mark E. Neely, Jr., "Politics Purified: Religion and the Growth of Antislavery Idealism in Re-

publican Ideology During the Civil War," ibid., 103–27; Wilentz, **Rise of American Democracy,** 679; 685.

87   "I AM NATURALLY"   Foner, **The Fiery Trial: Abraham Lincoln and American Slavery** (New York, 2010), 3.

88   A "MONSTROUS INJUSTICE"   Ibid., 66. Foner's treatment of the Peoria speech can be found ibid., 63–70.

88   "LET US RE-ADOPT"   Abraham Lincoln, "Speech at Peoria, Illinois," **Collected Works of Abraham Lincoln,** vol. 2, https://quod.lib.umich.edu/l/lin coln/lincoln2/1:282.1?rgn=div2;view=fulltext.

88   "IF ALL EARTHLY POWER"   Ibid.

88   MY FIRST IMPULSE   Ibid.

89   WAS "ALWAYS CALCULATING"   Goldsmith, **Growth of Presidential Power,** 2:894.

89   HE REJECTED ANY COMPROMISE   Foner, **Fiery Trial,** 144–57; and Ronald C. White, Jr., **A. Lincoln: A Biography** (New York, 2009), 360–61. See also Harold Holzer, **Lincoln President Elect: Abraham Lincoln and the Great Secession Winter** (New York, 2008); and William J. Cooper, Jr., **We Have the War Upon Us: The Onset of the Civil War, November 1860–April 1861** (New York, 2012).

89   BY THE SUMMER OF 1862   Foner, **Fiery Trial,** 206–47. The Second Confiscation Act, passed and signed in July 1862, was also a critical turning point. "The bill . . . authorized the president to warn all supporters of the Confederacy to abandon the rebellion or face the confiscation and sale

by federal courts of their property," Foner wrote. "The ninth section declared 'forever free of their servitude' all rebel-owned slaves who escaped to Union lines or lived in Confederate territory subsequently occupied by Union troops." Ibid., 215.

89 To prepare public opinion Ibid., 228–29.

89 "My paramount object"   "Letter to Horace Greeley," Abraham Lincoln Online.org, http://www.abrahamlincolnonline.org/lincoln/speeches/greeley.htm.

90 By speaking of   Foner, **Fiery Trial**, 229.

90 in the wake of the Confederate setback   Ibid., 230–31.

90 Lincoln told his cabinet   Ibid., 231.

90 He had drafted   Ibid.; Burlingame, **Abraham Lincoln**, 2:362–64.

90 He had, he told them   Ibid., 2:363.

90 With the Preliminary Emancipation Proclamation   Foner, **Fiery Trial**, 231. See also "Preliminary Emancipation Proclamation, 1862," American Originals, National Archives, https://www.archives.gov/exhibits/american_originals_iv/sections/preliminary_emancipation_proclamation.html. See also Foner, **Fiery Trial**, 206–89, for a complete treatment, as well as Allen Guelzo, **Lincoln's Emancipation Proclamation: The End of Slavery in America** (New York, 2004). The Proclamation, the twentieth-century historian C. Vann Woodward remarked, transformed the war for the North. "For one thing, it helped to elevate the war to a new plane," Woodward wrote. "It was still a war for union, but not as before—a war

for union with slavery. It was no longer merely a war against something [secession] but for something, a war for something greatly cherished in American tradition and creed, a war for freedom. What had started as a war for political ends had, by virtue of military necessity, undergone a metamorphosis into a higher and finer thing, a war for moral ends." Woodward, **The Burden of Southern History** (Baton Rouge, La., 1993), 73.

91 THE WORDS THAT JULIA WARD HOWE HAD WRITTEN   Julia Ward Howe, "Battle Hymn of the Republic," **The Atlantic Monthly,** February 1862.

92 "THE UNION"   Woodward, **Burden of Southern History,** 84.

92 "YOUR RACE ARE SUFFERING"   Abraham Lincoln, "Address on Colonization to a Deputation of Negroes," **Collected Works of Abraham Lincoln,** vol. 5, https://quod.lib.umich.edu/l/lincoln/lincoln5/1:812?rgn=div1;view=fulltext.

92 "BUT FOR YOUR RACE"   Ibid.

93 "WHEN WAS IT EVER"   Woodward, **Burden of Southern History,** 90.

93 HIS LAST PUBLIC SPEECH   Louis P. Masur, **Lincoln's Last Speech: Wartime Reconstruction and the Crisis of Reunion** (New York, 2013).

93 "WE MEET THIS EVENING"   Ibid., 5.

93 DESCRIBED AS "MISTY"   Noah Brooks, **Lincoln Observed: Civil War Dispatches of Noah Brooks,** ed. Michael Burlingame (Baltimore, 1998), 183.

93 "CHEERS UPON CHEERS"   Ibid.

93 AS TAD LINCOLN PICKED UP   Masur, **Lincoln's Last Speech,** 162.

93 HAD GIVEN THE UNION "HOPE"   Ibid., 189.

93 "WE SIMPLY MUST BEGIN"   Ibid. "The speech was longer and of a different character from what most people had expected," Noah Brooks wrote, "but it was well received, and it showed that the President had shared in, and had considered, the same anxieties which the people have had, as this struggle has drawn to a close." Brooks, **Lincoln Observed,** 183–84.

94 EDWARD ALFRED POLLARD   Pollard, **Lost Cause: A New Southern History** and **The Lost Cause Regained** (New York, 1868); Jack P. Maddex, Jr., **The Reconstruction of Edward A. Pollard: A Rebel's Conversion to Postbellum Unionism** (Chapel Hill, N.C., 1974); "Edward A. Pollard" in **The American Annual Cyclopedia and Register of Important Events, 1872** (New York, 1872), 676; James Southall Wilson, "Edward Alfred Pollard," in **Library of Southern Literature, Compiled Under the Direct Supervision of Southern Men of Letters,** ed. Edwin A. Alderman, Joel C. Harris, and Charles W. Kent (Atlanta, 1907), 9:4147–50; Joseph G. de Roulhac Hamilton, "Edward A. Pollard," in **Dictionary of American Biography,** ed. Allen Johnson and Dumas Malone (New York, 1928–37), 47–48; Connelly and Bellows, **God and General Longstreet,** 1–38; Brooks D. Simpson, "Continuous Hammering and Mere Attrition: Lost Cause Critics and the Military Reputation of Ulysses S.

Grant" in **Myth of the Lost Cause**, 147–69; Peter S. Carmichael, "New South Visionaries: Virginia's Last Generation of Slaveholders, the Gospel of Progress, and the Lost Cause," ibid., 119–26; James M. McPherson, "American Victory, American Defeat" in **Why the Confederacy Lost**, ed. Gabor S. Boritt (New York, 1992), 17–42.

94   "No one can read aright"   Pollard, **Lost Cause: A New Southern History**, 46. In a January 1856 speech at the Tremont Temple in Boston—approvingly cited by Pollard—Georgia senator Robert Toombs had declared: "The white is the superior race, and the black the inferior; and subordination, with or without law, will be the status of the African in this mixed society; and, therefore, it is the interest of both, and especially of the black race, and of the whole society, that this status should be fixed, controlled, and protected by law." Ibid., 49. To Pollard, "The whole ground is covered by these two propositions: that subordination is the necessary condition of the black man; and that the so-called 'slavery' in the South was but the precise adjustment of this subordination by law." Ibid.

95   "The people of the South"   Ibid., 750.

95   a " 'war of ideas' "   Ibid. See also Blight, **Race and Reunion**, 50–51.

95   "The war has left"   Pollard, **Lost Cause: A New Southern History**, 751. Pollard added: "It would be immeasurably the worst consequence of defeat in this war that the South should lose its moral and intellectual distinctiveness as a people,

and cease to assert its well-known superiority in civilization, in political scholarship, and in all the standards of individual character over the people of the North." Ibid.

95 "DID NOT DECIDE"   Ibid., 752.

95 HE WAS "PROFOUNDLY CONVINCED"   Pollard, **Lost Cause Regained,** 13.

96 THE "TRUE CAUSE"   Ibid., 14. It was, Pollard wrote, "the greater contest." Ibid., 154–55.

96 "MUST WEAR THE CROWN"   Ibid., 156. See also Wilson, **Baptized in Blood,** for the religious elements of the Lost Cause.

96 JUBAL A. EARLY, A VETERAN   For Early and his role in shaping the images of Lee and of the Lost Cause, see, for instance, Charles C. Osborne, **Jubal: The Life and Times of General Jubal A. Early, CSA, Defender of the Lost Cause** (Chapel Hill, N.C., 1992), 431–35, 438–40; Connelly, **Marble Man,** 55, 73–78; Blight, **Race and Reunion,** 264–70; Connelly and Bellows, **God and General Longstreet,** 3, 26, 33–35.

97 "WE CAN SCARCELY"   Alice Fahs and Joan Waugh, eds., **The Memory of the Civil War in American Culture** (Chapel Hill, N.C., 2004), 57.

97 THE NORTH HAD NOT OUTFOUGHT   See, for instance, Boritt, **Why the Confederacy Lost,** particularly McPherson, "American Victory, American Defeat," ibid., 17–42; Connelly and Bellows, **God and General Longstreet,** 1–38; Blight, **Race and Reunion,** 255–99. David Herbert Donald, ed., **Why the North Won the Civil War: Six Authoritative Views on the Economic,**

Notes 509

Military, Diplomatic, Social, and Political Reasons Behind the Confederacy's Defeat (New York, 2005), is also instructive. Boritt's collection, as Boritt put it, "follows in the footsteps" of the Donald book. Boritt, **Why the Confederacy Lost**, 13.

Henry A. Wise, the former Virginia governor and Confederate general, articulated this view in a speech on behalf of the Female Orphan Society in Richmond in the last days of January 1866, saying:

The noblest hands of men who ever fought or who ever fell in the annals of war, whose glorious deeds history ever took pen to record were, I exultingly claim, the private soldiers in the armies of the great Confederate cause. Whether right or wrong in the cause which they espoused, they were earnest and honest patriots in their convictions, who thought that they were right to defend their own, their native land, its soil, its altars and its honor. . . . They fought with a devout confidence and courage which was unconquerable save by starvation, blockade, overwhelming numbers, foreign dupes and mercenaries, Yankeedom, Negrodom and death! **Richmond Enquirer**, January 31, 1866.

In an address at Hanover, Virginia, in the summer of 1867, Wise said that the white South was not to be subjugated to blacks. "Are her lands and temples and groves to be dedicated to the Congo race?" Wise asked. Blacks were "naturally lazy and unsteady at work, and they are likely to be the slaves of crimes, engendered by their idleness, dissipation, destitution, and consequent degradation. They are unfit for self-government, and need training as mere pupils of liberty. . . . The white race everywhere cannot but heed our call to the rescue of our race. Let the appeal be at once made with a loud and long note, as of a trumpet making no uncertain sound." **NYT**, August 25, 1867.

In a discursive letter to a New York publishing house that was preparing a biographical sketch of him that he disliked, Wise wrote: "I said all I meant, meant all I said, and tried my best to do all I said and meant for '**the lost cause**.' What is the 'lost cause'?" The Confederacy, he said, "is not the only cause lost. The Constitution is lost; the Union, defined by it, is lost; the liberty of States and their people, which they both at first and for half a century guarded, are lost. I am anxious only that the truth shall be told and felt." Undated clip, Wise Family Papers, Virginia Historical Society.

The image of Robert E. Lee, as noted above in the discussion of Jubal Early, was an essential element in the Lost Cause. In a sense, as the decades passed, Lee **became** the Confederacy, far more so than his commander in chief, Jefferson Davis, or his brilliant colleague Thomas "Stonewall" Jackson. This was useful for adherents of the Lost Cause, for Lee would come to be seen in many quarters as a worthy American, rather than as a merely Southern, icon. For an examination of this subject, see Connelly, **Marble Man,** which traces Lee's evolving image from "Lee in His Time," Ibid., 11–26, through "The Making of a Southern Idol," Ibid., 62–98, to the "Birth of a National Hero," Ibid., 99–122, to "Lee and the Southern Renaissance, 1920–1940," Ibid., 123–40, to "The Middle-Class Hero: From Freeman to the Centennial," Ibid., 141–62.

To Theodore Roosevelt—whose mother grew up in antebellum Georgia and whose uncles fought for the Confederacy—Lee was "a matter of pride to all his countrymen." Connelly and Bellows, **God and General Longstreet,** 75. In 1904, when Robert E. Lee, Jr., published a popular volume entitled **Recollections and Letters of Robert E. Lee, The New York Times** was struck by the late general's "true character . . . the modesty, the courage, the humility and the grandeur of soul." Ibid.

In testimony before the Joint Committee on Reconstruction in Congress in Washington on Saturday, February 17, 1866, Lee was circumspect, answering lawmakers' questions laconically and briefly. Asked whether former Confederates might make common cause with England, France, or another foreign power in the event of war with the United States, Lee allowed: "It is possible. It depends upon the feelings of the individual." Of black suffrage, he said: "My own opinion is that, at this time, they cannot vote intelligently, and that giving them the right of suffrage would open the door to a great deal of demagogism, and lead to embarrassments in various ways."

Would a Virginia jury convict someone—the committee tactfully cited Davis as an example, not Lee himself—of treason for rebelling against the Union? "I think it is very probable that they would not consider that he had committed treason," Lee said.

"In what light would they view it?" Senator Jacob M. Howard of Michigan asked. "What would be their excuse or justification?"

"So far as I know, they look upon the action of the State, in withdrawing itself from the government of the United States, as carrying the individuals of the State along with it; that the State was responsible for the act, not the individual. . . . The act of Virginia, in withdrawing herself from the United States, carried me along as a citizen of Virginia, and that her law and her acts were binding on me."

"And that you felt to be your justification in taking the course you did?"

"Yes, sir," said Lee. Report of the Joint Committee on Reconstruction, at the First Session, Thirty-Ninth Congress (Washington, D.C., 1866), 131–34.

98   OLD TIMES THERE   Blight, **Race and Reunion,** 259, quotes Jefferson Davis on the point: "We may not hope to see the rebuilding of the temple as our Fathers designed it, but we can live on praying for that event and die with eyes fixed on the promised land." Ibid.

98   "The 'Lost Cause'"   Pollard, **Lost Cause Regained,** 214.

98   In the spring of 1866   Elaine Frantz Parsons, **Ku-Klux: The Birth of the Klan During Reconstruction** (Chapel Hill, N.C., 2015), 27–71; Blight, **Race and Reunion,** 108–22; Eric Foner, **Reconstruction: America's Unfinished Revolution, 1863–1877** (New York, 2014), 425–44; Allen W. Trelease, **White Terror: The Ku Klux Klan Conspiracy and Southern Reconstruction** (Baton Rouge, 1971), 3–27; David M. Chalmers, **Hooded Americanism: The History of the Ku Klux Klan** (New York, 1987), 8–21; Claude G. Bowers, **The Tragic Era: The Revolution After Lincoln** (New York, 1929), 306–12; Andrew Nelson Lytle, **Bedford Forrest and His Critter Company** (New York, 1931), 382–85.

On Reconstruction in general, see Foner, **Reconstruction,** and his **Forever Free: The Story of Emancipation and Reconstruction** (New York, 2005); Douglas R. Egerton, **The Wars of Reconstruction: The Brief, Violent History of America's Most Progressive Era** (New York, 2014); White, **Republic for Which It Stands;** Blight, **Race and Reunion,** especially 98–139; George C. Rable, **But There Was No Peace: The Role of Violence in the Politics of Reconstruction** (Athens, Ga., 1984); Gregory Downs, **After Appomattox: Military Occupation and the Ends of War** (Cambridge, Mass., 2015).

98   They were bored   Bowers, **Tragic Era,** 306.

98   derived from kuklos   Ibid.

98   "Boys, let's start something"   Ibid.

99 "EVERY ONE WAS" Ibid., 306-07.

99 "THE SCALAWAG-CARPETBAGGER REGIME" Lytle, **Bedford Forrest**, 382. The Unionist governor of Tennessee, William G. Brownlow, was furious about the vigilante violence. "I have no concessions to make to traitors, no compromises to offer to assassins and robbers; and if, in the sweep of coming events, retributive justice shall overtake the lawless and violent, their own temerity will have called it forth," Brownlow announced on Monday, February 25, 1867. "The outrages enumerated **must** and SHALL cease." Trelease, **White Terror**, 12.

99 AT A GATHERING AT THE MAXWELL HOUSE HOTEL Trelease, **White Terror**, 14–16.

99 INTRIGUED BY WHAT HE WAS HEARING Lytle, **Bedford Forrest**, 382–83.

100 "THERE WILL NEVER BE" Ibid., 305. The Klan and related groups waged a campaign of violence against blacks and federal officials, terrorizing those whom unrepentant Confederates believed to be threats. The Union general Carl Schurz, in his 1865 **Report on Conditions in the South,** wrote: "The pecuniary value which the individual negro formerly represented having disappeared, the maiming and killing of colored men seems to be looked upon by many as one of those venial offenses which must be forgiven to the outraged feelings of a wronged and robbed people." Trelease, **White Terror**, xvi–xvii.

The chaos and bloodshed were so widespread that Congress launched an investigation through a panel officially known as the Joint Select Committee to Inquire into the Condition of Affairs in the Late Insurrectionary States. Ibid., 392.

In 1872, the final majority report of the joint committee on the Klan struck reasonable notes. "The strong feeling which led to rebellion and sustained brave men, however mistaken, in resisting the Government which demanded their submission to its authority, the sincerity of whose belief was attested by their enormous sacrifice of life and treasure—this feeling cannot be expected to subside at once, nor in years," the Republicans wrote. "But while we invoke this forbearance and conciliation, fully recognizing that far from the largest part of the southern people a reluctant obedience is all that is to be hoped for, let it be understood that less than obedience the Government cannot accept." Ibid., 397. The "remnants of rebellious feeling, the antagonisms of race, or the bitterness of political partisanships" should not, the Republican majority wrote, "degrade the soldiers of Lee . . . into the cowardly midnight prowlers and assassins who scourge and kill the poor and defenseless." Ibid., 397–98.

100 ANDREW JOHNSON, THE TENNESSEE DEMOCRAT   Annette Gordon-Reed, **Andrew Johnson** (New York, 2011); Hans L. Trefousse, **Andrew Johnson: A Biography** (New York, 1989); Albert Castel, **The Presidency of Andrew Johnson** (Lawrence, Kan., 1979).

100 THE CIVIL RIGHTS ACT OF 1866   Foner, **Reconstruction**, 245–51.

100 RECONSTRUCTION LEGISLATION IN 1867   Ibid.,
      276–77.

101 THE PRESIDENT ALSO UNSUCCESSFULLY OP-
      POSED   Ibid., 260–61. See also White, **Repub-
      lic for Which It Stands**, 73–75.

101 "JOHNSON, WE HAVE FAITH"   Foner, **Recon-
      struction**, 177.

101 "I HOLD THIS"   Ibid.

101 "THE SINCERE FRIEND"   Ibid., 178.

101 HIS VIEW OF RECONSTRUCTION   Ibid., 176–
      227. See also White, **Republic for Which It
      Stands**, 37–42; and Gordon-Reed, **Andrew John-
      son**, 122–25.

102 "WHITE MEN ALONE"   Foner, **Reconstruction**,
      180.

102 "NO INDEPENDENT GOVERNMENT"   Ibid.

102 "PROBABLY THE MOST BLATANTLY RACIST"
      Ibid.

102 AN ANTEBELLUM FOOTING   Ibid., 189. "Every
      political right which the State possessed under
      the Federal Constitution [before the war] is hers
      today," said Alabama governor Lewis E. Parsons,
      "with the single exception relating to slavery."
      Ibid.

102 HE HAD VETOED THE   Ibid., 239–51.

102 "THE DISTINCTION OF RACE"   Ibid., 250.

102 JOHNSON WAS ULTIMATELY IMPEACHED
      Gordon-Reed, **Andrew Johnson**, 130–39; White,
      Republic for Which It Stands, 91–94. See also
      Hans L. Trefousse, **Impeachment of a President:
      Andrew Johnson, the Blacks, and Reconstruc-
      tion** (New York, 1999).

103 LASHING OUT AT OPPONENTS Foner, **Reconstruction**, 249, and **Forever Free**, 116–17.

103 TOO MUCH FORTIFYING WHISKEY Gordon-Reed, **Andrew Johnson**, 82–87. For a contemporary account, see Brooks, **Lincoln Observed**, 166–67. "I write these words in humiliation of spirit," Brooks noted, "for what honest American citizen does not feel his cheek tingle with shame at such a recital of the facts; but it cannot be denied." Ibid., 166.

103 JOHNSON RAMBLED IN REMARKS Brooks, **Lincoln Observed**, 166–67.

103 (DEFENDERS SAY HE WAS FIGHTING ILLNESS) Gordon-Reed, **Andrew Johnson**, 82–84.

103 (HE WAS DRUNK) Ibid., 83–84. "Johnson," Gordon-Reed wrote, "was like a drunken best man at a wedding giving an interminable and embarrassing toast." Ibid., 84.

103 AN ANGRY, SELF-PITYING SPEECH Foner, **Reconstruction**, 249. It was, Foner wrote, "Johnson at his worst—self-absorbed (in a speech one hour long he referred to himself over 200 times), intolerant of criticism, and out of touch with political reality." Ibid.

103 "WHO, I ASK, HAS SUFFERED MORE" Andrew Johnson, "Speech to the Citizens of Washington," February 22, 1866, TeachingAmericanHistory.org, http://teachingamericanhistory.org/library/document/speech-to-the-citizens-of-washington/.

103 HE ATTACKED RADICAL REPUBLICANS Foner, **Forever Free**, 117.

104 ASSERTED THAT FEDERAL STEPS Johnson, "Speech to the Citizens of Washington," February 22, 1866.

104 CONSIDERING HAVING HIM ASSASSINATED Ibid. See also Foner, **Reconstruction**, 249.

104 "IF MY BLOOD" Johnson, "Speech to the Citizens of Washington," February 22, 1866.

105 U. S. GRANT WON THE WHITE HOUSE For Grant's presidency, see Jean Edward Smith, **Grant** (New York, 2001), 455–605; Josiah Bunting III, **Ulysses S. Grant** (New York, 2004); Ron Chernow, **Grant** (New York, 2017), 614–858.

105–6 THE UNION GENERAL THOMAS EWING, JR. Pollard, **Lost Cause Regained**, 166.

106 "BLOOD IS THICKER" Ibid.

106 "THERE HAS NEVER BEEN" Joan Waugh, "Ulysses S. Grant, Historian" in **Memory of Civil War in American Culture**, 17.

106 "THE PRINCIPLE FOR WHICH WE CONTENDED" Pollard, **Lost Cause: A New Southern History**, 749.

107 RATIFICATION OF THE FIFTEENTH AMENDMENT Smith, **Grant**, 543.

107 WAS "A MEASURE OF" Ulysses S. Grant, "Special Message," March 30, 1870, American Presidency Project, http://www.presidency.ucsb.edu/ws/?pid=70628.

107 "TO THE RACE MORE FAVORED" Ibid.

107 PASSAGE OF THE ENFORCEMENT ACT Trelease, **White Terror**, 385; Smith, **Grant**, 543–48.

107 (IT WAS THE FIRST OF) Smith, **Grant**, 544.

108 "IF THAT IS" Foner, **Reconstruction**, 454.

108 GRANT INTERVENED ON CAPITOL HILL Smith, **Grant,** 546.

108 WRITING IN HIS OWN HAND Ibid.

108 "A CONDITION OF AFFAIRS" Ibid. The resulting legislation was known as the Ku Klux Klan bill. Ibid.

108 THOSE WHO "CONSPIRE" Trelease, **White Terror,** 388.

109 THE LAW WAS "UNCONSTITUTIONAL" Ibid., 390.

109 "AN OUTRAGE UPON" Ibid.

109 THE GRANT-ERA MANEUVERS Ibid., 418; Smith, **Grant,** 547; Chernow, **Grant,** 709–711.

109 "THOUGH REJOICED AT" Foner, **Reconstruction,** 458.

109 AN ECONOMIC DEPRESSION C. Vann Woodward, **The Strange Career of Jim Crow** (New York, 1974), 70–72; Foner, **Forever Free,** 190–91.

109 THE WITHDRAWAL OF FEDERAL FORCES Foner, **Forever Free,** 190.

109 THE DISPUTED 1876 PRESIDENTIAL ELECTION White, **Republic for Which It Stands,** 325–37. See also C. Vann Woodward, **Reunion and Reaction: The Compromise of 1877 and the End of Reconstruction** (Boston, 1951), and Michael F. Holt, **By One Vote: The Disputed Presidential Election of 1876** (Lawrence, Kan., 2008).

110 "I DON'T CARE" Woodward, **Reunion and Reaction,** 23–24.

110 "AS TO SOUTHERN AFFAIRS" Ibid., 24.

110 "NOTHING BUT GOOD WILL" Ibid.

110 "THE WHOLE SOUTH" Foner, **Forever Free,** 198–99.

110 "The purpose of" Stephen Budiansky, **The Bloody Shirt: Terror After the Civil War** (New York, 2008), 236. For the entire Hamburg episode, see ibid., 234–247.

111 "If," W.E.B. Du Bois wrote Du Bois, **Black Reconstruction in America,** 708.

111 Jim Crow laws were Woodward, **Strange Career of Jim Crow,** 67–109.

111 In 1894, Mississippi voted Coski, **Confederate Battle Flag,** 80–81.

111 "The white race" John Marshall Harlan, "Judge Harlan's Dissent," http://chnm.gmu.edu/courses/nclc375/harlan.html. See also Foner, **Forever Free,** 207–8.

113 "We fought," a Confederate veteran McPherson, "Southern Comfort."

THREE · With Soul of Flame and Temper of Steel

117 There must be Roosevelt, **Rough Riders and An Autobiography,** 243–44.

117 A great party Jane Addams, "Why I Seconded Roosevelt's Nomination," **Woman's Journal** 43 (August 17, 1912): 257.

117 Washington's Columbia Theater **The Washington Post,** October 10, 1908.

117 a lovely early autumn day **The Washington Times,** October 5, 1908. The weather in Washington was described as "fair" with a high of 69 and a low of 47. At 8 p.m. the temperature was about 56 degrees. (See also **The Washington Post,** October 6, 1908.)

117 WITH HIS WIFE, EDITH NYT, October 10, 1908.

117 THE PRESIDENT'S PARTY INCLUDED   Ibid.

117 ISRAEL ZANGWILL'S THE MELTING-POT   Israel Zangwill, **From the Ghetto to the Melting Pot: Israel Zangwill's Jewish Plays,** ed. Edna Nahshon (Detroit, 2006), 211–363; Dorsey, **We Are All Americans,** 16–17, 53–54; Joe Kraus, "How the Melting Pot Stirred America: The Reception of Zangwill's Play and Theater's Role in the American Assimilation Experience," **MELUS** 24, no. 3 (Fall 1999): 3–19; Philip Gleason, "The Melting Pot: Symbol of Fusion or Confusion?" **American Quarterly** 16, no. 1 (Spring 1964): 20–46. For an interesting viewpoint on the subtleties of the play, see Neil Larry Shumsky, "Zangwill's 'The Melting Pot': Ethnic Tensions on Stage," **American Quarterly** 27, no. 1 (March 1975), 29–41.

118 A "NON-JEWISH BOROUGH" Zangwill, **From the Ghetto to the Melting Pot,** 271.

118 AFFIXED A MEZUZAH   Ibid.

118 AN AMERICAN FLAG WAS PINNED   Ibid.

118 THERE WERE BOOKCASES   Ibid.

118 PICTURES OF WAGNER, COLUMBUS   Ibid.

119 WAS "GOD'S CRUCIBLE" Shumsky, "Zangwill's 'The Melting Pot,'" 29.

119 SEATED NEXT TO   Ibid.

119 "CERTAIN STRONG LINES" NYT, October 10, 1908.

119 PROMPTED THE PRESIDENT   Ibid.

119 "THERE SHE LIES" Dorsey, **We Are All Americans,** 16–17.

119 "IT'S GREAT" **The Washington Post,** Octo-

ber 18, 1908. See also Shumsky, "Zangwill's 'The Melting Pot,'" 29–30. TR did object to a line about divorce in the U.S. and wanted Zangwill to change it. Zangwill protested but obliged the president. **Washington Post,** October 18, 1908.

120 WOULD SEE "THAT"   Shumsky, "Zangwill's 'The Melting Pot,'" 30.

120 ZANGWILL LATER DEDICATED   Zangwill, **From the Ghetto to the Melting Pot,** 243.

120 THE PLAY WENT ON   Ibid., 243–52.

120 IN 1915 THE ACTOR   Ibid., 254.

120 "IT IS," TR SAID   Hans P. Vought, **The Bully Pulpit and the Melting Pot: American Presidents and the Immigrant, 1897–1933** (Macon, Ga., 2004), 31.

121 "THE RUDE, FIERCE SETTLER"   Thomas, **War Lovers,** 42.

121 HE WAS LARGELY UNINTERESTED   Ibid. As Thomas wrote, Roosevelt "brushed aside sympathy for the conquered." Ibid.

121 "DURING THE PAST CENTURY"   Ibid.

122 BORN IN A FOUR-STORY BROWNSTONE   Roosevelt, **Rough Riders and An Autobiography,** 256; Edmund Morris, **The Rise of Theodore Roosevelt** (New York, 1979), 4–29; Doris Kearns Goodwin, **The Bully Pulpit: Theodore Roosevelt, William Howard Taft, and the Golden Age of Journalism** (New York, 2013), 34–49; and Deborah Davis, **Guest of Honor: Booker T. Washington, Theodore Roosevelt, and the White House Dinner That Shocked a Nation** (New York, 2012), 11–19. See also Willard B. Gatewood, **Theodore**

Roosevelt and the Art of Controversy: Episodes of the White House Years (Baton Rouge, La., 1970); and David McCullough, **Mornings on Horseback: The Story of an Extraordinary Family, a Vanished Way of Life and the Unique Child Who Became Theodore Roosevelt** (New York, 1981).

122 A SICKLY CHILD   Goodwin, **Bully Pulpit**, 34–37. "I was a sickly, delicate boy," TR recalled, "suffered much from asthma, and frequently had to be taken away on trips to find a place where I could breathe." Roosevelt, **Rough Riders and An Autobiography**, 266.

122 "NOBODY SEEMED TO"   Goodwin, **Bully Pulpit**, 34.

122 FINDING SOLACE IN   Ibid., 37–38. "There was very little effort made to compel me to read books, my father and mother having the good sense not to try to get me to read anything I did not like, unless it was in the way of study," TR said, recalling some of his favorite literary pursuits. "I was given the chance to read books that they thought I ought to read, but if I did not like them I was then given some other good book that I did like." Roosevelt, **Rough Riders and An Autobiography**, 267–70.

122 "THE GREATEST OF"   Goodwin, **Bully Pulpit**, 43.

122 ALL THE NOVELS OF ANTHONY TROLLOPE   Morris, **Rise of Theodore Roosevelt**, xxxiii.

122 NICKNAMED "TEEDIE"   Goodwin, **Bully Pulpit**, 34.

122 "THERE WERE ALL"   Roosevelt, **Rough Riders and An Autobiography**, 306–7.

122 ("Most men") Ibid., 307.

122 The Revolutionary soldiers Ibid., 280.

122 His mother . . . had grown up Gatewood, **Theodore Roosevelt and the Art of Controversy**, 37.

122 "My earliest training" Ibid.

122 was "entirely 'unreconstructed'" Roosevelt, **Rough Riders and An Autobiography**, 263.

122 TR had heard Ibid., 254.

123 a visit in New York Ibid., 264–65.

123 Traveling under assumed Ibid., 264.

123 One, an admiral Ibid., 265.

123 "hearing of the" Ibid.

123 "I felt a great" Ibid., 280.

123 As he remembered it Ibid.

123 A miserable stagecoach ride Ibid., 280–81.

124 learn to box Ibid. TR could always recall every detail of the gym where he took boxing lessons from John Long. Roosevelt, **Rough Riders and An Autobiography**, 281.

124 under the tutelage Ibid.

124 lifting weights at Davis, **Guest of Honor**, 18.

124 He wrestled Roosevelt, **Rough Riders and An Autobiography**, 280–86.

124 "You never saw" James Bradley, **The Imperial Cruise: A Secret History of Empire and War** (New York, 2009), 35.

124 "Powerful, vigorous men" Roosevelt, **Rough Riders and An Autobiography**, 295.

124 "Do you know" Morris, **Rise of Theodore Roosevelt**, xxiv.

125 "THE BRIDE AT EVERY WEDDING"   Ibid., xxi.

125 ROOSEVELT WAS "A DAZZLING"   Ibid.

125 WATCHING HIM AT   White House, **Theodore Roosevelt and the Art of Controversy,** 17.

125 IN REMARKS AT GROTON   Peter Collier with David Horowitz, **The Roosevelts: An American Saga** (New York, 1994), 109.

125 HIS MOST QUOTED SPEECH   Theodore Roosevelt, "Citizenship in a Republic," Almanac of Theodore Roosevelt, April 23, 1910, http://www.theodore-roosevelt.com/trsorbonnespeech.html.

126 THE "MALEFACTORS OF"   Collier with Horowitz, **Roosevelts,** 119.

126 "THE RIGHTS OF THE WORKER"   Roosevelt, **Rough Riders and An Autobiography,** 728–29. See also Collier with Horowitz, **Roosevelts,** 114.

126 TO HIM, "PROGRESS"   Dyer, **Theodore Roosevelt and the Idea of Race,** 32.

127 A RICH NEW YORK WOMAN   Collier with Horowitz, **Roosevelts,** 113.

127 "THE BEST MAN"   Roosevelt, **Rough Riders and An Autobiography,** 258.

127 "I NEVER KNEW"   Ibid., 260.

127 A BOLD DRIVER OF HORSES   Ibid., 262.

127 "INTERESTED IN EVERY"   Ibid., 260.

127 "HE WAS A BIG"   Ibid., 260.

128 "LIKE ALL AMERICANS"   H. Paul Jeffers, **Commissioner Roosevelt: The Story of Theodore Roosevelt and the New York City Police, 1895–1897** (New York, 1994), 26.

128 HIS EMERGING CONVICTIONS   Roosevelt, **Rough Riders and An Autobiography,** 423–24.

128 A PIONEERING URBAN JOURNALIST Jeffers, **Commissioner Roosevelt**, 13–14; 27–28.

128 "BY THIS TIME" Roosevelt, **Rough Riders and An Autobiography**, 423.

129 "AN ENLIGHTENMENT AND" Ibid.

129 DESCRIBING GARMENT SWEATSHOPS Jeffers, **Commissioner Roosevelt**, 31–32.

129 TR WENT TO SEE Roosevelt, **Rough Riders and An Autobiography**, 424.

129 RIIS WAS OUT Jeffers, **Commissioner Roosevelt**, 32–33.

130 RIIS, TR RECALLED Roosevelt, **Rough Riders and An Autobiography**, 423.

130 "I HAVE ALWAYS" Ibid., 424.

130 TR ANTICIPATED THE WORK Milkis and Nelson, **American Presidency**, 218.

130 "THE NATION AND GOVERNMENT" Ibid.

132 ALIEN AND SEDITION ACTS "Alien and Sedition Acts (1798)," Our Documents, https://www
.ourdocuments.gov/doc.php?flash=true&doc=16. For this section, I drew on my "Our Historical Ambivalence About Immigration Is a Great Historical Paradox," **Time**, February 2, 2017.

132 "THE ALIEN BILL" James Madison to Thomas Jefferson, May 20, 1798, Founders Online, National Archives, https://founders.archives.gov/documents/Madison/01-17-02-0090.

133 "THE BOSOM OF" George Washington to Joshua Holmes, December 2, 1783, Founders Early Access, http://rotunda.upress.virginia.edu/founders/default.xqy?keys=FOEA-print-01-02-02-6127.

133 "THE INFLUX OF FOREIGNERS" Alexander Hamilton, "The Examination Number VIII," January 12, 1802, Founders Online, National Archives, https://founders.archives.gov/documents/Hamilton/01-25-02-0282.

133 THE KNOW-NOTHINGS HAD SPRUNG Jon Gjerde, ed., **Major Problems in American Immigration and Ethnic History** (New York, 1998), 152–60.

133 THE CHINESE EXCLUSION ACT "Chinese Exclusion Act (1882)," Our Documents, https://www.ourdocuments.gov/doc.php?flash=true&doc=47.

134 "WHATEVER BUSINESS OR TRADE" Gjerde, **Major Problems in American Immigration and Ethnic History,** 274–75.

134 "THE NEGRO SLAVE" Ibid., 276.

134 THE MOVEMENT FOR ECONOMIC JUSTICE Foner, **Forever Free,** 192–93; Woodward, **Strange Career of Jim Crow,** 93–96. See also Thomas C. Leonard, **Illiberal Reformers: Race, Eugenics and American Economics in the Progressive Era** (Princeton, N.J., 2016).

134 (SPENCER COINED THE PHRASE) Thomas, **War Lovers,** 55.

134 SENSE OF DESTINY White, **Republic for Which It Stands,** 570–73. See also Madison Grant, **The Passing of the Great Race** (LaVergne, Tenn., 2016); T. Lothrop Stoddard, **The Rising Tide of Color Against White World-Supremacy** (New York, 1920); Christopher Hitchens, **Blood, Class, and Nostalgia: Anglo-American Ironies** (New

York, 1990), 63–151; Thomas, **War Lovers**, especially 42–61.

134   CAPTURED IN LECTURES   White, **Republic for Which It Stands**, 447.

134–5   RUDYARD KIPLING'S 1899 POEM   David Gilmour, **The Long Recessional: The Imperial Life of Rudyard Kipling** (New York, 2002), is an illuminating treatment of Kipling and empire.

135   "THE ENGLISH-SPEAKING PEOPLES"   Winston S. Churchill, **The History of the English-Speaking Peoples** (New York, 1956–58).

135   KIPLING SENT TR   Hitchens, **Blood, Class, and Nostalgia**, 66.

135   "I SEND YOU"   Ibid.

135   "THE LANGUAGE OF SHAKESPEARE"   John Fiske, **American Political Ideas Viewed from the Standpoint of Universal History; Three Lectures Delivered at the Royal Institution of Great Britain in May, 1880** (New York, 1885), 67.

At a dinner party of Americans in Paris at the time of the American Civil War, Fiske said, there were a series of toasts to "the expected glories of the American nation" once it was clear that the Union would be saved, and with it the **"bigness"** of the country. "Here's to the United States of America," said the first guest, "bounded on the north by British America, on the south by the Gulf of Mexico, on the east by the Atlantic, and on the west by the Pacific Ocean."

Then a second guest spoke up. "But this is far too limited a view of the subject: in assigning boundaries we must look to the great and glorious future which is prescribed for us by the Manifest Destiny of the Anglo-Saxon Race. Here's to the United States—bounded on the north by the North Pole, on the south by the South Pole, on the east by the rising and on the west by the setting sun."

A third voice—an American from the West—was then heard. "If we are going to leave the historic past and present, and take our manifest destiny into the account," he said, "why restrict ourselves within the narrow limits assigned by our fellow countryman who has just sat down? I give you the United States—bounded on the north by the Aurora Borealis, on the south by the precession of the equinoxes, on the east by the primeval chaos, and on the west by the Day of Judgment!" Ibid., 45.

135 "Who can doubt" Ibid., 66.

136 "During the past" Morris, **Rise of Theodore Roosevelt**, 474–75. See also Dyer, **Theodore Roosevelt and the Idea of Race**, 45–68.

136 the rise of "the Slovak" Gjerde, **Major Problems in American Immigration and Ethnic History**, 282.

136 "Now we confront" Ibid., 283.

137 "Either the Anglo-Saxon race" Ibid., 277.

137 Longfellow's Nordic Saga of King Olaf Dyer, **Theodore Roosevelt and the Idea of Race**, 2.

138 "We freely extend" Theodore Roosevelt, **American Ideals and Other Essays, Social and Political** (New York, 1897), 28.

138 AMERICANISM IS A QUESTION   Ibid., 30.

139 DINNER WAS CALLED   Davis, **Guest of Honor,** 187. See also Gatewood, **Theodore Roosevelt and the Art of Controversy,** 32–61, and Dewey W. Grantham, Jr., "Dinner at the White House: Theodore Roosevelt, Booker T. Washington and the South," **Tennessee Historical Quarterly** 17, no. 2 (June 1958): 112–30.

139 DISPATCHED THAT VERY DAY   Ibid.

139 BORN A SLAVE   Davis, **Guest of Honor,** 8–10.

139 HAD NOT GIVEN "VERY MUCH"   Joseph Bucklin Bishop, **Theodore Roosevelt and His Time Shown in His Own Letters** (New York, 1920), 1:166.

139 "THERE IS A FEELING"   "Both Politically and Socially President Roosevelt Proposes to Coddle Descendants of Ham," Atlanta Constitution, October 18, 1901; http://www.c3teachers.org/ wp-content/uploads/2016/04/TPS_Booker_T _Washington_11-16.pdf. Chronicling America: Historic American Newspapers, Library of Congress, https://chroniclingamerica.loc.gov/lccn/ sn85034438/1901-10-20/ed-1/seq-1.pdf.

140 "PRESIDENT ROOSEVELT HAS COMMITTED"   "Booker T. Washington Dines with Theodore Roosevelt, Americans Outraged," November 15, 2015, Gilder Lehrman Institute of American History, https://www.gilderlehrman.org/content /booker-t-washington-dines-theodore-roosevelt- americans-outraged.

140 "POOR ROOSEVELT!"   Davis, **Guest of Honor,** 208. There were some voices of support. "Mr.

Washington is a colored man who enjoys the universal respect of all people in this country, black and white, on account of attainments, character, and deeds," the Philadelphia **Public Ledger** wrote. "As the President invited him to be his private guest, and did not attempt to force the companionship of a colored man upon anyone to whom the association could possibly be distasteful, any criticism of the President's act savors of very great impertinence." David Hicks, "Booker T. Washington in the White House," 9–12 Grade Teaching with Primary Sources, http://www.c3teachers .org/wp-content/uploads/2016/04/TPS_Booker _T_Washington_11-16.pdf.

141 "As things have"   Bishop, **Theodore Roosevelt and His Time,** 166.

142 "I have not"   Ibid.

142 I say that   Ibid.

142 Roosevelt had supported   Dyer, **Theodore Roosevelt and the Idea of Race,** 96–97. In a separate incident, TR, after an investigation, endorsed the dismissal of black soldiers accused of " 'shooting up' " Brownsville, Texas. He was excoriated by the black press, but stood by his decision, saying he would have done the same with white troops under the same circumstances. See ibid., 114–16, and Ann J. Lane, **The Brownsville Affair: National Crisis and Black Reaction** (Port Washington, N.Y., 1971).

143 a "fitting thing"   Ibid.

143 backed Minnie M. Cox   Ibid., 102–3.

143 He also refused   Ibid., 103–8.

143 "I KNOW OF"   Ibid., 107.

143 "IT SEEMS TO ME"   Ibid., 108.

143 PEOPLE OF COLOR ABROAD   Ibid., 89–122.

144 MIGHT LEAD TO "RACE SUICIDE"   Ibid., 143–167.

144 "I AM AN OPTIMIST"   Ibid., 149.

144 ROOSEVELT LAMENTED A   Ibid., 158.

144 "IN SPITE OF"   Ibid.

144 "HERE AGAIN, I"   Ibid., 100.

144 ROOSEVELT WAS WRONG   Ibid., 101. See also Thomas, **War Lovers,** 337.

144 STANDING CORRECTED   Dyer, **Theodore Roosevelt and the Idea of Race,** 101.

144 THE MISTAKE WAS   Ibid., 101.

144 "ROOSEVELT'S FREQUENT INVOCATION"   Ibid., 91–92.

145 WE OF TO-DAY   Theodore Roosevelt, "Lincoln and the Race Problem," February 13, 1905, BlackPast.org,   http://www.blackpast.org/1905 -theodore-roosevelt-lincoln-and-race-problem.

147 THE COFOUNDER OF HULL-HOUSE   See, for instance, Louise W. Knight, **Jane Addams: Spirit in Action** (New York, 2010); Jane Addams, **Twenty Years at Hull-House: With Autobiographical Notes,** ed. Victoria Bissell Brown (Boston, 1999); Addams, **Democracy and Social Ethics** (Urbana, Ill., 2002).

148 "JUSTICE AMONG THE NATIONS"   Roosevelt, **Rough Riders and An Autobiography,** 243–44.

149 SHE WAS DELIGHTED   Knight, **Jane Addams,** 173.

149 "WE FIGHT IN"   Collier with Horowitz, **Roosevelts,** 166.

149 "EXACTLY AS MUCH"   Roosevelt, **Rough Riders and An Autobiography**, 417.

149 BY HIS OWN ACCOUNT   Ibid.

149 "A VOTE IS"   Ibid., 417–18.

150 BECAUSE "HE IS"   William Draper Lewis, **The Life of Theodore Roosevelt** (Philadelphia, 1919), 377.

150 THE CROWD HAD   Knight, **Jane Addams**, 177–78.

150 "A GREAT PARTY HAS"   Addams, "Why I Seconded Roosevelt's Nomination," 257.

151 "I PRIZED YOUR ACTION"   "Telegram from Theodore Roosevelt to Jane Addams," Theodore Roosevelt Papers, Library of Congress Manuscript Division, Theodore Roosevelt Digital Library, Dickinson State University, http://www .theodorerooseveltcenter.org/Research/Digital -Library/Record?libID=o230361.

151 ISRAEL ZANGWILL WROTE ROOSEVELT   Dyer, **Theodore Roosevelt and the Idea of Race**, 131.

151 NOW AS A MATTER   Ibid.

152 LEAVING THE HOTEL GILPATRICK   Patricia O'Toole, "Assassination Foiled," **Smithsonian**, November 2012.

152 "THEY WANTED TO"   Frederick S. Wood, **Roosevelt as We Knew Him: The Personal Recollections of One Hundred and Fifty of His Friends and Associates** (Philadelphia, 1927), 278.

152 "AT ONE TIME"   Theodore Roosevelt, "It Takes More Than That to Kill a Bull Moose: The Leader and the Cause," October 14, 1912, Theodore Roosevelt Association, http://www.theodoroose

velt.org/site/c.elKSIdOWIiJ8H/b.9297449
/k.861A/It_Takes_More_Than_That_to_Kill_a
_Bull_Moose_The_Leader_and_The_Cause.htm.

153 "I ASK IN"   Ibid.

153 FROM AN EMBOLISM   "Theodore Roosevelt Dies
Suddenly at Oyster Bay Home; Nation Shocked,
Pays Tribute to Former President; Our Flag on All
Seas and in All Land at Half Mast," NYT, January
17, 1919.

153 "THERE CAN BE"   Wood, Roosevelt As We
Knew Him, 453.

FOUR · A New and Good Thing in the World

157 IT WAS WE, THE PEOPLE   Susan B. Anthony, "Is It
a Crime for a U.S. Citizen to Vote?" April 3, 1873,
Voices of Democracy: The U.S. Oratory Project,
http://voicesofdemocracy.umd.edu/anthony
-is-it-a-crime-speech-text/.

157 I WOULD BUILD A WALL OF STEEL   Clifford
Walker, "Americanism Applied," Proceedings of
the Second Imperial Klonvokation Held at Kansas City, Missouri, Sept. 23, 24, 25, and 26,
1924, 27.

157 TYPED THE SPEECH   Eleanor Flexner and Ellen
Fitzpatrick, Century of Struggle: The Woman's
Rights Movement in the United States (Cam-
bridge, Mass., 1996), 302.

157 HAD HARDLY BEEN AN ENTHUSIASTIC SUP-
PORTER   John Milton Cooper, Jr., Woodrow
Wilson: A Biography (New York, 2009), 335–36
and 411–15; A. Scott Berg, Wilson (New York,

2013), 486–94. "I . . . am tied to a conviction, which I have had all my life, that changes of this sort ought to be brought about state by state," Wilson said in 1915. Berg, **Wilson**, 487.

157 AFTER GENERATIONS OF ACTIVISM   Flexner and Fitzpatrick, **Century of Struggle;** Jean H. Baker, **Sisters: The Lives of America's Suffragists** (New York, 2005), and Baker's edited volume **Votes for Women: The Struggle for Suffrage Revisited** (New York, 2002); Sally G. McMillen, **Seneca Falls and the Origins of the Women's Rights Movement** (New York, 2008); Kathryn Kish Sklar, ed., **Women's Rights Emerges Within the Anti-Slavery Movement, 1830–1870: A Brief History with Documents** (Boston, 2000); Aileen S. Kraditor, **The Ideas of the Woman Suffrage Movement, 1890–1920** (New York, 1981); Elizabeth Frost-Knappman and Kathryn Cullen-DuPont, eds., **Women's Suffrage in America: An Eyewitness History** (New York, 2005).

158 A WAR FOR A MORE INCLUSIVE   Berg, **Wilson**, 493. Wilson's son-in-law William McAdoo, the secretary of the treasury, had told the president: "I felt that since no President of the United States had ever spoken in favor of woman's suffrage, and that since we were fighting a war for democracy, it seemed to me that we could not consistently persist in refusing to admit women to the benefits of democracy on an equality with men." Ibid.

158 "LOOKING TO THE GREAT"   Woodrow Wilson, "Address to the Senate on the Nineteenth Amendment," September 30, 1918, American Presi-

dency Project, http://www.presidency.ucsb.edu/ws/?pid=126468. He concluded: "That is my case. This is my appeal. Many may deny its validity, if they choose, but no one can brush aside or answer the arguments upon which it is based. The executive tasks of this war rest upon me. I ask that you lighten them and place in my hands instruments, spiritual instruments, which I do not now possess, which I sorely need, and which I have daily to apologize for not being able to employ." Ibid.

158 ON ARRIVING IN WASHINGTON   Baker, **Sisters,** 184.

158 "WHERE," WILSON ASKED   Ibid.

158 THE DEMONSTRATION THAT DAY   Ibid., 185. See also Flexner and Fitzgerald, **Century of Struggle,** 256–57.

159 ANGRY MEN TAUNTED   Flexner and Fitzgerald, **Century of Struggle,** 257.

159 THE **BALTIMORE AMERICAN** REPORTED   Ibid., 375.

159 "PRACTICALLY FOUGHT THEIR WAY"   Ibid., 256.

159 ONLY THE ARRIVAL OF CAVALRY TROOPS   Ibid., 256–57.

159 IN A SMALL MEETING   Baker, **Sisters,** 205.

159 ALICE PAUL, A LEADING ADVOCATE   Ibid., 183–220, is a useful sketch of Paul's life and work. See also Katherine H. Adams and Michael L. Keene, **Alice Paul and the American Suffrage Campaign** (Champaign, Ill., 2007); J. D. Zahniser and Amelia R. Fry, **Alice Paul: Claiming Power** (New York, 2014); Mary Walton, **A Wom-**

an's Crusade: Alice Paul and the Battle for the Ballot (New York, 2015); Christine Lunardini, Alice Paul: Equality for Women (New York, 2012); Bernadette Cahill, Alice Paul, the National Woman's Party and the Vote: The First Civil Rights Struggle of the 20th Century (Jefferson, N.C., 2015).

159 THE FACT THAT THE FIGHT   Baker, Sisters, 205.

159 THE FOUNDING CONVENTION   McMillen, Seneca Falls, 71–103.

159 "I DO NOT CARE"   Baker, Sisters, 205. "The president announced that he had never thought about women's suffrage," Baker wrote. "It had not, he said duplicitously, been brought to his attention. He did not know what his position might be on this new matter, but he hoped for more information. In the meantime the ladies must try to 'concert opinion.'" Ibid. For evidence of Wilson's anti-suffrage views, see ibid., 186–87.

159 ALICE PAUL HEADQUARTERED HERSELF   Ibid., 207.

159 A PERSISTENT CAMPAIGN   Ibid., 207. "Alice Paul intended to make the president, for the first time in American history, the specific target of a political movement," Baker wrote. Ibid., 187. See also Flexner and Fitzgerald, Century of Struggle, 256.

159 BORN IN 1885 TO A DISTINGUISHED QUAKER FAMILY   Baker, Sisters, 191–92.

159 HAD BEEN INFLUENCED BY   Flexner and Fitzgerald, Century of Struggle, 255–56.

159 THE MORE MILITANT BRITISH   Ibid., 243–47.

159 FROM 1907 TO 1910   Ibid., 255–56.

160 EMMELINE PANKHURST'S WOMEN'S SOCIAL AND POLITICAL UNION   Ibid., 244; Baker, Sisters, 194–98.

160 FACE-TO-FACE CHALLENGES   Baker, Sisters, 194–95.

160 WOULD REFUSE FOOD IN JAIL   Flexner and Fitzgerald, Century of Struggle, 244.

160 HIGHLY PUBLICIZED FORCE-FEEDINGS   Ibid.; Baker, Sisters, 196–97. To her mother in America, Paul wrote: "Force feeding is simply a policy of passive resistance. As a Quaker thee ought to approve of it." Ibid., 196.

160 THE GRUESOME DETAILS   Ibid., 197.

160 "THE ESSENCE OF THE CAMPAIGN"   Ibid., 197–98.

160 "I LONG TO HEAR"   Abigail Adams to John Adams, March 31–April 5 1776, Massachusetts Historical Society, https://www.masshist.org/digitaladams/archive/doc?id=L17760331aa. Mrs. Adams added:

That your Sex are Naturally Tyrannical is a Truth so thoroughly established as to admit of no dispute, but such of you as wish to be happy willingly give up the harsh title of Master for the more tender and endearing one of Friend. Why then, not put it out of the power of the vicious and the Lawless to use us with cruelty and indignity with impunity. Men of Sense in all Ages abhor those customs which treat us only as the vassals of your Sex. Regard us then as Beings placed by providence under your protection and in imitation of the Supreme Being make use of that power only for our happiness. Ibid.

162 THE JULY 1848 SENECA FALLS McMillen, **Seneca Falls,** 71–103, covers the gathering itself. "At Seneca Falls, for the first time, women and men gathered for the sole purpose of articulating female grievances and demanding women's equality," McMillen wrote. "As Susan B. Anthony observed in the early 1880s, 'Women had not been discovered fifty years ago.' Before Seneca Falls, no one could imagine that anyone would dare challenge, in such an organized manner, women's subservience or their legal, social, and political oppression." Ibid., 3–4.

162 "WE HOLD THESE TRUTHS" "Declaration of Sentiments and Resolutions, Woman's Rights Convention, Held at Seneca Falls, 19–20 July 1848," Elizabeth Cady Stanton and Susan B. Anthony Papers Project, Rutgers, State University of New Jersey, http://ecssba.rutgers.edu/docs/seneca.html.

162 "IT WAS WE, THE PEOPLE" Anthony, "Is It a Crime?" April 3, 1873.

162 DEMONSTRATORS KNOWN AS "SILENT SENTINELS" Baker, **Sisters,** 214.

162 WHEN ARRESTED (ON CHARGES OF INTERFERING WITH TRAFFIC) Ibid., 216–21.

162–3 DURING THE 1916 STATE OF THE UNION Ibid., 207.

163 For "the first time in American history" Ibid., 216–17.

163 "Will you take" Frost-Knappman and Cullen-DuPont, **Women's Suffrage in America,** 352.

164 "As I look back" Ibid.

165 Ellen, his beloved wife, had died Cooper, **Woodrow Wilson,** 260–61; Berg, **Wilson,** 334–35. "It is pathetic to see the President; he hardly knows where to turn." Francis B. Sayre, Sr., wrote. Berg, **Wilson,** 335. That August Wilson wrote: "I never understood before what a broken heart meant, and did for a man. It just means that he lives by the compulsion of necessity and duty only." Ibid., 338.

165 the president received a delegation Ibid., 345–47; Cooper, **Woodrow Wilson,** 270–72.

165 had promised African Americans For Wilson and segregation in the federal government, see Eric S. Yellin, **Racism in the Nation's Service: Government Workers and the Color Line in Woodrow Wilson's America** (Chapel Hill, N.C., 2013); Berg, **Wilson,** 305–12; Cooper, **Woodrow Wilson,** 205–26.

165 "absolute fair dealing" Yellin, **Racism in the Nation's Service,** 72–73. See also Nancy J. Weiss, "The Negro and the New Freedom: Fighting Wilsonian Segregation," **Political Science Quarterly** 84, no. 1 (March 1969), 63.

165 only to allow the segregation Sullivan, **Lift Every Voice,** 27–34. See also Yellin, **Racism**

in the Nation's Service. Wilson also gave in to a trio of Southern senators to block the appointment of an African American to a post traditionally held by a black man. Sullivan, **Lift Every Voice,** 27. Hearing reports of the institution of Jim Crow in government offices—which included segregated bathrooms and lunchrooms—Wilson approved, saying that he had "made no particular promises to Negroes, except to do them justice." Ibid., 28.

165 TROTTER HAD FOUNDED THE NIAGARA MOVEMENT   Kate Tuttle, "Niagara Movement," **Africana: The Encyclopedia of the African and African American Experience** (New York, 2005), 226. See also "Niagara Movement (1905–1909)," BlackPast.org, http://www.blackpast.org/aah/niagara-movement-1905-1909.

165 "WE REFUSE TO"   "Niagara Movement (1905–1909)," BlackPast.org.

166 IN 1909, IN THE AFTERMATH   Sullivan, **Lift Every Voice,** 3–15, details this period of the formation of the NAACP.

166 "'A HOUSE DIVIDED'"   "NAACP: A Century in the Fight for Freedom," Library of Congress, http://www.loc.gov/exhibits/naacp/founding-and-early-years.html#obj2.

166 ISSUED ON LINCOLN'S BIRTHDAY   Sullivan, **Lift Every Voice,** 6.

166 WHAT DU BOIS CALLED "DESPERATE ALTERNATIVES"   Ibid., 26.

166 NEITHER WILLIAM HOWARD TAFT   Ibid. See also Cooper, **Woodrow Wilson,** 170. "Taft had

made overtures toward the white South early in his administration, and Roosevelt had allowed the Progressives to organize in the South as a lily-white party," Cooper wrote. Ibid.

166 MANY GAMBLED, THEN   Sullivan, **Lift Every Voice**, 26.

167 THE NAACP . . . THROUGH ITS LEGAL BUREAU   Ibid., 42–50.

167 "ONLY TWO YEARS AGO"   Cooper, **Woodrow Wilson**, 270.

167 WILSON REPLIED THAT   Ibid.

167 "WE ARE NOT HERE"   Ibid.

167 "LET ME SAY THIS"   Ibid., 271.

168 "I AM FROM"   Ibid.

168 "YOU HAVE SPOILED"   Ibid.

168 "THAT UNSPEAKABLE FELLOW"   Woodrow Wilson to Joseph Tumulty, April 24, 1915, **Woodrow Wilson Papers**, 33:68.

168 "I WAS DAMN FOOL"   Cooper, **Woodrow Wilson**, 271.

169 JIM CROW REGULATIONS   Ibid., 205. A significant issue for white Southerners, Cooper wrote, was "racial mingling in federal offices, particularly in the case of black supervisors overseeing white clerks." Ibid. For Wilson and race more generally, see ibid., 409–11. I am also grateful to Professor Cooper for his guidance on these points.

169 "READILY . . . ACCEPTED"   Ibid., 410.

169 PURGED FROM THE PARTY   Ibid., 435–37.

169 STRONGLY DENOUNCED LYNCHING   Ibid., 409–10.

169 "GAVE A HINT"   Ibid., 410–11.

169 "EXCITED BY A FREEDOM"   Woodrow Wilson, "The Reconstruction of the Southern States," **The Atlantic Monthly,** January 1901.

170 AT THE FIFTIETH ANNIVERSARY   Blight, **Race and Reunion,** 6–12. Blight opens his book with the scene at Gettysburg half a century on.

170 "THESE VENERABLE MEN"   Woodrow Wilson, "Address at Gettysburg," July 4, 1913, American Presidency Project, http://www.presidency.ucsb.edu/ws/?pid=65370.

170 "WHOM DO I COMMAND?"   Ibid.

171 A TRILOGY OF NOVELS BY THOMAS W. DIXON, JR.   James Kinney, "Thomas Dixon, 1864–1946," Documenting the American South, http://docsouth.unc.edu/southlit/dixonclan/bio.html; Gerald R. Butters, Jr., **Black Manhood on the Silent Screen** (Lawrence, Kan., 2002), 64–65. See also Blight, **Race and Reunion,** 111–12; Cooper, **Woodrow Wilson,** 272; Berg, **Wilson,** 347–48. Christopher Hitchens remarked on the connection between Kipling's imperialism and Dixon's fiction: "There is evidence that Kipling's self-pitying interpretation of the race question was not lost on those whose main concern was the domestic front. D. W. Griffith's sinister film masterpiece **The Birth of a Nation** was based on a racist novel by Griffith's friend Thomas Dixon, a Baptist ranter from North Carolina whose tale **The Leopard's Spots** was published in 1902. Its subtitle was **A Romance of the White Man's Burden.** Evidently, the apple did not fall very far from the tree." Hitchens, **Blood, Class, and Nostalgia,**

74–75. Dixon also wrote novels designed to attack women's suffrage and socialism. Kinney, "Thomas Dixon."

171 THE BOOKS WERE WIDELY READ   Butters, **Black Manhood**, 64–65.

171 WHO BECAME A POPULAR FIGURE   Kinney, "Thomas Dixon."

171 "MY OBJECT IS"   Butters, **Black Manhood**, 65.

171 HE ADAPTED **The Clansman**   Ibid.

171 JOINED FORCES WITH   Ibid., 65–66. In addition to Griffith's movie, there were other film treatments of the Klan in these years: 1915's **A Mormon Maid** and 1919's **The Heart o' the Hills**, with Mary Pickford. Daniel Eagan, **America's Film Legacy: The Authoritative Guide to the Landmark Movies in the National Film Registry** (New York, 2010), 44.

172 OPENED A WORLD OF POSSIBILITIES   Butters, **Black Manhood**, 65–66.

173 "THE WHOLE PROBLEM"   Ibid.

173 A RUNNING TIME OF 187 MINUTES   Eagan, **America's Film Legacy**, 42.

173 THE TITLE CARDS INCLUDED   Allyson Hobbs, "A Hundred Years Later, 'The Birth of a Nation' Hasn't Gone Away," **The New Yorker**, December 13, 2015, https://www.newyorker.com/culture/culture-desk/hundred-years-later-birth-nation-hasnt-gone-away.

173 WILSON AND DIXON HAD OVERLAPPED   Cooper, **Woodrow Wilson**, 272; Berg, **Wilson**, 348.

173 WILSON AGREED TO HOST   Cooper, **Woodrow Wilson**, 272. It was, Scott Berg wrote, "the first

running of a motion picture in the White House."
Berg, **Wilson**, 348.

173 HE OFFERED LITTLE VISIBLE REACTION   Cooper, **Woodrow Wilson**, 272. "Another member of
the audience that night," Berg wrote, "reported
that the President seemed lost in thought during
the film and exited the East Room upon its completion without saying a word to anybody." Berg,
Wilson, 349.

174 YET WORD OF THE PRESIDENTIAL VIEW-
ING   Cooper, **Woodrow Wilson**, 272. "Regardless of what he did or did not say," Cooper wrote,
"Dixon and Griffith soon touted the event and
insinuated that **The Birth of a Nation** enjoyed a
presidential seal of approval." Ibid.

174 PROVOKED PROTESTS IN SEVERAL CITIES
Thomas Cripps, **Slow Fade to Black: The Negro
in American Film, 1900–1942** (New York,
1977), 53–69. William Monroe Trotter was arrested during the Boston protest; **The Washington Post** described Trotter as "the man whom
President Wilson practically ordered out of the
White House a short while ago when he was baiting the President at a conference with colored
leaders over alleged discrimination against colored government employees." "Race Riot at Theater," **The Washington Post**, April 18, 1915. See
also "Negroes Mob Photo Play," **NYT**, April 18,
1915.

174 OFFERED THE NASCENT NAACP   Cripps,
Slow Fade to Black, 52–69; Sullivan, **Lift Every
Voice**, 48–54.

174 DURING A DEMONSTRATION   Cripps, **Slow Fade to Black,** 63.

174 "AS I LOOKED"   Ibid.

174 "IT IS GRATIFYING"   Butters, **Black Manhood,** 83.

174 "IT IS TRUE THAT"   **The Papers of Woodrow Wilson,** ed. Arthur S. Link, (Princeton, N.J.) 33:86.

175 A SMALL GROUP OF MEN MET ON STONE MOUNTAIN   Lorraine Boissoneault, "What Will Happen to Stone Mountain, America's Largest Confederate Memorial?" Smithsonian.com, August 22, 2017. On the second Klan, see, for instance, Rory McVeigh, **The Rise of the Ku Klux Klan: Right-Wing Movements and National Politics** (Minneapolis, 2009); McVeigh, "Power Devaluation, the Ku Klux Klan, and the Democratic National Convention of 1924," **Sociological Forum** 16, no. 1 (March 2001): 1–31; Arnold S. Rice, **The Ku Klux Klan in American Politics** (New York, 1972); Richard K. Tucker, **The Dragon and the Cross: The Rise and Fall of the Ku Klux Klan in Middle America** (Hamden, Conn., 1991); Linda Gordon, **The Second Coming of the KKK: The Ku Klux Klan of the 1920s and the American Political Tradition** (New York, 2017); Chalmers, **Hooded Americanism,** 28–438; Nancy MacLean, **Behind the Mask of Chivalry: The Making of the Second Ku Klux Klan** (New York, 1994); William Rawlings, **The Second Coming of the Invisible Empire: The Ku Klux Klan of the 1920s** (Macon, Ga., 2016).

175 WILLIAM J. SIMMONS, AN ALABAMA-BORN Chalmers, **Hooded Americanism**, 28–29.

175 SIMMONS CLAIMED HIS FATHER   Ibid., 28.

175 "ON HORSEBACK IN"   Ibid.

176 SIMMONS'S CHOICE OF VENUE   Ibid., 29–30.

176 WERE CAMPAIGNING FOR THE CREATION   Boissoneault, "What Will Happen to Stone Mountain?" Smithsonian.com.

176 "THE BIRTH OF A NATION WILL GIVE US"   Ibid.

176 (IN THE END, THE MEMORIAL)   Ibid.

176 WHAT BEGAN ON   Chalmers, **Hooded Americanism**, 29–30.

176 FORTY-EIGHT STATES   McVeigh, "Power Devaluation," 1–3.

176 INDIANA WAS A STRONGHOLD   Ibid., 2–3. For Indiana, see Chalmers, **Hooded Americanism**, 162–74; for Oregon, see ibid., 85–91; for Colorado, see ibid., 126–34; for Kansas, see ibid., 143–48.

176 A COMBINATION OF FACTORS   Gordon, **Second Coming of the KKK**, 2–7, offers a useful overview.

176 UNEASE ABOUT CRIME   Jerry L. Wallace, "The Ku Klux Klan in Calvin Coolidge's America," July 14, 2014, Calvin Coolidge Presidential Foundation, https://coolidgefoundation.org/resources/essays-papers-addresses-23/231.

176 WORRY ABOUT ANARCHISTS   McVeigh, **Rise of the Ku Klux Klan**, 63; 104–6.

177 ANXIETY ABOUT COMMUNISM   MacLean, **Behind the Mask of Chivalry**, 25. See also Gordon, **Second Coming of the KKK**, 12.

177 DURING A KLAN MEETING   Chalmers, **Hooded Americanism,** 32–33.

177 "NOW LET THE"   Ibid., 33.

177 SIMMONS HIRED A PAIR   MacLean, **Behind the Mask of Chivalry,** 5–6.

177 WAS FINANCED BY   Chalmers, **Hooded Americanism,** 33–35.

177 "KING KLEAGLES"   Ibid., 33–34.

177 MONEY—INCLUDING REVENUE   Ibid., 34–35.

177 "THE KLAN OFFERED STRUCTURE"   Bennett, **Party of Fear,** 211.

178 KLANSMEN HELD GOVERNORSHIPS   Gordon, **Second Coming of the KKK,** 164.

178 (THE KLAN ITSELF)   MacLean, **Behind the Mask of Chivalry,** 17–18.

178 IN ALABAMA,   Chalmers, **Hooded Americanism,** 313–16.

178 A YOUNG HARRY TRUMAN   McCullough, **Truman,** 164–65.

178 THERE WAS LEGISLATION TO PROTECT   Cooper, **Woodrow Wilson,** 397–401.

178 TO "UTTER, PRINT, WRITE"   "The Sedition Act of 1918," Digital History, http://www.digital history.uh.edu/disp_textbook.cfm?smt ID=3&psid=3903.

179 UNDER WILSON AND THROUGH THE DIRECT OFFICES   Donald Johnson, "Wilson, Burleson, and Censorship in the First World War," **Journal of Southern History** 28 (February 1962): 46–58. Burleson issued a wide-ranging directive to his department: Local postmasters were to be on the watch for "matter which is calculated . . . to cause

insubordination, disloyalty, mutiny, or refusal of duty in the military or naval service, or to obstruct the recruiting, draft or enlistment services . . . or otherwise to embarrass or hamper the Government in conducting the war." Ibid., 48.

179 AS MANY AS FOUR HUNDRED PUBLICATIONS Anne Cipriano Venzon, ed., **The United States in the First World War: An Encyclopedia** (New York, 1999), 132–33.

179 "I SPENT THE WHOLE WINTER" Johnson, "Wilson, Burleson, and Censorship in the First World War," 49.

180 AT NIMISILLA PARK Ernest Freeberg, **Democracy's Prisoner: Eugene V. Debs, the Great War, and the Right to Dissent** (Cambridge, Mass., 2010), 72–78. See also Robert K. Murray, **Red Scare: A Study in National Hysteria, 1919–1920** (New York, 1964), 23–26, and David L. Sterling, "In Defense of Debs: The Lawyers and the Espionage Act Case," **Indiana Magazine of History** 83, no. 1 (March 1987): 17–42.

180 "AND HERE LET ME" Eugene V. Debs, **Debs and the War: His Canton Speech and His Trial in the Federal Court at Cleveland, September, 1918** (Chicago, 1923), 19.

180 SENTENCED TO TEN YEARS Murray, **Red Scare**, 25.

180 "I HAVE BEEN" Ibid.

180 WITH OLIVER WENDELL HOLMES, JR., WRITING Ibid., 25–26.

180 DISMISSED THE JUSTICES AS "BEGOWNED" Ibid., 26.

181 PRESIDENT WILSON REFUSED Ibid., 201. "No," Wilson said, "I will not release him." Attorney General Palmer supported the president's decision. Ibid.

181 IT FELL TO PRESIDENT WARREN G. HARDING Ibid., 273. Harding issued the pardon on Christmas Day 1921. Ibid.

181 AN ANARCHIST'S BOMB Ibid., 78–79. In the wake of the armistice in November 1918, a series of debilitating 1919 labor strikes from Seattle to Gary, Indiana, to Boston and beyond, as well as bombings and bomb threats, roiled the country. Bennett, **Party of Fear,** 188–89.

181 FRANKLIN D. ROOSEVELT, A NEIGHBOR OF PALMER'S Ward, **First-Class Temperament,** 455–56.

181 "AS WE WALKED ACROSS" Ibid.

181 "NOW WE ARE ROPED" Ibid., 456.

181 PALMER LAUNCHED AN ORGANIZED CAMPAIGN Murray, **Red Scare,** 80; 194–238.

182 SEVEN OTHER BOMBINGS Ward, **First-Class Temperament,** 457.

182 "MY INFORMATION SHOWED" Bennett, **Party of Fear,** 193.

182 "THE BLAZE OF REVOLUTION" Ward, **First-Class Temperament,** 457.

182 HIS ACTION OFFICER Murray, **Red Scare,** 193. See also Kenneth D. Ackerman, **Young J. Edgar: Hoover and the Red Scare, 1919–1920** (New York, 2011).

182 "THERE IS NO TIME" Samuel Walker, **In Defense of American Liberties: A History of the ACLU** (New York, 1990), 44.

182 THE IDEA OF "100 PERCENT AMERICANISM" Frederick Lewis Allen, **Only Yesterday: An Informal History of the 1920s** (New York, 2010), 51. Allen's book—he edited **Harper's** magazine—was originally published in 1931. See also Murray, **Red Scare**, 82–104.

182 "INNUMERABLE PATRIOTIC SOCIETIES" Allen, **Only Yesterday,** 58.

183 "INNUMERABLE OTHER GENTLEMEN" Ibid., 58–59.

184 "AMERICA IS NO LONGER" Ibid., 53–54.

184 PALMER, WHO CRAVED THE PRESIDENCY Murray, **Red Scare,** 260.

184 HIS RAIDS WERE NUMEROUS Ibid., 196–238.

184 WILSON SUFFERED A DEBILITATING STROKE Berg, **Wilson,** 626–52, charts Wilson's exhaustion during a tour in support of the League of Nations and the stroke itself, which felled the president in the White House on the morning of Thursday, October 2, 1919. Ibid., 640–42.

184 ("HE LOOKED AS IF") Ibid., 642. "For days his life hung in the balance," Edith Wilson, his second wife, recalled. Ibid.

185 THE PRESIDENT FAILED TO REIN Cooper, **Woodrow Wilson,** 546–47.

185 AFTER THE NEW YORK STATE LEGISLATURE Murray, **Red Scare,** 236–38. See also "Albany's Ousted Socialists," **Literary Digest,** January 24, 1920.

185 "ABSOLUTELY INIMICAL TO" Murrary, **Red Scare,** 236.

185 "SUGGESTED THEY OUGHT" Ibid., 237.

185 "AMERICANS ARE SAVAGES" **Literary Digest,** January 24, 1920, 19.

185 "Even the Czar of Russia"   Ibid.

185 Writing on behalf   Murray, **Red Scare,** 243–44.

186 "Is it not clear"   **Literary Digest,** January 24, 1920.

186 "And where will it"   Ibid. See also Murray, **Red Scare,** 242–43.

186 "The action of"   Murray, **Red Scare,** 244.

186 Signed by future Supreme Court justice Felix Frankfurter   Bennett, **Party of Fear,** 195.

187 "Talk about Americanization!"   Ibid.

187 "I hate"   Walker, **In Defense of American Liberties,** 53.

187 "In 1918 . . . we had to"   Du Bois, **Black Reconstruction,** 679.

187 Rudyard Kipling's 1897 imperial poem   Rudyard Kipling, "Recessional," 1897, Poetry Foundation, https://www.poetryfoundation.org/poems/46780/recessional. See also Gilmour, **Long Recessional.**

187 "Some . . . seem to see"   Du Bois, **Black Reconstruction,** 679.

187 a 1920 book by Lothrop Stoddard   Stoddard, **Rising Tide of Color.**

188 In 1925's **The Great Gatsby**   Hua Hsu, "The End of White America?" **The Atlantic,** January-February 2009. See also Lewis A. Turlish, "The Rising Tide of Color: A Note on the Historicism of The Great Gatsby," **American Literature** 43, no. 3 (November 1971): 442–44.

188 "Well, it's a fine book"   F. Scott Fitzgerald, **The Great Gatsby** (New York, 1992), 17.

188 An 1892 poem   Thomas Bailey Aldrich, "Unguarded Gates," Bartleby.com, http://www.bartleby.com/248/689.html.

189 Emma Lazarus had written a sonnet   Emma Lazarus, "The New Colossus," Poetry Foundation, https://www.poetryfoundation.org/poems/46550/the-new-colossus.

190 "Millions of Americans"   Hiram Wesley Evans, "The Klan of Yesterday and of Today," **Proceedings of the Second Imperial Klonvokation Held at Kansas City, Missouri,** 55. For more on Evans, see "Ku Klux Klan: Kleveland Konvention," **Time,** June 23, 1924; Evans appeared on the magazine's cover that week.

190 "The Klan, alone"   Evans, "Klan," 55–56.

191 "We are a movement"   Bennett, **Party of Fear,** 221. Such language made the Klan's meaning clear. "In its essence the thing was an authentic folk movement—at least as fully such as the Nazi movement in Germany, to which it was not without kinship," W. J. Cash wrote in his landmark 1941 study **The Mind of the South** (New York, 1941), 335. "It was, as is well known, at once anti-Negro, anti-Alien, anti-Red, anti-Catholic, anti-Jew, anti-Darwin, anti-Modern, anti-Liberal, Fundamentalist, vastly Moral, militantly Protestant." Ibid., 336–37.

191 Reliable numbers are hard to come by   Bennett, **Party of Fear,** 222–23; McVeigh, "Power Devaluation," 1; Gordon, **Second Coming of the KKK,** 2–3.

191 "If I am"   McVeigh, "Power Devaluation," 11.

192   THE ZANGWILL-TR "MELTING POT"   Evans, "Klan," 67.

192   "THE KLAN BELIEVES"   Ibid., 69.

192   ("JESUS WAS A PROTESTANT")   Bennett, **Party of Fear,** 215.

192   IN A SPEECH ENTITLED "AMERICANISM APPLIED,"   Walker, "Americanism Applied," 20–29.

192   A PHI BETA KAPPA GRADUATE   "Clifford Walker (1877–1954)," **New Georgia Encyclopedia,** https://www.georgiaencyclopedia.org/articles/government-politics/clifford-walker-1877-1954.

192   LEARNING HIS LESSON   Ibid.

193   SPEAKING IN KANSAS CITY   Walker, "Americanism Applied," 20–29.

193   "WHAT GOOD WILL IT DO"   Ibid., 25.

193   "I WOULD BUILD"   Ibid., 27.

193   THE "KLANBAKE"   Matthew Wills, "A Really Contested Convention: The 1924 Democratic Klanbake," JSTOR Daily, May 11, 2016, https://daily.jstor.org/contested-convention/. For an overview of the convention, see Chalmers, **Hooded Americanism,** 202–12. The fullest treatment is Robert K. Murray, **The 103rd Ballot: The Legendary 1924 Democratic Convention That Forever Changed Politics** (New York, 2016).

194   THE DELEGATES INCLUDED   McVeigh, "Power Devaluation," 5.

194   DEFEAT OF THE   Ibid. See also Bennett, **Party of Fear,** 233.

194   WITH THE IMPERIAL WIZARD   Chalmers, **Hooded Americanism,** 205.

194 "OUTNUMBERING THE ANTI-KLAN" McVeigh, "Power Devaluation," 8.

194 WE CONDEMN POLITICAL SECRET SOCIETIES Ibid., 6.

195 "IF YOU ARE OPPOSED" Chalmers, **Hooded Americanism,** 208.

195 "THIS UN-AMERICAN" **Official Proceedings of the Democratic National Convention Held at Madison Square Garden . . . Resulting in the Nomination of John W. Davis of West Virginia for President and Charles W. Bryan of Nebraska for Vice-President** (Indianapolis, 1924), 289–90.

195 "IF 343 MEMBERS" Chalmers, **Hooded Americanism,** 208.

196 "I SAY TO YOU" **Official Proceedings of the Democratic National Convention,** 285.

196 "WHAT WOULD YOU" Ibid.

196 "IF THE MEN" Ibid., 286.

197 "ARE WE, WITHOUT TRIAL" Ibid., 287–88.

197 "WILL MAKE HALF A MILLION" Ibid., 288.

197 "AND REMEMBER ONE THING" Ibid., 299.

197 TO NAME THE KLAN Ibid., 303–9.

197 "I CALL YOU BACK" Ibid., 308.

198 IN A VICTORY FOR THE KLAN McVeigh, "Power Devaluation," 6.

198 AND WHILE THE KLAN HELPED DENY Chalmers, **Hooded Americanism,** 203–4. Many in the Klan truly favored Senator Samuel Ralston of Indiana, but, as Chalmers wrote, he proved "no more than a dark-horse contender. McAdoo . . . was no bigot. His chief strategist, Bernard Baruch, was a Jew; his floor manager, Senator James

Phelan, was an Irish Catholic, but if McAdoo did not personally favor the Klan, he felt that he could not afford to alienate its support. His representatives solicited the Klan vote and he tacitly gave it shelter." Ibid., 204.

198 THE CRY OF "KU, KU, McADOO!"   Ibid., 206.

198 "BOOZE! BOOZE! BOOZE!"   Ibid.

198 THE CONVENTION WAS LEFT   Murray, **103rd Ballot,** 258–65.

198 AFTER THE 103RD BALLOT   Ibid., 265.

198 ON A DAY OF OCCASIONAL RAIN SHOWERS   "White-Robed Klan Cheered on March in Nation's Capital," **The Washington Post,** August 9, 1925.

198 "THE PARADE WAS GRANDER"   "The Klan Walks in Washington," **Literary Digest,** August 22, 1925.

199 "WHEN I GOT BACK"   Ibid.

199 THE SCOPES TRIAL IN DAYTON, TENNESSEE   See, for instance, Edward J. Larson, **Summer for the Gods: The Scopes Trial and America's Continuing Debate Over Science and Religion** (New York, 1997).

199 A SIGN HUNG OUTSIDE   "In Dayton Evolution Is a Dead Issue," **NYT,** August 14, 1927.

199 "I DO NOT THINK"   "The Scopes Trial: Examination of William Jennings Bryan by Clarence Darrow," Digital History, http://www.digital history.uh.edu/disp_textbook.cfm?smtID =3&psid=1160.

200 "DO YOU THINK"   Ibid.

200 (IN THE VIEWS)   The question of Mencken and anti-Semitism (and of racism) is a subject of great

literary and scholarly debates. See, for instance: Fred Hobson, **Mencken: A Life** (New York, 1994), x, xv–xvi, 26, 168–69, 224, 225, 275, 350, 404–414, 416–419, 424–425, 453–455, 457, 471, 477, 538–39 544–46; H. L. Mencken, **My Life as Author and Editor,** ed. Jonathan Yardley (New York, 1993), 20–23; Terry Teachout, "Mencken Unsealed," **NYT,** January 31, 1993; "Mencken Was Pro-Nazi, His Diary Shows," **Los Angeles Times,** December 5, 1989.

200 "SUCH OBSCENITIES AS" "Coverage of the Scopes Trial by H. L. Mencken from **The Baltimore Evening Sun,** June–September 1925," Internet Archive, https://archive.org/stream/Cover ageOfTheScopesTrialByH.l.Mencken/Scopes-TrialMencken.txt.

201 "SAT TIGHT-LIPPED" Ibid.

201 THE JURY SIDED "State of Tennessee v. Scopes," ACLU, https://www.aclu.org/other/state-tennessee-v-scopes.

201 "I THINK THIS CASE" Larson, **Summer for the Gods,** 193.

202 "NO ARGUMENTS YOU MAY USE" Bennett, **Party of Fear,** 230.

202 A KLAN WITH SUBSTANTIAL STRENGTH MacLean, **Behind the Mask,** 178–88. MacLean's book is largely about assessing the Klan in a global context with particular reference to the European fascist movements. She quoted Thomas Mann: "This story should convince us of one thing: that there are not two Germanys, a good one and a bad one, but only one. . . . Wicked Germany is

merely good Germany gone astray, good Germany in misfortune, in guilt, and ruin. For that reason it is quite impossible for one born there simply to renounce the wicked, guilty Germany and to declare, 'I am the good, the noble, the just Germany in the white robe; I leave it to you to exterminate the wicked one." Ibid., 177. See also James Q. Whitman, **Hitler's American Model: The United States and the Making of Nazi Race Law** (Princeton, N.J., 2017), for a provocative and thoughtful examination of what the Third Reich learned from the American example.

203 "THE KU KLUX KLAN"   MacLean, **Behind the Mask,** 179–80.

203 IN 1928, THE U.S. SUPREME COURT UPHELD The case was **People of the State of New York ex rel. Bryant v. Zimmerman et al.,** FindLaw, http://caselaw.findlaw.com/us-supreme-court/278/63.html. See also Chalmers, **Hooded Americanism,** 199.

203 "IT IS A MATTER"   **People of the State of New York ex rel. Bryant v. Zimmerman et al.**

203 "WAS CONDUCTING A CRUSADE"   Ibid.

204 IN 1925, A UNANIMOUS SUPREME COURT **Pierce v. Society of Sisters,** 268 U.S. 510 (1925), Justia, https://supreme.justia.com/cases/federal/us/268/510/case.html.

204 THE NEW YORK WORLD   Chalmers, **Hooded Americanism,** 35–36.

204 HOSTILITY FROM THE JOURNALISTS   Ibid., 38. "E. H. Loucks, in his seminal study of the Klan in Pennsylvania," Chalmers wrote, "suggested

that what New York attacked, rural America, with its belligerent inferiority complex, would stubbornly support." Ibid. See also E. H. Loucks, **The Ku Klux Klan in Pennsylvania** (Harrisburg, Pa., 1936), 23.

204 "IT WASN'T UNTIL" Chalmers, **Hooded Americanism,** 38.

204 WHEN THE HOUSE RULES COMMITTEE Ibid., 36–38.

205 "CERTAIN NEWSPAPERS ALSO" Ibid., 38.

205 "WEARING MASKS" Rawlings, **Second Coming of the Invisible Empire,** 246–47.

206 IN OCTOBER 1921, PRESIDENT HARDING "Harding Says Negro Must Have Equality in Political Life," NYT, October 27, 1921. See also Greg Bailey, "This Presidential Race Speech Shocked the Nation—in 1921," Narratively, October 26, 2016, http://narrative.ly/this-presi dential-speech-on-race-shocked-the-nation-in -1921/. For W.E.B. Du Bois's incisive critique of the speech, see Du Bois, "President Harding and Social Equality," December 1921, TeachingAmer icanHistory.org, http://teachingamericanhistory. org/library/document/president-harding-and -social-equality/.

206 SUPPORTED ANTI-LYNCHING LAWS Bailey, "This Presidential Race Speech." See also Robert K. Murray, **The Harding Era: Warren G. Harding and His Administration** (Minneapolis, 1969), 401–2.

206 IN BIRMINGHAM'S CAPITOL PARK "Harding Says Negro Must Have Equality in Political Life."

206 ("I would say")   Ibid.

206 ("Partnership of the races")   Ibid.

206 Harding, however, approvingly cited   Ibid.

206 "There are many"   Ibid.

206 "If the President's theory"   Bailey, "This Presidential Race Speech."

207 "a braver, clearer"   Du Bois, "President Harding and Social Equality."

207 The "pseudo-science"   Ibid.

207 "The absolute equality"   Ibid.

207 "To deny this fact"   Ibid.

208 "The nation which"   "Harding Says Negro Must Have Equality in Political Life."

208 The president was   Wallace, "The Ku Klux Klan in Calvin Coolidge's America."

208 "We have our factions"   Ibid.

209 The New York Times's headline   Ibid.

209 He made the same   Ibid.

209 In attempts to   Murray, Harding Era, 63–65; Peter Baker, "DNA Shows Warren Harding Wasn't America's First Black President," NYT, August 18, 2015.

209 In the 1920   Ibid., 63.

209 "By means of"   Ibid.

210 Harding chose to   Ibid., 64.

210 "I want you"   Ibid.

210 "How do I"   Ibid.

210 (In 2015, DNA testing)   Baker, "DNA Shows Warren Harding Wasn't America's First Black President."

210 After Harding's death   Wallace, "Ku Klux Klan in Calvin Coolidge's America."

210 "WE HAVE 227"   "Klan Boast Derided: Officials Call Claim of Initiation in White House 'Ridiculous,'" **NYT,** September 23, 1923.

210 SAID THE REPORTS WERE "TOO"   Wallace, "Ku Klux Klan in Calvin Coolidge's America."

210 COOLIDGE, THE NEW PRESIDENT   See, in particular, Amity Shlaes, **Coolidge** (New York, 2013), and Donald R. McCoy, **Calvin Coolidge: The Quiet President.** (New York, 1967).

210 TOOK THE OATH   Shlaes, **Coolidge,** 251–53. When Coolidge left Vermont as the thirtieth president, he remarked: "I believe I can swing it." Ibid., 253.

211 REFRAINED FROM TAKING   Wallace, "Ku Klux Klan in Calvin Coolidge's America." Coolidge was better on matters of race than is generally thought, if it is thought of at all. See, for instance, ibid.; Shlaes, **Coolidge,** 313–14; 336; Alvin S. Felzenberg, "Calvin Coolidge and Race: His Record in Dealing with the Racial Tensions of the 1920s," **The New England Journal of History** 55, no. 1 (Fall 1988): 83–96; Kurt Schmoke, "The Little Known History of Coolidge and Civil Rights," **Coolidge Quarterly,** 1, no. 3 (November 2016): 1–5. Jerry L. Wallace has written:

At a cabinet meeting, a discussion came up regarding the refusal of white government employees to work with their black counterparts. This, of course, was at a time when there was no legal framework that could be called upon to support an integrated workforce and no prospects for such whatsoever. This led President Coolidge to remark to his associates: "Well, I don't know what you can do, or how you will solve the question, but to me it seems a terrible thing for persons of intelligence, of education, of real character—as we know many colored people are—to be deprived of a chance to work because they happen to be born with a different colored skin. I think you ought to find a way to give them an even chance." Ibid. Wallace cited John S. Sargent, "Championing the Negro," in "The Real Calvin Coolidge," edited and with commentary by Grace Coolidge, **Good Housekeeping,** June 1935.

211 "GOVERNMENT CANNOT LAST" Charles C. Johnson, **Why Coolidge Matters: Leadership Lessons from America's Most Underrated President** (New York, 2013), 181.

211 DAWES TRIED TO SOFTEN Wallace, "Ku Klux Klan in Calvin Coolidge's America."

211 HAD "CONFOUND[ED THE] PARTY" Ibid. See also "General 'Opposed to' Klan," **NYT,** August 24, 1924.

211 AFTER CONFERRING WITH Wallace, "Ku Klux Klan in Calvin Coolidge's America."

211 "HE WAS PROBABLY" Ibid.

212 "MOREOVER," WALLACE WROTE Ibid.

212 "ONE POLITICAL CONSEQUENCE" Ibid.

212 A CORRESPONDENT HAD WRITTEN Bean, **Race and Liberty in America,** 147–49; Shlaes, **Coolidge,** 313–14.

212 "IT IS OF SOME CONCERN"   Bean, **Race and Liberty in America**, 148.

213 CITING THE SERVICE   Ibid.

213 THE AFRICAN AMERICAN CHICAGO DEFENDER   Ibid.

213 THE CAUSES OF THE KLAN'S FALL   MacLean, **Behind the Mask**, 184–85; Gordon, **Second Coming of the KKK**, 191–209; Chalmers, **Hooded Americanism**, 291–99.

214 RESTRICTIVE IMMIGRATION LAW   The chief piece of legislation was the National Origins Act of 1924. Gjerde, **Major Problems in American Immigration and Ethnic History**, 307–43. See also Bean, **Race and Liberty in America**, 137, and McVeigh, **Rise of the Ku Klux Klan**, 127–29.

214 (THE 805,228 IMMIGRANTS)   Gjerde, **Major Problems in American Immigration and Ethnic History**, 343.

214 COMMERCE WAS CULTURE   MacLean, **Behind the Mask**, 186–87. "Under conditions of economic uncertainty, sharply contested social relations, and political impasse," MacLean wrote, "assumptions about class, race, gender, and state power so ordinary as to appear 'common sense' to most WASP Americans could be refashioned and harnessed to the building of a virulent reactionary politics able to mobilize millions." Ibid., 186.

214 THE KLAN SABOTAGED ITSELF   Chalmers, **Hooded Americanism**, 171–74; Gordon, **Second Coming of the KKK**, 191–98; Rawlings, **Second Coming of the Invisible Empire**, 235–54. "The failure of the Ku Klux Klan to anchor itself as a

successful feature in American life," Chalmers wrote, "was due more to its own ineptness than any other cause or combination of factors," Chalmers wrote. "The decline of the Klan as a mass movement in America was its own fault, nobody else's." Chalmers, **Hooded Americanism,** 299.

214 "I'm a nobody from"   Gordon, **Second Coming of the KKK,** 17.

214 the revelation of depravity   Ibid., 191–94; MacLean, **Behind the Mask,** 177–78; Chalmers, **Hooded Americanism,** 298–99.

215 "Whether one traces"   Calvin Coolidge, "Address Before the American Legion Convention at Omaha, Nebraska," October 6, 1925, American Presidency Project, http://www.presidency.ucsb.edu/ws/?pid=438.

215 "I recognize the full"   Ibid.

216 If we are to have   Ibid.

216 Henry Hugh Proctor   "Henry Hugh Proctor (1868–1933)," **New Georgia Encyclopedia,** https://www.georgiaencyclopedia.org/articles/arts-culture/henry-hugh-proctor-1868-1933.

217 "Particularly do we"   Shlaes, **Coolidge,** 336.

FIVE · **The Crisis of the Old Order**

221 We must drive   Nathanael West, **Novels and Other Writings,** ed. Sacvan Bercovitch (New York, 1997), 174. I quoted this passage in "The Literature of Our Discontent," **NYT,** January 17, 2017.

221 The only limit   Franklin D. Roosevelt: "Un-

delivered Address Prepared for Jefferson Day," April 13, 1945, American Presidency Project, http://www.presidency.ucsb.edu/ws/?pid=16602.

221 ON CHRISTMAS EVE 1929 "Fire Wrecks the White House Offices," **NYT**, December 25, 1929. I drew on my essay "Literature of Our Discontent," originally published in **NYT**, January 17, 2017, for the description of the West Wing fire and its symbolic implications.

221 ACCORDING TO PUBLISHED REPORTS "Fire Wrecks the White House Offices." See also "Fire Fails to Halt White House Party," and "$60,000 Flames Eat West Wing of White House," **The Washington Post,** December 25, 1929.

221 "AT TIMES IT SEEMED" "Fire Wrecks the White House Offices."

222 "THE CRISIS OF THE OLD ORDER" Arthur M. Schlesinger, Jr., **Crisis of the Old Order, 1919– 1933,** The Age of Roosevelt, vol. 1 (Boston, 1957).

222 BERNARD M. BARUCH SAID "The Presidency: Prospect," **Time,** February 27, 1933.

223 NEARLY 20 PERCENT David M. Kennedy, **Freedom from Fear: The American People in Depression and War, 1929–1945** (New York, 1999), 86–88.

223 "THE COUNTRY HAD" Ibid., 87.

223 MOBS OF HUNGRY YOUTHS William Manchester, **Glory and the Dream: A Narrative History of America, 1932–1972** (Boston, 1974), 55.

223 ARMED STANDOFFS ROILED Ibid., 58–59.

223 "THERE ARE MANY SIGNS" Schlesinger, **Crisis of the Old Order,** 3.

223 HAD TOLD AN ADVISER   Rexford G. Tugwell, **The Democratic Roosevelt: A Biography of Franklin D. Roosevelt** (Garden City, N.Y., 1957), 349.

223 ("MACARTHUR HAS DECIDED")   Manchester, **Glory and the Dream,** 13.

224 THE LOUDEST CHEERS   Ibid., 77.

224 IN THE MIDDLE OF FEBRUARY 1933   Frank Freidel, **Franklin D. Roosevelt: A Rendezvous with Destiny** (Boston, 1990), 87–88; Sally Denton, **The Plots Against the President: FDR, a Nation in Crisis, and the Rise of the American Right** (New York, 2012), 71–77.

224 FROM ABOUT TEN YARDS AWAY   Freidel, **Franklin D. Roosevelt,** 87. Denton puts the distance at twenty-five feet. Denton, **Plots Against the President,** 71.

224 FDR HAD STOPPED OFF   Denton, **Plots Against the President,** 62; 68–69.

224 "IT WOULD BE EASY"   Ibid., 69–70.

224 WITHIN HALF AN HOUR   Ibid., 70.

224 AN EIGHT-DOLLAR PEARL-HANDLED .32 REVOLVER   Ibid., 71.

224 THE MAYOR OF CHICAGO, ANTON CERMAK   Ibid., 72.

225 "PEOPLE SEEMED TO FEEL"   Freidel, **Franklin D. Roosevelt,** 88. See also "The Presidency: Prospect."

225 "I'M ALL RIGHT"   Denton, **Plots Against the President,** 73.

225 "ROOSEVELT WAS SIMPLY HIMSELF"   Freidel, **Franklin D. Roosevelt,** 88.

225 BACK ON THE NOURMAHAL   Denton, **Plots Against the President**, 75–76.

225 DRANK A GLASS OF WHISKEY   Ibid.; Freidel, **Franklin D. Roosevelt**, 88.

225 ASKED WHETHER HISTORY HAD EVER   Manchester, **Glory and the Dream**, 31.

225 "I THINK BY 1933"   Arthur M. Schlesinger, Jr., **The Politics of Upheaval**, The Age of Roosevelt, vol. 3 (Boston, 1960), 17.

225 DESCRIBING THE PLIGHT OF   Manchester, **Glory and the Dream**, 31.

226 A SMALL GROUP OF   Denton, **Plots Against the President**, 176–217, is a full account, as is Jules Archer, **The Plot to Seize the White House: The Shocking True Story of the Conspiracy to Overthrow F.D.R.** (New York, 2015). See also Schlesinger, **Politics of Upheaval**, 82–83; 85.

226 THE "WALL STREET PUTSCH"   Denton, **Plots Against the President**, 201.

226 (ALSO KNOWN AS THE "BUSINESS PLOT")   Ibid.

226 "IF YOU GET"   Ibid., 200. See also Schlesinger, **Politics of Upheaval**, 83.

226 TOLD FBI DIRECTOR J. EDGAR HOOVER   Denton, **Plots Against the President**, 200–201.

226 REPORTS ABOUT THE WALL STREET   Ibid., 201.

226 IN LATE 1934, SECRET CONGRESSIONAL HEARINGS   Archer, **Plot to Seize the White House**, 139–40.

226 TWICE AWARDED THE   Ibid., 139. For Butler in general, see also Hans Schmidt, **Maverick Marine: General Smedley D. Butler and the Con-**

tradictions of American Military History (Lexington, Ky., 1998).

226 "May I preface" Ibid., 139–40.

227 "Nobody who has" Ibid., 140.

227 "Gen. Butler Bares" Ibid., 169. See also NYT, November 21, 1934.

227 "If General Butler" Archer, **Plot to Seize the White House,** 214. The McCormack interview with Archer took place in 1971. See also Denton, **Plots Against the President,** 212–13.

227 McCormack had little patience Archer, **Plot to Seize the White House,** 216. In a February 15, 1935, report to the full House on the committee's findings, McCormack wrote, "There is no question that these attempts were discussed, were planned, and might have been placed in execution if the financial backers had deemed it expedient. This committee received evidence from Maj. Gen. Smedley D. Butler (retired), twice decorated by the Congress of the United States. He testified before the committee as to conversations with one Gerald C. MacGuire in which the latter is alleged to have suggested the formation of a fascist army under the leadership of General Butler. MacGuire denied these allegations under oath, but your committee was able to verify all the pertinent statements made by General Butler, with the exception of the direct statement suggesting the creation of the organization. This, however, was corroborated in the correspondence of MacGuire with his principal, Robert Sterling Clark, of New York City, while MacGuire was abroad studying the various

forms of veterans organizations of Fascist character. . . . This committee asserts that any efforts based on lines as suggested in the foregoing and leading off to the extreme right, are just as bad as efforts which would lead to the extreme left. Armed forces for the purpose of establishing a dictatorship through the means of Fascism or a dictatorship through the instrumentality of the proletariat, or a dictatorship predicated on racial and religious hatreds, have no place in this country." Ibid., 192.

227 "The people were"   Ibid., 215.

228 "regarded the plot"   Ibid., 216.

228 "Why, there's no country"   Schlesinger, **Politics of Upheaval,** 89.

228 "Where in all history"   Ibid., 90.

228 "I was reading the other day"   Winston Churchill, "What Good's a Constitution?" **Collier's,** August 22, 1936. Churchill added: "This is an age in which the citizen requires more, and not less, legal protection in the exercise of his rights and liberties." Ibid.

228 a small novel by Nathanael West   I drew on my piece "Literature of Our Discontent" for this section about West's book.

229 "I'm a simple man"   West, **Novels and Other Writings,** 173–74.

230 At lunch one day at Hyde Park   T. Harry Williams, **Huey Long** (New York, 1969), 602. Long embellished the story of the lunch, telling his own family that the Roosevelt matriarch had said, "Frankie, you're not going to let Huey Long tell you what to do, are you?" Ibid.

230 FIVE DEMOCRATIC STATE CHAIRMEN   Ibid., 603.

230 LOST THE VOTE IN PENNSYLVANIA   Ibid.

230 "A MOB IS COMING"   Ibid., 626. On the eve of FDR's inauguration, Long stormed into a Roosevelt ally's hotel room, grabbed an apple, took a bite, then poked the FDR intimate with the fruit, saying, "I don't like you and your goddamned banker friends." Ibid., 625.

230 "I'M GOING TO ASK"   Ibid., 625.

231 "CERTAINLY WE ARE FACING COMMUNISM" Ibid., 557.

231 IN AN APRIL 1932 SPEECH TO THE SENATE   Huey P. Long, **Kingfish to America, Share Our Wealth: Selected Senatorial Papers of Huey P. Long,** ed. Henry M. Christman (New York, 1985), 9, 11.

232 "WHERE IS THE MIDDLE CLASS TODAY?" Schlesinger, **Politics of Upheaval,** 62.

232 "HE DELIGHTED IN"   Williams, **Huey Long,** 680.

232 "THINGS ARE AWFULLY QUIET"   Ibid.

232 "FRANKLY, WE ARE AFRAID"   Ibid., 681.

233 ONE DAY IN THE SENATE   Ibid., 680–81.

233 "HE WILL BE DIRECT"   Raymond Gram Swing, "The Menace of Huey Long: II. His Bid for National Power," **The Nation,** January 23, 1935, 98. Long defended his absolutist tendencies with candor.

   "They say they don't like my methods," Long once remarked. "Well, I don't like them either. I really don't like to have to do things the way I do.

I'd much rather get up before the legislature and say, 'Now this is a good law; it's for the benefit of the people, and I'd like for you to vote for it in the interest of the public welfare.' Only I know that laws ain't made that way. You've got to fight fire with fire." Williams, **Huey Long,** 748.

And he might have fought Roosevelt's fire with some of his own as early as 1936. "I might have a good parade to offer before we get through," Long told the Senate. "I am always open to propositions as they occur in these changing cycles of time." Ibid., 818.

233 As his "Share Our Wealth" message   Ibid., 692–702.

234 A banker from Montana   Schlesinger, **Politics of Upheaval,** 65.

234 Lawrence Dennis, a native of Georgia   Ibid., 76.

234 "I am in favor"   Ibid., 75–76. "No country has been better prepared for political and social standardization," Dennis added. Ibid.

234 "undoubtedly the easiest"   Ibid., 76–77.

234–35   Charles Coughlin, a Roman Catholic priest   See, for instance, ibid., 16–28; Brinkley, **Voices of Protest,** 82–106.

236 when Alexander Hamilton   Schlesinger, **Politics of Upheaval,** 27. A typical Coughlin message: "Christian parents, do you want your daughter to be the breeder of some lustful person's desires, and, when the rose of her youth has withered, to be thrown upon the highways of Socialism?" he would ask. "Choose to-day! It is ei-

ther Christ or the Red Fog of Communism."
Ibid., 17.

236 "I HAIL THESE MOVEMENTS"   Ibid., 77.

237 HUGH S. JOHNSON, A RETIRED GENERAL   Williams, **Huey Long**, 807–8.

237 "OUR SOLE HOPE"   Ibid., 808.

237 THE NEW YORK GOVERNOR WAS "NOT A MAN"
Manchester, **Glory and the Dream**, 47.

237 "FRANKLIN D. ROOSEVELT IS NO CRUSADER"
Freidel, **Franklin D. Roosevelt**, 68.

237 "HE HAS SPOKEN OF"   Manchester, **Glory and the Dream**, 51.

238 "WILD RADICALISM HAS MADE"   Franklin D. Roosevelt, "Address Accepting the Presidential Nomination at the Democratic National Convention in Chicago," July 2, 1932, American Presidency Project, http://www.presidency.ucsb.edu/ws/?pid=75174.

238 "TO MEET BY REACTION"   Ibid.

239 "I PLEDGE YOU"   Ibid.

239 "HIS IMPULSE"   Winston S. Churchill, **Great Contemporaries: Churchill Reflects on FDR, Hitler, Kipling, Chaplin, Balfour, and Other Giants of His Age**, ed. James W. Muller with Paul H. Courtenay and Erica L. Chenoweth (Wilmington, Del., 2012), 368.

239 ("MAMA LEFT THIS MORNING")   Ward, **First-Class Temperament**, 628.

239 HIS MARRIAGE SURVIVED   Ibid., 411–17.

240 THE FORCE OF "A PHYSICAL BLOW"   Jon Meacham, **Franklin and Winston: An Intimate Portrait of an Epic Friendship** (New York, 2003), 344.

240 "PRESIDENT ROOSEVELT'S PHYSICAL AFFLIC-
TION" Ibid., 353.

241 LYNDON JOHNSON WEPT Manchester, **Glory
and the Dream,** 355.

241 "HE WAS JUST LIKE A DADDY" Ibid.

241 "MEN WILL THANK GOD" Ibid., 354. See also
"Franklin D. Roosevelt," **NYT,** April 13, 1945.
"It is a hard and stunning blow," the **Times**
wrote, "to lose the genius and the inspiration of
his leadership in this decisive moment of the
war. . . . Gone is the exuberance and the enthusiasm and the indomitable courage that conquered the hardest of personal afflictions and the
worst handicaps of physical misfortune. Gone is
the fresh and spontaneous interest which this
man took, as naturally as he breathed air, in the
troubles and the hardships and the disappoint-
ments and the hopes of little men and humble
people." Ibid.

242 "THIS GREAT NATION WILL ENDURE" Franklin D. Roosevelt, "Inaugural Address," March 4,
1933, American Presidency Project, http://www
.presidency.ucsb.edu/ws/?pid=14473.

242 FDR HAD DRAWN ON Samuel I. Rosenman,
Working with Roosevelt (New York, 1952), 91.
For other speculation on the origin of the phrase
and its inclusion in FDR's speech, see "First Inaugural Address," https://fdrlibrary.org/first-inaugu
ral-curriculum-hub.

242 THOREAU HAD WRITTEN "Thoreau & FDR,"
Thoreau Society, https://www.thoreausociety.org/
news-article/thoreau-fdr.

242 FDR HAD THE BOOK   Rosenman, **Working with Roosevelt**, 91.

242 SUITE 776 OF THE MAYFLOWER HOTEL   "Mayflower Hotel," National Park Service, https://www.nps.gov/nr/travel/wash/dc59.htm.

242 "ROOSEVELT FREQUENTLY PICKED UP"   Rosenman, **Working with Roosevelt**, 91.

243 "WE DO NOT DISTRUST THE FUTURE"   Franklin D. Roosevelt, "Inaugural Address," March 4, 1933.

243 A FRIEND TOLD HIM   Manchester, **Glory and the Dream**, 80.

243 "IF I FAIL"   Ibid.

243 (HE CALLED IT "STUMPING")   Meacham, **Franklin and Winston**, 114.

244 "IT WAS PART OF"   Schlesinger, **Coming of the New Deal**, 575.

244 SAY THAT CIVILIZATION   Schlesinger, **Politics of Upheaval**, 648–49.

244 "FRANKLIN, DARLING, WHY IS"   Ward, **First-Class Temperament**, 527.

244 "MUMMY, I THINK I KNOW"   Ibid.

245 "YOU'LL NEVER BE"   Freidel, **Franklin D. Roosevelt**, 94.

245 ROOSEVELT PARRIED A QUESTIONER   Schlesinger, **Coming of the New Deal**, 529.

245 "I HAVE NO EXPECTATION"   Ibid., 531. Also in "Second Fireside Chat," May 7, 1933, American Presidency Project, http://www.presidency.ucsb.edu/ws/?pid=14636.

246 "THE COUNTRY NEEDS"   Franklin D. Roosevelt, "Address at Oglethorpe University in

Atlanta, Georgia," May 22, 1932, American Presidency Project, http://www.presidency.ucsb.edu/ws/?pid=88410.

246 "AT THE TIME FRANKLIN ROOSEVELT BECAME PRESIDENT" Schlesinger, **Coming of the New Deal,** 570–71.

246 "IT IS A GREAT THING" Ibid., 571.

247 "YOU AND I" Robert E. Sherwood, **Roosevelt and Hopkins: An Intimate History** (New York, 1948), 266.

247 "OH—HE SOMETIMES TRIES" Ibid.

247 "WE SHALL STRIVE" Franklin D. Roosevelt, "Inaugural Address," January 20, 1945.

248 "YOU AND I HAVE GOT" Sherwood, **Roosevelt and Hopkins,** 880–81.

248 REPORTING FROM NORTH CAROLINA IN 1934 Schlesinger, **Coming of the New Deal,** 572.

249 "MORE THAN ANY MAN" Ibid.

249 "THE NEW DEAL IS SIMPLY" Gunther, **Roosevelt in Retrospect,** 281.

249 ROOSEVELT'S INITIAL TWO YEARS Kennedy, **Freedom from Fear,** 131–217.

249 THE SECOND NEW DEAL Ibid., 241–87; Schlesinger, **Politics of Upheaval,** 211–424.

249 "I WOULD SAY" Freidel, **Franklin D. Roosevelt,** 189.

250 THE KINGFISH'S ASSASSINATION Williams, **Huey Long,** 848–72.

250 ATTEMPTED TO ALTER THE MAKEUP Freidel, **Franklin D. Roosevelt,** 221–39.

250 THE REPUBLICANS SAY OFFICIALLY Ibid., 200.

251 THE TELEPHONE IN THE PRESIDENT'S BED-

ROOM   Michael R. Beschloss, **Kennedy and Roosevelt: The Uneasy Alliance** (New York, 1980), 190.

251 "WELL, BILL"   Ibid.

252 95 PERCENT OF THOSE POLLED   Manfred Jonas, **Isolationism in America, 1935–1941** (Chicago, 1990), 1.

252 "HE IS A GENTLEMAN"   Wayne S. Cole, **Roosevelt and the Isolationists, 1932–45** (Lincoln, Neb., 1983), 24.

252 THE REICH'S SEARCH FOR LEBENSRAUM   David Reynolds, **From Munich to Pearl Harbor: Roosevelt's America and the Origins of the Second World War** (Chicago, 2001), 14–15.

252 CONSTRAINED BY NEUTRALITY LEGISLATION   Ibid., 12–40.

253 DID THE BEST HE COULD   See, for instance, Cole, **Roosevelt and the Isolationists;** Jonas, **Isolationism in America;** Reynolds, **From Munich to Pearl Harbor;** Steven Casey, **Cautious Crusade: Franklin D. Roosevelt, American Public Opinion, and the War Against Nazi Germany** (New York, 2001).

253 "THE GREATEST SAFEGUARD"   Jonas, **Isolationism in America,** 34.

253 CONGRESSMAN LOUIS LUDLOW OF INDIANA   Manchester, **Glory and the Dream,** 177.

253 THE AMENDMENT CAME TO A VOTE   Ibid.

253 "OUR GOVERNMENT IS CONDUCTED"   Franklin D. Roosevelt, "Letter to the Speaker of the House on a Proposed Referendum to Declare War," January 6, 1938, American Presidency

Project, http://www.presidency.ucsb.edu/ws/?pid
=15616.

254 THE HOUSE VOTED THE MEASURE DOWN
James M. Lindsay, "TWE Remembers: The Ludlow Amendment," January 10, 2011, Council on
Foreign Relations, https://www.cfr.org/blog/twe-
remembers-ludlow-amendment.

254 "WE MUST NOT"   Manchester, **Glory and the
Dream,** 200.

254 ROOSEVELT'S VIEW WAS SUBTLER   See, for instance, Franklin D. Roosevelt, "Annual Message to
Congress on the State of the Union," January 6,
1941, American Presidency Project, http://www.
presidency.ucsb.edu/ws/?pid=16092. "I have re-
cently pointed out how quickly the tempo of
modern warfare could bring into our very midst
the physical attack which we must eventually expect if the dictator nations win this war," Roosevelt said.

> There is much loose talk of our immunity
> from immediate and direct invasion from
> across the seas. Obviously, as long as the Brit-
> ish Navy retains its power, no such danger ex-
> ists. Even if there were no British Navy, it is
> not probable that any enemy would be stupid
> enough to attack us by landing troops in the
> United States from across thousands of miles
> of ocean, until it had acquired strategic bases
> from which to operate. But we learn much
> from the lessons of the past years in Europe—
> particularly the lesson of Norway, whose es-

sential seaports were captured by treachery
and surprise built up over a series of years. The
first phase of the invasion of this hemisphere
would not be the landing of regular troops.
The necessary strategic points would be occupied by secret agents and their dupes—and
great numbers of them are already here, and in
Latin America. As long as the aggressor nations maintain the offensive, they—not we—
will choose the time and the place and the
method of their attack. Ibid.

254 In late July 1939 the president met   Manchester, **Glory and the Dream**, 202.

254 "Well, Captain"   Ibid.

254 "Now that war"   Charles Lindbergh, "America and European Wars," September 15, 1939,
CharlesLindbergh.com, http://www.charleslind
bergh.com/pdf/9_15_39.pdf.

255 "Passionately though we may desire"
Franklin D. Roosevelt, "Fireside Chat," September 3, 1939, American Presidency Project, http://
www.presidency.ucsb.edu/ws/?pid=15801.

255 running against the Republican Wendell
Willkie   See, for instance, Charles Peters, **Five
Days in Philadelphia: The Amazing "We Want
Willkie!" Convention of 1940 and How It Freed
FDR to Save the Western World** (New York, 2005).

255 "And while I am talking"   Gunther, **Roosevelt in Retrospect**, 312.

255 Listening on the radio   Freidel, **Franklin D.
Roosevelt**, 355.

255 "THAT HYPOCRITICAL SON OF A BITCH!" Ibid.

256 WON REPEAL OF THE EMBARGO Reynolds, **From Munich to Pearl Harbor,** 66.

256 TO EXCHANGE OLD AMERICAN DESTROYERS Freidel, **Franklin D. Roosevelt,** 333–36; 351–52.

256 HE WAGED AN UNDECLARED NAVAL WAR Joseph P. Lash, **Roosevelt and Churchill, 1939– 1941: The Partnership That Saved the West** (New York, 1976), 415–30.

256 A BROAD PLAN, CALLED LEND-LEASE Freidel, **Franklin D. Roosevelt,** 358–63.

256 THE IDEA HAD COME TO HIM Manchester, **Glory and the Dream,** 229–30.

256 A SEAPLANE HAD BROUGHT Ibid.

256 "ALTHOUGH THE PRESENT GOVERNMENT" Meacham, **Franklin and Winston,** 62.

257 "WE SHALL GO ON" Ibid., 57. For an incisive account of Churchill's early war leadership, see John Lukacs, **Five Days in London: May 1940** (New Haven, Conn., 1999).

257 "UNLESS WE CAN ESTABLISH" Meacham, **Franklin and Winston,** 78.

257 THE PRESIDENT PROPOSED Reynolds, **From Munich to Pearl Harbor,** 104–8.

258 "TODAY, THINKING OF" Franklin D. Roosevelt, "Annual Message to Congress on the State of the Union."

259 CHARLES LINDBERGH STEPPED Justus E. Doenecke, ed., **In Danger Undaunted: The Anti-Interventionist Movement of 1940–41 as Revealed in the Papers of the America First Committee** (Stanford, Calif., 1990), 37–38.

259 FOUNDED BY LAW STUDENTS   Ibid., 7.

259 "AMERICAN DEMOCRACY CAN BE PRESERVED" Ibid., 9.

260 IN LATE 1940   Ibid., 12.

260 BY ONE ESTIMATE SIXTY THOUSAND   Ibid.

260 FOR "THAT SILENT MAJORITY"   Manchester, **Glory and the Dream**, 220.

260 "IT IS NOT DIFFICULT TO UNDERSTAND"   Doenecke, **In Danger Undaunted**, 37–38.

261 "IF I SHOULD DIE TOMORROW"   Lynne Olson, **Those Angry Days: Roosevelt, Lindbergh, and America's Fight Over World War II, 1939–1941** (New York, 2013), 103.

261 "LINDBERGH'S ANTI-JEWISH SPEECH"   Ibid., 38.

261 NORMAN THOMAS, THE SOCIALIST LEADER   Ibid.

261 "IT SEEMS INCREDIBLE"   Ibid., 395.

262 HENRY FORD'S **DEARBORN INDEPENDENT** Ibid., 237.

262 "WHEN WE GET THROUGH"   Manchester, **Glory and the Dream**, 176.

262 THE GERMAN-AMERICAN BUND   Olson, **Those Angry Days**, 124.

262 "THE PRINCIPLES OF"   MacLean, **Behind the Mask**, 180.

262 A BUND LEADER   Chalmers, **Hooded Americanism**, 323.

262 THE THIRD REICH HAD SOUGHT   Olson, **Those Angry Days**, 182–83.

262 GERALD L. K. SMITH, A FORMER ALLY   Gerald L. K. Smith, "This Is Christian Nationalism," The Cross and Flag, http://www.thecrossandflag.com/articles/christian_nationalism.html.

263 "THE CHRISTIAN NATIONALIST CRUSADE" Ibid.

263 WOULD "RATHER DIE ON OUR FEET" Franklin D. Roosevelt, "Message to the Special Convocation of the University of Oxford," June 19, 1941, American Presidency Project, http://www.presidency.ucsb.edu/ws/?pid=16131.

263 AFTER NEWS OF THE JUNE 1940 LYNCHING Sullivan, **Lift Every Voice**, 237–39.

263 "THERE IS SOMETHING DEFINITELY WRONG" Ibid.

263 "MY IMPRESSION OF" Schlesinger, **Coming of the New Deal**, 587–88.

264 AS A YOUNGER WOMAN Richard Breitman and Allan J. Lichtman, **FDR and the Jews** (Cambridge, Mass., 2013), 17.

264 WHEN THE NEW YORK TIMES PUBLISHED A DISPATCH Joseph P. Lash, **Eleanor and Franklin: The Story of Their Relationship, Based on Eleanor Roosevelt's Private Papers** (New York, 1971), 512.

265 "THE PERSONAL TOUCH" Ibid., 532.

265 THERE HAD BEEN 3,500 SUCH ATTACKS Sullivan, **Lift Every Voice**, 196.

265 ONLY 67 INDICTMENTS AND 12 CONVICTIONS Ibid.

266 "WE KNOW THAT IT IS MURDER" Franklin D. Roosevelt, "Address Before the Federal Council of Churches of Christ in America," December 6, 1933, American Presidency Project, http://www.presidency.ucsb.edu/ws/?pid=14574.

266 MRS. ROOSEVELT AND THE NAACP PRESSED

THE PRESIDENT   Lash, **Eleanor and Franklin,** 515–16. On Mrs. Roosevelt and the lynching issue, see also Melissa Cooper, "Reframing Eleanor Roosevelt's Influence in the 1930s Anti-Lynching Movement Around a 'New Philosophy of Government,'" **European Journal of American Studies** 12, no. 1 (Spring 2017), https://ejas .revues.org/11914.

266 "IF I COME OUT"   Lash, **Eleanor and Franklin,** 515–16. See also Freidel, **Franklin D. Roosevelt,** 246.

266 "YOU CAN SAY ANYTHING"   Freidel, **Franklin D. Roosevelt,** 246.

266 FDR SUPPORTED   Ibid., 247.

266 "I AM SO SORRY"   Lash, **Eleanor and Franklin,** 518.

267 WHEN A YOUNG AIDE, WILL ALEXANDER   Ibid., 528.

267 "WILL, DON'T YOU THINK"   Ibid.

267 MRS. ROOSEVELT RESIGNED   Ibid., 525–26.

267 WAS "IN LINE WITH"   Ibid., 526.

267 ANDERSON WAS INSTEAD INVITED   Ibid., 527. For details of the program, including her opening song, see "The Sound of Freedom: Marian Anderson at the Lincoln Memorial," https://blogs .loc.gov/loc/2014/04/the-sound-of-freedom-marian -anderson-at-the-lincoln-memorial/.

267 HE HAD "NEVER HEARD"   Lash, **Eleanor and Franklin,** 527.

267 "ONE OF THE MOST"   Ibid.

268 THE NAACP, AMONG OTHERS   See Sullivan, **Lift Every Voice,** for a thorough and engaging account of the civil rights group's decades of work.

268 IN EARLY 1941, A. PHILIP RANDOLPH   Ibid., 254. See also Manchester, **Glory and the Dream,** 244.

268 RANDOLPH ARGUED THAT "SOMETHING DRAMATIC"   Sullivan, **Lift Every Voice,** 254.

268 THE FIRST LADY WAS ALSO URGING   Lash, **Eleanor and Franklin,** 532.

268 "MRS. ROOSEVELT'S INTRUSIVE"   Ibid.

268 ROOSEVELT DISPATCHED HIS WIFE   Ibid., 534.

268 "YOU KNOW WHERE"   Ibid.

269 THE REWARD FOR CALLING OFF   Ibid., 534–35. See also Manchester, **Glory and the Dream,** 244. Randolph understood the magnitude of the moment. "There never has been issued in America an executive order affecting Negroes in this country since the Proclamation of Emancipation," he told an NAACP convention in Houston. Sullivan, **Lift Every Voice,** 255.

269 "I HOPE FROM"   Lash, **Eleanor and Franklin,** 535.

269 BEGINNING IN 1942, ABOUT 117,000   "Japanese Relocation During World War II," National Archives, https://www.archives.gov/education/lessons/japanese-relocation. See also Manchester, **Glory and the Dream,** 297, and Kennedy, **Freedom from Fear,** 748–60.

269 "JAPS LIVE LIKE RATS"   Manchester, **Glory and the Dream,** 298.

269 THE ATTORNEY GENERAL OF CALIFORNIA   Walker, **In Defense of American Liberties,** 136–37.

269 WHILE HE UNDERSTOOD "THE UNWILLINGNESS"   Walter Lippmann, "The Fifth Column

on the Coast," **The Washington Post,** February 12, 1942.

269 "The Pacific Coast"   Ibid. See also Manchester, **Glory and the Dream,** 299.

270 Roosevelt issued Executive Order 9066 Kennedy, **Freedom from Fear,** 753; Manchester, **Glory and the Dream,** 297–302.

270 "Enforcing this on"   Walker, **In Defense of American Liberties,** 138. Seeing no alternative short of a favorable legal ruling, which would doubtless take a great deal of time, the Japanese-American Citizens League stoically accepted the outrages. "We are going into exile," the group wrote, "as our duty to our country." Ibid.

270 A majority of the Supreme Court   Ibid., 144–49.

270 "Hardships are part"   Ibid., 147–48.

270 The military did allow   Manchester, **Glory and the Dream,** 301–2.

270 On the porch   Ronald Reagan, "Remarks on Signing the Bill Providing Restitution for the Wartime Internment of Japanese-American Civilians," August 10, 1988, American Presidency Project, http://www.presidency.ucsb.edu/ws/?pid =36240.

271 There were some   Ibid.

271 "Blood that has soaked"   Ibid.

272 Eloquent words, and Ronald Reagan Ibid.

272 "For here," Reagan said   Ibid.

272 Scholars continue to argue   Breitman and Lichtman, **FDR and the Jews,** is a recent—

and comprehensive—treatment of the subject. See also, for instance, Richard Breitman, **Official Secrets: What the Nazis Planned, What the British and Americans Knew** (New York, 1998); Richard Breitman and Alan M. Kraut, **American Refugee Policy and American Jewry, 1933–1945** (Bloomington, Ind., 1987); David S. Wyman, **The Abandonment of the Jews: America and the Holocaust, 1941–1945** (New York, 1998); Michael Berenbaum and Abraham J. Peck, eds., **The Holocaust and History: The Known, the Unknown, the Disputed, and the Reexamined** (Bloomington, Ind., 1998); Robert H. Abzug, ed., **America Views the Holocaust, 1933–1945: A Brief Documentary History** (Boston, 1999); Michael Beschloss, **The Conquerors: Roosevelt, Truman, and the Destruction of Hitler's Germany, 1941–1945** (New York, 2002); William D. Rubinstein, **The Myth of Rescue: Why the Democracies Could Not Have Saved More Jews from the Nazis** (New York, 1997); Arthur M. Schlesinger, Jr., "Did FDR Betray the Jews? Or Did He Do More Than Anyone Else to Save Them?" in **FDR and the Holocaust**, ed. Verne W. Newton (New York, 1996), 159–61; Schlesinger, **A Life in the 20th Century: Innocent Beginnings, 1917–1950** (Boston, 2000), 306–12; William J. Vanden Heuvel, "America and the Holocaust," **American Heritage**, July-August 1999, 34–52; Meacham, **Franklin and Winston**, 189–92; 418–19.

272 EDWARD R. MURROW OF CBS   I drew on my

account of this scene in my **Franklin and Winston**, 355–56, for the section on Murrow and Buchenwald.

273 THE PRISONERS MURROW SAW   Ibid., 355.

273 INMATES SHOWED MURROW   Ibid.

273 "THERE WERE TWO ROWS"   Ibid., 355–56. He was visiting on the day FDR died in Warm Springs. "If I've offended you by this rather mild account of Buchenwald, I'm not in the least sorry," Murrow said. "I was there on Thursday, and many men in many tongues blessed the name of Roosevelt. For long years his name had meant the full measure of their hope. These men who had kept close company with death for many years did not know that Mr. Roosevelt would, within hours, join their comrades who had laid their lives on the scales of freedom."

Murrow recalled a moment, early in the war, when an emotional Churchill had told him: "One day the world and history will recognize and acknowledge what it owes to your President." From the concentration camp, Murrow added, "I saw and heard the first installment of that at Buchenwald on Thursday. It came from men from all over Europe. Their faces, with more flesh on them, might have been found anywhere at home. To them the name 'Roosevelt' was a symbol, a code word from a lot of guys named 'Joe' who are somewhere out in blue with the armor heading east." Ibid., 355–56.

273 "THE THINGS I SAW"   "Ohrdruf," **Holocaust Encyclopedia**, U.S. Holocaust Memorial Mu-

seum, https://www.ushmm.org/wlc/en/article. php?ModuleId=10006131.

273 "For us, it is a problem"   The quotation is from an August 1920 speech of Hitler's. "Statements by Hitler and Senior Nazis Concerning Jews and Judaism," Pratique de l'Histoire et Dévoiements Négationnistes, www.phdn.org/ archives/www.ess.uwe.ac.uk/genocide/state ments.htm.

274 The Nuremberg Laws   Breitman and Lichtman, **FDR and the Jews,** 1.

274 Roosevelt combined the Austrian   Ibid., 101–2.

274 one that led to   Ibid., 102–10.

274 Roosevelt slowed his efforts   Ibid., 123–24.

275 believed that Roosevelt began thinking   Ibid., 124.

275 "The more Roosevelt risked"   Ibid.

275 The German authorities   "11 Allies Condemn Nazi War on Jews," **NYT,** December 18, 1942.

276 established the War Refugee Board   Breitman, **Official Secrets,** 200–204.

276 Every single life counts   Gerhard L. Weinberg, "The Allies and the Holocaust" in **Holocaust and History,** 490. The key question: Could more have been done? Certainly on rescue and refugee policy, yes. It would have been difficult, but Franklin Roosevelt was equal to the task of rescuing democracy—so why couldn't he control his own bureaucracy?

Part of the answer to that is that the full, consuming urgency of the Holocaust was not as clear then as it is now. This is a different thing from **not knowing.** They knew, it's just that during the war itself the Final Solution—as difficult as this is to grasp—was an element of the evil the Allies were fighting, not the whole compound. It was only in the 1960s that the Holocaust came to play the central role in our memory of World War II that it plays now.

Part of this is because of the Cold War; almost immediately after V-E Day the Germans became our quasi-allies against the Soviets. And part of it was the rise, in the 1960s, of a historical sensibility that focused more on the experiences of the common person than on the actions of Great Men. And another part of it was the increasing awareness that the world needed to be reminded why a Jewish homeland was so important. For my conclusions I am indebted, in part, to Breitman and Lichtman, **FDR and the Jews,** 315–29, and Peter Novick, **The Holocaust in American Life** (Boston, 1999), as well as the books cited above.

277 ELEANOR ROOSEVELT BROUGHT　Eleanor Roosevelt Oral History, Session 12, 2, Robert D. Graff Papers Collection, Franklin D. Roosevelt Presidential Library and Museum. I drew on my **Franklin and Winston,** 281–84, for this section, as well as my "FDR's D-Day Prayer," **Time,** June 5, 2014.

277 "ON D-DAY"　Eleanor Roosevelt Oral History,

Session 12, 2, Graff Papers, Franklin D. Roosevelt Presidential Library and Museum.

278 "THE MOST DIFFICULT AND COMPLICATED"   See my "FDR's D-Day Prayer," **Time,** June 5, 2014.

278 ROOSEVELT "WAS TENSE"   Eleanor Roosevelt, **This I Remember** (New York, 1949), 252.

278 "I WONDER HOW"   Ibid.

278 RUSSELL LINAKA   Ibid.

278 (HE MADE IT)   For correspondence about Linaka's future assignments, see PPF: 7548: Linaka, Russell W., December 11, 1944, Franklin D. Roosevelt Library and Museum.

278 WHO LOVED THE KING JAMES   See my "FDR's D-Day Prayer," **Time,** June 5, 2014.

278 HIS DAUGHTER, ANNA   Geoffrey C. Ward, ed., **Closest Companion: The Unknown Story of the Intimate Friendship Between Franklin Roosevelt and Margaret Suckley** (Boston, 1995), 309–10.

278 THE WHITE HOUSE RELEASED   "Let Our Hearts Be Stout: A Prayer by the President of the United States," **NYT,** June 7, 1944.

278 TO THE AFTERNOON NEWSPAPERS   Stephen E. Ambrose, **D-Day: June 6, 1944** (New York, 1994), 491.

278 ONE HUNDRED MILLION AMERICANS   "War-Matured Nation Hears D-Day News with Restraint," **Newsweek,** June 19, 1944, 38.

279 ONE OF THE LARGEST MASS PRAYERS   This is my estimation. See my "FDR's D-Day Prayer," **Time,** June 5, 2014.

279 ALMIGHTY GOD   Franklin D. Roosevelt: "Prayer

on D-Day," June 6, 1944, http://www.presidency
.ucsb.edu/ws/?pid=16515.

280 "BEAUTIFULLY READ BY"   Ward, **Closest Companion**, 310.

280 "I COULDN'T BELIEVE IT"   Sherwood, **Roosevelt and Hopkins**, 880.

281 TO RESEMBLE THE PROW OF A SHIP   Author observation. See also William B. Rhoads, "Franklin D. Roosevelt and the Architecture of Warm Springs," **Georgia Historical Quarterly** 67, no. 1 (Spring 1983), 70–87.

281 "TODAY, SCIENCE HAS BROUGHT"   Franklin D. Roosevelt, "Undelivered Address Prepared for Jefferson Day." For details about the drafting of the speech—including the point that FDR wrote the last line himself—see Rosenman, **Working with Roosevelt**, 551.

SIX · Have You No Sense of Decency?

285 THE FACT THAT   Harry S. Truman: "Remarks at the National Health Assembly Dinner," May 1, 1948, American Presidency Project, http://www.presidency.ucsb.edu/ws/?pid=13170.

285 HE WAS IMPATIENT   Roy Cohn, **McCarthy** (New York, 1968), 275.

285 AT EIGHT O'CLOCK   Harry S. Truman, "Rear Platform and Other Informal Remarks in Michigan," October 30, 1952, American Presidency Project, http://www.presidency.ucsb.edu/ws/?pid=14325.

286 HARDLY A FRIEND   Ibid.

286 THE COVER STORY "Building a Business for War or Peace," **Business Week,** October 18, 1952.

286 "IT USED TO BE TRUE" Ibid.

286 "THE DEMOCRATIC PARTY" Truman, "Rear Platform and Other Informal Remarks in Michigan."

286 "THE ARTICLE POINTS OUT" Ibid.

287 " 'HIGH LEVELS OF' " Ibid.

287 "NOW THERE YOU" Ibid.

288 HE GAVE HIS CHAPTER James T. Patterson, **Grand Expectations: The United States, 1945– 1974** (New York, 1996), 61.

288 "THE GREATEST PROSPERITY" Ibid.

288 AVERAGE WEEKLY EARNINGS Manchester, **Glory and the Dream,** 397.

288 SAVED ABOUT $136 BILLION Ibid.

288 BY 1949 PER-CAPITA INCOME Patterson, **Grand Expectations,** 61.

288 BIRTH AND EMPLOYMENT RATES Ibid., 61–81.

288 "OF THE THREE" Lawrence R. Samuel, **The American Middle Class: A Cultural History** (New York, 2014), epigraph.

288 "HERE INDIVIDUALS OF" J. Hector St. John Crèvecoeur, "What Is an American," in **Letters from an American Farmer** (New York, 1904), 55.

289 "THE MOST VALUABLE" Samuel, **American Middle Class,** epigraph.

289 "THE BEST AMERICANISM" Theodore Roosevelt, "Sixth Annual Message," December 3, 1906, American Presidency Project, http://www .presidency.ucsb.edu/ws/?pid=29547.

289 WILLIAM HOWARD TAFT SAID THAT William

Howard Taft, "Address Accepting the Republican Presidential Nomination," July 28, 1908, American Presidency Project, http://www.presidency.ucsb.edu/ws/?pid=76222.

289 "THE FACT THAT" Truman, "Remarks at the National Health Assembly Dinner."

289 "THE CLASS STRUGGLE" Dwight D. Eisenhower, "Telephone Broadcast to the AFL-CIO Merger Meeting in New York City," December 5, 1955, American Presidency Project, http://www.presidency.ucsb.edu/ws/?pid=10394.

290 AS LONG AGO AS Sitaraman, **Crisis of the Middle-Class Constitution**, 3–12; 59–104. See also Barrington Moore, Jr., **Social Origins of Dictatorship and Democracy: Lord and Peasant in the Making of the Modern World** (Boston, 1966), for an examination of the role of the Revolution and, chiefly, of the Civil War in the story of American capitalism.

290 DEFINITIONS OF "MIDDLE-CLASS" Samuel, **American Middle Class**, 4–8. "The difficulty in defining the middle class reflects Americans' discomfort with the idea of class in general," Samuel wrote. "Even the U.S. Department of Commerce—an organization intimately familiar with facts and statistics—concluded that being middle class 'is as much a state of mind and aspirations as it is a set of income levels' after conducting a study in 2008. The Department found that owning a car, having a retirement nest egg, and being able to take a family vacation were other common criteria among Americans." Ibid., 4.

290 THE SCHOLAR GANESH SITARAMAN Sitara-

man, **Crisis of the Middle-Class Constitution,** 13. **The Economist** wrote this in its February 14, 2009, issue.

290 WHAT HENRY CLAY HAD CALLED   Cullen, **American Dream,** 69.

291 THE PACIFIC RAILROAD AND HOMESTEAD This section draws on my essay "Keeping the Dream Alive," **Time,** June 12, 2012. See also Harold Hyman, **American Singularity: The 1787 Northwest Ordinance, the 1862 Homestead and Morrill Acts, and the 1944 G.I. Bill** (Athens, Ga., 2008).

292 THE MORRILL ACT CREATED   Hyman, **American Singularity,** 35–61.

292 "THE GREAT ARSENAL"   Franklin D. Roosevelt, "Fireside Chat," December 29, 1940, American Presidency Project, http://www.presidency.ucsb.edu/ws/?pid=15917.

292 THE GI BILL OF RIGHTS   See, for instance, Suzanne Mettler, **Soldiers to Citizens: The G.I. Bill and the Making of the Greatest Generation** (New York, 2007), and Hyman, **American Singularity,** 62–76.

293 (AFTER A 1965 LAW)   Sitaraman, **Crisis of the Middle-Class Constitution,** 208–9.

293 THE INTERSTATE HIGHWAY SYSTEM   Patterson, **Grand Expectations,** 274.

293 "NOW IT IS TRUE"   Dwight D. Eisenhower to Edgar Newton Eisenhower, November 8, 1954, TeachingAmericanHistory.org, http://teachingamericanhistory.org/library/document/letter-to-edgar-newton-eisenhower/.

295 "THERE WAS AN ATMOSPHERE"   J. Ronald

Oakley, **God's Country: America in the Fifties** (New York, 1986), 49.

295 IN THE CLOSING WEEKS   Robert Welch, **The Politician** (Belmont, Mass., 1964), vii–viii.

295 CONSERVATIVE CANDY MANUFACTURER   Michael Seiler, "Robert Welch, Founder of Birch Society, Dies at 85," **Los Angeles Times,** January 8, 1985.

295 (TWO OF HIS MOST POPULAR)   Ibid.

295 EISENHOWER WAS TO BLAME   Welch, **Politician,** vii–viii.

296 HIS FRIENDS EXPRESSED SURPRISE   Ibid., viii.

296 AN "AGENT" OF   Seiler, "Robert Welch," **Los Angeles Times,** January 8, 1985.

296 WITH A RISING WORRY   Welch, **Politician,** 5.

296 "THE AMERICAN PEOPLE"   Ibid. "They were, at long last, realizing the crime of 'containment' and the folly of appeasement," Welch wrote. "And without the American government to hold over the Kremlin the umbrella of its protection, against storms rising on every side, the Kremlin faced a very precarious future." Ibid.

296 "THE SAD TRUTH IS"   Ibid., 6.

297 GUILTY OF "A VERY SINISTER"   Ibid., 6; 13.

297 HAD BEEN "SWEPT ALONG"   Ibid.

297 "A CONSCIOUS, DELIBERATE"   Ibid., 15.

297 ANOTHER "COMMUNIST AGENT"   Ibid., 223.

297 "THERE IS NOTHING"   Ibid., epigraph.

298 A MEETING IN INDIANAPOLIS   Seiler, "Robert Welch," **Los Angeles Times,** January 8, 1985.

298 "WITH HIS DEATH"   Ibid.

298 "TODAY WE ARE ENGAGED"   Joseph McCarthy,

"'Enemies from Within' Speech Delivered in Wheeling, West Virginia (1950)," Digital History Project, University of Houston, https://liberalarts.utexas.edu/coretexts/_files/resources/texts/1950%20McCarthy%20Enemies.pdf. See also David M. Oshinsky, **A Conspiracy So Immense: The World of Joe McCarthy** (New York, 2005), 108–11. I am grateful to Professor Oshinsky for his guidance on my treatment of the era.

299　HAD FORMED A　Oshinsky, **Conspiracy So Immense,** 92–93.

299　PASSED THE SMITH ACT　Ibid., 93.

299　"THE MOOD OF"　Ibid.

300　ABROAD, EVIDENCE OF　Ibid., 103.

300　BY 1949 MOSCOW HAD　Ibid., 106.

300　"WE CANNOT SIT IDLE"　Ibid.

300　THE ARRESTS OF KLAUS FUCHS　Ibid.

300　JULIUS AND ETHEL ROSENBERG　Ibid., 103.

300　CHINA, MEANWHILE, FELL　Ibid.

300　CELEBRATED CASE OF ALGER HISS　Ibid., 98–100; Richard Nixon, **Six Crises** (New York, 1962), 1–71; Patterson, **Grand Expectations,** 194–95. See also Sam Tanenhaus, **Whittaker Chambers: A Biography** (New York, 1997).

301　AN "INTIMATE" AND "HOMEY"　Frank Desmond, "McCarthy Charges Reds Hold U.S. Jobs," **The Wheeling Intelligencer,** February 10, 1950.

301　MARKET AND TWELFTH STREETS　Cohn, **McCarthy,** 1.

301　"WHILE I CANNOT TAKE"　McCarthy, "Enemies from Within."

301 THE NUMBER OF Oshinsky, **Conspiracy So Immense**, 110.

301 "TALKING TO JOE" David Halberstam, **The Fifties** (New York, 1994), 51.

302 "JOE MCCARTHY BOUGHT" Cohn, **McCarthy**, 8.

302 AS COHN TELLS THE STORY Ibid., 8–9.

302 THE SOVIETS HAD Oshinsky, **Conspiracy So Immense**, 85–102.

302 A LOYALTY PROGRAM Ibid., 97–98.

302 "BUYING THE PACKAGE" Cohn, **McCarthy**, 10.

302 "THE FIRST WAS PATRIOTIC" Ibid.

303 MCCARTHY, COHN SAID, "SAW" Ibid., 10–11.

303 A TRIO OF Edwin R. Bayley, **Joe McCarthy and the Press** (Madison, Wis., 1981), 36.

303 "LISTEN, YOU BASTARDS" Ibid.

303 "MCCARTHY'S METHODS" Richard H. Rovere, **Senator Joe McCarthy** (Berkeley, Calif., 1996), 18.

303 "THERE IS NO DIFFERENCE" Correspondence Between President Harry S. Truman and A. Barr Comstock, October 18, 1951, Truman Papers, President's Personal File, PPF 5866: Comstock, A. Barr. President Truman drafted, but chose not to send, a reply to a McCarthy telegram after Wheeling. McCarthy's charges, the president wrote, marked:

the first time in my experience, and I was ten years in the Senate, that I ever heard of a Senator trying to discredit his own Government before the world. You know that isn't done by honest public officials. Your telegram is not only not true and an insolent approach to a situation that should have been worked out between man and man but it shows conclusively that you are not even fit to have a hand in the operation of the Government of the United States. I am very sure that the people of Wisconsin are extremely sorry that they are represented by a person who has as little sense of responsibility as you have." Telegram from Senator Joseph McCarthy to President Harry S. Truman, National Archives, https://www.archives.gov/education/lessons/mccarthy-telegram.

304 ADDED A PARAGRAPH   Rovere, **Senator Joe McCarthy**, 10.

304 "PARLIAMENTARY INSTITUTIONS"   Queen Elizabeth II, Coronation Speech, June 2, 1953, Archives of Women's Political Communication, Iowa State University, https://awpc.cattcenter.iastate.edu/2017/03/09/coronation-speech-june-2-1953/.

305 THURSDAY, MARCH 30, 1950, AT A PRESS CONFERENCE   Harry S. Truman, "The President's News Conference at Key West," March 30, 1950, American Presidency Project, http://www.presidency.ucsb.edu/ws/?pid=13755.

306 "FOR POLITICAL BACKGROUND"   Ibid.

306 "NOW, IF ANYBODY"   Ibid.

307 "TO TRY TO SABOTAGE"   Ibid.

307 SENATOR MARGARET CHASE SMITH   Margaret Chase Smith, **Declaration of Conscience**, ed.
William C. Lewis, Jr. (New York, 1972), 3–61.

307 "JOE BEGAN TO GET"   Oshinsky, **Conspiracy
So Immense**, 164.

307 AS SMITH RECALLED IT   Ibid.

308 "I WOULD LIKE TO SPEAK"   Smith, **Declaration
of Conscience**, 12–18.

309 McCARTHY DISMISSED THEM   Margaret Chase
Smith, "A Declaration of Conscience," June 1,
1950, Classic Senate Speeches, U.S. Senate, https://
www.senate.gov/artandhistory/history/common/
generic/Speeches_Smith_Declaration.htm.

309 "JOE, YOU'RE A REAL"   Halberstam, **Fifties**,
250.

309 "HE'S UNBEATABLE NOW"   Oshinsky, **Conspiracy So Immense**, 161.

309 "FROM A DISTANCE"   Rovere, **Senator Joe
McCarthy**, 10.

311 "WILL YOU PLEASE"   Eleanor Roosevelt, **On
My Own** (New York, 1958), 125–26.

311 HE WAS FRIENDLY   Evan Thomas, **Robert Kennedy: His Life** (New York, 2000), 64–65.

311 POPULAR IN MASSACHUSETTS   Michael Beschloss, **Presidential Courage** (New York, 2007),
248.

311 A HOSPITALIZED SENATOR JOHN F. KENNEDY
Oshinsky, **Conspiracy So Immense**, 489–91. See
also Eleanor Roosevelt, "On My Own," **Saturday
Evening Post**, March 8, 1958, https://www2.
gwu.edu/~erpapers/mep/displaydoc.cfm?docid
=jfk15.

312 CHOSE TO REMAIN SILENT Oshinsky, **Conspiracy So Immense,** 490. JFK did not openly support the censure, Oshinsky pointed out, until 1958, when he was seeking support for the Democratic presidential nomination. On another front, "some critics complained," Michael Beschloss wrote, "that **Profiles** [**in Courage,** Kennedy's 1956 book] was an attempt to deflect attention from Kennedy's failure to endorse the Senate's censure" of McCarthy. Beschloss, **Presidential Courage,** 248–49.

312 "WELL, AT THE TIME" Thomas, **Robert Kennedy,** 64. The exchange between RFK and the writer Peter Maas took place "in the mid-1960s." Ibid.

312 (BUT, . . . "I WAS WRONG") Ibid.

312 SAVORING SUPERLATIVES Oshinsky, **Conspiracy So Immense,** 145.

312 "I HAVE JUST BEGUN" Ibid.

313 THE "GROWTH OF THE MASS MEDIA" Hofstadter, **Paranoid Style in American Politics,** 63.

313 "THINGS HAVE TO BE DONE" Oshinsky, **Conspiracy So Immense,** 188.

314 "INVENTED THE MORNING" Rovere, **Senator Joe McCarthy,** 164.

315 HIS OFFICE PRODUCED Bayley, **Joe McCarthy and the Press,** 179–80.

315 THE NUMBER OF TV SETS "Series R 93-105. Radio and Television Stations, Sets Produced, and Households With Sets: 1921 to 1970," **Historical Statistics of the United States, Colonial Times to 1970,** part 2. U.S. Department of Commerce, Bu-

reau of the Census (1975), 796. See also Bayley, **Joe McCarthy and the Press**, 176.

315 "PEOPLE AREN'T GOING" Sidney Zion, **The Autobiography of Roy Cohn** (Secaucus, N.J., 1988), 148.

316 HE WOULD ADJOURN FOR LUNCH "Investigations: The First Day," **Time**, May 3, 1954.

316 "MY OWN IMPRESSION" Bayley, **Joe McCarthy and the Press**, 186.

316 "MCCARTHY'S CHARGES" Ibid., 187.

317 PALMER HOYT, THE EDITOR AND PUBLISHER Ibid., 145–46. The Hoyt memo is found in the Joseph Pulitzer II Papers, Library of Congress, Washington, D.C.

317 "APPLY ANY REASONABLE" Ibid., 146.

317 IF A MCCARTHY STATEMENT Ibid.

317 "IT SEEMS OBVIOUS" Ibid.

317 "BELIEVE ME" Ibid., 147.

317 MCCARTHY DID NOT Oshinsky, **Conspiracy So Immense**, 182–85.

318 "KEEP IN MIND" Ibid., 184.

318 THE WASHINGTON POST HAD ASSIGNED Halberstam, **Fifties**, 250.

319 "IT IS THIS NEWSPAPER'S HOPE" Rovere, **Senator Joe McCarthy**, 14.

319 EISENHOWER HAD FLINCHED David A. Nichols, **Ike and McCarthy: Dwight Eisenhower's Secret Campaign Against Joe McCarthy** (New York, 2017), 3. For an excellent treatment of Eisenhower, McCarthy, and the atmosphere of the time, see William I. Hitchcock, **The Age of Eisenhower: America and the World in the 1950s** (New York, 2018), 81–83; 119–47.

319 In the text of a speech   Halberstam, **Fifties**, 251.

320 Talked out of it by political advisers
Nichols, **Ike and McCarthy**, 4–5.

320 Eisenhower always regretted   Ibid., 6.

320 ("It turned my stomach")   Halberstam, **Fifties**, 251.

320 "Nothing will be"   Nichols, **Ike and McCarthy**, 10.

320 "I had made up my mind"   Oshinsky, **Conspiracy So Immense**, 259.

320 "Getting in the gutter"   Nichols, **Ike and McCarthy**, 30.

320 "I would not"   Oshinsky, **Conspiracy So Immense**, 259.

321 In 1953, McCarthy deplored   Ibid., 277–79.

321 Among other titles   Nicholas von Hoffman, **Citizen Cohn** (New York, 1988), 153. See also Oshinsky, **Conspiracy So Immense**, 277.

321 the writer Dashiell Hammett   Sally Cline, **Dashiell Hammett: Man of Mystery** (New York, 2014), 174–75, 182–88; Robert L. Gale, **A Dashiell Hammett Companion** (Westport, Conn., 2000), 42–43.

321 They also complained   Von Hoffman, **Citizen Cohn**, 153.

321 "What is America"   Ibid., 171.

321 "Don't join the"   Nichols, **Ike and McCarthy**, 40.

322 At ten-thirty   Joseph Wershba, "Murrow vs. McCarthy: See It Now," **NYT**, March 4, 1979.

322 "We must not confuse"   Edward R. Mur-

row, "A Report on Senator Joseph R. McCarthy," **See It Now,** March 9, 1954, CBS-TV, http://www.lib.berkeley.edu/MRC/murrowmccarthy.html.

322 "THE ACTIONS OF"   Ibid.

323 THE BROADCAST ROOM   "North Hall," White House Museum, http://www.whitehousemuseum.org/floor0/north-hall.htm.

323 HE HAD DECIDED   Nichols, **Ike and McCarthy,** 221–22. See also Jack Gould, "Television in Review: New 'Format' Brings Out the President's Warmth and Charm Before Cameras," **NYT,** April 6, 1954.

323 THERE WOULD BE CUE CARDS   Gould, "Television in Review." See also "Robert Montgomery Presents: President as a Pro," **Life,** April 19, 1954, 28–29.

323 THE FIRST DATES FROM   Carlos D'Este, **Eisenhower: A Soldier's Life** (New York, 2002), 527.

323 HIS JANUARY 1961 FAREWELL ADDRESS   Dwight D. Eisenhower, "Farewell Radio and Television Address to the American People," January 17, 1961, American Presidency Project, http://www.presidency.ucsb.edu/ws/?pid=12086.

323 HIS APRIL 1954 SPEECH ABOUT FEAR   Dwight D. Eisenhower, "Radio and Television Address to the American People on the State of the Nation," April 5, 1954, American Presidency Project, http://www.presidency.ucsb.edu/ws/?pid=10201.

325 BEHIND THE SCENES   Nichols, **Ike and McCarthy,** 113–15; 121–24; 161–96; 199–216; 233; 287–88; 296–97. See also William Bragg Ewald, **Who Killed Joe McCarthy?** (New York, 1984).

325 TO SECURE FAVORS   Oshinsky, **Conspiracy So Immense,** 400–401; 416.

325 ITS IMPLICATION OF AN ILLICIT RELATION-SHIP   Von Hoffman, **Citizen Cohn,** 188–90; 202; 226; 230–31.

325 ALWAYS DENIED BY COHN   Zion, **Autobiography of Roy Cohn,** 245–46.

325 MCCARTHY PERFORMED POORLY   Cohn, **McCarthy,** 207–11.

325 IN AN ICONIC MOMENT   Oshinsky, **Conspiracy So Immense,** 461–64.

325 MCCARTHY BLUNDERED FORWARD   Nichols, **Ike and McCarthy,** 281.

326 GALLUP FOUND THAT . . . 34 PERCENT   Oshinsky, **Conspiracy So Immense,** 464. See also Zion, **Autobiography of Roy Cohn,** 150.

326 "UNLESS WE CAN"   Zion, **Autobiography of Roy Cohn,** 150.

326 THE REPUBLICANS, COHN BELIEVED   Ibid., 150–51.

326 A "RIGHT-WING THIRD PARTY TICKET"   Ibid..

326 THE SENATE CENSURED MCCARTHY   Oshinsky, **Conspiracy So Immense,** 472–94.

326 SENATOR RALPH FLANDERS   Ibid., 475.

327 THE SENIOR SENATOR FROM CONNECTICUT   "Resolution of Censure, Remarks of Senator Prescott Bush," December 1, 1954, 83rd Cong., 2nd sess., **Congressional Record** 100, pt. 12: 16268. See also my **Destiny and Power: The American Odyssey of George Herbert Walker Bush** (New York, 2015), 108. His son George H. W. Bush, then in the oil business in Texas, watched from afar as anti-McCarthy senators were attacked by the far

right. "I realize that anybody who takes a stand against McCarthy is apt to be subjected through the lunatic fringe to all sorts of abuse," the future president wrote at the time. George H. W. Bush to Senator William Fulbright, September 3, 1954, Jean Becker, "All the Best, George Bush" File, Post-Presidential Materials, George Bush Presidential Library and Museum, College Station, Texas.

327 Two YEARS EARLIER   Mickey Herskowitz, **Duty, Honor, Country: The Life and Legacy of Prescott Bush** (Nashville, 2003), 128; Meacham, **Destiny and Power,** 95–96. One could approve of anti-Communism, Bush had said at Bridgeport, without endorsing McCarthy's means. "But, I must say in all candor," Bush said, "that some of us, while we admire his objectives in his fight against Communism, we have very considerable reservations concerning the methods which he sometimes employs." Ibid.

327 "HAS CAUSED DANGEROUS"   "Resolution of Censure, Remarks of Senator Prescott Bush," December 1, 1954, 83rd Cong., 2nd sess., **Congressional Record** 100, pt. 12: 16268.

327 OF ACUTE HEPATITIS—HIS LIVER WAS   Oshinsky, **Conspiracy So Immense,** 505. "The official cause of death was listed as acute hepatitis—or inflammation of the liver," Oshinsky wrote. "There was no mention of cirrhosis or delirium tremens, though the press hinted, correctly, that he drank himself to death." Ibid. See also Nichols, **Ike and McCarthy,** 296.

328 "Undoubtedly the hearings" Cohn, **McCarthy,** 211.

328 "Human nature being" Ibid.

328 "I was fully aware" Ibid., 275.

329 "He was selling" Ibid., 275–76.

330 "modern American conservatism" Geoffrey Kabaservice, **Rule and Ruin: The Downfall of Moderation and the Destruction of the Republican Party, from Eisenhower to the Tea Party** (New York, 2012), 13–14.

330 Writing in the inaugural issue **National Review,** November 19, 1955.

330 In January 1961, during a meeting William F. Buckley, Jr., "Goldwater, the John Birch Society, and Me," **Commentary,** March 1, 2008.

331 Richard Hofstadter delivered Hofstadter, **Paranoid Style in America Politics,** 41–42.

332 Who is the pseudo-conservative Ibid., 44–45.

333 Political life is not Ibid., 52–53.

334 When Joe McCarthy died **NYT,** May 3, 1957.

334 "Years will pass" Ibid.

334 "The harmful influence" Ibid., May 4, 1957.

334 There is an element Ibid.

335 At a requiem mass Ibid., May 7, 1957.

335 McCarthy's casket was Ibid.

335 "I don't want" Marie Brenner, "How Donald Trump and Roy Cohn's Ruthless Symbiosis Changed America," **Vanity Fair,** August 2017.

335 ONE OF HIS MORE CELEBRATED CLIENTS   Ibid.
See also Von Hoffman, **Citizen Cohn**, 378–80.

SEVEN · What the Hell Is the Presidency For?

339 NIGGUHS HATE WHITES   Marshall Frady, **Wallace** (New York, 1968), 14.

339 AT THE MOMENT   Author interview.

339 "VERY FRANKLY, MR. SPEAKER"   Michael Beschloss, ed. **Taking Charge: The Johnson White House Tapes 1963–1964** (New York, 1997), 26.

339 "LYNDON ACTS AS IF"   Manchester, **Glory and the Dream**, 1010.

339 ON THIS LONG FRIDAY EVENING   Merle Miller, **Lyndon, an Oral Biography** (New York, 1980), 397–98. See also Robert A. Caro, **The Passage of Power**, vol. 4, **The Years of Lyndon Johnson** (New York, 2012), 371–72.

340 "LYNDON," LADY BIRD REMARKED   Nick Kotz, **Judgment Days: Lyndon Baines Johnson, Martin Luther King Jr., and the Laws That Changed America** (New York, 2005), 11.

340 "WELL, I'M GOING"   Ibid., 16.

340 "OH, DADDY," SHE SAID   Ibid., 9.

341 "WE'RE STILL A TEN-DAY NATION"   Ibid., 18.

342 "WELL, WHAT THE HELL"   Miller, **Lyndon**, 411. See also Caro, **Passage of Power**, xiv–xv.

342 HAD HARDLY BEEN   For an overview of Johnson's evolution on civil rights, see, for instance, Kotz, **Judgment Days**, 59–64.

342 THOUGH HE HAD DECLINED   Kotz, **Judgment Days**, 45; 38.

342 (Though he would point out) Richard N. Goodwin, **Remembering America: A Voice from the Sixties** (Boston, 1988), 316.

342 "I've never felt" Kotz, **Judgment Days**, 88.

343 "I wasn't a crusader" Goodwin, **Remembering America**, 316.

343 "Now I represent" Ibid.

343 "Let me make" Beschloss, **Taking Charge**, 29–30.

344 right-wing demonstrators Bill Minutaglio and Steven L. Davis, **Dallas 1963** (New York, 2013), 66.

344 texas traitor Ibid., 64–65.

344 In October 1963 a similar crowd Ibid., 243–47.

344 One protestor shouted Ibid., 244.

344 Pulling away from Ibid., 247.

344 "John Kennedy's death" Lyndon B. Johnson, "Address Before a Joint Session of the Congress," November 27, 1963, American Presidency Project, http://www.presidency.ucsb.edu/ws/?pid =25988. The "bloodstream" imagery was prevalent in Washington. On the Sunday after the assassination, Chief Justice Earl Warren, speaking in the Rotunda, said, "What moved some misguided wretch to do this horrible deed may never be known to us, but we do know that such acts are commonly stimulated by forces of hatred and malevolence, such as today are eating their way into the bloodstream of American life. What a price we pay for such fanaticism!" Beschloss, **Taking Charge**, 64.

344 "WE KNOW THAT" Jon Meacham, ed., **Voices in Our Blood: America's Best on the Civil Rights Movement** (New York, 2001), 19.

345 HAD NOTHING ELSE Ibid., 20. "Sometimes, fleetingly, like a rainbow that comes and vanishes in its coming," Wright wrote, "the wan faces of the poor whites make us think that perhaps we can join our hands with them and lift the weight of the Lords of the Land off our backs. But, before new meanings can bridge the chasm that has been long created between us, the poor whites are warned by the Lords of the Land that they must cast their destiny with their own color, that to make common cause with us is to threaten the foundations of civilization." Ibid.

345 "GET OUT OF THE SHADOW" Hubert H. Humphrey, **The Education of a Public Man: My Life and Politics** (New York, 1976), 112.

345 WORRIED ABOUT COMMUNISTS AND CIVIL RIGHTS Coski, **Confederate Battle Flag**, 98–109.

345 IMPEACH EARL WARREN SIGNS Alden Whitman, "Earl Warren, 83, Who Led High Court in Time of Vast Social Change, Is Dead," **NYT**, July 10, 1974. The signs were driven by the integration decisions, the court's opposition to internal-security measures such as the McCarran Act, and an overall fear of centralized power; the right-wing John Birch Society was a prime mover behind the billboards. "It was kind of an honor to be accused by the John Birch Society," Warren said. "It was a little rough on my wife, but it never bothered me." Ibid.

345 GEORGIA INCORPORATED THE   "State Flags of Georgia," **New Georgia Encyclopedia,** https://www.georgiaencyclopedia.org/articles/government-politics/state-flags-georgia.

346 SOUTH CAROLINA HOISTED   Sidney Blumenthal, "The Star-Spangled Banner in South Carolina," **The Atlantic,** June 24, 2015, https://www.theatlantic.com/politics/archive/2015/06/confederate-flag-south-carolina-history/396695/.

346 AND GEORGE WALLACE ORDERED   Coski, **Confederate Battle Flag,** 152–53.

346 SHE AND HER BROTHER   Meacham, **Voices in Our Blood,** 63.

346 HEARING THE HOOFBEATS   Ibid., 68–69.

346 LISTENING FROM THE SIDE   Ibid., 69.

347 "IF ON JUDGMENT DAY"   Ibid.

348 ACCEPTED AN ASSIGNMENT FROM LIFE   Ibid., 107.

348 ENRAGED WHITE SOUTHERNERS   Ibid., 113. The detail is from a column of Murray Kempton's, filed from Nashville and published on September 10, 1957, under the headline "Upon Such a Day." Ibid.

348 "I'M GLAD IT'S YOU"   Ibid., 167.

348 "THE AWFUL RESPONSIBILITY"   Robert Penn Warren, **All the King's Men** (New York, 1981), 546.

348 A 1930 ESSAY HE NOW REPUDIATED   Woodward, **Burden of Southern History,** 287.

348 SUSPICION OF "THE NEW YORK PRESS"   Meacham, **Voices in Our Blood,** 173.

348 "WELL, BY GOD"   Ibid.

348 "You hear some white men"   Ibid., 174–75.

349 "Lord, that man's"   Ibid., 177.

349 The Great Alibi "explains"   Warren, **Legacy of the Civil War**, 54.

349 "Even now, any common lyncher"   Ibid.

350 Did the Southern "man who"   Ibid., 57–58.

350 "The Treasury of Virtue"   Ibid., 59.

351 "In the happy contemplation"   Ibid., 61–63. He quoted the clergyman and abolitionist James T. Ayers, who worried that emancipated blacks would move north and soon "the Bucks will be wanting to galant our Daughters Round." Ibid., 63.

351 "The crusaders themselves"   Ibid., 64–65.

351 "We have to deal"   Meacham, **Voices in Our Blood**, 202. This remark came in a self-interview Warren conducted as he worked out his own conclusions. He added, "If the South is really able to face up to itself and its situation, it may achieve identity, moral identity. Then in a country where moral identity is hard to come by, the South, because it has had to deal concretely with a moral problem, may offer some leadership. And we need any we can get. If we are to break out of the national rhythm, the rhythm between complacency and panic." Ibid.

352 "Nigguhs hate whites"   Frady, **Wallace**, 14.

352 "You know, we just can't"   Ibid., 141.

352 In 1948 he sought election   Stephan Lesher, **George Wallace: American Populist** (New York, 1994), 79.

352 Yet in 1958   Ibid., 125–26.

352 "JOHN PATTERSON OUT-NIGGUHED"   Frady, **Wallace,** 127.

352 (WALLACE DENIED THIS OFT-REPEATED) Lesher, **George Wallace,** 128–29.

352 "HE USED TO BE"   Frady, **Wallace,** 141.

353 WALLACE WAS INAUGURATED   For video of the address, see "George Wallace 1963 Inauguration Address," YouTube, https://www.youtube.com/watch?v=_RC0EjsUbDU.

353 "THIS CRADLE OF THE CONFEDERACY"   "Inaugural Address of Governor George Wallace," Alabama Department of Archives and History, http://digital.archives.alabama.gov/cdm/ref/col lection/voices/id/2952.

353 THE CROWD ERUPTED   "George Wallace 1963 Inauguration Address," YouTube. "This nation was never meant to be a unit of one," Wallace said, "but a united of the many. . . .

> And so it was meant in our racial lives. Each race, within its own framework has the freedom to teach, to instruct, to develop, to ask for and receive deserved help from others of separate racial stations. This is the great freedom of our American founding fathers. But if we amalgamate into the one unit as advocated by the communist philosophers, then the enrichment of our lives, the freedom for our development, is gone forever. We become, therefore, a mongrel unit of one under a single all powerful government and we stand for everything, and for nothing. "Inaugural Address of Governor George Wallace."

353 "I'm gonna make race"   Frady, **Wallace**, 140.

354 (he privately admired)   Ibid., 243. "He asked a reporter once, in a low, earnest voice, 'How come you reckon Bobby Kennedy wants to wear all that hair? I mean, I been wondering about it. You reckon that's why he's so big with all these college kids?' And unconsciously, he touched his own limp, oil-combed streaks with the heel of his hand, as if he were fleetingly considering whether he himself could muster a mane." Ibid.

354 "simply more alive"   Ibid., 5–6.

354 Educated people in Alabama   Ibid., 212.

354 One woman whom Frady described   Ibid.

354 A federal court ordered   Branch, **Parting the Waters**, 821–22.

355 "whose gray head"   Frady, **Wallace**, 149. "Wallace seemed to regard his career as governor merely as an invocation and projection of the old aboriginal glory and valor," Frady wrote. "It was all still happening to him. In fact, one got the feeling that, for him, what was happening was not quite as **real** as the great primeval conflict." Ibid.

356 "Today," the president said   John F. Kennedy, "Radio and Television Report to the American People on Civil Rights," June 11, 1963, American Presidency Project, http://www.presidency.ucsb.edu/ws/?pid=9271.

356 "This is not"   Ibid.

356 "If an American"   Ibid.

356 Wallace was forced   Frady, **Wallace**, 170–71.

357 Title II of the proposed bill   Miller, **Lyndon**, 366–67.

359 ON THE EVENING OF KENNEDY'S FUNERAL Kotz, **Judgment Days**, 19.

359 "PRESIDENT JOHNSON WILL"   Ibid., 18.

359 "WE KNOW WHAT"   Beschloss, **Taking Charge**, 37.

360 HE WAS CALLED   Branch, **Parting the Waters**, 111.

360 WHEN ROSA PARKS   Ibid., 132–33. King was elected leader of the boycott less because of his evident skill—though he would prove more than worthy of the assignment—than for his relative newness to town. "Idealists would say afterward that King's gifts made him the obvious choice," Branch wrote. "Realists would scoff at this, saying that King was not very well known, and that his chief asset was lack of debts or enemies. Cynics would say that the established preachers stepped back for King only because they saw more blame and danger ahead than glory." Ibid., 137.

360 ON THE NIGHT HE FIRST SPOKE   Ibid., 138.

361 "THIS," KING REMARKED TO A FRIEND   Ibid.

361 "WE ARE HERE THIS EVENING"   Ibid., 139–40.

361 "AND WE ARE DETERMINED"   Ibid., 141.

362 HIS HOUSE IN MONTGOMERY   Kotz, **Judgment Days**, 47.

362 "LORD, I'M DOWN HERE"   Ibid., 48.

362 "I COULD HEAR"   Ibid.

363 KING'S ADDRESS TO THE MARCH   The following section is a lightly edited version of my essay "Martin Luther King Jr.: Architect of the 21st Century," **Time**, August 26, 2013. I also owe much to Branch, **Parting the Waters**, 875–83.

363 A TEXT THAT HAD BEEN DRAFTED   Clarence B. Jones and Stuart Connelly, **Behind the Dream: The Making of the Speech That Transformed a Nation** (New York, 2011), especially 54–62.

363 "AND SO TODAY"   Branch, **Parting the Waters,** 882.

363 KING HAD ALREADY BEGUN   Ibid.

364 "TELL 'EM ABOUT THE DREAM"   Ibid.

364 A "NEW FOUNDING FATHER"   Ibid., 887. Branch's full observation: "More than his words, the timbre of his voice projected him across the racial divide and planted him as a new founding father. It was a fitting joke on the races that he achieved such statesmanship by setting aside his lofty text to let loose and jam, as he did regularly from two hundred podiums a year." Ibid.

364 "I SAY TO YOU TODAY"   Martin Luther King, Jr., "I Have a Dream . . ." National Archives, https://www.archives.gov/files/press/exhibits/dream-speech.pdf.

364 "I HAVE A DREAM"   Ibid.

366 "THERE WAS GREAT FEAR"   Author interview.

367 BOB DYLAN   Meacham, **Voices in Our Blood,** 288–92.

367 "FOR MANY, THE DAY SEEMED"   Ibid., 285.

367 IN THE WHITE HOUSE   Beschloss, **Presidential Courage,** 275–76.

367 LISTENED WITH APPRECIATION   Branch, **Parting the Waters,** 883. "He's damn good," Kennedy remarked. Ibid. For JFK during King's speech, see also Beschloss, **Presidential Courage,** 275–76.

367 THE CONVERSATION DID NOT   Branch, **Parting the Waters**, 883–87.

368 "IN THE PROCESS"   King, "I Have a Dream . . ."

368 "THE DEMONSTRATION IMPRESSED"   Meacham, **Voices in Our Blood**, 286.

369 "I HAVE A DREAM"   King, "I Have a Dream . . ."

370 PRESIDENT JOHNSON ASKED KING   Kotz, **Judgment Days**, 66–67.

370 "NOW EVERY PERSON"   Beschloss, **Taking Charge**, 83–84.

371 JOHNSON WENT TO WORK   See, for instance, Kotz, **Judgment Days**, 112–55; Todd S. Purdum, **An Idea Whose Time Has Come: Two Presidents, Two Parties, and the Battle for the Civil Rights Act of 1964** (New York, 2014); Clay Risen, **The Bill of the Century: The Epic Battle for the Civil Rights Act** (New York, 2014).

371 "THEY TELL [THIS] STORY"   Miller, **Lyndon**, 342.

372 "I HAVE NO DOUBT"   Ibid., 369.

372 "I MADE MY POSITION"   Ibid.

372 THE PRESIDENT WOULD NOT BEND   Kotz, **Judgment Days**, 38.

373 HE TASKED SENATOR HUBERT HUMPHREY   Miller, **Lyndon**, 368–69.

373 "WE WERE WELL ORGANIZED"   Ibid., 370.

374 "UNLESS WE HAVE"   Kotz, **Judgment Days**, 141.

374 "WE DON'T WANT"   Ibid.

374 JOHNSON WON THE CLOTURE VOTE   Ibid., 151–52.

374 "IT'S JUST A MIRACLE"   Ibid., 151.

374 "THERE WAS A GLORIOUS" Miller, **Lyndon,** 372.

375 ONE SOUTHERN MEMBER Kotz, **Judgment Days,** 153.

375 "I WOULD URGE" Ibid.

375 HE SIGNED THE CIVIL RIGHTS ACT E. W. Kenworthy, "President Signs Civil Rights Bill; Bids All Back It," **NYT,** July 3, 1964.

375 KENNEDY CALLED JOHNSON Kotz, **Judgment Days,** 155.

375 "I WANT YOU" Miller, **Lyndon,** 375.

376 "HE USED TO" Ibid.

376 "IT IS AN" Kotz, **Judgment Days,** 154.

376 ("NOTHING EXCEPT A BATTLE LOST") Christopher Hibbert, **Wellington: A Personal History** (New York, 1999), 185.

376 HE MUSED FOR Miller, **Lyndon,** 389–90.

376 "YOU ARE AS" Ibid., 391.

377 WE'RE ALL AMERICANS Transcript of LBJ and Theodore Sorensen telephone conversation, June 3, 1963, Collections of the Lyndon B. Johnson Presidential Library, 1–2.

378 "I BELIEVE THAT" Ibid., 2. Johnson specifically referred to George Wallace and Ross Barnett, the segregationist Democratic governor of Mississippi. Ibid.

378 "THEN A MAN" Ibid., 3.

378 "THIS AURA" Ibid., 2.

378 "I THINK THE PRESIDENCY" Ibid., 8.

379 "I'VE BEEN IN" Ibid., 9–10.

379 THE PRESIDENT IS Ibid., 19.

380 IN THE 1964 GENERAL ELECTION Theodore

H. White, **Making of the President, 1964** (New York, 1965), is a wonderful account of the campaign—in some ways, I think, a more important book than White's fabled account of the 1960 campaign, for the forces in play in 1964, particularly the triumph of movement conservatism in securing the nomination for Goldwater, continue to shape our politics.

380 THE PRESIDENT WAS DUE Leuchtenburg, **White House Looks South**, 320.

380 "SEVERAL PEOPLE IN" Ibid.

380 HAD OTHER IDEAS Ibid., 320–22.

380 "IF WE ARE" Lyndon B. Johnson, "Remarks at a Fundraising Dinner in New Orleans," October 9, 1964, American Presidency Project, http://www.presidency.ucsb.edu/ws/?pid=26585.

380 "NOW, THE PEOPLE" Ibid.

381 "WHATEVER YOUR VIEWS" Ibid.

381 THE "APPLAUSE WAS" Johnson, **Vantage Point**, 109.

381 "ONLY SAY WHAT" Ibid.

381 AN OLD DEMOCRATIC SENATOR Johnson, "Remarks at a Fundraising Dinner."

382 SENATOR JOE BAILEY, SR. Johnson, **Vantage Point**, 110.

382 "HE WAS TALKING" Johnson: "Remarks at a Fundraising Dinner."

382 "NIGRA, NIGRA, NIGRA!" Leuchtenburg, **White House Looks South**, 321. Other versions of the speech render Johnson's peroration as "Negro, negro, negro!" Johnson, "Remarks at a Fundraising Dinner." Johnson himself candidly recalled

that he had said "'Nigger, nigger, nigger.'" Johnson, **Vantage Point,** 110.

382 THE CROWD WAS Kotz, **Judgment Days,** 224.

382 A PROLONGED OVATION Ibid. Kotz reported the cheers lasted eight minutes. In William Leuchtenburg's telling, the audience "let out a gasp. . . . Then, led by blacks in the room, the audience rose to its feet and the hall was 'rocked by a thunderous cheer' that lasted fully five minutes." Leuchtenburg, **White House Looks South,** 321.

382 "MANY OF HIS" Leuchtenburg, **White House Looks South,** 321–322.

382 "NOT IN NEW YORK" Johnson, **Vantage Point,** 109.

382 IN NOVEMBER LBJ WON "United States presidential election of 1964," **Encyclopaedia Britannica,** https://www.britannica.com/event/United-States-presidential-election-of-1964.

383 "I'VE JUST BEEN" Kotz, **Judgment Days,** 260.

383 JOHNSON REACHED OUT TO CONGRESSMAN GERALD FORD Ibid., 261.

384 KING MARKED HIS THIRTY-SIXTH BIRTHDAY Ibid., 251.

384 "THERE IS NOT" Ibid.

384 HAD LAUNCHED A VOTING-RIGHTS DRIVE Ibid., 254.

384 ON SUNDAY, MARCH 7, 1965 My account of Bloody Sunday is drawn from interviews with John Lewis and from his memoir, with Michael D'Orso, **Walking with the Wind: A Memoir of the Movement** (New York, 1998), 323–47,

among other sources. This account of Lewis's experiences was the heart of an essay I wrote for **Garden & Gun,** "The G&G Interview: Congressman John Lewis," February-March, 2015.

384 TRAPPED BETWEEN ASPHALT Author interview with John Lewis.

385 "PEOPLE ARE GOING TO DIE HERE" Ibid.

385 IMAGES OF THE Lewis, **Walking with the Wind,** 331.

385 "AT THE MOMENT" Author interview with John Lewis.

386 BORN IN 1940 TO SHARECROPPER PARENTS Ibid.

386 LEWIS HAD PREPARED Ibid.

386 THEN HE HEARD THE COMMANDER'S ORDER Ibid.

386 "THE TROOPERS AND POSSEMEN" Lewis, **Walking with the Wind,** 327.

386 LEWIS MADE IT BACK Ibid., 329–30.

387 HE STILL REMEMBERS Author interview with John Lewis.

387 "I ALWAYS FELT" Ibid.

387 "THE MARCH OF 1965" Ibid.

388 "IN THE FINAL ANALYSIS" Ibid.

389 "IF I JUST SEND" Kotz, **Judgment Days,** 303.

389 WORKING THROUGH HIS FRIEND Ibid., 304.

389 THE PRESIDENT SEATED WALLACE Ibid. "It was an intimidating Johnson maneuver that Hubert Humphrey called a 'nostril inspection,'" Kotz wrote. "The psychological warfare had begun." Ibid. See also Goodwin, **Remembering America,** 321–24.

389 "I kept my eyes"   Johnson, **Vantage Point,** 162.

391 "Why don't you"   Kotz, **Judgment Days,** 305.

391 "Oh, Mr. President"   Ibid.

391 "Don't you shit me"   Ibid.

392 "George, why are"   Ibid.

392 He described the   Ibid., 305–6.

392 "Now, listen, George"   Ibid., 306.

392 Under pressure from   Johnson, **Vantage Point,** 163. In the end, Wallace told Johnson that the state could not afford the financial costs of mobilizing the National Guard. "It needed federal assistance," Johnson recalled. "I gave such assistance immediately. I signed an Executive Order federalizing the Alabama National Guard. So the troops went in after all. They went in by order of the President, because the Governor said Alabama couldn't afford them financially. But they were not intruders forcing their way in; they were citizens of Alabama. That made all the difference in the world." Ibid.

392 "Hell, if I'd stayed"   Kotz, **Judgment Days,** 306.

393 with a purposeful stride   "President Johnson's Special Message to the Congress: The American Promise," LBJ Presidential Library, http://www.lbjlibrary.org/lyndon-baines-johnson/speeches-films/president-johnsons-special-message-to-the-congress-the-american-promise.

393 He did not pause   Ibid.

393 the president opened a folder   Ibid.

393 "I speak tonight"   Lyndon B. Johnson, "Spe-

cial Message to the Congress: The American Promise," March 15, 1965, American Presidency Project, http://www.presidency.ucsb.edu/ws/?pid=26805.

394 Here, for the first time "President Johnson's Special Message to the Congress: The American Promise," LBJ Presidential Library.

395 There is no Negro problem Lyndon B. Johnson, "Special Message to the Congress: The American Promise," American Presidency Project.

396 "It is ironic, Mr. President" Kotz, **Judgment Days,** 314.

397 "It is difficult to fight for freedom" Lyndon B. Johnson, "Remarks in the Capitol Rotunda at the Signing of the Voting Rights Act," August 6, 1965, American Presidency Project, http://www.presidency.ucsb.edu/ws/?pid=27140.

397 On Sunday, March 31, 1968 Miller, **Lyndon,** 618–25. I also drew on my essay "Fifty Years After 1968, We Are Still Living in Its Shadow," **Time,** January 18, 2018.

397 He had a draft Miller, **Lyndon,** 619.

397 The president had talked Ibid., 619–21.

398 Johnson stopped in Ibid., 621.

398 "After spending all day" Ibid.

398 Only a few hours Lyndon B. Johnson: "The President's Address to the Nation Announcing Steps to Limit the War in Vietnam and Reporting His Decision Not to Seek Reelection," March 31, 1968, American Presidency Project, http://www.presidency.ucsb.edu/ws/?pid=28772.

398 "I had already" Miller, **Lyndon,** 621.

398 MORE THAN HALF A MILLION "Vietnam War: Allied Troop Levels, 1960–1973," American War Library, http://www.americanwarlibrary.com/vietnam/vwatl.htm.

399 ABOUT 46 U.S. TROOPS "Vietnam War U.S. Military Fatal Casualty Statistics: Electronic Records Reference Report," National Archives, https://www.archives.gov/research/military/vietnam-war/casualty-statistics.

399 THE SETTING WAS SPLENDID This section appeared, in slightly different form, in my **Martin Luther King Jr.: His Life and Legacy, Time** special edition, 2018.

399 "WE ARE TIED TOGETHER" King, "Remaining Awake Through a Great Revolution."

400 HIS EVENING ADDRESS Johnson: "The President's Address to the Nation Announcing Steps to Limit the War in Vietnam."

401 "EVER ANCIENT, EVER NEW" The phrase is from book 10 of **The Confessions of Saint Augustine**, http://www.leaderu.com/cyber/books/augconfessions/bk10.html.

402 "ONE DAY WE" King, "Remaining Awake Through a Great Revolution."

403 "IT SEEMS THAT I CAN HEAR" Ibid.

403 HE TELEPHONED CORETTA SCOTT KING Kotz, **Judgment Days,** 415.

403 THE PRESIDENT ATTENDED Lyndon B. Johnson, "Address to the Nation Upon Proclaiming a Day of Mourning Following the Death of Dr. King," April 5, 1968, American Presidency Project, http://www.presidency.ucsb.edu/ws/?pid=28783.

403 "The dream of"   Ibid.

403 learned about the assassination   Thomas, **Robert Kennedy**, 366.

403 Wearing an overcoat   Ibid.

404 "What we need"   "Robert Kennedy: Delivering News of King's Death," National Public Radio, April 4, 2008. https://www.npr.org/2008/04/04/89365887/robert-kennedy-delivering-news-of-kings-death.

404 "Do you know"   Thomas, **Robert Kennedy**, 361.

404 Back in the ballroom   Ibid., 391.

404 The dynamics of the '68 campaign   See, for instance, Theodore H. White, **The Making of the President, 1968** (New York, 1969); Joe McGinniss, **The Selling of the President, 1968** (New York, 1969); Lewis Chester, Geoffrey Hodgson, and Bruce Page, **An American Melodrama: The Presidential Campaign of 1968** (New York, 1969).

405 George Wallace carried   "1968 Presidential Election," 270 to Win, https://www.270towin.com/1968_Election/.

405 "The magnitude of"   Johnson, **Vantage Point**, 565–66.

406 Immigration and Nationality Act   Lyndon B. Johnson: "Remarks at the Signing of the Immigration Bill, Liberty Island, New York," October 3, 1965, American Presidency Project, http://www.presidency.ucsb.edu/ws/?pid=27292.

406 And a single word   Sitaraman, **Crisis of the Middle-Class Constitution**, 206–8.

406 THE ADDITION OF WOMEN   Ibid. "After the
Civil Rights act was passed," Sitaraman wrote, "the
civil rights movement became a model for women,
and equal opportunity became the approach to
combating sex discrimination." Ibid., 207–8.

406 SPOKE OUT IN THE SPIRIT   Representative Shirley Chisholm of New York, "Equal Rights for
Women," Address to the U.S. House of Representatives, May 21, 1969, Washington, D.C.,
Archives of Women's Political Communication,
Iowa State University, https://awpc.cattcenter.ia-
state.edu/2017/03/21/equal-rights-for-women
-may-21-1969/.

407 AS A BLACK PERSON   Ibid.

408 JOHNSON'S LAST PUBLIC APPEARANCE   Kotz,
Judgment Days, 424; Miller, **Lyndon,** 681–85.

408 THE HUBERT HUMPHREYS   Miller, **Lyndon,**
681–83.

408 HE WAS SICK   Ibid., 681–82.

408 A HIGHLY UNUSUAL WINTER STORM   Ibid.

408 THE SNOW AND THE ICE   Ibid., 681.

408 "I WAS JUST"   Ibid.

408 HE OVERRULED HIS DOCTORS   Ibid., 681–82.

408 "FOR JOHNSON"   Ibid., 682.

409 "I WAS DETERMINED"   Ibid.

409 "PUT ON HIS"   Ibid.

409 JOHNSON GREW FRUSTRATED   Ibid., 681.

409 IN HIS REMARKS   Kotz, **Judgment Days,** 424.

409 TWO MEMBERS OF THE AUDIENCE   Ibid., 425.

410 "THE FATIGUE OF"   Miller, **Lyndon,** 685.

410 "LET'S TRY TO"   Kotz, **Judgment Days,** 425.

410 AND HE DIED   Ibid., 425–26.

CONCLUSION · **The First Duty of an American Citizen**

413 THE PEOPLE HAVE   Truman, **Mr. Citizen**, 27.

413 BEGIN WITH THE   Theodore Roosevelt, "The Duties of American Citizenship," Buffalo, New York, January 26, 1893, Gilder Lehrman Center for the Study of Slavery, Resistance, and Abolition, Yale University, https://glc.yale.edu/duties -american-citizenship.

413 GREAT LEADERS WE HAVE HAD   Press release of speech given by Eleanor Roosevelt before the Democratic National Convention, August 13, 1956; correspondence between Eleanor Roosevelt and Harry S. Truman, Eleanor Roosevelt Papers, Part II, 1945–1960, FDRL.

413 KNEW THERE'D BE HELL TO PAY   Gardner, **Harry Truman and Civil Rights**, 80–81. "He knew very well that this was a great risk, political risk, as indeed it was," Truman assistant George Elsey recalled. "But as President, he saw what he thought was his duty, and he went right ahead with it." Ibid.

413 "OUR AMERICAN FAITH"   Truman, "Special Message to the Congress on Civil Rights," February 2, 1948.

413 TRUMAN USED RACIAL SLURS   McCullough, **Truman**, 83; 86; 247; 980. See also Leuchtenburg, **White House Looks South**, 151–52, and Leuchtenburg, "The Conversion of Harry Truman," **American Heritage**, November 1991.

413 IN 1911, WHILE COURTING   "Truman's Racial

Ideas Changed, Letters Show," **NYT,** April 11, 1983; Leuchtenburg, "Conversion of Harry Truman." Truman was twenty seven at the time he wrote the letter.

414 THE DESCENDANT OF SLAVE OWNERS   Leuchtenburg, "Conversion of Harry Truman." McCullough described the ethos of the Independence, Missouri, of Truman's childhood this way: "The atmosphere remained pervadingly southern— antebellum Old South, unreconstructed. Handkerchiefs were waved whenever the band played 'Dixie.' The United Daughters of the Confederacy thrived, and such formal parties as attended by genteel young folk like Bessie Wallace and her friends were hardly different from those put on in Macon or Tuscaloosa. . . . The biggest memorial in Woodland Cemetery was the Confederate monument. Portraits of Lee and Jackson were displayed prominently in many front parlors." McCullough, **Truman,** 53.

414 THE MARCH ON WASHINGTON AS "SILLY" Leuchtenburg, **White House Looks South,** 223.

414 INSPIRED BY COMMUNISTS   Martin Luther King, Jr., **The Papers of Martin Luther King, vol. 5, Threshold of a New Decade, January 1959–December 1960,** (Berkeley, Calif.) 5:437.

414 HIS HORROR OVER BRUTAL ATTACKS   Leuchtenburg, **White House Looks South,** 165–66.

414 IN SOUTH CAROLINA   "Resonant Ripples in a Global Pond: The Blinding of Isaac Woodard," https://faculty.uscupstate.edu/amyers/conference .html.

414 "My God!" Truman said   Leuchtenburg, **White House Looks South**, 166.

414 "My forebears were"   Ibid., 366. See also McCullough, **Truman**, 588.

415 "We believe that"   Truman, "Special Message to the Congress on Civil Rights," February 2, 1948.

415 "damnable, communistic, unconstitutional"   Gardner, **Harry Truman and Civil Rights**, 80.

415 At a White House luncheon   Alfred Steinberg, **The Man from Missouri: The Life and Times of Harry S. Truman** (New York, 1962), 303–4; Miller, **Plain Speaking**, 80–81; William Lee Miller, **Two Americans**, 337–38.

415 "I want to take"   Steinberg, **Man from Missouri**, 303–4.

416 The president thought   Ibid., 304; Miller, **Plain Speaking**, 80–81; Leuchtenburg, **White House Looks South**, 366.

416 Taking a copy of the Constitution   Leuchtenburg, **White House Looks South**, 366.

416 "I'm everybody's president"   Steinberg, **Man from Missouri**, 304.

416 A White House waiter   Ibid.; Leuchtenburg, **White House Looks South**, 366–67.

416 "Those—the Bill of Rights"   Miller, **Plain Speaking**, 80.

417 "I was just thinking"   Ibid., 80–81.

417 Dictating to his secretary   Truman, **Where the Buck Stops**, ix.

417 "You never can"   Ibid., 79.

419 "THE NEXT GENERATION"   Samuel W. Rushay, Jr., "Harry Truman's History Lessons," **Prologue** 41, no. 1 (Spring 2009).

420 "RIGHTEOUSNESS IS EASY"   Arthur M. Schlesinger, Jr., **Life in the 20th Century,** 311.

421 "THE PRESIDENT," WOODROW WILSON WROTE   Wilson, **Constitutional Government,** 40.

421 "MAN CAN BE"   John F. Kennedy: "Commencement Address at American University in Washington," June 10, 1963, American Presidency Project, http://www.presidency.ucsb.edu/ws/?pid=9266. "No problem of human destiny is beyond human beings," Kennedy added. "Man's reason and spirit have often solved the seemingly unsolvable—and we believe they can do it again." Ibid.

421 "THE METHOD OF"   Du Bois, **Black Reconstruction in America,** 677–78.

422 CODED RACIAL APPEALS   See, for instance, Timothy Nels Thurber, **Republicans and Race: The GOP's Frayed Relationship with African Americans, 1945–1974** (Lawrence, Kan., 2013), and Thomas Byrne Edsall with Mary D. Edsall, **Chain Reaction: The Impact of Race, Rights, and Taxes on American Politics** (New York, 1992).

422 A "CRISIS OF CONFIDENCE"   Jimmy Carter, "Address to the Nation on Energy and National Goals: 'The Malaise Speech,'" July 15, 1979, American Presidency Project, http://www.presidency.ucsb.edu/ws/?pid=32596.

422 A REMARKABLE ABILITY   See, for instance, William Ker Muir, Jr., **The Bully Pulpit: The Presi-**

dential Leadership of Ronald Reagan (Berkeley, Calif., 1992).

422 "Sometimes I want"   Ronald Reagan, "Remarks at a Fund-raising Reception for the John F. Kennedy Library Foundation," June 24, 1985, American Presidency Project, http://www.presidency.ucsb .edu/ws/?pid=38816.

423 that John Kennedy had   John F. Kennedy, "Address to Massachusetts State Legislature," January 9, 1961, National Archives Catalog, https:// catalog.archives.gov/id/193879.

423 "I've spoken of"   Ronald Reagan, "Farewell Address to the Nation," January 11, 1989, American Presidency Project, http://www.presidency .ucsb.edu/ws/?pid=29650.

424 killing 168   "Oklahoma City Bombing," FBI .gov, https://www.fbi.gov/history/famous-cases/ oklahoma-city-bombing.

424 "Let us let"   William J. Clinton, "Remarks at a Memorial Service for the Bombing Victims in Oklahoma City, Oklahoma," April 23, 1995, American Presidency Project, http://www.presi dency.ucsb.edu/ws/?pid=51265.

424 In those terrible weeks   George Bush, All the Best, George Bush: My Life in Letters and Other Writings (New York, 2013), 591–92.

425 "The terrorists are"   George W. Bush, "Address Before a Joint Session of the Congress on the United States Response to the Terrorist Attacks of September 11," September 20, 2001, American Presidency Project, http://www.presi dency.ucsb.edu/ws/?pid=64731.

426 "Our purpose as"   George W. Bush, "Remarks at the National Day of Prayer and Remem-
brance Service," September 14, 2001, American
Presidency Project, http://www.presidency.ucsb
.edu/ws/?pid=63645.

426 "This world He created"   Ibid.

426 A young white supremacist   Glenn Smith,
Jennifer Berry Hawes, and Abigail Darlington,
"SLED analysts: Dylann Roof's prints found on
gun that killed nine at Emanuel AME Church,"
The Post and Courier (Charleston, S.C.), December 12, 2016, https://www.postandcourier
.com/church_shooting/sled-analysts-dylann
-roof-s-prints-found-on-gun-that/article
_dbe60122-bfef-11e6-9ba5-5f9142dfcf38.html.

427 "According to the"   Barack Obama, "Eulogy
at the Funeral Service for Pastor Clementa C.
Pinckney of the Emanuel African Methodist Episcopal Church in Charleston, South Carolina,"
June 26, 2015, American Presidency Project,
http://www.presidency.ucsb.edu/ws/?pid=110387.

428 "For too long"   Ibid.

428 Obama began to sing   Ibid.

428 "We may not"   Ibid.

429 "Our nation was"   Barack Obama, "Remarks
by the President on the Supreme Court Decision
on Marriage Equality," June 26, 2015, Obama
White House Archive, https://obamawhitehouse
.archives.gov/the-press-office/2015/
06/26/remarks-president-supreme-court-decision
-marriage-equality.

429 "I know change"   Ibid.

430 "THE COUNTRY HAS TO"   Truman, **Where the Buck Stops,** 111.

430 TRUMAN HAD IMMENSE   Sherwood, **Roosevelt and Hopkins,** 883.

430 "GOD DAMN IT"   Ibid., 881.

431 "COMMERCE, LUXURY, AND"   Schlesinger, **Cycles of American History,** 7.

431 "THE LAST RED"   William Faulkner, "Banquet Speech," December 10, 1950, NobelPrize.org, https://www.nobelprize.org/nobel_prizes/litera ture/laureates/1949/faulkner-speech.html.

432 "THE FIRST DUTY"   Roosevelt, "Duties of American Citizenship."

432 THE "PASSION AND ACTION"   Oliver Wendell Holmes, Jr., "In Our Youth Our Hearts Were Touched with Fire," Memorial Day Address, May 30, 1884, Keene, New Hampshire.

432 "EVERY MAN WHO"   Roosevelt, **Rough Riders and An Autobiography,** 407–8.

433 "THE SECRET PERVADING"   Bagehot, **English Constitution,** 73.

433 "HEREDITARY MONARCHS WERE"   Bryce, **American Commonwealth,** 1:67.

433 "THE SPIRIT OF RESISTANCE"   Thomas Jefferson to Abigail Adams, February 22, 1787, Founders Online, National Archives, https://founders .archives.gov/documents/Jefferson/01-11 -02-0182.

434 "WE KNOW INSTINCTIVELY"   Addams, **Democracy and Social Ethics,** 8.

434 "IT IS NOT ONLY"   Roosevelt, **You Learn by Living,** 174.

435 "I HAVE BEEN"   Truman, **Mr. Citizen,** 113.

435 FACTS, AS JOHN ADAMS   "Speech by John Adams at the Boston Massacre Trial," Boston Massacre Historical Society, http://www.boston massacre.net/trial/acct-adams3.htm.

436 "THE DICTATORS OF"   Truman, **Where the Buck Stops,** 100.

436 "WHEREVER THE PEOPLE"   Thomas Jefferson to Richard Price, January 8, 1789, Founders Online, National Archives, https://founders.archives .gov/documents/Jefferson/01-14-02-0196.

437 AS PART OF A SERIES   I am indebted to Michael Beschloss, who discussed the evening long afterward with Professor Donald, for the details about the Hickory Hill series. For notes about the evenings, see also Arthur M. Schlesinger, Jr., Papers, Manuscripts and Archives Division, New York Public Library.

437 "NO ONE HAS"   Donald, **Lincoln,** 13.

438 "THE POLITICIAN'S OPTIC"   White, **Making of the President, 1964,** 55.

438 "THIS IS AN"   Ibid.

438 "TO ANNOUNCE THAT"   "Roosevelt in the Kansas City Star," May 7, 1918, Theodore Roosevelt Association, http://www.theodoreroosevelt.org/ site/c.elKSIdOWIiJ8H/b.9297493/k.7CB9/ Quotations_from_the_speeches_and_other _works_of_Theodore_Roosevelt.htm.

438 "PUBLICITY IS THE"   Jeremy Bentham, **Benthamiana; or, Select Extracts from the Works of Jeremy Bentham,** ed. John Hill Burton (Philadelphia, 1844), 139.

439 I THINK [THE PRESS] IS INVALUABLE   John F. Kennedy, "Television and Radio Interview: 'After Two Years—a Conversation with the President,'" December 17, 1962, American Presidency Project, http://www.presidency.ucsb.edu/ws/?pid=9060.

439 "WHEN THE MARINER"   Pollard, **Lost Cause Regained,** 159.

440 "I CANNOT EASILY"   Rovere, **Senator Joe McCarthy,** 256.

440 "BUT IF I AM"   Ibid., 258–59.

440 WARNED OF THE DANGERS   Bryce, **American Commonwealth,** 1:68.

441 "A BOLD PRESIDENT"   Ibid.

441 "THE PEOPLE HAVE"   Truman, **Mr. Citizen,** 27.

441 "HE WAS A"   Truman, **Where the Buck Stops,** 11–12.

442 IN THE SUMMER OF 1864   Burlingame, **Abraham Lincoln,** 2:655–58; Thomas A. Lewis, "When Washington, D.C. Came Close to Being Conquered by the Confederacy," Smithsonian .com, July 1988, https://www.smithsonianmag .com/history/when-washington-dc-came-close-to -being-conquered-by-the-confederacy -180951994/; Osborne, **Jubal,** 261–93.

442 HAD SEEN ACTION   "166th Regiment, Ohio Infantry (National Guard)," National Park Service, https://www.nps.gov/civilwar/search-battle-units -detail.htm?battleUnitCode=UOH0166RIN.

442 HEADQUARTERED AT SILVER SPRING   Osborne, **Jubal,** 284–85.

442 "IN SIGHT OF THE DOME"   Lewis, "When Washington, D.C. Came Close."

442 THE FEDERAL TROOPS MOUNTED   Ibid.; Burlingame, **Abraham Lincoln,** 2:656–57.

442 LINCOLN, WHO OBSERVED   Ibid., 2:656. At Fort Stevens, Lincoln "became the first and only sitting American president to come under serious enemy fire." Ibid.

442 "A MAN," HIS SECRETARY   John Hay, **Inside Lincoln's White House: The Complete Civil War Diary of John Hay,** ed. Michael Burlingame and John R. Turner Ettlinger (Carbondale, Ill., 1997), 222.

442 "HE STOOD THERE"   Donald, **Lincoln,** 518–19.

442 "GET DOWN, YOU"   Lewis, "When Washington, D.C. Came Close."

443 HIS FACE HEAVILY LINED   See the portrait taken by Alexander Gardner in Washington on February 5, 1865. Abraham Lincoln, **The Annotated Lincoln,** ed. Harold Holzer and Thomas A. Horrocks (Cambridge, Mass., 2016), 562.

443 "IT IS," HE SAID   Lincoln, "Address to the 166th Ohio Regiment."

Bibliography

|||||||||||||||||||||||||||||||||||||||||||||||||||||||

Manuscript Collections

Adams Family Papers, Massachusetts Historical Society, Boston, Mass.

Jane Addams Papers Project, Ramapo College of New Jersey, Mahwah, N.J.

Jean Becker, "All the Best, George Bush" File, Post-Presidential Materials, George Bush Presidential Library and Museum, College Station, Tex.

Prescott S. Bush Papers, Archives and Special Collections, Thomas J. Dodd Research Center, University of Connecticut Libraries, Storrs, Conn.

The Reminiscences of Prescott S. Bush (1966–67), Columbia Center for Oral History Archives, Rare Book and Manuscript Library, Columbia University in the City of New York.

Frederick Douglass Papers, Library of Congress, Washington, D.C.

The Dwight D. Eisenhower Presidential Library, Abilene, Kan.

Ulysses S. Grant Papers, Digital Collection, Mississippi State University, Starkville, Miss.

Richard Hofstadter Papers, Columbia University, New York.

Andrew Johnson Papers, Library of Congress, Washington, D.C.

Collections of the Lyndon B. Johnson Presidential Library, Austin, Tex.

Martin Luther King, Jr., Papers Project, Stanford University, Palo Alto, Calif.

Edward Livingston Papers, Manuscripts Division, Department of Rare Books and Special Collections, Princeton University Library, Princeton, N.J.

Joseph Pulitzer II Papers, Library of Congress, Washington, D.C.

Eleanor Roosevelt Oral History, Robert D. Graff Papers Collection, Franklin D. Roosevelt Presidential Library and Museum, Hyde Park, N.Y.

Eleanor Roosevelt Papers Project, George Washington University, Washington, D.C.

Franklin D. Roosevelt Papers, Franklin D. Roosevelt Presidential Library and Museum, Hyde Park, N.Y.

Theodore Roosevelt Papers, Library of Congress, Washington, D.C.

Arthur M. Schlesinger, Jr., Papers, Manuscripts and Archives Division, New York Public Library, New York.

Harry S. Truman Papers, Harry S. Truman Presidential Library and Museum, Independence, Mo.

Woodrow Wilson Papers, Library of Congress, Washington, D.C.

Wise Family Papers, Virginia Historical Society, Richmond, Va.

Books and Essays Consulted

Abel, Donald C. **Theories of Human Nature: Classical and Contemporary Readings.** New York: McGraw-Hill, 1992.

Abernethy, George L. **The Idea of Equality: An Anthology.** Richmond, Va.: John Knox Press, 1959.

Abzug, Robert H. **America Views the Holocaust, 1933–1945: A Brief Documentary History.** The Bedford Series in History and Culture. Boston: Bedford / St. Martin's, 1999.

Ackerman, Kenneth D. **Young J. Edgar: Hoover and the Red Scare, 1919–1920.** Falls Church, Va.: Viral History Press, 2011.

Adams, James Truslow. **The Epic of America.** Boston: Little, Brown, 1931.

Adams, John. **The Works of John Adams, Second President of the U.S. With a Life of the Author, Notes and Illustrations, by His Grandson Charles Francis Adams.** Vol. 6. Boston: Little, Brown, 1851.

Adams, Katherine H., and Michael L. Keene. **Alice Paul and the American Suffrage Campaign.** Urbana: University of Illinois Press, 2007.

Addams, Jane. **Democracy and Social Ethics.** Urbana: University of Illinois Press, 2002. First published 1902.

———. **Twenty Years at Hull-House: With Autobiographical Notes.** Edited by Victoria Bissell Brown. Boston: Bedford / St. Martin's, 1999. First published 1910.

Alexander, Shawn Leigh. **An Army of Lions: The Civil Rights Struggle Before the NAACP.** Politics and

Culture in Modern America. Philadelphia: University of Pennsylvania Press, 2012.

Allen, Frederick Lewis. **Only Yesterday: An Informal History of the 1920s.** New York: Harper Perennial Modern Classics, 2010. First published 1931.

Alter, Jonathan. **The Defining Moment: FDR's Hundred Days and the Triumph of Hope.** New York: Simon & Schuster, 2006.

Ambrose, Stephen E. **D-Day: June 6, 1944.** New York: Simon & Schuster, 1994.

Angelou, Maya. **I Know Why the Caged Bird Sings.** Foreword by Oprah Winfrey. New York: Random House, 2015.

Archer, Jules. **The Plot to Seize the White House: The Shocking True Story of the Conspiracy to Overthrow F.D.R.** New York: Skyhorse Publishing, 2015.

Aristotle. **The Works of Aristotle.** Translated into English under the editorship of W. D. Ross. Vol. 11. Oxford: Clarendon Press, 1928.

Augustine of Hippo, Saint. **The City of God.** Translated by Marcus Dods. New York: Modern Library, 1993.

Bagehot, Walter. **The English Constitution.** Ithaca, N.Y.: Cornell University Press, 1966. First published 1867.

Baillie, John. **The Belief in Progress.** London: Oxford University Press, 1950.

Baker, Jean H. **Sisters: The Lives of America's Suffragists.** New York: Hill and Wang, 2005.

———, ed. **Votes for Women: The Struggle for Suffrage Revisited.** Viewpoints on American Culture. Oxford: Oxford University Press, 2002.

Bass, Jack, and Marilyn W. Thompson. **Strom: The Complicated Personal and Political Life of Strom Thurmond.** New York: PublicAffairs, 2005.

Bayley, Edwin R. **Joe McCarthy and the Press.** Madison: University of Wisconsin Press, 1981.

Bean, Jonathan, ed. **Race and Liberty in America: The Essential Reader.** Lexington: University Press of Kentucky, 2009.

Beard, Charles A. **An Economic Interpretation of the Constitution of the United States.** New York: Macmillan, 1935.

Beasley, Vanessa B. **You, the People: American National Identity in Presidential Rhetoric.** Presidential Rhetoric Series, no. 10. College Station: Texas A & M University Press, 2004.

————, ed. **Who Belongs in America? Presidents, Rhetoric, and Immigration.** Presidential Rhetoric Series, no. 16. College Station: Texas A & M University Press, 2006.

Beeman, Richard. **Plain, Honest Men: The Making of the American Constitution.** New York: Random House, 2009.

Beitzinger, A. J. **A History of American Political Thought.** New York: Dodd, Mead, 1972.

Bellah, Robert N. **The Broken Covenant: American Civil Religion in Time of Trial.** 2nd ed. Chicago: University of Chicago Press, 1992.

Bellah, Robert N, and Phillip E. Hammond. **Varieties of Civil Religion.** San Francisco: Harper & Row, 1980.

Belz, Herman. **The Webster-Hayne Debate on the Nature of the Union: Selected Documents.** Indianapolis, Ind.: Liberty Fund, 2000.

Bennett, David H. **The Party of Fear: From Nativist Movements to the New Right in American History.** 2nd Vintage Books ed., rev. and updated. New York: Vintage Books, 1995.

Bentham, Jeremy. **Benthamiana; or, Select Extracts from the Works of Jeremy Bentham** [. . .]. Edited by John Hill Burton. Philadelphia: Lea & Blanchard, 1844.

Bercovitch, Sacvan. **The American Jeremiad.** Madison: University of Wisconsin Press, 1978.

Berenbaum, Michael, and Abraham J. Peck, eds. **The Holocaust and History: The Known, the Unknown, the Disputed, and the Reexamined.** Bloomington: Indiana University Press, 1998.

Berg, A. Scott. **Wilson.** New York: G. P. Putnam's Sons, 2013.

Berkin, Carol. **A Brilliant Solution: Inventing the American Constitution.** New York: Harcourt, 2002.

Beschloss, Michael. **The Conquerors: Roosevelt, Truman, and the Destruction of Hitler's Germany, 1941–1945.** New York: Simon & Schuster, 2002.

———. **Kennedy and Roosevelt: The Uneasy Alliance.** New York: W. W. Norton, 1980.

———. **Presidential Courage: Brave Leaders and How They Changed America, 1789–1989.** New York: Simon & Schuster, 2007.

Bishop, Joseph Bucklin. **Theodore Roosevelt and His Time Shown in His Own Letters.** 2 vols. New York: C. Scribner's Sons, 1920.

Blight, David W. **Race and Reunion: The Civil War in American Memory.** Cambridge, Mass.: Harvard University Press, 2002.

Boorstin, Daniel J. **The Genius of American Politics.** 1st Phoenix ed. Charles R. Walgreen Foundation Lectures. Chicago: University of Chicago Press, 1958.

Boritt, Gabor S., ed. **Why the Confederacy Lost.** New York: Oxford University Press, 1992.

Bourke, Joanna. **Fear: A Cultural History.** Emeryville, Calif.: Shoemaker Hoard, 2006.

Bowen, Catherine Drinker. **Miracle at Philadelphia: The Story of the Constitutional Convention, May to September, 1787.** Foreword by Warren E. Burger. Boston: Little, Brown, 1986.

Bowers, Claude G. **The Tragic Era: The Revolution after Lincoln.** Blue Ribbon Books. Cambridge, Mass.: Houghton Mifflin, 1929.

Bradley, James. **The Imperial Cruise: A Secret History of Empire and War.** New York: Little, Brown, 2009.

Branch, Taylor. **At Canaan's Edge: America in the King Years, 1965–68.** New York: Simon & Schuster, 2006.

———. **Parting the Waters: America in the King Years, 1954–63.** New York: Simon & Schuster, 1988.

———. **Pillar of Fire: America in the King Years, 1963–65.** New York: Simon & Schuster, 1998.

Breitman, Richard. **Official Secrets: What the Nazis Planned, What the British and Americans Knew.** New York: Hill and Wang, 1998.

Breitman, Richard, and Alan M. Kraut. **American Refugee Policy and European Jewry, 1933–1945.** Bloomington: Indiana University Press, 1987.

Breitman, Richard, and Allan J. Lichtman. **FDR and the Jews.** Cambridge, Mass.: Belknap Press of Harvard University Press, 2013.

Bremer, Francis J. **John Winthrop: America's Forgotten Founding Father.** New York: Oxford University Press, 2003.

Brendon, Piers. **The Dark Valley: A Panorama of the 1930s.** London: Jonathan Cape, 2000.

Brinkley, Alan. **Voices of Protest: Huey Long, Father Coughlin, and the Great Depression.** New York: Alfred A. Knopf, 1982.

Brooks, Noah. **Lincoln Observed: Civil War Dispatches of Noah Brooks.** Edited by Michael Burlingame. Baltimore: Johns Hopkins University Press, 1998.

Brundage, William Fitzhugh. **The Southern Past: A Clash of Race and Memory.** Cambridge, Mass.: Belknap Press of Harvard University Press, 2005.

Bryce, James. **The American Commonwealth.** 3rd ed., completely rev. 3 vols. New York: Macmillan, 1893–95.

Buckley, William F., Jr. **Getting It Right: A Novel.** Washington, D.C.: Regnery Publishing, 2003.

———. **Let Us Talk of Many Things: The Collected Speeches.** Roseville, Calif.: Forum, 2000.

———. **The Redhunter: A Novel Based on the Life of Senator Joe McCarthy.** Boston: Little, Brown, 1999.

Buckley, William F., Jr., and L. Brent Bozell. **McCarthy and His Enemies: The Record and Its Meaning.** Great Debate Books. Chicago: Henry Regnery, 1954.

Budiansky, Stephen. **The Bloody Shirt: Terror After the Civil War.** New York: Viking, 2008.

Bunting, Josiah, III. **Ulysses S. Grant.** The American Presidents Series. New York: Times Books, 2004.

Burke, Edmund. **Complete Writings on America.** With an introduction by Bruce Frohnen. Tacoma, Wash.: Cluny Media, 2016.

————. **Reflections on the Revolution in France, and Other Writings.** Edited by Jesse Norman. Everyman's Library, no. 365. New York: Alfred A. Knopf, 2015.

Burlingame, Michael. **Abraham Lincoln: A Life.** 2 vols. Baltimore: Johns Hopkins University Press, 2008.

Burns, Edward McNall. **The American Idea of Mission: Concepts of National Purpose and Destiny.** Westport, Conn.: Greenwood Press, 1973.

Burns, James MacGregor. **Leadership.** New York: Harper & Row, 1978.

————. **Presidential Government: The Crucible of Leadership.** Boston: Houghton Mifflin, 1965.

Bury, John B. **The Idea of Progress: An Inquiry into Its Origin and Growth.** New York: Dover, 1932.

Bush, George. **All the Best, George Bush: My Life in Letters and Other Writings.** New York: Scribner, 2013.

Butters, Gerald R., Jr. **Black Manhood on the Silent Screen.** Culture America. Lawrence: University Press of Kansas, 2002.

Cahill, Bernadette. **Alice Paul, the National Woman's Party and the Vote: The First Civil Rights Struggle of the 20th Century.** Jefferson, N.C.: McFarland, 2015.

Calhoun, John C. **The Papers of John C. Calhoun.** Edited by Robert L. Meriwether. 28 vols. Columbia: Published by the University of South Carolina Press for the South Carolinian Society, 1959–2003.

Carleton, Don E. **Red Scare!: Right-Wing Hysteria, Fifties Fanaticism, and Their Legacy in Texas.** Austin: Texas Monthly Press, 1985.

Caro, Robert A. **Passage of Power.** Vol. 4 of The Years of Lyndon Johnson. New York: Alfred A. Knopf, 1982–2012.

Casey, Steven. **Cautious Crusade: Franklin D. Roosevelt, American Public Opinion, and the War Against Nazi Germany.** New York: Oxford University Press, 2001.

Cash, W. J. **The Mind of the South.** New York: Alfred A. Knopf, 1941.

Cashman, Sean Dennis. **America in the Gilded Age: From the Death of Lincoln to the Rise of Theodore Roosevelt.** 3rd ed. New York: New York University Press, 1993.

Castel, Albert. **The Presidency of Andrew Johnson.** American Presidency Series. Lawrence: Regents Press of Kansas, 1979.

Chalmers, David M. **Hooded Americanism: The History of the Ku Klux Klan.** 3rd ed. Durham: Duke University Press, 1981

Chernow, Ron. **Alexander Hamilton.** New York: Penguin Press, 2004.

———. **Grant.** New York: Penguin Press, 2017.

———. **Washington: A Life.** New York: Penguin Press, 2010.

Chester, Lewis, Geoffrey Hodgson, and Bruce Page. **An American Melodrama: The Presidential Campaign of 1968.** New York: Viking Press, 1969.

Chesterton, G. K. **Orthodoxy.** New York: Doubleday, 2001. First published 1908.

———. **What I Saw in America.** London: Hodder and Stoughton, 1923.

Churchill, Winston. **Great Contemporaries: Churchill Reflects on FDR, Hitler, Kipling, Chaplin, Balfour, and Other Giants of His Age.** Edited by James W. Muller with Paul H. Courtenay and Erica L. Chenoweth. Wilmington, Del.: ISI Books, 2012. First published 1937.

———. **A History of the English-Speaking Peoples.** 4 vols. London: Cassell, 1956–58.

Cline, Sally. **Dashiell Hammett: Man of Mystery.** New York: Arcade Publishing, 2014.

Cohen, Mitchell, and Nicole Fermon, eds. **Princeton Readings in Political Thought: Essential Texts Since Plato.** Princeton, N.J.: Princeton University Press, 1996.

Cohn, Roy M. **McCarthy.** New York: New American Library, 1968.

Cohodas, Nadine. **Strom Thurmond and the Politics of Southern Change.** New York: Simon & Schuster, 1993.

Cole, Wayne S. **America First: The Battle Against Intervention, 1940–41.** Madison: University of Wisconsin Press, 1953.

———. **Roosevelt and the Isolationists, 1932–45.** Lincoln: University of Nebraska Press, 1983.

Collier, Christopher, and James Lincoln Collier. **Decision in Philadelphia: The Constitutional Convention of 1787.** New York: Ballantine Books, 1986.

Collier, Peter, with David Horowitz. **The Roosevelts: An American Saga.** New York: Simon & Schuster, 1994.

Commager, Henry Steele. **The Empire of Reason: How Europe Imagined and America Realized the Enlightenment.** Garden City, N.Y.: Anchor Press / Doubleday, 1977.

Condorcet, Jean-Antoine-Nicolas de Caritat. **Condorcet: Political Writings.** Edited by Steven Lukes and Nadia Urbinati. Cambridge: Cambridge University Press, 2012.

Connelly, Thomas L. **The Marble Man: Robert E. Lee and His Image in American Society.** Baton Rouge: Louisiana State University Press, 1977.

Connelly, Thomas L., and Barbara L. Bellows. **God and General Longstreet: The Lost Cause and the Southern Mind.** Baton Rouge: Louisiana State University Press, 1982.

Coolidge, Calvin. **The Autobiography of Calvin Coolidge.** New York: Cosmopolitan Book Corporation, 1929.

Cooper, John Milton, Jr., ed. **Reconsidering Woodrow Wilson: Progressivism, Internationalism, War, and Peace.** Washington, D.C.: Woodrow Wilson Center Press, 2008.

——. **Woodrow Wilson: A Biography.** New York: Alfred A. Knopf, 2009.

Cooper, William J., Jr. **We Have the War Upon Us: The Onset of the Civil War, November 1860–April 1861.** New York: Alfred A. Knopf, 2012.

Cooper, William J., Jr., and John M. McCardell Jr., eds. **In the Cause of Liberty: How the Civil War Redefined American Ideals.** Baton Rouge: Louisiana State University Press, 2009.

Cornuelle, Richard C. **Reclaiming the American Dream.** New York: Random House, 1965.

Corwin, Edward S. **The President, Office and Powers: History and Analysis of Practice and Opinion**. 2nd ed. New York: New York University Press, 1941.

Coski, John M. **The Confederate Battle Flag: America's Most Embattled Emblem**. Cambridge, Mass.: Belknap Press of Harvard University Press, 2005.

Crespino, Joseph. **Strom Thurmond's America**. New York: Hill and Wang, 2012.

Crèvecoeur, J. Hector St. John. **Letters from an American Farmer**. New York: Fox, Duffield & Co., 1904.

Cripps, Thomas. **Slow Fade to Black: The Negro in American Film, 1900–1942**. New York: Oxford University Press, 1977.

Cronin, Thomas E., ed. **Inventing the American Presidency**. Studies in Government and Public Policy. Lawrence: University Press of Kansas, 1989.

Cullen, Jim. **The American Dream: A Short History of an Idea That Shaped a Nation**. New York: Oxford University Press, 2003.

Davis, Deborah. **Guest of Honor: Booker T. Washington, Theodore Roosevelt, and the White House Dinner That Shocked a Nation**. New York: Atria Books, 2012.

Debs, Eugene V. **Debs and the War: His Canton Speech and His Trial in the Federal Court at Cleveland, September 1918**. Chicago: National Office Socialist Party, 1923.

Denton, Sally. **The Plots Against the President: FDR, a Nation in Crisis, and the Rise of the American Right**. New York: Bloomsbury Press, 2012.

Descartes, René. **The Passions of the Soul: And Other Late Philosophical Writings**. Translated with an introduction and notes by Michael Moriarty. Oxford

World's Classics. Oxford: Oxford University Press, 2015.

D'Este, Carlo. **Eisenhower: A Soldier's Life.** New York: Henry Holt, 2002.

Doenecke, Justus D., ed. **In Danger Undaunted: The Anti-Interventionist Movement of 1940–41 as Revealed in the Papers of the America First Committee.** Hoover Archival Documentaries. Stanford, Calif.: Hoover Institution Press, 1990.

Donald, David Herbert. **Charles Sumner and the Rights of Man.** New York: Alfred A. Knopf, 1970.

———. **Lincoln.** New York: Simon & Schuster, 1995.

———, ed. **Why the North Won the Civil War: Six Authoritative Views on the Economic, Military, Diplomatic, Social, and Political Reasons Behind the Confederacy's Defeat.** New York: Simon & Schuster, 2005.

Dorsey, Leroy G. **We Are All Americans, Pure and Simple: Theodore Roosevelt and the Myth of Americanism.** Tuscaloosa: University of Alabama Press, 2007.

Douglass, Frederick. **Autobiographies.** Edited by Henry Louis Gates, Jr. New York: Library of America, 1994.

———. **Oration by Frederick Douglass, Delivered on the Occasion of the Unveiling of the Freedmen's Monument in Memory of Abraham Lincoln, in Lincoln Park, Washington, D.C., April 14th, 1876.** Washington, D.C.: Gibson Brothers, 1876.

———. **Selected Speeches and Writings.** Edited by Philip S. Foner. Chicago: Lawrence Hill, 1999.

Downs, Gregory P. **After Appomattox: Military Oc-**

cupation and the Ends of War. Cambridge, Mass.: Harvard University Press, 2015.

Dozier, Rush W., Jr. Why We Hate: Understanding, Curbing, and Eliminating Hate in Ourselves and Our World. Chicago: Contemporary Books, 2002.

Du Bois, W.E.B. Black Reconstruction in America: An Essay Toward a History of the Part Which Black Folk Played in the Attempt to Reconstruct Democracy in America, 1860–1880. Studies in American Negro Life. New York: Atheneum, 1983. First published 1935.

———. The Souls of Black Folk. Everyman's Library. New York: Alfred A. Knopf, 1993. First published 1903.

Dunn, Susan. 1940: FDR, Willkie, Lindbergh, Hitler—The Election Amid the Storm. New Haven, Conn.: Yale University Press, 2013.

Dyer, Thomas G. Theodore Roosevelt and the Idea of Race. Baton Rouge: Louisiana State University Press, 1980.

Eagan, Daniel. America's Film Legacy: The Authoritative Guide to the Landmark Movies in the National Film Registry. New York: Continuum, 2010.

Ebony (Chicago, Illinois). The White Problem in America. By the editors of Ebony. First published as a special issue of Ebony magazine, August 1965. Chicago: Johnson Publishing, 1966.

Edelstein, Ludwig. The Idea of Progress in Classical Antiquity. Baltimore: Johns Hopkins Press, 1967.

Edsall, Thomas Byrne, with Mary D. Edsall. Chain Reaction: The Impact of Race, Rights, and Taxes on American Politics. New York: W. W. Norton, 1992.

Egerton, Douglas R. The Wars of Reconstruction: The Brief, Violent History of America's Most Progressive Era. New York: Bloomsbury, 2014.

Eisenhower, Dwight D. The White House Years. 2 vols. Garden City, N.Y.: Doubleday, 1963–65.

Eliot, Charles William, ed. Harvard Classics. Vol. 43, American Historical Documents, 1000–1904. New York: Collier, 1910.

Eliot, George. Middlemarch: A Study of Provincial Life. 4 vols. London: William Blackwood and Sons, 1872.

Ellis, Richard J. The Development of the American Presidency. New York: Routledge, 2012.

Emerson, Ralph Waldo. Essays and Lectures. Edited by Joel Porte. New York: Library of America, 1983.

Engs, Robert F., and Randall M. Miller, eds. The Birth of the Grand Old Party: The Republicans' First Generation. Philadelphia: University of Pennsylvania Press, 2002.

Ewald, William Bragg, Jr. Who Killed Joe McCarthy? New York: Simon & Schuster, 1984.

Fahs, Alice, and Joan Waugh, eds. The Memory of the Civil War in American Culture. Civil War America. Chapel Hill: University of North Carolina Press, 2004.

Fariello, Griffin. Red Scare: Memories of the American Inquisition; an Oral History. New York: W. W. Norton, 1995.

Faust, Drew Gilpin. This Republic of Suffering: Death and the American Civil War. New York: Alfred A. Knopf, 2008.

Feller, Daniel. The Jacksonian Promise: America,

1815–1840. *The American Moment*. Baltimore: Johns Hopkins University Press, 1995.

———. "Rediscovering Jacksonian America." In *The State of U.S. History*, edited by Melvyn Stokes, 69–82. New York: Berg, 2002.

Felzenberg, Alvin S. *A Man and His Presidents: The Political Odyssey of William F. Buckley Jr.* New Haven, Conn.: Yale University Press, 2017.

Ferguson, Robert A. *The American Enlightenment, 1750–1820*. Cambridge, Mass.: Harvard University Press, 1997.

Fiske, John. *American Political Ideas Viewed from the Standpoint of Universal History: Three Lectures Delivered at the Royal Institution of Great Britain in May, 1880*. New York: Harper & Brothers, 1885.

Fitzgerald, F. Scott. *The Great Gatsby*. New York: Collier Books, 1992. First published 1925.

Flexner, Eleanor, and Ellen F. Fitzpatrick. *Century of Struggle: The Woman's Rights Movement in the United States*. Cambridge, Mass.: Belknap Press of Harvard University Press, 1996.

Foner, Eric. *The Fiery Trial: Abraham Lincoln and American Slavery*. New York: W. W. Norton, 2010.

———. *Forever Free: The Story of Emancipation and Reconstruction*. New York: Alfred A. Knopf, 2005.

———. *Reconstruction: America's Unfinished Revolution, 1863–1877*. Updated ed. New York: HarperCollins, 2014.

Foote, Shelby. *The Civil War: A Narrative*. 3 vols. New York: Random House, 1958–74.

Ford, Henry Jones. *The Rise and Growth of American*

Politics: A Sketch of Constitutional Development. New York: Da Capo Press, 1967. First published 1898.

Foster, Gaines M. **Ghosts of the Confederacy: Defeat, the Lost Cause, and the Emergence of the New South, 1865 to 1913.** New York: Oxford University Press, 1987.

Frady, Marshall. **Wallace.** New York: World Publishing, 1968.

Frank, Gerold. **An American Death: The True Story of the Assassination of Dr. Martin Luther King, Jr. and the Greatest Manhunt of Our Time.** Garden City, N.Y.: Doubleday, 1972.

Fraser, James W. **A History of Hope: When Americans Have Dared to Dream of a Better Future.** New York: Palgrave Macmillan, 2002.

Freeberg, Ernest. **Democracy's Prisoner: Eugene V. Debs, the Great War, and the Right to Dissent.** Cambridge, Mass.: Harvard University Press, 2010.

Freeman, Douglas Southall. **R. E. Lee: A Biography.** 4 vols. New York: Charles Scribner's Sons, 1934–35.

Freidel, Frank. **Franklin D. Roosevelt: A Rendezvous with Destiny.** Boston: Little, Brown, 1990.

Friedländer, Saul. **Prelude to Downfall: Hitler and the United States, 1939–1941.** Translated from the French by Aline B. and Alexander Werth. New York: Alfred A. Knopf, 1967.

Frost-Knappman, Elizabeth, and Kathryn Cullen-DuPont, eds. **Women's Suffrage in America: An Eyewitness History.** Updated ed. New York: Facts on File, 2005.

Galbraith, John Kenneth. **The Affluent Society and**

Other Writings, 1952–1967. Edited by James K. Galbraith. New York: Library of America, 2010.

Gale, Robert L. **A Dashiell Hammett Companion.** Westport, Conn.: Greenwood, 2000.

Gallagher, Gary W., **The Union War.** Cambridge, Mass.: Harvard University Press, 2011.

Gallagher, Gary W., and Alan T. Nolan, eds. **The Myth of the Lost Cause and Civil War History.** Bloomington: Indiana University Press, 2000.

Gardner, Michael R. **Harry Truman and Civil Rights: Moral Courage and Political Risks.** Carbondale: Southern Illinois University Press, 2002.

Garrow, David J. **Bearing the Cross: Martin Luther King, Jr., and the Southern Christian Leadership Conference.** New York: William Morrow, 1986.

Gatewood, Willard B., Jr. **Theodore Roosevelt and the Art of Controversy: Episodes of the White House Years.** Baton Rouge: Louisiana State University Press, 1970.

Geldard, Richard G. **Remembering Heraclitus.** Hudson, N.Y.: Lindisfarne Books, 2000.

Gerber, David A. **American Immigration: A Very Short Introduction.** Very Short Introductions, no. 274. Oxford: Oxford University Press, 2011.

Geselbracht, Raymond H., ed. **The Civil Rights Legacy of Harry S. Truman.** The Truman Legacy Series, vol. 2. Kirksville, Mo.: Truman State University Press, 2007.

Gilmour, David. **The Long Recessional: The Imperial Life of Rudyard Kipling.** New York: Farrar, Straus and Giroux, 2002.

Gjerde, Jon, ed. **Major Problems in American Immi-**

gration and Ethnic History: Documents and Essays. Major Problems in American History Series. Boston: Houghton Mifflin, 1998.

Goetz, Stewart, and Charles Taliaferro. **A Brief History of the Soul.** Hoboken, N.J.: Wiley-Blackwell, 2011.

Goldsmith, William M. **The Growth of Presidential Power: A Documented History.** 3 vols. New York: Chelsea House Publishers, 1974.

Goodwin, Doris Kearns. **The Bully Pulpit: Theodore Roosevelt, William Howard Taft, and the Golden Age of Journalism.** New York: Simon & Schuster, 2013.

———. **Lyndon Johnson and the American Dream.** New York: Harper & Row, 1976.

Goodwin, Richard N. **Remembering America: A Voice from the Sixties.** Boston: Little, Brown, 1988.

Gordon, Linda. **The Second Coming of the KKK: The Ku Klux Klan of the 1920s and the American Political Tradition.** New York: Liveright Publishing, 2017.

Gordon-Reed, Annette. **Andrew Johnson.** American Presidents Series. New York: Times Books, 2011.

Gorski, Philip. **American Covenant: A History of Civil Religion from the Puritans to the Present.** Princeton, N.J.: Princeton University Press, 2017.

Grant, Madison. **The Passing of the Great Race.** LaVergne, Tenn.: Ostara Publications, 2016.

Green, Joshua. **Devil's Bargain: Steve Bannon, Donald Trump, and the Storming of the Presidency.** New York: Penguin Press, 2017.

Guelzo, Allen C. **Lincoln's Emancipation Proclama-**

tion: The End of Slavery in America. New York: Simon & Schuster, 2004.

Gunther, John. Roosevelt in Retrospect: A Profile in History. New York: Harper & Brothers, 1950.

Halberstam, David. The Children. New York: Random House, 1998.

———. The Fifties. New York: Villard Books, 1993.

Hamby, Alonzo L. For the Survival of Democracy: Franklin Roosevelt and the World Crisis of the 1930s. New York: Free Press, 2004.

Hamilton, Alexander. Writings. Edited by Joanne B. Freeman. New York: Library of America, 2001.

Hamilton, Alexander, James Madison, and John Jay. The Federalist Papers. Edited by Isaac Kramnick. New York: Penguin Books, 1987.

H[amilton], J[oseph] G. de R[oulhac]. "Pollard, Edward Alfred." In Dictionary of American Biography, edited by Allen Johnson and Dumas Malone. Vol. 8, 47–48. New York: Charles Scribner's Sons, 1935.

Hargrove, Erwin C. The President as Leader: Appealing to the Better Angels of Our Nature. Lawrence: University Press of Kansas, 1998.

Harper, Ida Husted. How Women Got the Vote: The Story of the Women's Suffrage Movement in America. Originally published in Encyclopedia Americana in 1920. N.p.: A. J. Cornell Publications, 2013.

Hart, Roderick P. The Political Pulpit. West Lafayette, Ind.: Purdue University Press, 1977.

Hay, John. Inside Lincoln's White House: The Complete Civil War Diary of John Hay. Edited by Michael Burlingame and John R. Turner Ettlinger. Carbondale: Southern Illinois University Press, 1997.

Herskowitz, Mickey. **Duty, Honor, Country: The Life and Legacy of Prescott Bush.** Nashville: Rutledge Hill Press, 2003.

Hibbert, Christopher. **Wellington: A Personal History.** Reading, Mass.: Perseus Books, 1999.

Himmelfarb, Gertrude. **Victorian Minds.** New York: Alfred A. Knopf, 1968.

Historical Statistics of the United States, Colonial Times to 1970. Part 2. Washington, D.C.: U.S. Department of Commerce, Bureau of the Census, 1975.

Hitchcock, William I. **The Age of Eisenhower: America and the World in the 1950s.** New York: Simon & Schuster, 2018.

Hitchens, Christopher. **Blood, Class, and Nostalgia: Anglo-American Ironies.** New York: Farrar, Straus & Giroux, 1990.

Hobson, Fred. **Mencken: A Life.** New York: Random House, 1994.

Hochschild, Arlie Russell. **Strangers in Their Own Land: Anger and Mourning on the American Right.** New York: New Press, 2016.

Hoffer, Williamjames. **The Caning of Charles Sumner: Honor, Idealism, and the Origins of the Civil War.** Witness to History. Baltimore: Johns Hopkins University Press, 2010.

Hofstadter, Richard. **The Age of Reform: From Bryan to F.D.R.** New York: Alfred A. Knopf, 1955.

———. **The American Political Tradition and the Men Who Made It.** New York: Alfred A. Knopf, 1948.

———. **The Paranoid Style in American Politics, and Other Essays.** New York: Alfred A. Knopf, 1965.

Hogeland, William. **The Whiskey Rebellion: George Washington, Alexander Hamilton, and the Frontier Rebels Who Challenged America's Newfound Sovereignty.** New York: Scribner, 2006.

Holt, Michael F. **By One Vote: The Disputed Presidential Election of 1876.** American Presidential Elections. Lawrence: University Press of Kansas, 2008.

Holzer, Harold. **Lincoln at Cooper Union: The Speech That Made Abraham Lincoln President.** New York: Simon & Schuster, 2004.

———. **Lincoln President-Elect: Abraham Lincoln and the Great Secession Winter, 1860–1861.** New York: Simon & Schuster, 2008.

Holzer, Harold, and Norton Garfinkle. **A Just and Generous Nation: Abraham Lincoln and the Fight for American Opportunity.** New York: Basic Books, 2015.

Horn, James. **A Land as God Made It: Jamestown and the Birth of America.** New York: Basic Books, 2005.

Houston, Alan Craig. **Algernon Sidney and the Republican Heritage in England and America.** Princeton, N.J.: Princeton University Press, 2014.

Hughes, Emmet John. **The Ordeal of Power: A Political Memoir of the Eisenhower Years.** New York: Atheneum, 1963.

Humphrey, Hubert H. **The Education of a Public Man: My Life and Politics.** Edited by Norman Sherman. Garden City, N.Y.: Doubleday, 1976.

Huntington, Samuel P. **American Politics: The Promise of Disharmony.** Cambridge, Mass.: Belknap Press, 1981.

————. Who Are We? The Challenges to America's National Identity. New York: Simon & Schuster, 2005.

Hyman, Harold M. American Singularity: The 1787 Northwest Ordinance, the 1862 Homestead and Morrill Acts, and the 1944 G.I. Bill. The Richard B. Russell Lectures, no. 5. Athens: University of Georgia Press, 1986.

Isenberg, Nancy. White Trash: The 400-Year Untold History of Class in America. New York: Viking, 2016.

Jackson, Andrew. Correspondence of Andrew Jackson. Edited by John Spencer Bassett. 7 vols. Washington, D.C.: Carnegie Institution of Washington, 1926–35.

————. The Papers of Andrew Jackson. Edited by Sam B. Smith et al. Vol. 4, 1816–1820, edited by Harold D. Moser et al. Knoxville: University of Tennessee Press, 1994.

Jacoby, Susan. Freethinkers: A History of American Secularism. New York: Metropolitan Books, 2004.

Janney, Caroline E. Remembering the Civil War: Reunion and the Limits of Reconciliation. The Littlefield History of the Civil War Era. Chapel Hill: University of North Carolina Press, 2013.

Jeffers, H. Paul. Commissioner Roosevelt: The Story of Theodore Roosevelt and the New York City Police, 1895–1897. New York: J. Wiley & Sons, 1994.

John Birch Society. The Blue Book of the John Birch Society. Boston: Western Islands, 1961.

Johnson, Charles C. Why Coolidge Matters: Leadership Lessons from America's Most Underrated President. New York: Encounter Books, 2013.

Johnson, Lyndon B. **Reaching for Glory: Lyndon Johnson's Secret White House Tapes, 1964–1965.** Edited by Michael R. Beschloss. New York: Simon & Schuster, 2001.

———. **Taking Charge: The Johnson White House Tapes, 1963–1964.** Edited by Michael Beschloss. New York: Simon & Schuster, 1997.

———. **The Vantage Point: Perspectives of the Presidency, 1963–1969.** New York: Holt, Rinehart and Winston, 1971.

Jonas, Manfred. **Isolationism in America, 1935–1941.** Chicago: Imprint, 1990. First published 1966.

Jones, Clarence B., and Stuart Connelly. **Behind the Dream: The Making of the Speech That Transformed a Nation.** New York: Palgrave Macmillan, 2011.

Kabaservice, Geoffrey. **Rule and Ruin: The Downfall of Moderation and the Destruction of the Republican Party, from Eisenhower to the Tea Party.** Studies in Postwar American Political Development. New York: Oxford University Press, 2012.

Karabell, Zachary. **The Last Campaign: How Harry Truman Won the 1948 Election.** New York: Alfred A. Knopf, 2000.

Kaus, Mickey. **The End of Equality.** New York: Basic Books, 1992.

Kendi, Ibram X. **Stamped from the Beginning: The Definitive History of Racist Ideas in America.** New York: Nation Books, 2016.

Kennedy, David M. **Freedom from Fear: The American People in Depression and War, 1929–1945.** The Oxford History of the United States, vol. 9. New York: Oxford University Press, 1999.

Ketchum, Richard M. **The Borrowed Years, 1938–1941: America on the Way to War.** New York: Random House, 1989.

King, Martin Luther, Jr. **The Papers of Martin Luther King, Jr.** Edited by Clayborne Carson et al. 7 vols. Berkeley: University of California Press, 1992–2014. Vol. 1, **Called to Serve, January 1929–June 1951,** 1992. Vol. 2, **Rediscovering Precious Values, July 1951–November 1955,** 1994. Vol. 3, **Birth of a New Age, December 1955–December 1956,** 1997. Vol. 4, **Symbol of the Movement, January 1957–December 1958,** 2000. Vol. 5, **Threshold of a New Decade, January 1959–December 1960,** 2005. Vol. 6, **Advocate of the Social Gospel, September 1948–March 1963,** 2007. Vol. 7, **To Save the Soul of America, January 1961–August 1962,** 2014.

———. **A Testament of Hope: The Essential Writings and Speeches of Martin Luther King, Jr.** Edited by James Melvin Washington. San Francisco: HarperOne, 2003.

Klosko, George. **History of Political Theory: An Introduction.** 2nd ed. Vol. 1, **Ancient and Medieval.** Oxford: Oxford University Press, 2012.

Knight, Louise W. **Jane Addams: Spirit in Action.** New York: W. W. Norton, 2010.

Kotz, Nick. **Judgment Days: Lyndon Baines Johnson, Martin Luther King, Jr., and the Laws That Changed America.** Boston: Houghton Mifflin, 2005.

Kraditor, Aileen S. **The Ideas of the Woman Suffrage Movement, 1890–1920.** New York: W. W. Norton, 1981.

Ladner, Gerhart B. **The Idea of Reform: Its Impact on**

Christian Thought and Action in the Age of the Fathers. Santa Fe, N.M.: Gannon, 1970.

Lakoff, Sanford A. **Equality in Political Philosophy.** Harvard Political Studies. Cambridge: Harvard University Press, 1964.

Lane, Ann J. **The Brownsville Affair: National Crisis and Black Reaction.** Port Washington, N.Y.: Kennikat Press, 1971.

Larson, Edward J. **Summer for the Gods: The Scopes Trial and America's Continuing Debate Over Science and Religion.** New York: Basic Books, 1997.

Lash, Joseph P. **Eleanor and Franklin: The Story of Their Relationship, Based on Eleanor Roosevelt's Private Papers.** New York: W. W. Norton, 1971.

———. **Roosevelt and Churchill, 1939–1941: The Partnership That Saved the West.** New York: W. W. Norton, 1976.

Lee, Harper. **Go Set a Watchman.** New York: Harper, 2015.

———. **To Kill a Mockingbird.** Philadelphia: Lippincott, 1960.

Leonard, Thomas C. **Illiberal Reformers: Race, Eugenics, and American Economics in the Progressive Era.** Princeton, N.J.: Princeton University Press, 2016.

Lesher, Stephan. **George Wallace: American Populist.** Reading, Mass.: Addison-Wesley, 1994.

Leuchtenburg, William E. **The White House Looks South: Franklin D. Roosevelt, Harry S. Truman, Lyndon B. Johnson.** Walter Lynwood Fleming Lectures in Southern History. Baton Rouge: Louisiana State University Press, 2005.

Lewis, Anthony. **Freedom for the Thought That We Hate: A Biography of the First Amendment.** New York: Basic Books, 2007.

Lewis, John, with Michael D'Orso. **Walking with the Wind: A Memoir of the Movement.** New York: Simon & Schuster, 1998.

Lewis, Sinclair. **It Can't Happen Here.** New York: Signet Classics, 2014. First published 1935.

Lewis, William Draper. **The Life of Theodore Roosevelt.** Philadelphia: John C. Winston, 1919.

Lincoln, Abraham. **The Annotated Lincoln.** Edited by Harold Holzer and Thomas A. Horrocks. Cambridge, Mass.: Belknap Press of Harvard University Press, 2016.

——. **Lincoln on Democracy.** Edited by Mario M. Cuomo and Harold Holzer. New York: HarperCollins, 1990.

Lipset, Seymour Martin. **American Exceptionalism: A Double-Edged Sword.** New York: W. W. Norton, 1996.

Long, Huey P. "The Doom of America's Dream." In **Share Our Wealth: Every Man a King,** 30–32. Washington, D.C.: N.p., 1935.

——. **Kingfish to America, Share Our Wealth: Selected Senatorial Papers of Huey P. Long.** Edited by Henry M. Christman. New York: Schocken Books, 1985.

——. **My First Days in the White House.** Harrisburg, Penn.: Telegraph Press, 1935.

Loucks, Emerson Hunsberger. **The Ku Klux Klan in Pennsylvania: A Study in Nativism.** Harrisburg, Penn.: Telegraph Press, 1936.

Lukacs, John. **Five Days in London: May 1940**. New Haven, Conn.: Yale University Press, 1999.

Lunardini, Christine. **Alice Paul: Equality for Women**. Lives of American Women. New York: Westview Press, 2012.

Lytle, Andrew Nelson. **Bedford Forrest and His Critter Company**. New York: Minton, Balch, 1931.

MacLean, Nancy. **Behind the Mask of Chivalry: The Making of the Second Ku Klux Klan**. New York: Oxford University Press, 1994.

Maddex, Jack P., Jr. **The Reconstruction of Edward A. Pollard: A Rebel's Conversion to Postbellum Unionism**. James Sprunt Studies in History and Political Science, vol. 54. Chapel Hill: University of North Carolina Press, 1974.

Madison, James. **Notes of Debates in the Federal Convention of 1787 Reported by James Madison**. Athens: Ohio University Press, 1984. First published 1840.

Maier, Pauline. **American Scripture: Making the Declaration of Independence**. New York: Alfred A. Knopf, 1997.

———. **Ratification: The People Debate the Constitution, 1787–1788**. New York: Simon & Schuster, 2010.

Manchester, William. **American Caesar: Douglas MacArthur, 1880–1964**. Boston: Little, Brown, 1978.

———. **The Death of a President: November 20–November 25, 1963**. New York: Harper & Row, 1967.

———. **The Glory and the Dream: A Narrative History of America, 1932–1972**. Boston: Little, Brown, 1974.

Mansfield, Harvey C., Jr. **Taming the Prince: The Ambivalence of Modern Executive Power.** New York: Free Press, 1989.

Marable, Manning, and Leith Mullings, eds. **Let Nobody Turn Us Around: Voices of Resistance, Reform, and Renewal: An African American Anthology.** Lanham, Md.: Rowman & Littlefield, 2003.

Marty, Martin E. **The One and the Many: America's Struggle for the Common Good.** Cambridge, Mass.: Harvard University Press, 1997.

Masur, Louis P. **Lincoln's Last Speech: Wartime Reconstruction and the Crisis of Reunion.** Pivotal Moments in American History. New York: Oxford University Press, 2015.

Matthews, Chris. **Bobby Kennedy: A Raging Spirit.** New York: Simon & Schuster, 2017.

———. **Kennedy and Nixon: The Rivalry That Shaped Postwar America.** New York: Simon & Schuster, 1996.

McCardell, John. **The Idea of a Southern Nation: Southern Nationalists and Southern Nationalism, 1830–1860.** New York: W. W. Norton, 1979.

McCoy, Donald R. **Calvin Coolidge: The Quiet President.** New York: Macmillan, 1967.

McCullough, David. **Mornings on Horseback: The Story of an Extraordinary Family, a Vanished Way of Life and the Unique Child Who Became Theodore Roosevelt.** New York: Simon & Schuster, 1981.

———. **Truman.** New York: Simon & Schuster, 1992.

McDonald, Forrest. **The American Presidency: An Intellectual History.** Lawrence: University Press of Kansas, 1994.

McFeely, William S. **Frederick Douglass.** New York: W. W. Norton, 1991.

McGeer, Michael. **A Fierce Discontent: The Rise and Fall of the Progressive Movement in America, 1870–1920.** Oxford: Oxford University Press, 2003.

McGinniss, Joe. **The Selling of the President, 1968.** New York: Trident Press, 1969.

McMahon, Kevin J. **Reconsidering Roosevelt on Race: How the Presidency Paved the Road to Brown.** Chicago: University of Chicago Press, 2004.

McMillen, Sally G. **Seneca Falls and the Origins of the Women's Rights Movement.** Pivotal Moments in American History. New York: Oxford University Press, 2008.

McPherson, James M. **Battle Cry of Freedom: The Civil War Era.** The Oxford History of the United States, vol. 6. New York: Oxford University Press, 1988.

———. **For Cause and Comrades: Why Men Fought in the Civil War.** New York: Oxford University Press, 1997.

McVeigh, Rory. **The Rise of the Ku Klux Klan: Right-Wing Movements and National Politics.** Social Movements, Protest, and Contention, vol. 32. Minneapolis: University of Minnesota Press, 2009.

Meacham, Jon. **American Gospel: God, the Founding Fathers, and the Making of a Nation.** New York: Random House, 2006.

———. **American Lion: Andrew Jackson in the White House.** New York: Random House, 2008.

———. **Destiny and Power: The American Odyssey of George Herbert Walker Bush.** New York: Random House, 2015.

————. **Franklin and Winston: An Intimate Portrait of an Epic Friendship.** New York: Random House, 2003.

————. **Thomas Jefferson: The Art of Power.** New York: Random House, 2012.

————, ed. **Voices in Our Blood: America's Best on the Civil Rights Movement.** New York: Random House, 2001.

Mencken, H. L. **My Life as Author and Editor.** Ed. Jonathan Yardley. New York: Alfred A. Knopf, 1993.

————. **A Religious Orgy in Tennessee: A Reporter's Account of the Scopes Monkey Trial.** Introduction by Art Winslow. Hoboken, N.J.: Melville House Publishing, 2006.

Mettler, Suzanne. **Soldiers to Citizens: The G.I. Bill and the Making of the Greatest Generation.** New York: Oxford University Press, 2007.

Milkis, Sidney M., and Michael Nelson. **The American Presidency: Origins and Development, 1776–2007.** 5th ed. Washington, D.C.: CQ Press, 2008.

Miller, Merle. **Lyndon, an Oral Biography.** New York: G. P. Putnam's Sons, 1980.

————. **Plain Speaking: An Oral Biography of Harry S. Truman.** New York: Berkley Pub. Corp., 1974.

Miller, William Lee. **The First Liberty: Religion and the American Republic.** New York: Alfred A. Knopf, 1986.

————. **Two Americans: Truman, Eisenhower, and a Dangerous World.** New York: Alfred A. Knopf, 2012.

Mills, C. Wright. **White Collar: The American Middle Classes.** New York: Oxford University Press, 1953.

Minutaglio, Bill, and Steven L. Davis. **Dallas 1963.** New York: Twelve, 2013.

Moore, Barrington, Jr. **Social Origins of Dictatorship and Democracy: Lord and Peasant in the Making of the Modern World.** Boston: Beacon Press, 1966.

Morel, Lucas E. **Lincoln's Sacred Effort: Defining Religion's Role in American Self-Government.** Applications of Political Theory. Lanham, Md.: Lexington Books, 2000.

Morris, Edmund. **The Rise of Theodore Roosevelt.** New York: Random House, 1979.

Muir, William Ker, Jr. **The Bully Pulpit: The Presidential Leadership of Ronald Reagan.** Berkeley, Calif.: Institute for Contemporary Studies Press, 1992.

Murray, Robert K. **The Harding Era: Warren G. Harding and His Administration.** Minneapolis: University of Minnesota Press, 1969.

———. **The 103rd Ballot: The Legendary 1924 Democratic Convention That Forever Changed Politics.** New York: Harper, 2016.

———. **Red Scare: A Study in National Hysteria, 1919–1920.** Minneapolis: University of Minnesota Press, 1955.

Myrdal, Gunnar. **An American Dilemma: The Negro Problem and Modern Democracy.** 20th anniversary ed. New York: Harper & Row, 1962.

Needleman, Jacob. **The American Soul: Rediscovering the Wisdom of the Founders.** New York: J. P. Tarcher / Putnam, 2003.

Nelson, Craig. **Thomas Paine: Enlightenment, Revolution, and the Birth of Modern Nations.** New York: Penguin Books, 2007.

Nelson, Michael, ed. **The Evolving Presidency: Landmark Documents, 1787–2015.** 5th ed. Thousand Oaks, Calif.: CQ Press, 2016.

Neustadt, Richard E., and Ernest R. May. **Thinking in Time: The Uses of History for Decision Makers.** New York: The Free Press, 1986.

Nevins, Allan. **James Truslow Adams: Historian of the American Dream.** Urbana: University of Illinois Press, 1968.

Nichols, David A. **Ike and McCarthy: Dwight Eisenhower's Secret Campaign Against Joseph McCarthy.** New York: Simon & Schuster, 2017.

———. **A Matter of Justice: Eisenhower and the Beginning of the Civil Rights Revolution.** New York: Simon & Schuster, 2007.

Niebuhr, Reinhold. **Reinhold Niebuhr: Major Works on Religion and Politics.** Edited by Elisabeth Sifton. New York: Library of America, 2015.

Nisbet, Robert A. **History of the Idea of Progress.** New York: Basic Books, 1980.

———. **Social Change and History: Aspects of the Western Theory of Development.** A Galaxy Book, no. 313. London: Oxford University Press, 1970.

Nixon, Richard M. **Six Crises.** Garden City, N.Y.: Doubleday, 1962.

Novak, Michael. **Choosing Presidents: Symbols of Political Leadership.** New Brunswick, N.J.: Transaction Publishers, 1992.

Novick, Peter. **The Holocaust in American Life.** Boston: Houghton Mifflin, 1999.

Nye, Russel B. **This Almost Chosen People: Essays in the History of American Ideas.** [East Lansing]: Michigan State University Press, 1966.

Oakley, J. Ronald. **God's Country: America in the Fifties.** New York: Dembner Books, 1986.

O'Donnell, Lawrence. **Playing with Fire: The 1968 Election and the Transformation of American Politics.** New York: Penguin Press, 2017.

Official Report of the Proceedings of the Democratic National Convention Held in Madison Square Garden, New York City, June 24, 25, 26, 27, 28, 30, July 1, 2, 3, 4, 5, 7, 8, and 9, 1924 [. . .]. Compiled by Charles A. Greathouse. Indianapolis: Bookwalter-Ball-Greathouse Printing Co., 1924.

Olson, Lynne. **Those Angry Days: Roosevelt, Lindbergh, and America's Fight Over World War II, 1939–1941.** New York: Random House, 2013.

Osborne, Charles C. **Jubal: The Life and Times of General Jubal A. Early, CSA, Defender of the Lost Cause.** Chapel Hill, N.C.: Algonquin Books of Chapel Hill, 1992.

Oshinsky, David M. **A Conspiracy So Immense: The World of Joe McCarthy.** Oxford: Oxford University Press, 2005.

O'Toole, Patricia. **The Moralist: Woodrow Wilson and the World He Made.** New York: Simon & Schuster, 2018.

———. **When Trumpets Call: Theodore Roosevelt After the White House.** New York: Simon & Schuster, 2005.

Paine, Thomas. **Collected Writings.** New York: Library of America, 1995.

Painter, Nell Irvin. **Sojourner Truth: A Life, a Symbol.** New York: W. W. Norton, 1996.

Parker, Theodore. "Speech at the New England Anti-Slavery Convention in Boston, May 29, 1850." In

Speeches, Addresses, and Occasional Sermons, vol. 2, 174–208. Boston: W. Crosby and H. P. Nichols, 1852.

Parsons, Elaine Frantz. **Ku-Klux: The Birth of the Klan During Reconstruction.** Chapel Hill: University of North Carolina Press, 2015.

Parton, James. **Life of Andrew Jackson.** 3 vols. Boston: Ticknor and Fields, 1866.

Patterson, James T. **Grand Expectations: The United States, 1945–1974.** The Oxford History of the United States, vol. 10. New York: Oxford University Press, 1996.

Pauley, Garth E. **The Modern Presidency and Civil Rights: Rhetoric on Race from Roosevelt to Nixon.** Presidential Rhetoric Series, no. 3. College Station: Texas A & M University Press, 2001.

Percy, Walker. **Signposts in a Strange Land.** Edited by Patrick Samway. New York: Farrar, Straus, and Giroux, 1991.

Perlmutter, Philip. **Legacy of Hate: A Short History of Ethnic, Religious, and Racial Prejudice in America.** Armonk, N.Y.: M. E. Sharpe, 1999.

Pessen, Edward. **Riches, Class, and Power Before the Civil War.** New York: Routledge, 1990.

Peters, Charles. **Five Days in Philadelphia: The Amazing "We Want Willkie!" Convention of 1940 and How It Freed FDR to Save the Western World.** New York: PublicAffairs, 2005.

———. **We Do Our Part: Toward a Fairer and More Equal America.** New York: Random House, 2017.

Pocock, J. G. A. **The Machiavellian Moment: Florentine Political Thought and the Atlantic Republican**

Tradition. Princeton, N.J.: Princeton University Press, 1975.

Pollard, Edward A. The Lost Cause: A New Southern History of the War of the Confederates; Comprising a Full and Authentic Account of the Rise and Progress of the Late Southern Confederacy [. . .]. New York: E. B. Treat, 1866.

———. The Lost Cause Regained. New York: G. W. Carleton, 1868.

"Pollard, Edward A." In The American Annual Cyclopaedia and Register of Important Events of the Year 1872. Vol. 12, 676. New York: D. Appleton, 1873.

Pringle, Henry F. Theodore Roosevelt: A Biography. Rev. ed. A Harvest Book, no. 15. New York: Harcourt, Brace, 1956.

Proceedings of the Second Imperial Klonvokation: Held in Kansas City, Missouri, Sept. 23, 24, 25, and 26, 1924. [Atlanta, Ga.]: Knights of the Ku Klux Klan, 1924.

Prucha, Francis Paul. The Great Father: The United States Government and the American Indians. 2 vols. Lincoln: University of Nebraska Press, 1984.

Purdum, Todd S. An Idea Whose Time Has Come: Two Presidents, Two Parties, and the Battle for the Civil Rights Act of 1964. New York: Henry Holt, 2014.

Rable, George C. But There Was No Peace: The Role of Violence in the Politics of Reconstruction. Athens: University of Georgia Press, 1984.

Rakove, Jack N. Original Meanings: Politics and Ideas in the Making of the Constitution. New York: Vintage Books, 1997.

Rawlings, William. **The Second Coming of the Invisible Empire: The Ku Klux Klan of the 1920s.** Macon, Ga.: Mercer University Press, 2016.

Reeves, Richard. **President Kennedy: Profile of Power.** New York: Simon & Schuster, 1993.

Remini, Robert V. **Andrew Jackson and the Course of American Democracy, 1833–1845.** New York: Harper & Row, 1984. Vol. 3 of the author's biography of Andrew Jackson.

Reynolds, David. **From Munich to Pearl Harbor: Roosevelt's America and the Origins of the Second World War.** The American Ways Series. Chicago: Ivan R. Dee, 2001.

Rice, Arnold S. **The Ku Klux Klan in American Politics.** New York: Haskell House Publishers, 1972.

Risen, Clay. **The Bill of the Century: The Epic Battle for the Civil Rights Act.** New York: Bloomsbury Press, 2014.

Robin, Corey. **Fear: The History of a Political Idea.** Oxford: Oxford University Press, 2004.

———. **The Reactionary Mind: Conservatism from Edmund Burke to Sarah Palin.** New York: Oxford University Press, 2011.

Rollins, Peter C., and John E. O'Connor, eds. **Hollywood's White House: The American Presidency in Film and History.** Lexington: University Press of Kentucky, 2005.

Roosevelt, Eleanor. **The Autobiography of Eleanor Roosevelt.** New York: Harper & Brothers, 1961.

———. **My Day: The Best of Eleanor Roosevelt's Acclaimed Newspaper Columns, 1936–1962.** Edited by David Emblidge. New York: Da Capo Press, 2001.

———. **On My Own.** New York: Harper & Brothers, 1958.

———. **This I Remember.** New York: Harper & Brothers, 1949.

———. **Tomorrow Is Now.** New York: Penguin Books, 2012. First published 1963.

———. **You Learn by Living.** New York: Harper & Brothers, 1960.

Roosevelt, Franklin D. **F.D.R.: His Personal Letters, 1928–1945.** Edited by Elliott Roosevelt. 2 vols. New York: Duell, Sloan, and Pearce, 1950.

Roosevelt, Theodore. **American Ideals and Other Essays, Social and Political.** New York: G. P. Putnam's Sons, 1897.

———. **Fear God and Take Your Own Part.** New York: George H. Doran Co., 1916.

———. **The Letters of Theodore Roosevelt.** Edited by Elting E. Morison. Vol. 3, **The Square Deal, 1901–1903.** Cambridge, Mass.: Harvard University Press, 1951.

———. **The Rough Riders and An Autobiography.** Edited by Louis Auchincloss. New York: Library of America, 2004. First published 1899.

Rosenman, Samuel I. **Working with Roosevelt.** New York: Harper & Brothers, 1952.

Ross, Lawrence. **Blackballed: The Black and White Politics of Race on American Campuses.** New York: St. Martin's Press, 2016.

Rovere, Richard H. **Senator Joe McCarthy.** Berkeley: University of California Press, 1996. First published 1959.

Rubinstein, William D. **The Myth of Rescue: Why

the Democracies Could Not Have Saved More Jews from the Nazis. New York: Routledge, 1997.

Samuel, Lawrence R. The American Middle Class: A Cultural History. New York: Routledge, Taylor & Francis, 2014.

Sargent, John S. "Championing the Negro" (excerpted from Good Housekeeping, June 1935). In The Real Calvin Coolidge, edited by Grace Coolidge. N.p.: N.p., 1935.

Schlesinger, Arthur M., Jr. The Coming of the New Deal. The Age of Roosevelt, vol. 2. Boston: Houghton Mifflin, 1958.

———. The Crisis of the Old Order, 1919–1933. The Age of Roosevelt, vol. 1. Boston: Houghton Mifflin, 1957.

———. The Cycles of American History. Boston: Houghton Mifflin, 1986.

———. "Did FDR Betray the Jews? Or Did He Do More Than Anyone Else to Save Them?" In FDR and the Holocaust, edited by Verne W. Newton, 159–61. New York: St. Martin's Press, 1996.

———. The Disuniting of America. New York: W. W. Norton, 1992.

———. The Imperial Presidency. 1st Mariner Books ed. Boston: Houghton Mifflin, 2004.

———. Journals, 1952–2000. Edited by Andrew Schlesinger and Stephen C. Schlesinger. New York: Penguin Press, 2007.

———. A Life in the Twentieth Century: Innocent Beginnings, 1917–1950. Boston: Houghton Mifflin, 2000.

———. The Politics of Hope: And, the Bitter Heritage; American Liberalism in the 1960s. The James Madison Library in American Politics. Princeton, N.J.: Princeton University Press, 2008.

———. The Politics of Upheaval. The Age of Roosevelt, vol. 3. Boston: Houghton Mifflin, 1960.

———. A Thousand Days: John F. Kennedy in the White House. Boston: Houghton Mifflin, 1965.

———. War and the American Presidency. New York: W. W. Norton, 2004.

Schmidt, Hans. Maverick Marine: General Smedley D. Butler and the Contradictions of American Military History. Lexington: University Press of Kentucky, 1998.

Schrag, Peter. Not Fit for Our Society: Nativism and Immigration. Berkeley: University of California Press, 2010.

Schurz, Carl. The Condition of the South: Extracts from the Report of Major-General Carl Schurz, on the States of South Carolina, Georgia, Alabama, Mississippi and Louisiana; Addressed to the President. [Philadelphia, Penn.]: N.p., 1865.

Seneca, Lucius Annaeus. Anger, Mercy, Revenge. Translated by Robert A. Kaster and Martha C. Nussbaum. Chicago: University of Chicago Press, 2010.

Shakespeare, William. The Merchant of Venice. Edited by Jay L. Halio. Oxford: Clarendon Press, 1993.

Sharp, James Roger. American Politics in the Early Republic: The New Nation in Crisis. New Haven, Conn.: Yale University Press, 1993.

Sherwood, Robert E. Roosevelt and Hopkins: An Intimate History. New York: Harper & Brothers, 1948.

Shlaes, Amity. **Coolidge.** New York: Harper, 2013.

Sitaraman, Ganesh. **The Crisis of the Middle-Class Constitution: Why Economic Inequality Threatens Our Republic.** New York: Alfred A. Knopf, 2017.

Sklar, Kathryn Kish. **Women's Rights Emerges Within the Anti-Slavery Movement, 1830–1870: A Brief History with Documents.** The Bedford Series in History and Culture. Boston: Bedford / St. Martin's, 2000.

Smith, Adam. **The Theory of Moral Sentiments.** Edited by Ryan Patrick Hanley. New York: Penguin Books, 2009. First published 1759.

Smith, Jean Edward. **Eisenhower: In War and Peace.** New York: Random House, 2012.

———. **Grant.** New York: Simon & Schuster, 2001.

Smith, Margaret Chase. **Declaration of Conscience.** Edited by William C. Lewis, Jr. New York: Doubleday, 1972.

Sorel, Georges. **The Illusions of Progress.** Translated by John and Charlotte Stanley. Berkeley: University of California Press, 1969.

Sorensen, Theodore C. **Decision-Making in the White House: The Olive Branch or the Arrows.** New York: Columbia University Press, 1963.

———. **Kennedy.** New York: Harper & Row, 1965.

Southern, Ed, ed. **The Jamestown Adventure: Accounts of the Virginia Colony, 1605–1614.** Real Voices, Real History Series. Winston-Salem, N.C.: John F. Blair, 2004.

Stampp, Kenneth M. **The Peculiar Institution: Slavery in the Ante-Bellum South.** New York: Alfred A. Knopf, 1956.

Steinberg, Alfred. **The Man from Missouri: The Life and Times of Harry S. Truman.** New York: G. P. Putnam's Sons, 1962.

Stevenson, Leslie, et al. **Thirteen Theories of Human Nature.** 7th ed. New York: Oxford University Press, 2018.

Stewart, David O. **The Summer of 1787: The Men Who Invented the Constitution.** New York: Simon & Schuster, 2007.

Stoddard, Lothrop. **The Rising Tide of Color Against White World-Supremacy.** New York: Charles Scribner's Sons, 1920.

Stone, Geoffrey R. **Perilous Times: Free Speech in Wartime from the Sedition Act of 1798 to the War on Terrorism.** New York: W. W. Norton, 2004.

Sullivan, Patricia. **Lift Every Voice: The NAACP and the Making of the Civil Rights Movement.** New York: New Press, 2009.

Swinburne, Richard. **The Evolution of the Soul.** Oxford: Clarendon Press, 1986.

Taft, William Howard. **Our Chief Magistrate and His Powers.** New York: Columbia University Press, 1916.

Tanenhaus, Sam. **The Death of Conservatism.** New York: Random House, 2009.

———. **Whittaker Chambers: A Biography.** New York: Random House, 1997.

Teggart, Frederick John. **Theory and Processes of History.** Berkeley: University of California Press, 1977.

———, ed. **The Idea of Progress: A Collection of Readings.** University of California Syllabus Series, no. 223. Berkeley: University of California Press, 1929.

Thach, Charles C. **The Creation of the Presidency, 1775–1789: A Study in Constitutional History.** Farmington Hills, Mich.: Thomson Gale, 2010.

Thomas, Aquinas Saint. **St. Thomas Aquinas on Politics and Ethics: A New Translation, Backgrounds, Interpretations.** Translated and edited by Paul E. Sigmund. A Norton Critical Edition. New York: W. W. Norton, 1988.

——. **The "Summa Theologica" of St. Thomas Aquinas.** Vol. 4. Translated by Fathers of the English Dominican province. London: R. & T. Washbourne, 1914.

Thomas, Evan. **Robert Kennedy: His Life.** New York: Simon & Schuster, 2000.

——. **The War Lovers: Roosevelt, Lodge, Hearst, and the Rush to Empire, 1898.** New York: Little, Brown, 2010.

Thurber, Timothy N. **Republicans and Race: The GOP's Frayed Relationship with African Americans, 1945–1974.** Lawrence: University Press of Kansas, 2013.

Tocqueville, Alexis de. **Democracy in America.** Edited by J. P. Mayer and translated by George Lawrence. Garden City, N.Y.: Doubleday, 1969. First published in two volumes in 1835 and 1840.

To Secure These Rights: The Report of Harry S. Truman's Committee on Civil Rights. Edited by Steven F. Lawson. The Bedford Series in History and Culture. New York: Bedford / St. Martin's, 2003.

Trefousse, Hans L. **Andrew Johnson: A Biography.** New York: W. W. Norton, 1989.

——. **Impeachment of a President: Andrew John-**

son, the Blacks, and Reconstruction. New York: Fordham University Press, 1999.

Trelease, Allen W. White Terror: The Ku Klux Klan Conspiracy and Southern Reconstruction. New York: Harper & Row, 1971.

Truman, Harry S. Memoirs. 2 vols. Garden City, N.Y.: Doubleday, 1955–56. Vol. 1, Year of Decisions, 1955. Vol. 2, Years of Trial and Hope, 1956.

———. Mr. Citizen. New York: Geis Associates, 1960.

———. Where the Buck Stops: The Personal and Private Writings of Harry S. Truman. Edited by Margaret Truman. New York: Warner Books, 1989.

Tuchman, Barbara W. The March of Folly: From Troy to Vietnam. New York: Alfred A. Knopf, 1984.

———. Practicing History: Selected Essays. New York: Alfred A. Knopf, 1981.

———. The Proud Tower: A Portrait of the World before the War, 1890–1914. New York: Macmillan, 1966.

Tucker, Richard K. The Dragon and the Cross: The Rise and Fall of the Ku Klux Klan in Middle America. Hamden, Conn.: Archon Books, 1991.

Tugwell, Rexford G. The Democratic Roosevelt: A Biography of Franklin D. Roosevelt. Garden City, N.Y.: Doubleday, 1957.

Tulis, Jeffrey K. The Rhetorical Presidency. Princeton, N.J.: Princeton University Press, 1987.

Turgot, Anne-Robert-Jacques. Turgot on Progress, Sociology and Economics: A Philosophical Review of the Successive Advances of the Human Mind [. . .]. Translated and edited by Ronald L. Meek. Cambridge Studies in the History and Theory of

Politics. Cambridge: Cambridge University Press, 1973.

Turner, Frederick Jackson. "The Significance of the Frontier in American History." In **Annual Report of the American Historical Association for the Year 1893,** 199–227. Washington, D.C.: Government Printing Office, 1894.

Tuttle, Kate. "Niagara Movement." In **Africana: The Encyclopedia of the African and African American Experience,** 2nd ed., ed. Kwame Anthony Appiah and Henry Louis Gates, Jr., 4:226–27. Oxford: Oxford University Press, 2005.

Unger, Harlow Giles. **"Mr. President": George Washington and the Making of the Nation's Highest Office.** Boston: Da Capo Press, 2013.

United States Congress Joint Committee on Reconstruction. **Report of the Joint Committee on Reconstruction, at the First Session, Thirty-Ninth Congress.** Washington, D.C.: U.S. Government Printing Office, 1866.

Varon, Elizabeth R. **Appomattox: Victory, Defeat, and Freedom at the End of the Civil War.** New York: Oxford University Press, 2014.

Venzon, Anne Cipriano, ed. **The United States in the First World War: An Encyclopedia.** Garland Reference Library of the Humanities, vol. 1205. New York: Garland Publishing, 1999.

Von Hoffman, Nicholas. **Citizen Cohn.** New York: Doubleday, 1988.

Vought, Hans P. **The Bully Pulpit and the Melting Pot: American Presidents and the Immigrant, 1897–1933.** Macon, Ga: Mercer University Press, 2004.

Walker, Samuel. **In Defense of American Liberties: A

History of the ACLU. New York: Oxford University Press, 1990.

Walters, Ronald G. **American Reformers, 1815–1860.** Rev. ed. New York: Hill and Wang, 1997.

Walton, Hanes, Jr., and Robert C. Smith. **American Politics and the African American Quest for Universal Freedom.** New York: Longman, 2000.

Walton, Mary. **A Woman's Crusade: Alice Paul and the Battle for the Ballot.** New York: St. Martin's Griffin, 2015.

Walzer, Michael. **What It Means to Be an American.** New York: Marsilio, 1992.

Ward, Geoffrey C. **Before the Trumpet: Young Franklin Roosevelt, 1882–1905.** New York: Harper & Row, 1985.

———. ed., **Closest Companion: The Unknown Story of the Intimate Friendship Between Franklin Roosevelt and Margaret Suckley.** Boston: Houghton Mifflin, 1995.

———. **A First-Class Temperament: The Emergence of Franklin Roosevelt.** New York: Harper & Row, 1989.

———. **Not for Ourselves Alone: The Story of Elizabeth Cady Stanton and Susan B. Anthony: An Illustrated History.** Based on a documentary film by Ken Burns and Paul Barnes. New York: Alfred A. Knopf, 1999.

Warner, Michael, ed. **American Sermons: The Pilgrims to Martin Luther King Jr.** New York: Library of America, 1999.

Warren, Robert Penn. **All the King's Men.** New York: Harcourt, Brace, 1946.

———. **The Legacy of the Civil War: Meditations**

on the Centennial. New York: Random House, 1961.

———. Segregation: The Inner Conflict in the South. New York: Random House, 1956.

Washington, George. Writings. Edited by John H. Rhodehamel. New York: Library of America, 1997.

Weinberg, Gerhard L. "The Allies and the Holocaust." In The Holocaust and History: The Known, the Unknown, the Disputed, and the Reexamined, edited by Michael Berenbaum and Abraham J. Peck, 480–91. Bloomington: Indiana University Press, 1998.

Welch, Robert. The Politician. Belmont, Mass.: Privately printed, 1964.

West, Nathanael. Novels and Other Writings. Edited by Sacvan Bercovitch. New York: Library of America, 1997.

Westen, Drew. The Political Brain: The Role of Emotion in Deciding the Fate of the Nation. New York: PublicAffairs, 2007.

White, Richard. The Republic for Which It Stands: The United States During Reconstruction and the Gilded Age, 1865–1896. The Oxford History of the United States. New York: Oxford University Press, 2017.

White, Ronald C., Jr. A. Lincoln: A Biography. New York: Random House, 2009.

———. American Ulysses: A Life of Ulysses S. Grant. New York: Random House, 2016.

White, Theodore H. The Making of the President, 1964. New York: Atheneum, 1965.

———. The Making of the President, 1968. New York: Atheneum, 1969.

Whitman, James Q. **Hitler's American Model: The United States and the Making of Nazi Race Law.** Princeton, N.J.: Princeton University Press, 2017.

Wilentz, Sean. **The Rise of American Democracy: Jefferson to Lincoln.** New York: W. W. Norton, 2005.

Williams, T. Harry. **Huey Long.** New York: Alfred A. Knopf, 1969.

Wills, Garry. **Explaining America: The Federalist.** His America's Political Enlightenment. Garden City, N.Y.: Doubleday, 1981.

———. **Inventing America: Jefferson's Declaration of Independence.** His America's Political Enlightenment. Garden City, N.Y.: Doubleday, 1978.

———. **Lincoln at Gettysburg: The Words That Remade America.** New York: Simon & Schuster, 1992.

Wilson, Charles Reagan. **Baptized in Blood: The Religion of the Lost Cause, 1865–1920.** Athens: University of Georgia Press, 1980.

Wilson, Glenn D., ed. **The Psychology of Conservatism.** London: Academic Press, 1973.

Wilson, James Southall. "Edward Alfred Pollard." In **Library of Southern Literature,** edited by Edwin A. Alderman, Joel C. Harris, and Charles W. Kent. Vol. 9, 4147–50. Atlanta, Ga.: Martin and Hoyt, 1907.

Wilson, Woodrow. **Constitutional Government in the United States.** New York: Columbia University Press, 1908.

———. **The Papers of Woodrow Wilson.** Edited by Arthur S. Link. Vol. 33, **April 17–July 21, 1915.** Princeton, N.J.: Princeton University Press, 1980.

Winthrop, John. **The Journal of John Winthrop, 1630–1649.** Edited by Richard S. Dunn, James Savage, and Laetitia Yeandle. The John Harvard Library. Cambridge, Mass.: Harvard University Press, 1996.

———. **Winthrop Papers.** Edited by Malcolm Freiburg. Vol. 2, **1623–1630.** Boston: Massachusetts Historical Society, 1931.

Wofford, Harris. **Of Kennedys and Kings: Making Sense of the Sixties.** New York: Farrar, Straus, Giroux, 1980.

Wolfe, Alan. **One Nation, After All: What Middle-Class Americans Really Think About God, Country, and Family, Racism, Welfare, Immigration, Homosexuality, Work, the Right, the Left, and Each Other.** New York: Viking, 1998.

Wood, Frederick S. **Roosevelt as We Knew Him: The Personal Recollections of One Hundred and Fifty of His Friends and Associates.** Philadelphia: John C. Winston, 1927.

Wood, Gordon S. **The Idea of America: Reflections on the Birth of the United States.** New York: Penguin Press, 2011.

Woodward, C. Vann. **The Burden of Southern History.** 3rd ed. Baton Rouge: Louisiana State University Press, 1993.

———. **Reunion and Reaction: The Compromise of 1877 and the End of Reconstruction.** Boston: Little, Brown, 1951.

———. **The Strange Career of Jim Crow.** 3rd rev. ed. New York: Oxford University Press, 1974.

Wyman, David S. **The Abandonment of the Jews: America and the Holocaust, 1941–1945.** New York: New Press, 1998.

Yellin, Eric S. **Racism in the Nation's Service: Government Workers and the Color Line in Woodrow**

Wilson's America. Chapel Hill: University of North Carolina Press, 2013.

Zahniser, J. D., and Amelia R. Fry. **Alice Paul: Claiming Power.** Oxford: Oxford University Press, 2014.

Zakaria, Fareed. **The Future of Freedom: Illiberal Democracy at Home and Abroad.** Rev. ed. New York: W. W. Norton, 2007.

Zangwill, Israel. **From the Ghetto to the Melting Pot: Israel Zangwill's Jewish Plays; Three Playscripts.** Edited by Edna Nahshon. Detroit: Wayne State University Press, 2006.

Zinn, Howard. **A People's History of the United States.** New York: Harper & Row, 1980.

Zion, Sidney. **The Autobiography of Roy Cohn.** Secaucus, N.J.: Lyle Stuart, 1988.

Selected Articles

Abbott, Lyman. "A Review of President Roosevelt's Administration IV: Its Influence on Patriotism and Public Service." **The Outlook,** February 27, 1909, 430-34.

Addams, Jane. "Why I Seconded Roosevelt's Nomination." **Woman's Journal** 43 (August 17, 1912): 257, in JAMC (reel 47-0469), Special Collections, University Library, University of Illinois at Chicago.

Baker, Peter. "DNA Shows Warren Harding Wasn't America's First Black President," **The New York Times,** August 18, 2015.

Brenner, Marie. "How Donald Trump and Roy Cohn's Ruthless Symbiosis Changed America." **Vanity Fair,** August 2017.

Buckley, William F., Jr. "Goldwater, the John Birch

Society, and Me." **Commentary,** March 1, 2008, 52–54.

Churchill, Winston S. "What Good's a Constitution?" **Collier's,** August 22, 1936, 386–93.

Cooper, Melissa. "Reframing Eleanor Roosevelt's Influence in the 1930s Anti-Lynching Movement Around a 'New Philosophy of Government.'" **European Journal of American Studies** 12, no. 1 (Spring 2017), https://ejas.revues.org/11914.

Desmond, Frank. "McCarthy Charges Reds Hold U.S. Jobs." **The Wheeling** (W.V.) **Intelligencer,** February 10, 1950.

Douglass, Frederick. "An Appeal to Congress for Impartial Suffrage." **The Atlantic Monthly,** January 1867, 112–17.

Fairbanks, James David. "The Priestly Functions of the Presidency: A Discussion of the Literature on Civil Religion and Its Implications for the Study of Presidential Leadership." **Presidential Studies Quarterly** 11, no. 2 (Spring 1981): 214–32.

Felzenberg, Alvin S. "Calvin Coolidge and Race: His Record in Dealing with the Racial Tensions of the 1920s." **The New England Journal of History** 55, no. 1 (Fall 1988), 83–96.

Gleason, Philip. "The Melting Pot: Symbol of Fusion or Confusion?" **American Quarterly** 16, no. 1 (Spring 1964): 20–46.

Goldman, Eric F. "The Presidency as Moral Leadership." In **Ethical Standards in American Public Life,** ed. Clarence N. Callender and James C. Charlesworth, special issue, **Annals of the American Academy of Political and Social Science** 280 (March 1952): 37–45.

Gould, Jack. "Television in Review: New 'Format' Brings Out the President's Warmth and Charm Before Cameras." **The New York Times,** April 6, 1954, 41.

Graham, Sally Hunter. "Woodrow Wilson, Alice Paul, and the Woman Suffrage Movement." **Political Science Quarterly** 98, no. 4 (Winter 1983–84): 665–79.

Grantham, Dewey W., Jr. "Dinner at the White House: Theodore Roosevelt, Booker T. Washington, and the South." **Tennessee Historical Quarterly** 17, no. 2 (June 1958): 112–30.

Hacker, J. David. "A Census-Based Count of the Civil War Dead." **Civil War History** 57, no. 4 (December 2011): 307–48.

Hobbs, Allyson. "A Hundred Years Later, 'The Birth of a Nation' Hasn't Gone Away." **The New Yorker,** December 13, 2015.

Howe, Julia Ward. "Battle Hymn of the Republic." **The Atlantic Monthly,** February 1862, 145.

Hsu, Hua. "The End of White America?" **The Atlantic,** January–February 2009.

Johnson, Donald. "Wilson, Burleson, and Censorship in the First World War." **Journal of Southern History** 28, no. 1 (February 1962): 46–58.

Kraus, Joe. "How the Melting Pot Stirred America: The Reception of Zangwill's Play and Theater's Role in the American Assimilation Experience." **MELUS** 24, no. 3 (Fall 1999): 3–19.

Lawson, Steven F. " 'I Got It from the **New York Times**': Lyndon Johnson and the Kennedy Civil Rights Program." **Journal of Negro History** vol. 67, no. 2 (Summer 1982): 159-73.

Leuchtenburg, William E. "The Conversion of Harry

Truman." **American Heritage,** November 1991, 55–58.

McCormick, Anne O'Hare. "Roosevelt's View of the Big Job: The Presidency Is 'a Superb Opportunity for Applying the Simple Rules of Human Conduct,' Says the Democratic Candidate, Interviewed in the Midst of a Whirl of Varied Activity." **The New York Times,** September 11, 1932.

McPherson, James M. "Southern Comfort." **New York Review of Books,** April 12, 2001, 28, 30–32.

McVeigh, Rory. "Power Devaluation, the Ku Klux Klan, and the Democratic National Convention of 1924." **Sociological Forum** 16, no. 1 (March 2001): 1–30.

O'Toole, Patricia. "Assassination Foiled." **Smithsonian,** November 2012, 64–65.

Rhoads, William B. "Franklin D. Roosevelt and the Architecture of Warm Springs." **Georgia Historical Quarterly** 67, no. 1 (Spring 1983): 70–87.

"Robert Montgomery Presents: President as a Pro," **Life,** April 19, 1954, 28–29.

Rushay, Samuel W., Jr., "Harry Truman's History Lessons." **Prologue** 41, no. 1 (Spring 2009), https://www .archives.gov/publications/prologue/2009/spring/ truman-history.html.

Schlesinger, Arthur M., [Sr.]. "The Lost Meaning of 'The Pursuit of Happiness.'" **William and Mary Quarterly** 21, no. 3 (July 1964): 325–27.

Schmoke, Kurt. "The Little Known History of Coolidge and Civil Rights." **Coolidge Quarterly** 1, no. 3 (November 2016), 1–5.

Shumsky, Neil Larry. "Zangwill's 'The Melting Pot':

Ethnic Tensions on Stage." **American Quarterly** 27, no. 1 (March 1975): 29–41.

Sterling, David L. "In Defense of Debs: The Lawyers and the Espionage Act Case." **Indiana Magazine of History** 83, no. 1 (March 1987): 17–42.

Swing, Raymond Gram. "The Menace of Huey Long: II. A Monarch in Pajamas." **The Nation,** January 16, 1935, 69–71.

Teachout, Terry. "Mencken Unsealed." **The New York Times,** January 31, 1993.

Teggart, Frederick J. "The Argument of Hesiod's Works and Days." **Journal of the History of Ideas** 8, no. 1 (January 1947): 45–77.

Turlish, Lewis A. "The Rising Tide of Color: A Note on the Historicism of **The Great Gatsby**." **American Literature** 43, no. 3 (November 1971): 442–44.

United States Congress. "Resolution of Censure, Remarks of Senator Prescott Bush." 83rd Cong., 2nd sess. **Congressional Record** 100, pt. 12 (December 1, 1954): 162–68.

Vanden Heuvel, William J. "America and the Holocaust." **American Heritage,** July–August 1999, 34–52.

Weiss, Nancy J. "The Negro and the New Freedom: Fighting Wilsonian Segregation." **Political Science Quarterly** 84, no. 1 (March 1969): 61–79.

Wilson, Woodrow. "The Reconstruction of the Southern States." **The Atlantic Monthly,** January 1901, 1–15.

Dissertation

Deaver, Jean Franklin. "A Study of Senator Joseph R. McCarthy and 'McCarthyism' as Influences upon the News Media and the Evolution of Reportorial Method." PhD diss., University of Texas at Austin, 1969.

Online Resources

Bailey, Greg. "This Presidential Speech on Race Shocked the Nation . . . in 1921." Narratively, October 26, 2016. http://narrative.ly/this-presidential -speech-on-race-shocked-the-nation-in-1921/.

Baker's Evangelical Dictionary of Biblical Theology. Edited by Walter A. Elwell. Grand Rapids, Mich.: Baker Books, 1996. https://www.biblestudytools .com/dictionaries/bakers-evangelical-dictionary/.

Boissoneault, Lorraine. "What Will Happen to Stone Mountain, America's Largest Confederate Memorial?" Smithsonian.com, August 22, 2017. https:// www.smithso nianmag.com/history/what-will -happen-stone-mountain-americas-largest-con federate-memorial-180964588/.

Chisholm, Shirley. "Equal Rights for Women." Address to the U.S. House of Representatives, May 21, 1969. https://awpc.cattcenter.iastate.edu/2017/03/21/ equal-rights-for-women-may-21-1969/.

"Declaration of Sentiments and Resolutions: Woman's Rights Convention, Held at Seneca Falls, 19–20 July 1848." The Elizabeth Cady Stanton and Susan B. Anthony Papers Project, Rutgers, State University of New Jersey. http://ecssba.rutgers.edu/docs/seneca .html.

Douglass, Frederick. "Oration in Memory of Abraham Lincoln." April 14, 1876. TeachingAmerican

History.org. http://teachingamericanhistory.org/
library/document/oration-in-memory-of
-abraham-lincoln/.

Du Bois, W.E.B. "President Harding and Social Equality." December 1921. TeachingAmericanHistory.org.
http://teachingamericanhistory.org/library/
document/president-harding-and-social-equality.

King Institute Encyclopedia. Martin Luther King, Jr.,
and the Global Freedom Struggle. Stanford, Calif.:
The Martin Luther King, Jr. Research and Education Institute, Stanford University. http://kingency
clopedia.stanford.edu/encyclopedia/encyclopedia
_contents.html.

Lewis, Thomas A. "When Washington, D.C. Came
Close to Being Conquered by the Confederacy."
Smithsonian.com, July 1988. https://www.smith
sonianmag.com/history/when-washington-dc
-came-close-to-being-conquered-by-the-confederacy
-180951994/.

"Resonant Ripples in a Global Pond: The Blinding of
Isaac Woodard." University of South Carolina Upstate.
https://faculty.uscupstate.edu/amyers/conference
.html.

Robin, Corey. "Forget About It," **Harper's** magazine
(April 2018): 5–7.

Rogers, James R. "The Meaning of 'The Pursuit of
Happiness.'" First Things, June 19, 2012. https://
www.firstthings.com/web-exclusives/2012/06/the-
meaning-of-the-pursuit-of-happiness.

Roosevelt, Theodore. "Citizenship in a Republic." Almanac of Theodore Roosevelt. http://www.theodore
-roosevelt.com/trsorbonnespeech.html.

———. "Lincoln and the Race Problem." BlackPast. Org: Remembered and Reclaimed; An Online Reference Guide to African American History. http://www.blackpast.org/1905-theodore-roosevelt-lincoln-and-race-problem.

The Stanford Encyclopedia of Philosophy. Edited by Edward N. Zalta et al. Stanford, Calif.: Metaphysics Research Lab, Center for the Study of Language and Information, Stanford University, 2016. https://plato.stanford.edu/.

Wallace, Jerry L. "The Ku Klux Klan in Calvin Coolidge's America." Calvin Coolidge Presidential Foundation, July 14, 2014. https://coolidgefoundation.org/blog/the-ku-klux-klan-in-calvin-coolidges-america/.

Wills, Matthew. "A Really Contested Convention: The 1924 Democratic Klanbake." JSTOR Daily, May 11, 2016. https://daily.jstor.org/contested-convention/.

Woolley, John T., and Gerhard Peters. The American Presidency Project. University of California, Santa Barbara. http://www.presidency.ucsb.edu/index.php.

Magazines, Journals, and Newspapers

American Heritage
American Literature
American Quarterly
The Atlanta Constitution
The Atlantic Monthly
The Birmingham News
Business Week
Chicago Tribune
Civil War History
Coolidge Quarterly
Collier's
The Commercial Appeal (Memphis, Tenn.)

The Daily Progress
  (Charlottesville, Va.)
The Economist
The Georgia Historical
  Quarterly
Good Housekeeping
Harper's Magazine
Indiana Magazine of
  History
Journal of Negro
  History
The Journal of Southern
  History
Life
The Literary Digest
Los Angeles Times
MELUS
The Memphis Press-
  Scimitar
The Nation
Newsweek
The New York Times
New-York Tribune
The New Yorker

The Outlook
Political Science
  Quarterly
The Post and Courier
  (Charleston, S.C.)
Presidential Studies
  Quarterly
Prologue
Richmond (Va.)
  Enquirer
Smithsonian
Sociological Forum
Tennessee Historical
  Quarterly
Time
USA Today
Vanity Fair
The Washington Post
The Washington Times
The Wheeling (W.V.)
  Intelligencer
The William and Mary
  Quarterly
Woman's Journal

Illustration List and Credits

Index

ABOUT THE AUTHOR

||||||||||||||||||||||||||||||||||||||||||||||||||||

JON MEACHAM is a Pulitzer Prize–winning biographer. The author of the **New York Times** bestsellers **Thomas Jefferson: The Art of Power, American Lion: Andrew Jackson in the White House, Franklin and Winston,** and **Destiny and Power: The American Odyssey of George Herbert Walker Bush,** he is a distinguished visiting professor at Vanderbilt University, a contributing writer for **The New York Times Book Review,** and a fellow of the Society of American Historians. Meacham lives in Nashville with his wife and children.